PAUL KENNETH CHRISTIANSON is a member of the Department of History at Queen's University.

Starting in the 1530s with John Bale, English reformers found in the apocalyptic mysteries of the Book of Revelation a framework for reinterpreting the history of Christianity and explaining the break from the Roman Catholic Church. Identifying the papacy with antichrist and the Roman Catholic Church with Babylon, they pictured the reformation as a departure from the false church that derived its jurisdiction from the devil. Those who took the initiative in throwing off the Roman yoke acted as instruments of God in the cosmic warfare against the power of evil that raged in the latter days of the world. The reformation ushered in the beginning of the end as prophesied by St John.

Reformers and Babylon examines the English apocalyptic tradition as developed in the works of religious thinkers both within and without the Established Church and distinguishes the various streams into which the tradition split. By the middle of Elizabeth's reign the mainstream apocalyptic interpretation was widely accepted within the Church of England. Under Charles I, however, it also provided a vocabulary of attack for critics of the Established Church. Using the same weapons that their ancestors had used to justify the reformation in the first place, reformers like John Bastwick, Henry Burton, William Prynne, and John Lilburne attacked the Church of England's growing sympathies with Romish ways and eventually prepared parliamentarians to take up arms against the royalist forces whom they saw as the forces of antichrist.

Scholars of sixteenth- and seventeenth-century intellectual history will welcome this closely reasoned study of the background of religious dissent which underlay the politics of the time.

PAUL CHRISTIANSON

Reformers and Babylon: English apocalyptic visions from the reformation to the eve of the civil war

UNIVERSITY OF TORONTO PRESS
TORONTO BUFFALO LONDON

© University of Toronto Press 1978
Toronto Buffalo London
Printed in Canada

The cover woodcut is from the title page of
Newes from Rome, London 1641.

Library of Congress Cataloging in Publication Data
Christianson, Paul, 1937–
Reformers and Babylon.

Based on the author's thesis, University of Minnesota,
1971.
Bibliography: p.
Includes index.
1. England – Church history – 16th century.   2. England
– Church history – 17th century.   3. Eschatology – History
of doctrines.   4. Dissenters, Religious – England.
I. Title.
BR757.C47   274.2   77-16706
ISBN 0-8020-5365-3

To my parents

Contents

Preface

In the beginning was the Word, and the Word was with God,
and the Word was God ... And the Word was made flesh,
and dwelt among us ...

John i:1,14

By rendering the *logos* of John i as the Word, those scholars who prepared the authorized version of the Bible announced the Christian
message of salvation in a manner that expressed a deep reverence for the
mystery and power of language. Sixteenth- and seventeenth-century
protestants believed that they could change the world with the Word.
The following study analyses one aspect of the way in which they
carried out that intention. Concentrating upon the publicly expressed
ideas and feelings of individuals, it draws almost exclusively upon
printed treatises, sermons, and pamphlets as sources. To avoid deficient
generalizations, an effort was made to analyse the complete contemporary works of each individual discussed and to include well-known or
representative figures as well as more obscure authors. The need to keep
footnotes to a manageable length prevented the citation of all secondary
works consulted and of each source analysed, even of many deemed
relevant to the topic. Fairly exhaustive notes, therefore, appear only in
sections that present controversial points.

The technological innovations of microfilm and photocopy greatly
facilitated my research. Many of the sixteenth- and seventeenth-
century editions cited below were read in the reproductions made by
University Microfilms of items listed in the short-title catalogues of
Pollard and Redgrave and Wing. In addition, the libraries of Harvard

University, Union Theological Seminary, the British Museum, and the Henry E. Huntington Library and Art Gallery generously made available microfilm or photocopy reproductions of other works. Visits to Dr Williams's Library, the Guildhall Library, the Congregational Library, Wilson Library at the University of Minnesota, a prolonged stay in the North Library of the British Library, and, of course, the Douglas Library at Queen's University completed my research itinerary. I wish to thank the staff of each of these institutions for their courteous and efficient help.

The principal portion of this study is a substantially revised version of my doctoral thesis 'English Protestant Apocalyptic Visions, c. 1536–1642,' University of Minnesota, 1971. Those who wish to consult it may obtain a copy from University Microfilms or may read the photocopy version available at Dr Williams's Library in London. An earlier, shortened version of chapter five appeared as an article in the *Journal of Ecclesiastical History*. A sabbatical leave granted by the principal and trustees of Queen's University, aided by a leave fellowship from the Canada Council (no. w72 0254), provided the time for additional research and revision. This book has been published with the help of a grant from the Social Science Research Council of Canada, using funds provided by the Canada Council, and a grant to University of Toronto Press from the Andrew W. Mellon Foundation. I thank each of these bodies for its generous support.

It is a pleasure to record personal thanks to those who have extended special favour and guidance. Dr David Harris Willson, Dr Stanford E. Lehmberg, Dr Richard Bauckham, Dr Katherine Firth, Mr John K. Graham, Dr William M. Lamont, Dr George A. Rawlyk, and Dr James A. Stayer all deserve my thanks for reading and commenting upon various stages of the manuscript. Mr Gerald Hallowell of the University of Toronto Press and Mr A.R. Hazelwood, who compiled the index, also deserve my thanks for their expert contributions. Any errors that remain are my responsibility. Finally, I wish to thank my parents, brothers, sister, and their families for the immeasurable help and support that they have provided over the years.

In quotations, spelling and capitalization are modernized, but punctuation follows the original. Titles retain the spelling of the original.

Kingston, Ontario
September 1976

REFORMERS AND BABYLON:
ENGLISH APOCALYPTIC VISIONS FROM THE REFORMATION
TO THE EVE OF THE CIVIL WAR

Introduction

That James was but a middling writer may be allowed ... If he has composed a commentary on the Revelations, and proved the Pope to be Antichrist; may not a familiar reproach be extended to the famous Napier; and even to Newton, at a time when learning was much more advanced than during the reign of James? From the grossness of its superstitions, we may infer the ignorance of an age; but never should pronounce concerning the folly of an individual, from his admitting popular errors, consecrated with the appearance of religion.

David Hume, *The History of Great Britain: The Reigns of James I and Charles I*, ed. Duncan Forbes, Harmondsworth 1970, p. 252

Simple words seem to have clear meanings, but after analysis the deception of simplicity often vanishes. The 'ignorance' and 'superstitions' of others strike one as more complex when examined in context – what the outsider calls 'folly' sometimes contains deep emotional and intellectual meaning for others. One experiences great difficulties when attempting to communicate with someone who inhabits a different perceptual world. Just as the social anthropologist tries to translate his experience of unaccustomed cultural patterns into language understood by those who inhabit a contemporary but vastly dissimilar world of thought, so the historian of ideas must attempt the same task when reconstructing the world views of those who lived in the past. The analysis and history of language provides the historian with a significant tool for such a job. This approach helps one begin to discover the layers of meaning attached to words and works by people who lived before us and thereby to ascertain the ways in which they perceived the

world and the paradigms which guided their thoughts and sensations.[1]
Early in his career, the student of seventeenth-century England learns
that Charles I, Oliver Cromwell, and John Lilburne gave quite distinct
meanings to the words 'liberty' and 'reformation,' that they put forth
disparate and conflicting conceptions of religion and politics under the
umbrella of these two words. Likewise, Tudor and Stuart Englishmen
applied the term 'puritan' – whether with positive or negative value – to
a wide spectrum of thought expounded by such diverse representatives
as Anglican bishops and tub preachers.[2] Studies of the variety of meanings expressed by these words have grown so numerous that it would
constitute a major task just to list and comment upon all of them.

Another word which seems simple at first sight, but which acted as a
significant symbol in the language of sixteenth- and seventeenth-
century Britain, has received less serious scrutiny. Until very recently,
'popery' got the same simplistic treatment accorded to 'liberty,' 'reformation,' and 'puritanism' in the more distant past. Historians, it is true,
observed the emotive response elicited by 'popery,' but usually they
remained satisfied with its most obvious level of meaning.[3] They dismissed the feelings of their forefathers by branding them prejudices
or superstition. Interpretation, reduced to its barest and perhaps most
crude form, ran along these lines: Scots and Englishmen strongly disliked Roman catholicism; they feared that their protestant churches
might be endangered by the forced reimposition of catholicism; these
fears gained cogency with the Marian burnings, the assassination of
William of Orange, the St Bartholomew's day massacre, the Armada,
the Gunpowder Plot, the pre-Gustavian phase of the Thirty Years War,
and the Irish rebellion – to mention a few outstanding events fresh in the
minds of mid-century Britons. These understandable anxieties produced
an irrational, intolerant, anti-catholic fanaticism which always lay
under the surface and actively erupted upon the political scene in

1 This study attempts to apply the analytical framework of Kuhn, *Structure*, to a
different area of intellectual history and in a chronological manner. My research
employed some of the techniques discussed in Holsti, *Content Analysis*.
2 Cf. Hill, *Society and Puritanism*, ch. 1, and Russell, *Origins*, ch. 4
3 See Wiener, 'Beleaguered isle,' Clifton, 'Popular fear,' and Miller, *Popery and Politics*.
For general accounts of apocalyptic thought in this period, see Froom, *Prophetic Faith*,
II, Tuveson, *Millennium and Utopia*, Lamont, *Godly Rule*, Hill, *Antichrist*, Ball, *Great
Expectation*, and the unpublished studies by Bauckham, 'Prophecy,' and Firth,
'Apocalyptic Tradition.' Drs Bauckham and Firth kindly made their typescripts avail-
able to me.

occasional but crucial outbursts of action. While something of a straw man, this summary exaggerates only slightly. It contains a good deal of truth, but it ignores the most important component of the 'ideological filter' through which British reformers and reformed viewed the church of Rome and its supporters. One can grasp the intense hatred of 'popery' shown by contemporaries by placing it firmly within the context of that standard justification of a break with Rome, the apocalyptic interpretation of the reformation. The very nature of this approach to human action strengthened its appeal to men and women engaged in the strain of confessional strife.

Apocalyptic thought in general contains three characteristics which help explain its importance in Tudor and Stuart England: a polarized view of the universe, a catastrophic explanation of events, and a firm concern with prophecy and its fulfilment. Like apocalyptic writers since the days of Daniel, English protestants of our period viewed the actions of their fellow human beings through polarized spectacles. They believed that transcendent forces of good and evil strove to control the universe and linked each individual to one side or the other, whether or not he exercised a choice in the matter. Eventually, the conflict between these two powers and their instruments would lead to the triumph of good and the eternal destruction of evil. An overwhelming importance, therefore, infused the task of distinguishing between the institutional form taken by either side on earth. No compromise existed between them! If one wished to share in the glories of the victory, one had to align oneself explicitly with the allies of the good (or recognize that the Almighty had elected one to that position). In a period of fierce confessional debate, apocalyptic thought accustomed people to conceive of conflict as the natural law of a sinful world and to view opponents as mortal enemies linked with supernatural evil. It helped to establish an attitude of mind which stressed differences not similarities, which made militance likely, and which acted to accentuate rather than to heal tensions in times of crisis. Apocalyptic visions strengthened people to take action. Paradoxically, action could mean supplication through prayer as well as more obvious outward striving. Supernatural forces controlled the destiny of mankind, the very timing and course of human events.

The belief in an imminent catastrophic end to evil separates apocalyptic thought from other polarizing ideologies, such as Manicheanism. Although the end itself appeared certain, the exact means and date of its accomplishment remained matters for debate. The forces of good and evil normally worked their ends on earth through human instruments, but the final victory could bypass such vessels and suddenly arrive through the direct intervention of the Almighty. Until that day, evil often seemed successful and might well reign ascendant in the world. Those who considered themselves the sons and daughters of light fervently sought the destruction of darkness, especially when the end of their suffering appeared to loom just ahead. To this catastrophic character of apocalyptic thought, British protestants brought a particularly well-developed historical consciousness. They poured a great deal of learned energy into working out the chronology of this plan of the Lord, first for the past and later for future events. By the late sixteenth century, scholars replaced vague feelings about the imminence of the end with more precise calculations of its arrival. The apocalyptic calculators not only doubled the urgency of their message, but they provided clues employed by the next generations to demonstrate the veracity of the theory as a whole. Interpreters transformed themselves into prophets and thus increased expectations that great events would happen soon.

Prophecy and its fulfilment play a major role in apocalyptic thought, as in many other facets of the Judeo-Christian tradition. Not all prophets espoused an apocalyptic framework, but all apocalyptic thinkers acted, to a greater or lesser degree, as prophets. Prediction was built into the very nature of the system, otherwise certainty of the outcome would not obtain. The whole framework gained enormous strength by confirmation of its previous prophecies, whether in history or in current events. Some disconfirmation did not immediately disprove such a framework for the converted, but confirmation created a more palatable proof. British reformers employed the biblical books of Daniel and Revelation as primary sources for constructing their apocalyptic interpretation. As Keith V. Thomas recently demonstrated in his study of popular beliefs, ancient prophecies exercised a potent influence in Tudor and Stuart England. Even in the peak years of 1588 and 1641–2, these consisted of many types.[4] However, those based upon the Bible carried the added weight of an immediately apparent divine sanction which increased their authority. The seeming fulfilment of specific apocalyptic prophecies added persuasive force to the theory, especially when people saw the predictions of a previous generation coming true before their very eyes, as they believed they could in the early seventeenth century.

4 Thomas, *Religion*, ch. 13

Through the confirmation of their prophecies, then, apocalyptic interpreters exercised a powerful, persuasive hold over the way in which contemporaries viewed events in the world.

Many sociologists, anthropologists, theologians, and historians prefer to refer to this type of thought and the movements it engenders as millennial, rather than apocalyptic. Their overly subtle terminology, with its differentiations between 'premillennial' versus 'postmillennial,' 'millenialists' versus 'millenarians,' 'chiliast' versus 'millenialist,' has reached a state of confusion.[5] Only the first of these pairs works very well in practice and one can express it in terms more easily understood by the non-specialist. In this study, 'apocalyptic' denotes the generic term and 'millennial' that species which posits a future, collective, imminent transformation of life on earth through a supernatural agency.[6] Only those who expected a literal thousand-year reign of the saints on earth will merit the term 'millenarian.' This terminology should add some clarity and still allow proper distinctions.

In itself, apocalyptic thought displayed neither revolutionary nor conservative characteristics in its social and political thrust. It was a creed of action, if only in the form of prayer. It certainly worked to reinforce existing attitudes toward social and political action. With its polarized view of the universe, its stress upon an imminent catastrophic end to the normal world, and its propensity toward prophecy, apocalyptic thought operated as a powerful rational and emotional weapon in ideological dispute. The combination of retribution for enemies with the creation of a new order of righteousness provided an inspirational mixture with explosive potential. People who view the church and society in which they live in black and white terms, who convince themselves that their cause will triumph despite seeming odds against it, and who detect signs that the victory of the ages draws near, make

5 In Christian theology 'premillennial' indicates a rule of the saints on earth inaugurated by the second advent of Christ, while 'postmillennial' posits a millennium followed by the return of Christ. As Bryan Ball has shown, these categories remain useful when judiciously applied; however, they are a little refined for the few truly millennial thinkers discussed in this study. 'Apocalyptic' seems preferable to the broader 'eschatological' or the confusing 'amillennial' favoured by Ball; cf. *Great Expectation*, introduction, ch. 1, 5, pp. 160–1, Firth, 'Apocalyptic Tradition,' and Capp, *'Godly Rule'* and 'Millennium.' For an example of the confusion of categories, see Tuveson, *Redeemer Nation*, pp. 33–5; also see Barkun, *Disaster and the Millennium*, Burridge, *New Heaven, New Earth*, Hobsbawm, *Primitive Rebels*, Lanternari, *Religions of the Oppressed*, and Thrupp, *Millennial Dreams*.

6 Thrupp, *Millennial Dreams*, p. 31

formidable friends or foes, hopeless compromisers or moderates.

Long before Christianity began, apocalyptic visions gave hope to the ancient Jews, especially those oppressed in exile or under the thumb of conquerors in the holy land. Babylon became the symbol of sin and evil on earth by design, not by chance, when an exile there composed the prophecies of Daniel. Under the early Christians those messianic expectations, often found mingled with apocalyptic visions, took the form of longing for the imminent return of Christ. St John's Apocalypse took Babylon as the symbol of perdition and charged it with even greater depths of imagery. The Book of Revelation joined that of Daniel in the canon of holy prophecy. Medieval commentators, whether orthodox or heretical, attempted to unlock the meaning of the murky metaphors of these scriptures to apply them to current events. Without ignoring Babylon, they tended to focus their attention upon the shadowy figure of antichrist – mentioned only in I John ii:18,22 and II John 7 – to such a degree that he came to personify the human leader of the forces of evil in the last days of the earth. Medieval heretics applied this image against the pope, papalists against some emperors, long before the sixteenth century. By the time that the reformation began in England, antichrist had long acted as a well-worn weapon in the armoury of spiritual warfare.[7]

It should cause no surprise, then, that English protestants of the sixteenth and seventeenth centuries believed that the Herculean task of reformation – of rooting out catholic 'superstition' and planting the gospel – formed part of an unfolding cosmic combat which engaged those on earth as well as in the heavens. Like those medieval heretics and continental reformers with whom they identified, they felt the need of making a clear break with the orthodox Christian tradition of the middle ages, or of reinterpreting that tradition. This they did by concluding that the medieval church and its continuation at Rome represented the worldly manifestation of cosmic darkness. They conceived their struggle, therefore, as being not only against the pope and his agents – catholic princes, prelates, and priests – but also against the very might of Satan, the ultimate source of catholic power. English reformers identified themselves with the saints of God and branded catholics as the hordes of antichrist or the brats of Babylon.

Predecessors paved the way, but John Bale forged the link between a

---

7 For the ancient and medieval background, see Bousset, *Antichrist*, Cohn, *Pursuit of the Millennium*, and Reeves, *Influence of Prophecy*.

new reformation apocalyptic tradition and that of the past. He endowed the British protestant version with its particular historical cast. For the first time, the history of the Christian church and society were employed systematically to elucidate the prophecies of St John and unlock the mysteries of Revelation. Bale's interpretation seems to have acted as a paradigm. He framed his insight into the nature of reality into a coherent system or framework of thought with its own inner logic and vocabulary. Central to it was the discernment of a true and a false church operating in inexorable opposition throughout history and especially in the history of Christianity. Crucial was the identification of the medieval church and its successors at Rome with the false church of the latter days and of protestant churches with the true. Bale took the nebulous implicit historical thrust of apocalyptic thought and made it explicit. He took an identification of antichrist with the pope as a single man leading the forces of evil on earth at the very end of time, extended it to the institution of the papacy, and demonstrated how the historical consequences of this redefinition contained great contemporary relevance. Bale's successors applied and refined his framework and solved the exegetical, historical, and chronological problems that it posed. Although some dissenters remained, Bale saw an ubiquitous acceptance of his apocalyptic explanation of the reformation by English protestants before he died.

Within this new historical paradigm, prophecies about the beasts of Daniel vii and of Revelation, the whore of Babylon portrayed in Revelation, the New Jerusalem of Revelation xxi, and antichrist – to name a few of the most powerful biblical images – became identifiable puzzles awaiting systematic solution and application. These images took on a wide variety of meanings, but they fell into a few discernible categories. English reformers, for example, normally reserved the term 'antichrist' for the leading human instrument of evil on earth, 'Babylon' for the institutional form of his power. With the one exception noted below, the word 'antichrist' unfailingly appeared in an apocalyptic context during the sixteenth century; it lost this precision and became a general term of abuse only in the 1640s. However, the derivative term 'antichristian' lacked apocalyptic content more frequently. Contemporaries sometimes applied it to practices deemed contrary to those instituted by Christ (viz., 'anti' meaning against, hence 'anti-Christ' or 'antichristian'). Most commonly, however, English protestants used 'antichristian' in an apocalyptic context either to disparage the practices of the contemporary allies of antichrist or to condemn practices which arose when antichrist ruled over the Christian church (that is, during the middle ages). The language of apocalyptic writers operated within a complex web of nuances and contexts. Those intellectuals who wrote treatises on antichrist or commentaries on Daniel, Revelation, or II Thessalonians employed it with clarity and precision. Such scholars worked within an international Latin tradition. They included some of the best minds of the age and built up a sophisticated, systematic interpretation of holy history.[8] Other advocates assumed such a theory or made brief allusions to it, but concentrated their concern upon applying apocalyptic insights to their church and society, sometimes with startling results. Each of these intellectual levels deserves some attention.

Even within the general application of Bale's framework, several streams of interpretation arose. Apocalyptic thought provided English protestants with a valuable tool for differentiating and defending their various ecclesiastical positions.[9] With the exception of the Arminian innovators of the early seventeenth century, Anglicans justified their break with Rome by equating it with Babylon and the corrupted papacy with antichrist. This category included conforming puritans as well as Archbishops Cranmer, Parker, Grindal, Whitgift, Bancroft, and Abbot. Separatists turned the language of these reformers against the Established Church and condemned it as a part of Babylon, its governors as antichrists. They separated from it because they believed that England had not yet witnessed a true reformation. Radical puritans attempted to maintain a position between the previous two by identifying the Church of England with Laodicea the lukewarm (one of the churches addressed by St John), an institution with proper doctrine but improper government. While essentially negative, the image of Laodicea held forth the promise of better things as well as the threat of rejection. Some radical puritans took a further step which brought them very close to the separatists by linking episcopacy with antichrist and by demanding its 'root and branch' abolition. Starting from the same premise – a shared apocalyptic condemnation of Rome based upon Bale's framework – these four streams of interpretation arrived at strikingly different con-

---

8 Bauckham and Firth and Ball deal primarily with the intellectuals and show how they operated within an international, as well as a national, context. For biblical symbols, see Ball, *Great Expectation*, pp. 68–70.
9 This idea came from Wilson, 'Another look,' pp. 45–6; cf. Hill, *Antichrist*, ch. 1 and 2.

clusions. The way in which each of them unfolded provides one of the main themes of the following account.

Not only did different ecclesiological streams of interpretation develop within the apocalyptic tradition in England, adherents also disagreed on the means which the Lord would use to overthrow the powers of darkness. While all believed, except in times of extreme crisis, that Christ would work through human instruments to accomplish this task, some reformers stressed the role of magistrates (be they princes or parliaments) as leaders of church reform. For them, the Almighty exercised his will primarily through existing structures of power, especially through the 'godly prince.' Looking back to the example of Constantine I and glorying in the imperial crown of England, these men advocated an 'imperial tradition' of apocalyptic thought. Others believed that God would purge the existing church through human instruments who lacked power and prestige in the eyes of the world. Convinced that the present authority structure lacked righteousness, these interpreters stressed an apocalyptic 'tradition of the persecuted and oppressed.' These two basic views of the means by which the Lord reformed his visible church, paradoxically, did not appear contradictory to contemporaries. Most English protestants held both but gave greater weight to one or the other.[10] Either could produce radical political and social consequences, the imperial tradition by demanding actions from the godly prince that he proved unable or unwilling to perform, that of the oppressed and persecuted by attacking established authority. In either case, apocalyptic warfare generally remained a spiritual contest fought with the word, not the sword, throughout most of the sixteenth century in England, if not in Scotland. The Armada experience changed this and introduced a new element which would come into its own in the early 1640s.

Some of the complexities of the apocalyptic interpretation of the reformation should now begin to become apparent, how it made events seem to fit together as parts of a pattern, how it gave 'popery' a stinging depth of powerful meaning. 'Popery' in any of its forms merged into a whole chain of cosmic evil and formed a part of the age-old struggle between the minions of antichrist and the saints of Christ. Looking back

10 The concept of an imperial tradition derived from Lamont, *Marginal Prynne*, pp. 16–17, 59–60, 66–8, while the tradition of the oppressed came from Lanternari, *Religions of the Oppressed*; cf. Lamont, *Godly Rule*, p. 32.

from the Augustan calm of the eighteenth century, David Hume could only describe the apocalyptic visions of his predecessors as 'superstitions.' For English protestants who lived in the turmoil of the previous two centuries, these beliefs stood as an article of faith which helped them to explain and act upon the important and bewildering events of their time. The historian who desires to understand those events can ignore the apocalyptic tradition only at the peril of missing the meaning it gave to contemporaries.

I

Forming the English protestant apocalyptic tradition

He that looketh but a little into the world, shall espy just cause to move us to prayer, if any men; now, if ever. The great devil in these our later days is let loose. Antichrist rageth and seeketh our confusion.

Edwin Sandys, *Sermons*, p. 398

Even before Henry VIII and his Parliament removed the pope's jurisdiction from England, exiles like Robert Barnes, John Frith, and William Tyndale had proclaimed apocalyptic explanations of the reformation. These early reformers enunciated individual elements of what became the English protestant apocalyptic tradition, however, not its overall framework.[1] Shortly after the break with Rome it appeared that a protestant perspective had arrived as official policy. As part of the anti-papal campaign of 1536, for example, Archbishop Cranmer preached a sermon at St Paul's Cross in which he identified the contemporary pope as antichrist and derided the authority of the emperor. From the account contained in the report of the imperial ambassador, it appears that Cranmer envisioned antichrist in the medieval way, as the earthly leader of evil in the very last days of the world.[2] The floodgates of reform, however, stood open only for a short time. When reaction set in after the fall of Thomas Cromwell, John Bale – an able writer for the anti-papal campaign – joined those who fled to the continent. From his place of

1 Clebsch, *England's Earliest*, pp. 65–73, 85–8, 152, 169, Bauckham, 'Prophecy,' ch. 1, Firth, 'Apocalyptic Tradition,' ch. 1, and Hill, *Antichrist*, pp. 9–10, 41–2
2 *Letters and Papers, Henry VIII*, X, no. 283 (Chapuys to Granvelle); see Maclure, *Paul's Cross Sermons*. For the propaganda campaign against the papacy, see Anglo, 'Early Tudor programme,' and Pineas, *Anti-Catholic Drama*.

refuge, Bale broke with the medieval past – whether orthodox or heretical – and pulled together a new framework of explanation, one that showed how the history of the Christian church fulfilled the prophecies of St John and how the contemporary reformation represented the beginning of the final triumph of good.

Carmelite prior turned reformer, Bale had studied at Jesus College, Cambridge, obtained a BD in 1528–9, and most probably advanced to a DD not long thereafter. Best known to historians as a playwright, a bibliographer, an antiquarian and chronicler, and a vigorous religious controversialist, Bale qualified as an impeccable Renaissance humanist.[3] Although his polemical writings abound with apocalyptic imagery, Bale explained his vision of the reformation most cogently in his weighty verse-by-verse paraphrase and commentary upon the Book of Revelation, *The image of bothe churches*. His condition provided him with time to write and gave him a special affinity toward the prophecy of St John.

In exile was it [the Book of Revelation] first written ... In exile are the powers thereof most earnestly proved of them that have faith ... The forsaken wretched sort hath the Lord provided always to rebuke the world of sin for want of true faith ... for nought is it not therefore, that he hath exiled a certain number of believing brethren of the realms of England; of the which afflicted family my faith is that I am one. Whereupon I have considered it no less than my bound duty, under pain of damnation, to admonish Christ's flock by this present revelation of the perils past, and the dangers to come for contempt of the gospel ...[4]

The Lord called Bale into a wretched exile and placed upon him the task of revealing the judgments of Revelation upon his generation – a terrible responsibility. Almost with relief, however, Bale cut himself off from the cares of the world, turned his attention to the ways of the spirit, and began his prophetic authorship. Some would call him an 'alienated intellectual,'[5] but his sense of duty ran at least as deep as his sense of alienation.

3 Bale's literary career has received a good deal of attention and discussions of his apocalyptic thought appear in Bauckham, 'Prophecy,' ch. 1, Firth, 'Apocalyptic Tradition,' pp. 67–94, 103–7, 116–19, Gilsdorf, 'Puritan Apocalypse,' pp. 14–20, and Haller, *Foxe's Book*, pp. 61–4, 68–70.
4 Bale, *Works*, pp. 154–5, cf. 260. Part one of the *Image* appeared in 1541, part two in 1545, part three in 1547, and further full editions in 1551 and 1560.
5 Cf. Walzer, *Revolution*, ch. 2

In the introduction to his commentary and in its marginal notes, Bale placed himself firmly within a long tradition of exegesis of St John's Apocalypse. With some exceptions, he most frequently cited either contemporary reformed scholars or medieval heretics – François Lambert (48), Sebastian Meyer (26), Martin Luther (14), and Johannes Oecolampadius (11) in the one category, John Wycliffe (20), John Hus (17), and Joachim of Flora (7) in the other. These men partook in a Latin anti-papal stream of apocalyptic interpretation that applied the prophecies of St John loosely to past, present, and future events. Bale made this scholarly Latin tradition readily available to the lay public in vernacular form, as well as giving it a new thrust.[6] He wrote his commentary on the Book of Revelation because of its contemporary relevance but also because it was central to the scriptures as a whole and therefore a mandatory frame for constructing a biblical theology. Bale's marginal notes overwhelmingly referred to other passages in the Bible. Revelation formed a veritable microcosm of holy writ and provided the Christian believer with a mirror in which he could discern his own true estate and the type of church to which he belonged: 'He that knoweth not this book, knoweth not what the church is whereof he is a member ... Either we are citizens in the New Jerusalem with Jesus Christ, or else in the old superstitious Babylon with antichrist the vicar of Satan.'[7]

Bale took St Augustine's idea of the two cities and transformed it into that of the two churches – one headed by Christ and the other by antichrist. He thereby institutionalized Tyndale's designation of antichrist as the representative of evil on earth through all ages. A differentiation of this type solved one of the key problems of the reformation – the tracing of legitimate authority, a problem faced by protestants especially, for they could not rely upon an unbroken institutional tradition for their defence. By applying the idea of the two churches, Bale stood history on its head. The church establishment of the middle ages, headed by the papacy, became the vassals of antichrist, while many hounded as heretics in the same period became the small, pure, persecuted elect of the true church. Bale obtained the facts to make his case from chronicles, his interpretation from a hitherto unique reading of the Apocalypse. Since most of the historical sources he drew upon purported

6 Bale, *Works*, pp. 255–9. Sebastian Meyer was an obscure reformer in Berne; the others need no comment. Important continental influences upon the English tradition appeared in Bullinger, *A hundred sermons*, and Junius, *A brief commentary*; see note 48 below. Hill places an unwarranted stress upon Martin Bucer's *De Regno Christi*, a work with little apocalyptic content, in *Antichrist*, pp. 13, 60, 62, 67–8, 80, 88.

7 Bale, *Works*, p. 252

to establish the very opposite viewpoint, scripture had to provide the primary test for his explanation. 'Yet is the text of Revelation a light to the chronicles, and not the chronicles to the text.' Holy history provided the framework for his exegesis, but the mystery of unlocking sacred tropes preserved Bale from too direct an application of specific prophecies to individual historical events. The chronology mattered most, not the minute details: 'For we must consider that this revelation [the Book of Revelation] is in all points *no story* [that is, historical account] ... But it is a *mystery* ...'[8] The prophecies of St John provided a framework for a proper understanding of history. Caught up in the task of convincing his compatriots that they lived under the mantle of the false church, Bale sometimes ignored his own dictum and descended to specifics. Compared to many future commentators, however, his most specialized applications seem general indeed.

According to Bale, St John's Apocalypse portrayed a spiritual struggle between good and evil that began with the creation of time and ended only on the judgment day. The Almighty preordained both sides from all eternity: 'For like as all the faithful (which have been from the beginning) belong to one mystical body in Christ, and shall be preserved by him; so doth the wicked pertain with one mystical antichrist, having all one spirit with him, and so shall with him perish.' The communion of saints – an old, familiar Christian concept – opposed what one could call a communion of devils united under the one form of antichrist. Contrary to most previous commentators, Bale did not perceive antichrist as one particular person, born near the end of the world; instead, all enemies of the elect made up the image of the beast. Bale made this point explicitly in a key passage quoted in part above:

For we must consider that this revelation is in all points no story, specially here, as many writers have thought it to be, in supposing an antichrist to be born at the latter end of the world. But it is a mystery comprehending in it but one general antichrist for all, which hath reigned in the church in a manner since the ascension of Christ. And in this one point are all the commentators that I have seen most foully deceived; yea, the best learned of them. I know well, if there be any yet to come, he shall be but a member of this.[9]

---

8 *Ibid.*, pp. 253, 442; the emphasis in the latter quotation is mine.
9 *Ibid.*, pp. 461 (upon Rev. xiv:11), 442 (upon Rev. xiii:14–15). In his sermon of 1536, Cranmer saw antichrist as a single individual. For some medieval examples, see *Here begynneth* and Cohn, *Pursuit of the Millennium*, passim.

In short, antichrist ruled in the world from eternity and infiltrated the church after the ascension of Christ.

The shift of antichrist from a specific to a universal context, of course, threatened to remove the apocalyptic content from this powerful image and even to turn it into a vague, mystical umbrella term. Bale consciously avoided these dangers, however, by concentrating antichrist into two historical institutions – one headed by the pope, the other by Mohammed – and by linking these to the prophecies of St John: 'The beast of the bottomless pit is the cruel, crafty, and cursed generation of antichrist, the pope with his bishops, prelates, priests, and religious in Europe, Mahomet with his doting douzepers* in Africa, and so forth in Asia and India ...'[10] The seven seals and vials of the Book of Revelation gave Bale the chronology for his framework, while history provided the evidence for the actions prophesied under specific seals and vials.

The first three seals represented the sufferings of the true church from the ascension of Christ to the sixth century. With the arrival of Mohammed and the claim of Pope Boniface III to be the vicar of Christ on earth, the opening of the fourth seal ushered in a maturation of the power of antichrist. 'The antichrists thus spread, and their kingdoms well set forward, the light was clearly extincted, and darkness overwent the whole world.'[11] Bale concentrated upon popery, the enemy at hand, and brought in Mohammed to extend the jurisdiction of antichrist beyond Europe and to explain the shadowy figures of Gog and Magog. The hierarchical structure and the descending theory of the papal monarchy helped him to show how corruption reached from the top to the bottom of the false church. After all, even the parish priest received his authority and jurisdiction from the pope. By the turn of the first millennium, the power of the papacy had so grown that the pontificate of Sylvester II marked the point when Satan broke his bindings and began to rage in the world again. Persecution increased and the true church continued only among those saints whom the pope and his officials tried to destroy as heretics.[12] Just at this low point, light began to dawn again, however, and the last ages of the world started to unfold.

The opening of the sixth seal commenced with the work of Wycliffe.

---

10 *Ibid.*, p. 392 (upon Rev. xi:7); cf. 261–3, 283, 291, 319–20, 571. Bale did not mention the new world. *douzepers: twelve peers of France, hence any illustrious grandees, *Oxford English Dictionary (OED)*
11 *Ibid.*, p. 320; see 312–14, 316–17, 319–20
12 *Ibid.*, pp. 322, 559–63

The pouring of the sixth vial clearly corresponded to the dissolution of the monasteries and the preaching of the gospel in Henry VIII's England. Popery now represented the beast out of the sea and the names of blasphemy emblazoned upon its head spelled out the offices of the Roman church. The reformation on the continent and the enactment of Henrician supremacy in England wounded the head of that beast, while the continued usage of popish ceremonies in reformed churches showed how that wound would heal. The fall of Thomas Cromwell led to the recovery of the English portion of the beast, as seen in the conservative religious reaction which followed. This stage would not last long, however. As Bale wrote to the now ascendant Bishop Gardiner, a man who turned from writing against the pope to persecuting protestants: 'You shall be overcome ... at the latter day ... which is not far off.'[13] Holy history flowed from the past, through contemporary events, on into the imminent future.

With ardent expectation, Bale awaited the opening of the seventh seal, the opening of that time when the elect would glory in the fall of Babylon and the erection of a New Jerusalem. In his discussion of the New Zion, however, Bale employed purposely studied and ambiguous language. The commentary in this section, unlike that in the rest of the book, consisted almost entirely of a literal paraphrase of the text. Bale conceived of this glorious estate of the saints as a spiritual kingdom – that is, a reformed church – but he cautioned his readers on this point to 'submit your weak judgments with Paul, confessing God's secret counsels to be unsearchable, and his ways past finding out.'[14] While hesitant to become a detailed architect of Zion, Bale threw caution aside when dealing with the fall of Babylon and describing the forces involved.

A sign of the opening of the seventh seal would be an upsurge of preaching, not only by ministers as in the age of the sixth seal but by the multitudes as well. Bale explained the passage 'and there were great voices in heaven' by pointing out that after the seventh angel blew his trumpet the oppressed and persecuted would step forth as the instruments of the Almighty: 'Many (the congregation or kingdom of God, his gospel once purely published by preachers,) shall speak godly things to the edification of others. The simple, poor weaklings, idiots, and infants shall utter the hidden wisdom of God to the confusion of the great wise men and sage seniors of this world. Yea, the stones in the street, the

13 *Ibid.*, p. 433; see 326, 358, 421–2, 426 ff., 563–4
14 *Ibid.*, pp. 594 (upon Rev. xxi:9–10), 588 (upon Rev. xxi:5–6)

outcasts of the world, the forsaken people, shall wonderfully praise the Lord.' Bale's prophecy came true in the mouths of the mechanic martyrs of Mary's reign, of the gathered separatist saints of Elizabeth's reign, and of the tub preachers of the seventeenth century. This passage heralded the tradition of the persecuted and oppressed, for it placed the overthrow of the unreformed church into the hands of all protestants and it especially emphasized the role of the lower social orders. The reformed church waxed powerful in the word, the old church in the world. God gave the victory in the spiritual combat raging between them. The oppressed elect must strive manfully against the persecuting establishment, but they must remember that they best fought with weapons of the spirit: 'Let us pray ... unto the Lord for grace, and then amend our lives, and the plague shall cease. Only hath he promised to destroy them [Gog and Magog] with the breath of his mouth, and with no bodily armour nor strength of men ...'[15] The plague of popery ceased with the spread of the reformation. Speaking through his witnesses – preachers in the sixth age, the lowly and oppressed in the seventh and last age – the Almighty had started to smash the power of the pope and Mohammed, those twin manifestations of antichrist, with the word. Babylon was falling through the efforts of protestants.

The call for a godly prince echoed faintly through the pages of *The image of bothe churches*. Compared to other protestant contemporaries, Bale placed very little reliance in the apocalyptic leadership of established social or political forces. Repeatedly, he noted that princes possessed insufficient strength to overcome the hordes of antichrist: 'For unto kings hath not God given it to subdue these beasts. Only is it reserved to the victory of his living word.' Unlike Tyndale who supposedly asked the Lord to 'open the eyes of the King of England' when bound to the stake, Bale escaped from reliance on a reformation from above. Magistrates, princes, bishops, established power in general, proved weaker reeds than preachers, the persecuted, and the oppressed in the troubles of the last days. A godly prince might still help to open the light of the Lord in England, but Bale – despite his belief that God sent Prince Edward 'for the singular comfort of England' – believed that the reformation would come through other channels if necessary.[16] References to England and English history abounded in *The image of bothe churches*, but Bale did not single out his country for any special

---

15 *Ibid.*, pp. 400–1 (upon Rev. xi:15), 575 (upon Rev. xx:8)
16 *Ibid.*, pp. 365, 443, cf. 164–5, 450, 486–7; cf. Morris, *Political Thought*, ch. 2

apocalyptic role. Instead, he explained the concentration upon England by pointing out that 'this book is written in that language.' During the 1530s, when he wrote anti-papal propaganda under the aegis of Thomas Cromwell and John, Earl of Oxford, Bale portrayed king and nation in a much more favourable light in his popular plays. Cromwell, however, fell from power in 1540 and Edward VI ascended the throne only in 1547.[17] *The image of bothe churches* reflects the great disappointment for English protestants of the intervening period. It carried the attitudes of an interlude into the future.

John Bale created a new apocalyptic tradition, but he also stood at the end of an old one. *The image of bothe churches* formed a link between the medieval Latin and the protestant vernacular interpretation of the Apocalypse. A critical scholar not blindly reliant upon his sources, Bale consciously applied the insights of Joachim, Wycliffe, and Hus within a new context and from them forged a truly historical approach to the prophecies of St John. His good friend John Foxe would pile up mounds of evidence in support. Bale's chronological framework gave depth to his generic conception of antichrist. It delineated the eternal struggle against evil in a way which directly applied to the history of the Christian church and to contemporary events. This combat was 'like still to continue to the end of the world, both by this prophecy Revelation, and also by the prophecy of Daniel.' So long as people read and believed in Bale's exegesis, the threat remained. Drawing upon a tradition which identified individual popes with antichrist, he transformed it into an even more potent critique of popery. Popery consisted not merely in allegiance to the pope and his officers, it included the whole fabric of unreformed Christianity. Hence, Bishop Gardiner who accepted the Henrician supremacy none the less acted as an agent of antichrist in Bale's eyes by upholding traditional doctrine and ceremony.[18] Pope was not the only name of blasphemy written on the head of the beast – others appeared there as well: 'cardinal, patriarchy, legate, metropolitan, primate, archbishop, diocesan, prothonorary, archdeacon, official, chancellor, dean, prebend, parson, vicar, my lord abbot, master doctor and such like ... For offices they are not appointed by the Holy Ghost, nor once mentioned in the scriptures.'

17 *Ibid.*, p. 450
18 *Ibid.*, p. 323; see 433, 510. Bale's attack upon Gardiner has been criticized in Hughes, *Reformation*, II, pp. 121 n. 2, 287–8. While not logically consistent to a modern Roman catholic, Bale's position made sense to many British protestants in the sixteenth and seventeenth centuries.

Only by removing the ceremonies and nomenclature of the past and by working out a godly church ordinance from the Bible could popery be removed. Such sentiments echoed often down the following hundred years! The English church of the early 1540s (and many still thought in the early 1640s) remained sorely in danger; 'Nothing is brought as yet to Christ's clear institution and sincere ordinance, but all remaineth still as the antichrists left it.'[19] Like his successors, Bale firmly upheld the primacy of scripture both for doctrine and for polity. Although he became a bishop under Edward VI, his identification of the ceremony, polity, and doctrine of the medieval church with popery provided English protestants with a powerful apocalyptic tool for criticizing the retention of any of these elements within a reformed English church. After all, Bale not only called for a full and thorough reformation of the church, he also branded those who opposed such action as the devil's disciples.

By conjoining the prophecies of St John with historical and contemporary events, John Bale created an important method of biblical exegesis and a new view of the past. Furthermore, he established a fruitful framework which placed the contemporary call for reformation in chronological cosmic perspective, which emphasized the necessity of spiritual strife, and which promised the preordained triumph of those who fought for the true protestant church. Bale clearly employed this method in other works as well and he made his message available even to the common people by publishing it in English. Without downgrading the contributions of other early English reformers, one must still award priority of place to *The image of bothe churches* in the formation of a protestant apocalyptic tradition in England.[20] It imposed a method and a key historical thrust upon that tradition. With its emphasis upon the sanctity of the oppressed and its almost complete absence of reference to the godly prince, *The image of bothe churches* – in these aspects – lay outside of the mainstream of English protestant thought in the reigns of Edward VI and Elizabeth I. Instead of the magisterial reformation so beloved by sixteenth-century reformers, it portrayed the preacher and the poor, the oppressed and the persecuted, as the champions of God's

19 *Ibid.*, p. 422 (upon Rev. xiii:1), 427 (upon Rev. xiii:3). This position anticipated that of many who became dissatisfied with the Elizabethan settlement; see Knappen, *Tudor Puritanism*, ch. 3.
20 For the importance of Bale's articulation of this historical apocalyptic paradigm, see Firth, Bauckham, and Fairfield, 'John Bale,' p. 150; cf. Ball, *Great Expectation*, pp. 18–21, for an emphasis upon George Joye's translations of Lutheran writings.

work on earth. This basic theme struck up a leitmotif which never completely faded away during the next generations of English protestants, a motif that swelled in power and tone whenever times of crisis threatened to undermine the reformation until it finally reached a crescendo in the 1640s. It soon received copious illustration in the acts of the Marian martyrs and in the stories collected by John Foxe. At the same time, Bale's overall framework struggled for acceptance against other apocalyptic visions.

The change of monarch in England in 1547 brought into existence a new world for protestant action. Although exiles, including John Bale, and continental reformers like Martin Bucer, helped to reform the English church under Edward vi, control of this magisterial reformation remained in the hands of those in England who had weathered the stormy last years of the reign of Henry viii. Led by a truly godly prince, they established protestantism through the channels of creative governmental action. In a change of role, John Bale became bishop of Ossory, sent to bring the gospel to the outer fringes of Ireland. Bishop Bale tried to use his authority to enforce right religion upon the 'superstitious' natives, a surprising turn of events for the earlier champion of those oppressed by the Henrician bishops. Even in authority he felt himself to be one of the persecuted. Caught up in the excitement of returning to power, however, Bale took up the imperial tradition. At the end of the 1550 edition of his commentary on Revelation he implored the godly to pray daily for King Edward vi, who 'hath so sore wounded the beast, that he may throw all his superstition into the bottomless lake again (from whence they have come) to the comfort of his people ...'[21] The cosmic theme of the struggle against antichrist continued, but now it seemed that the Almighty worked through the prince and his consecrated preachers.

A full investigation of the writings and sermons of the divines of the short reign of Edward vi might disclose that the apocalyptic explanation of the reformation continued to be a major element in the defence of protestantism. Archbishop Cranmer, for example, used it against the Devon rebels in 1549, who demanded restoration of the old ceremonies of the church. Cranmer, after defending baptism and communion in both kinds (that is, giving both bread and wine to laymen) as sacraments ordained by Christ, condemned other so-called sacraments and

21 Bale, *Vocacyon*, passim, and *Image of bothe*, sig. L1 3v (last page). Bale remoulded medieval traditions to a new purpose in more than one way; see Fairfield. '*Vocacyon*.'

sacramentals, for these had been 'ordained by the bishops of Rome; adversaries to Christ, and therefore rightly called antichrist.' From his identification of antichrist with an individual pope in 1536, Cranmer now broadened the term to include the papacy. He went on to point out: 'But antichrist ... hath set up his superstitions under the name of holiness to none other intent but as the devil seeketh all means to draw us from Christ, so doth antichrist advance his holy superstitions to the intent that we should take him in the stead of Christ ...' While not spelled out at length, Cranmer's remarks implied an historical apocalyptic outlook. The medieval accretions of doctrine and practice upheld by the conservative rebels arose during that period when antichrist ruled the visible church, according to the archbishop. When Cranmer's turn arrived, one of his last statements reaffirmed his belief that the papacy was antichrist.[22] Popular religious rebellions could be repressed only so long as the reformers retained the backing of the crown. The greatest threat to the English reformation followed from the death of Edward vi. Suddenly governmental policy reversed. The leaders and followers of Edward's reign, cast from their seats of authority by Queen Mary, swung the cudgel prepared by their predecessors to beat against their oppressors.

Marian exiles and Marian martyrs returned to the themes sounded by Barnes, Tyndale, and Frith and systematically synthesized by Bale. Babylon reared its head in England, so combat against its power and the jurisdiction of a government that upheld it once again became a strident theme in religious controversy. Cast into the Tower and removed from his bishopric of London by Mary, Nicholas Ridley wrote, disputed, and finally died to uphold his fellow protestants in their faith. William Haller viewed the campaign of 'organized and sustained propaganda' against the Marian reaction as being 'set in motion by Ridley's directing hand and soon taken up by certain of his personal associates in exile on the Continent.' One of Ridley's militant and skilful products was *Certain godly, learned, and comfortable conferences between Nicholas Ridley ... and Hugh Latimer*. Because they feared that the authorities would stop his pen, his friends held it back from publication until after Ridley's death.[23] The pamphlet portrayed two of England's leading pro-

---

22 Cranmer, 'Answer to the fifteen articles of the rebels of Devon,' in Williams, *English Documents*, v, p. 375, and Cranmer, *Works*, pp. 295–6, 338. The latter come from Foxe. Cranmer never accepted Bale's framework fully.
23 Haller, *Foxe's Book*, p. 30

testants steeling themselves for the inevitable results of Mary's accession to the throne. In dialogue, they answered catholic objections to their actions, especially to Ridley's support of the Northumberland plot. Accused of stirring up sedition – that worst of crimes which challenged the framework of order in the Tudor and early Stuart universe – Ridley prevaricated by answering: 'Were these men as they were called, seditious persons, Christ, Paul, and the prophets? God forbid!' As the Bible provided him with examples of proper action in adversity, so would he create a model for future reformers. Accused of breaking the laws of the realm, he replied that 'a man ought to obey his prince, but in the Lord, and never against the Lord.' Neither the appeal from the law of the land to the law of God nor the comparison of himself to biblical heroes was unprecedented. Rarely had it such a skilful and vivid presentation in the vernacular, however. Both became standard arguments used against the authorities by religious dissidents. Ridley ended this work with militant images drawn from his boyhood home of Tynedale as well as from St Paul.[24] When this pamphlet was composed, England had not yet been received back into the fold of Rome. This act of reconciliation took place, however, before Ridley wrote his last major works. In these, the militant protestant tone of the *Conferences* turned apocalyptic in interpretation, fierce in force.

With England officially restored to papal supremacy and with the persecutions of 'Bloody Mary' begun, the apocalyptic tradition gained cogency and relevance for English protestants. Ridley, awaiting a martyr's death, lashed out in fury against antichrist in his last major work, *A piteous lamentation of the miserable estate of the church in England*. He despised the new changes in the English church: prayer in ignorance rather than in the vernacular, abuse of communion by restoring the idolatry of the mass and withholding the cup from laymen, the withdrawal of the Bible, and a whole host of other abominations. '... The false prophets of antichrist, which are past all shame, do openly preach in the pulpits unto the people of God, that the catechism is to be counted heresy; whereby their old blindness is brought home again ...'[25] The

24 Ridley, *Works*, pp. 143, 144, 145. Haller stretched the evidence in his assessment of this section of the *Conferences*; 'the saint was to put on the armour of faith and fight the good fight under Christ's banner against Antichrist.' *Foxe's Book*, p. 35. Ridley made no mention of antichrist.

25 Ridley, *Works*, p. 49. *A piteous lamentation* was first printed in London in 1566 and reprinted in Foxe's *Actes and monuments*. Jasper Ridley argued that it was written in the winter of 1554–5 and smuggled abroad; *Nicholas Ridley*, p. 369.

government of Mary was part of a cosmic conspiracy to pull the English people of God away from the right path into the ways of perdition. 'The head, under Satan, of all mischief is antichrist and his brood; and the same is he which is the Babylonical beast.' Like Bale, Ridley equated Babylon with 'the whole trade of the Romish religion ... which is contrary to the only rule of all true religion, that is, God's word.' Lest any miss the intent of his application of Revelation to the contemporary situation, Ridley wrote that Rome, 'that wicked see ... maketh indeed the body of the beast, whereupon the abominable whore doth sit.'[26] The restoration of Babylon fulfilled the prophecies of doom that he and others had preached at the court of Edward VI.

God punished England with a return to the Roman Babylon because the Edwardian reformation had brought forth too few fruits. Godly preachers had failed sufficiently to change the corrupt ways of the people. Magistrates modified the laws of the land and established the outward signs of a purified church, but English hearts by remaining sinful brought on retribution. So it seemed to Ridley, who advised the godly remaining in England to follow one of two courses. Those still enjoying liberty 'in the time of the reign of antichrist's abominations, [were] to fly unto the mountains: which signifieth places of stronghold,' that is, they should 'depart the realm' for the safety of the continent. Those who could not flee must trust in the Lord. In the past, God had provided help – sometimes deliverance – to his persecuted elect. Ridley admonished those in immediate danger of persecution to remember that one could aspire to no higher honour than martyrdom; his own actions followed this advice. Whatever course one followed, each individual – above all else – must stand fast in his faith. Ridley did not even hint that God might raise up another godly prince (or princess) to deliver England from its oppression. He became very pessimistic about the future of protestantism in his country. The imminent return of Christ provided the only ray of hope for the future of the English elect. 'The world without doubt (this I do believe and therefore I say) draweth towards an end ...'[27] The battle of protestants against the Marian régime became fused with the second coming of Christ. In Ridley's view, direct divine intervention seemed the only way to win the war against Babylon. His apocalyptic vision, if joined with the battle images of his earlier work,

---

26 *Ibid.*, pp. 53, 55. Ridley followed Bale's notion of popery.
27 *Ibid.*, pp. 63 (Rev. xviii), 65, 75. Ridley feared the birth of an heir to Queen Mary, a
   possibility in the winter of 1554–5; see Prescott, *Mary Tudor*, pp. 314–17.

might have produced an ideology of rebellion or revolution. He came very close to extending spiritual warfare to the political arena, but passive resistance remained his quietist solution. Ridley advocated either flight or martyrdom to English protestants. Neither godly prince nor rebellion could save them. Their only real hope lay in the sudden return of their Saviour.

Among the eight hundred Englishmen who took Ridley's advice and sailed to the continent were two friends who had been bishops under Edward VI, John Bale and John Ponet. Bale made a tortuous voyage from Ossory to safety and once again engaged in his paper war with the wily old foe. His former patron, John Ponet (successively bishop of Rochester and Winchester), trod a different but equally stormy path to the haven of Frankfurt. Having participated in Wyatt's rebellion, Ponet practised the theme of his most important work, *A shorte treatise of politike power*: 'It is better to trust in the Lord, than to trust in princes.' Ponet transformed Ridley's militant reaction to Mary into a call for political rebellion. By justifying the deposition of rulers who became tyrants, he broke sharply with the passive resistance to rulers advocated by previous English protestants.[28] Although he wrote about political power, Ponet clearly saw the reformation in an apocalyptic context.

When preaching at the court of Edward VI, Ponet stressed the necessity 'for every man to have eyes of his own, whereby he may discern the true church from the false, and the good doctrine from the bad ... Christian learning from papistry, and Christ from antichrist.' This came straight from Bale. Ponet went on to warn against the 'subversion of the kingdom of Christ, and all Christian doctrine and setting up again of the doctrine of the Romish antichrist to God's great dishonour.' After being forced into exile, he slashed at the ministers of Queen Mary for re-establishing the 'beastly popish mass' in England. With sharp, mocking tones he derided the real power of the pope, pointed to its source, and deplored the methods of its establishment: 'For all men, yea half wise women and babes can well judge, that his power is not worthy to be laughed at; and were it not bolstered and propped up with sword and faggot, it would (as it will notwithstanding) shortly lie in the mire, for it is not built on the rock, but on sand, not planted by the father of heaven, but by the devil of hell, as the fruits do manifestly declare.'[29] The exiled

28 P[onet], *A shorte treatise*, p. 1 (quoting Psalm 118); see Hudson, *John Ponet*, and Morris, *Political Thought*, pp. 146–56
29 *A shorte treatise*, pp. 19, 63, 21–2, and Ponet, *A notable sermon*, sig. F 7V, F 8V–GI, cf. E 4V–5

bishop showed no respect for the wordly might of the 'high seat of antichrist,' as he still called the papacy. However, his castigation reached beyond Rome, beyond churchmen, to include the queen and lesser magistrates of England. They forfeited their trust to God and the realm by bringing back catholicism. Ponet rebuked them with stinging irony: '... Hath not the realm good cause to thank and trust the potentates, prelates, and Parliament men for banishing the sacred testament and gospel of God with sincerer administration of his holy sacraments, and for bringing in the devilish power of the Romish antichrist into England again with his miserable mass and all popish slavery? By the which they have ... broken their oath and loyalty to God, and to the imperial crown of England ... and are guilty of the innocent blood of ... true Christian natural English men and women.' Although Ponet displayed no confidence in those magistrates who betrayed their trust by resurrecting popery, he still paid tribute to the sovereign realm of England and its imperial crown. Like other Marian exiles, including Bale, Ponet lamented the fall of reformed England with a nationalistic jeremiad: 'In what nation under the cope of heaven, hath God shewed greater tokens, and it so little set by; as in England?'[30] Mary and her advisers sorely misused their responsibility to God and man by reversing the reformation. The people of England failed to prevent them and now suffered under the judgment of the Lord. Ponet's anger stemmed from a strong sense of betrayal.

Such pessimism, ironically, evaporated when the results of persecution became known. Both Marian officials and protestant exiles marvelled at the many martyrs produced in England. The courageous men and women who lost their blood in defence of their faith offered indisputable proof that reformed religion, while established by statute, clearly had penetrated into the fabric of society. The preachers of Edward VI's reign, it became evident, had not laboured in vain. A vicarious sense of success reinforced the nationalistic nostalgia experienced by the exiles. So strongly did the acts of the martyrs influence the mind of Ponet that he identified the elect of God almost entirely with the persecuted and oppressed: 'God will have *his* tried by *persecution*, that the world may see ... Yea he hath no other way to let the difference appear to men's eyes between his servants and princes' parasites, than only by persecution. [To be] killed of the worldly princes and tyrants, rather than they would disobey God, and forsake Christ: this can neither papists nor Turks, Jews

30 *A shorte treatise*, pp. 172, 139–40, 157; cf. Ponet, *An apologie*, pp. xxxii, cxviii–ix

nor gentiles, nor none other do, but only the elects of God.'[31] Only the true saints could withstand the test of merciless cruelty. This argument could easily redound against protestants, of course, for it ignored the considerable bravery displayed as well by catholic and anabaptist martyrs in early sixteenth-century England. One might expect some prophet from the lower orders to claim that only the persecuted constituted the elect, but it sounds singularly inappropriate in the mouth of a bishop who had, himself, enforced religious change from a position of authority. Perhaps Ponet's concentration upon the persecuted was the natural reaction of a person who had fled his country for ideological reasons; after all, Bale had presented a similar point of view. Having viewed the fruits of reformation and responsibility from afar, influential Marian exiles like Ponet longed to return to England that they might finish forging a godly nation.

A religious conservative who always remained faithful to the second Edwardian prayer book, to that Anglican church enacted by Parliament, Ponet none the less became a political radical. Certain that the godly must triumph over the minions of antichrist, he did not fear to advocate, or even to participate in, political rebellion. Civil war threatened England with as bleak a future as its worst trials of the past. 'Oh miserable England, that once thus wast by a tyrant and outward enemies plagued [that is, by William the Conqueror]. But how much more miserable shalt thou be by the wars that are to come shortly on thee. God be merciful unto thee.' Bishop Ponet both urged the people of England to repent to prepare themselves for the coming cosmic combat and also implored them to overthrow their ruling tyrant. Without losing hope that God might grant mercy to the realm, perhaps by direct intervention, Ponet concentrated most of his energy upon advocating temporal warfare. The last paragraph of his treatise cleared up any remaining ambiguities by explicitly distinguishing between 'variable England' and 'constant Jerusalem,' between the 'company of men' and the 'fellowship of angels,' between 'your earthly country' and the 'heavenly paradise.'[32] The transcendent context of reform came close to blending Ponet's categories, but his fight against Rome remained in the realm of spiritual strife, waged with the weapons of the spirit, and his call for the deposition of tyrants retained a classical, temporal cast. In the 1640s

31 *Ibid.*, p. 74 (my emphasis). This statement represented almost a *reductio ad absurdum* of the tradition of the persecuted and oppressed.
32 *Ibid.*, pp. 170, 183

readers of *A shorte treatise* had no difficulty in blending the two together, something the author, himself, refused to do.

Ponet carried forward several of the important themes enunciated in
Bale's interpretation. These included his view of the reformation as a
struggle against antichrist, his discovery of the elect among those persecuted, and his distrust of the prince as an instrument of God's action
upon earth. By advocating actual revolt against princes, Ponet travelled
beyond Bale into the realm of active resistance. Of course, Ponet's
treatise was not a commentary on the Book of Revelation and, therefore,
contained no lengthy unravelling of the prophecies of St John. The
apocalyptic tradition, however, ran like a thread throughout this work
and provided a significant part of the context in which Ponet expounded
his theories of political power. John Ponet died before the deliverance of
England from the 'mist of popery' which enshrouded the kingdom during
the reign of Mary. Had he lived to see the dawning of the new day, his
voice might then have mingled with those who sang the praises of the
godly princess Elizabeth.

Most of the Marian exiles returned to their homeland and became
leaders in the protestant church enacted by the first Parliament of
Elizabeth I.[33] Many of Elizabeth's bishops came from their ranks. During
the formative part of their lives, the reformation in England (or its
reversal) depended upon the tenuous contingency of the life or death of
individual Tudors. In a very real sense, this unsettled state of affairs
continued to exist during the first decades of Elizabeth's reign. This
common experience of anxiety, heightened by exile, helped to shape a
consensus interpretation of the reformation in apocalyptic terms. Representative bishops of the Church of England, such as John Aylmer, John
Jewel, and Edwin Sandys, helped to mould this tradition. Like Ponet,
they faced exile in the reign of Mary. Unlike Ponet, they published their
works after the end of the period of despair.

One can readily detect the change of tone in that paean of Elizabeth,
England, Englishmen, and English mixed monarchy written by John
Aylmer, *An harborowe for faithfull and true subjects*. This pamphlet
tried to defend Elizabeth's right to the throne against those blasts trum-
peted forth by men like John Knox and John Ponet. It made a key
contribution to the origins of the notion that England might become an
'elect nation' and it also helped to revivify protestant predilections

toward the godly prince. Aylmer dedicated his tract to Francis, Earl of Bedford and Lord Robert Dudley, councillors of the new queen, who,

with a singular favour and desire to advance and promote the true doctrine of Christ's cross, which of late through the power of darkness, the members of antichrist's and Satan's guard, hath not only been obscured, but clean defaced and was like still to be if God inspired not the heart of our English Helena, and such as be about her, to seek out and dig up his son's cross out of the dunghill of the devil's doctrine, and to rear [it] up again in the eyes of her subjects, to the unspeakable comfort of all Christ's members and the wonderful confusion of the adversaries.[34]

Long, rolling sentences, full of allusions but clearly based upon an apocalyptic vision, expressed Aylmer's belief that God, once again, worked through the political élite. The new queen and her aristocratic advisers had returned England to the proper path of reformation.

Aylmer's vision extended back through holy history. Like Bale, he portrayed contemporary events within the context of an eternal combat between the forces of good and those of evil. Before the reformation 'antichrist ruled and revelled in the temple of God (which is men's hearts and conscience), armed and guarded with the power of emperors, kings, princes and laws ...' This described the medieval church. The new dawning of the gospel, starting only after the papacy reached the zenith of its domination, first shone forth in God's special nation. Aylmer, foreshadowing the nineteenth-century Russian novelists with their spirit of 'Mother Russia,' personified his religiously inspired nationalism. He made England say: 'God hath brought forth in me, the greatest treasure that he hath for your comfort and all the world's. He would that out of my womb should come that servant of his, your brother John Wycliffe, who begat Hus, who begat Luther, who begat truth.' Many future authors would repeat Aylmer's genealogy of truth and share his sense of national potential, especially in the heady days of the 1640s. Smothered in the past by 'both the spiritual and temporal

---

34 [Aylmer], An harborowe, sig. A 4r. Constantine the Great's mother was believed to have been a British princess named Helena, hence Aylmer was comparing Elizabeth to Constantine. Aylmer shared the religious and social attitudes of a man like Ponet. The differences between their treatises sprang from the fact that Aylmer wrote after the death of Mary. For similar praise of Elizabeth by contemporaries, see Haller, Foxe's Book, ch. 3, Morris, Political Thought, ch. 4, and Smith, 'Elizabethan doctrine of the prince.'

antichrist, the pope and the Turk,' the true light of Christ, revived by Wycliffe, now beamed forth under the aegis of Elizabeth.[35] Aylmer transformed Bale's interpretation into a celebration of queen and country.

Ponet the exile and Ridley the martyr-to-be ended their pamphlets by attacking their monarch and praying that the Lord would save his persecuted elect. Aylmer finished his with effusive praise for Queen Elizabeth and a call for her preservation:

Let us seek to requite her with thankfulness, which studieth to keep us in quietness. Let us daily call to God with lifted up hearts and hands for her preservation and long life; that she may many years carry the sword of our defence, and therewith cut off the head of that Hydra, the antichrist of Rome, in such sort, as it [may] never grow again in this realm of England; that God's glory may flourish, good men's conscience may be at rest, this noble realm in honour and the queen's majesty in long felicity, which God grant. Amen.

With an original mixture of metaphors that blended the beast with seven heads from Revelation with the hydra of anarchy into a powerful image of the popish antichrist, Aylmer emphasized the role of Elizabeth and reformed religion in upholding order. In the flush of the restoration of protestantism in England through the agency of the Queen-in-Parliament, the call for rebellion seemed neither desirable nor necessary. Aylmer embraced the reformation as keenly as Bale, Ridley, or Ponet, but the new situation called for the rhetoric of order, obedience, and thanksgiving – an example upon the imperial tradition. Aylmer even played down the imminent return of Christ to some extent in the wonder of the work performed by the Almighty through his godly queen. She carried on the torch lit by Wycliffe. To help this happen, John Aylmer toiled energetically within the Established Church, so much so that he never published another book.[36] The dominant orders of society regained the initiative in the spiritual warfare of the latter days. For most Elizabethan reformers, God's imperial instrument replaced the oppressed and persecuted. As bishop of London, Aylmer himself became a target and scourge of those who felt that the Elizabethan settlement had not purged the church of enough medieval elements.

35 *An harborowe*, sig. B 4r, R IV, Q Ir. Milton's *Aeropagitica* contained the most famous repetition of this genealogy.
36 *Ibid.*, sig. R 3r. For Aylmer's role as bishop of London, see Collinson, *Elizabethan Puritan*.

With Aylmer's hand busy in the enormous task of administering the most important and difficult bishopric in the land, the task of defending the Church of England from its critics passed to the bishop of Salisbury, John Jewel. Jewel clearly used an historical apocalyptic interpretation of the reformation to uphold the Established Church. However, he stood outside of the chronological matrix of Bale and tended to see antichrist as an individual in the medieval tradition. 'There is none,' he noted in his commentary upon II Thessalonians, 'neither old nor young, neither learned nor unlearned, but he hath heard of antichrist. They hate his name, and detest him, before they know him.' The problem was to identify antichrist. In his ironic way, Jewel liked to pretend that it was one of tact.

I know many men are offended to hear the pope pointed out for antichrist, and think it an uncharitable kind of doctrine, therefore I refrain to use any such names, and only will report to you other, by what tokens antichrist, when he cometh, may be known ... 'Whosoever calleth himself the universal priest, or desireth so to be called, in the pride of his heart is the forerunner of antichrist.' These words were written by Gregory I, against John the patriarch of Constantinople more than 900 years since.[37]

Fear of causing offence never prevented Jewel from going on at length in several of his works to demonstrate that the tokens of antichrist applied only to popes, those of Babylon to the church of Rome. Nor had the reformers of the sixteenth century first proclaimed this fact. Bernard of Clairvaux, Lorenzo Valla, Marsiglio of Padua, Petrarch, Savonarola, Joachim of Flora, and Baptist of Mantua all gave 'the world sometime to understand that the bishop of Rome himself (by your leave) is very antichrist.' In his *Apology of the Church of England*, Jewel put this forth as one of the basic beliefs of the Established Church: 'We believe that he [the pope] does give unto himself ... a profane, a sacreligious, and an antichristian name; that he is also the king of pride; that he is Lucifer, which preferreth himself before his brethren; that he has forsaken the faith, and is the forerunner of antichrist.'[38] For all of his tact, the conclusion presented itself with clarity, even though the reader had to

---

37 Jewel, *Works*, II, p. 902, *Certaine sermons*, sig. E 6v–7r; see *Apology*, pp. 118, 132; also see Bauckham, 'Prophecy,' and Booty, *John Jewel*

38 Jewel, *Apology*, pp. 75, 26; see *Works*, pp. 902–33. Jewel drew upon history for examples, not to establish a chronology of Revelation. Most of the figures he mentioned also appeared in the preface of Bullinger, *A hundred sermons* (unpaginated), between the marginal notes: 'The eldest and most common doctrine is that the pope is antichrist' and 'All good men at all times have spoken against the pope.'

draw it for himself. Good authorities had called popes antichrist for at least four centuries, the shoe still fit, so logic demanded an identification of the papacy with antichrist. Jewel, however, explicitly reserved this judgment for Christ, who would reveal the nature of the papacy at his second coming: 'He will overthrow the whole power of antichrist by his presence and by the glory of his coming. Then shall it appear who is the successor of Peter, who is the true vicar of Christ, and who is antichrist.' That day drew near. Like Constantine at Nicaea, the godly princes of the sixteenth century prepared the way for their Saviour by restoring the gospel in its purity. Certainty might elude one until the end, but even catholics should be able to 'see that now all their subtle practices will soon fall down headlong upon the sight of the Gospel. For antichrist is not overthrown but with the brightness of Christ's coming.'[39] Until the final end, the Lord would work through his imperial instruments to reform the church on earth.

Jewel and Aylmer reverted to the early protestant call for a godly prince to explain that miracle which called them forth from exile into positions of power to carry on the work of the Lord. The death of Mary and accession of Elizabeth appeared to be a direct intervention of the hand of God. No wonder Jewel, Aylmer, and others like them preached obedience to the higher powers and revived the imperial tradition of apocalyptic thought! Although he drew upon history for examples, Jewel remained outside of Bale's chronological framework. This was so unusual that those who operated within it would read it by implication into Jewel's works – as this author did at an earlier stage. More typical of the Elizabethan hierarchy was Edwin Sandys, another Marian exile, who fused Bale's interpretation with the imperial tradition.

Before being elevated to the archbishopric of York, Sandys preceded Aylmer at London. After more than a quarter century of service he published a collection of twenty-two sermons in 1585. 'Rome,' he boldly affirmed at St Paul's, 'is a sink of all abomination' not 'a fountain from whence those living waters ... may be had.'[40] He returned to this theme at St Paul's Cross, ending a lengthy attack upon popery with the following invective:

We gladly grant that we are fallen away from the bishop of Rome, who long ago

39 Jewel, *Works*, II, p. 933, and *Apology*, p. 81; cf. *Certaine sermons*, sig. n 8v

40 Sandys, *Sermons*, p. 20. Edwin Sandys served as bishop of Worcester 1559–70, bishop of London 1570–7, and archbishop of York 1577–88. Most of the collected sermons were preached in the latter two posts. See Maclure, *Paul's Cross Sermons*, pp. 207, 209, 210, 215, 224.

fell from Christ; we do utterly abandon his usurped and proud authority; we have happily forsaken that synagogue of Satan, that den of thieves, that polluted church, that simoniacal temple; and we joyfully confess that we have no society or fellowship with his darkness. In our sermons we preach Christ, and none else but him; we know nothing, we believe nothing, but Christ and him crucified. In our sacraments we shew forth the Lord's death in no other sort, than he himself hath done and commanded us to do ... This is our apostasy. We have forsaken him that hath forsaken God, and whom God hath forsaken; we have left that man of sin, that rose-coloured harlot with whom the kings of the earth have committed fornication, that triple-crowned beast, that double-sworded tyrant, that thief and murderer, who hath robbed so many souls of salvation, and sucked so much innocent blood of Christian martyrs, that adversary unto Christ, that pretensed vicar, who hath displaced the person, not only taking upon him Christ's room and office, but also boasting himself as if he were a god, and being content of his parasites so to be called. This wicked man of sin is at last revealed by the sincere preaching of the gospel. Daniel in his prophecies, Paul in his epistles, and John in his revelations, have most lively described and pointed him forth even as it were with the finger. Yea, through his pride and ambition, his usurping authority and worldly rule, his tyranny and persecuting of Christ in his members, he hath sufficiently revealed and detected himself, if none had done it for him.

This wicked man the Lord shall destroy with the breath of his mouth; and then shall be the end. The blast of God's trump hath made him already stagger ... his falsehood is espied; many princes refuse to taste any more of his poisoned cup; he is fallen from being the head, and come almost to be the tail; he was too cruel and too violent to continue.

Such fierce imagery represented a more typical strain on the Elizabethan bench than the ironic coyness of Jewel. One may safely say that many of Sandys' contemporaries matched the vitriolic tone of this attack on the papacy.[41]

An apocalyptic interpretation of the history of the church, probably derived from Bale, provided the context for Sandys' view of contemporary events. Sandys accepted Bale's image of the two churches. Combat between them raged throughout time: 'Christ hath always had a church here on earth: it was begun in paradise; sithence it hath ... continued

41 Sandys, *Sermons*, pp. 389–90; from a sermon preached in the 1570s, probably shortly after the papal bull of 1570 was promulgated. See Bauckham, 'Prophecy,' for a host of analogous examples.

even unto this day ... So hath antichrist his also. Wherefore it behoveth us to know ... the one from the other.'[42] He also spread the power of antichrist across the earth through the twin agencies of the pope and Mohammed. Like Bale and other exiles, Sandys placed emphasis upon the persecuted elect as instruments of the Lord. However, he clearly differentiated between times when the forces of evil commanded the church and those in which the godly exercised control. For 'when the church is infected and polluted with idolatry and superstition then we are to serve him as we conveniently may.' On the other hand, when monarchs like Edward vi and Elizabeth legally settled the true religion, men 'may lawfully and in right reason ought to be constrained thereunto.'[43] As shall be seen, contemporary religious radicals thought this a dubious distinction. None the less, one expects an archbishop to support the disciplinary rights of the monarch and church he serves. The distinction made by Sandys allowed him to combine the tradition of the oppressed and persecuted with the imperial tradition. He gloried in the humble martyrs of the past and still upheld the reforming leadership of his queen.

On the commemoration of her coming to the throne, Sandys lavished fulsome praise upon Elizabeth: 'For as this day, now twenty years fully finished, the Lord in his mercy remembering us, when we little hoped and less deserved, delivered us from the state of miserable servitude, and gave us our gracious sovereign, his own elect, Elizabeth by his grace our prince and governor, the restorer of our religion and liberty.' Her reign marked the culmination of that heroic struggle against the papacy initiated by previous English monarchs. However, Sandys was not slavish in his praise of the godly queen. When preaching in her presence he openly criticized the government for not being forward enough in promoting the gospel. Nevertheless, God chose Elizabeth to dislodge the popish antichrist from England forever, to remove the realm from Babylon. The nation, therefore, should rejoice in the favour thus bestowed. 'If any church, any people, any nation in the world,' Sandys contended, 'have cause to praise the Lord for their prince; this land hath more than any ...' In his wisdom, the Lord thrust his hand into the affairs of England, selecting it for special treatment. Sandys hoped it might become an elect nation before the end of the world arrived. The time of

42 *Sermons*, p. 371; see 261–3, 283, 319–20, 392, 571. Sandys may have derived this through Foxe.
43 *Ibid.*, pp. 191, 192 (preached at York in 1577); for persecution, see 11–12, 29–30, 65–7, 116–17, 180, 377–8

deliverance for all the saints – not only the English – would soon be felt, for 'the coming of Christ [was] at hand.'[44]

Thomas Cranmer, Nicholas Ridley, John Ponet, John Aylmer, John Jewel, and Edwin Sandys, all important bishops, form as representative a group of spokesmen for the reformed Church of England as one could assemble. John Bale sat as a bishop in Ireland. Aside from Bale, whose contribution could not be ignored, these men were selected deliberately to show that an apocalyptic interpretation of the reformation represented a consensus view among the first English protestants, not one confined to 'proto-puritans,' or some other imaginary minority group. The author chose them before reading their works. The group could be enlarged by extending discussion to other divines, including Archbishop Whitgift.[45] All viewed the reformation as a cosmic conflict between the forces of Christ and those of antichrist. Their disagreements came in matters of emphasis or detail, such as the instruments used by the Lord on earth or the relationship of spiritual strife to political action. All wrote and preached in the vernacular to spread their message to the people. All took positions of responsibility to enforce it. However, most of the works so far discussed received only limited circulation. Jewel's *Apology* formed a significant exception, being frequently printed and chained in parish churches. Bale's *The image of bothe churches* also went through several editions. But this group of men really represent the wide acceptance of apocalyptic visions among leading English reformers, not the availability of such interpretations to the population at large. Wide dissemination of Bale's apocalyptic framework followed from its integration into the two most popular books of Elizabethan and early Stuart England, the Geneva Bible and John Foxe's *Actes and monuments*.

Confident in the wonder-working ability of the unleashed word, a group of Marian exiles in Geneva concentrated their scholarly energies upon the creation of a new translation of the Bible into English. In

44 *Ibid.*, pp. 56, 80, 171; see 75, 80–1, 154–5, 158–9, 213, 388, 398
45 In order to show that those who established the mainstream were not 'proto-puritans,' some influential reformers – such as Bishop John Hooper – deliberately have been excluded from this account. Although Archbishop John Whitgift and Thomas Cartwright differed in dating the time when antichrist first fully corrupted the church, both shared the apocalyptic interpretation of the reformation put forth by Bale. Cf. Whitgift, *An answere*, pp. 56–7, 67, 233, 238, *The defense*, pp. 73, 318, 349, C[artwright], *A replye*, pp. 63, 78, 164, and Cartwright, *Second replie*, pp. 285, 508, 510, and *The rest*, p. 171

similar circumstances, John Foxe first conceived and began his rewriting of holy history, an enormous undertaking that finally culminated in the lengthy vernacular editions of the *Actes and monuments*. The vast influence exercised by these two works in shaping the English protestant mind of the next century cannot be denied. Both applied Renaissance humanist learning to the production of books meant for the common man as well as the scholar. They carried forward the famous hope of Erasmus 'that the gospels might be read by wayfaring men, "that the husbandman may sing parts of them at his plow, that the weaver may warble them at his shuttle."'[46] Even the illiterate could and did listen and understand. Like many Renaissance treatises, these were produced to educate and uplift men – to mould their minds – to bring them to a realization of truth at its highest level. Humanist study of ancient languages produced the Geneva Bible. Humanist interest in and techniques of studying history produced Foxe's great collection. These two works, in many ways, stood in the mainstream of the new learning. Both also took the apocalyptic interpretation of Bale and brought it to the widest possible audience.

The vernacular Bible probably acted as the most important vehicle for the spread of reformed religion. Sermons, pamphlets, treatises, acts of Parliament, all played an important role in the English reformation, but the open Bible, read at church or at home, formed the crucial part of the religious life of the people. It encouraged literacy and it helped men and women to think for themselves – to hear with their own ears and see with their own eyes. For most people in Tudor and early Stuart Britain the Bible meant the Geneva translation – the best, cheapest, and most widely used version. In Elizabeth's reign alone, it went through seventy complete editions, plus another thirty of the New Testament, more than three times as many printings as the nearest competitor, the Bishops' Bible. It remained in print until 1644, well after the authorized version of 1611.[47] The copious marginal notes of this edition gave guidance to the reader for those many difficult parts of the text and especially to those who could not afford other commentaries. '... For half a century the people of England and Scotland, who read the Geneva Bible in preference to any other version, learned much of their biblical exegesis from these notes.' For the common people, the marginal notes acquired an

46 Quoted in Rupp, *Six Makers*, p. 15
47 Greenslade, *Cambridge History of the Bible*, ch. 4, and Bruce, *English Bible*, ch. 7, pp. 91–2, 94

authority almost equal to that of the text itself – notes and text fused into one interpretive whole. Much of the commentary reflected a Genevan environment, but that on the Book of Revelation derived from Heinrich Bullinger and Bale.[48] Although the interpretation put forth in these notes will seem familiar, it is worth citing because of the great impact which they had on the common mind.

The notes applied the prophecies of St John to the history of the church and the contemporary situation, tersely noting that 'Antichrist [was] the pope, king of hypocrites and Satan's ambassador.'[49] Following Bale, they equated the locusts from the bottomless pit with the offices of popery: 'Locusts are false teachers, heretics, and worldly subtle prelates, with monks, friars, cardinals, patriarchs, archbishops, bishops, doctors, bachelors, and masters which forsake Christ to maintain false doctrine' (Rev. ix:3). They also carefully maintained the distinction between the outward glory and inward corruption of the unreformed church: 'Antichrist is compared to an harlot because he seduceth the world with vain words, doctrines of lies, and outward appearance' (Rev. xvii:1). The thousand-year binding of Satan dated 'from Christ's nativity to the time of Pope Sylvester the second,' another variation on Bale. This circumscribed the period in which 'pure doctrine should after a sort remain' (Rev. xx:3). The followers of Mohammed came in to join with the papacy in explanation of the figures of Gog and Magog (Rev. xx:8). The New Jerusalem appeared in spiritual terms, equated with heaven: 'All things shall be renewed and restored to a most excellent and perfect estate, and therefore the day of resurrection is called the day of restoration of all things. For all things shall be purged from their corruption, and the faithful shall enter into heaven with their head Christ' (Rev. xxi:1). James VI and I disliked some of the marginal notes of the Geneva Bible, especially those on certain Old Testament texts, but even he could not have quarrelled with the following upon the coming Zion: 'Here we see as in infinite other places that kings and princes (contrary to that wicked opinion of the anabaptists) are partakers of the heavenly

---

48 Bruce, English Bible, p. 90. Bauckham has established that most editions of the Geneva Bible derived their notes on Revelation from Bale and Bullinger, but that from 1599 onward some editions had notes taken from the commentary of Junius. Hill, Antichrist, pp. 3–6, 42–3, incorrectly implies that these notes came from Calvin; since Calvin wrote no commentary on Revelation, this would have taken extraordinary insight.

49 Bible, upon Rev. ix:11; henceforth the chapter and verse commented upon will be noted within parentheses in the text.

glory, if they rule in the fear of the Lord' (Rev. xxi:24). The caveat of the last phrase represented no threat to a magisterial reformation – it was a commonplace.

In the notes on Revelation the Geneva Bible took no stand on God's instruments for reformation. It stressed neither the imperial tradition nor that of the oppressed and persecuted. It portrayed princes in a far more favourable manner than either Bale's commentary or Ponet's treatise. The notes on Revelation, then, fit squarely into the mainstream English protestant interpretation of the reformation. The reformation represented that spiritual conflict of the latter days prophesied by St John. It opened the way for the imminent return of Christ and his final annihilation of popery – 'The overthrow of the beast and his [supporters] which shall be accomplished at the second coming of Christ' (Rev. xix:20). Surprisingly, the marginal notes on Daniel contained little historical apocalyptic content (cf. Daniel vii:8). The only significant difference between the marginal notes of the Geneva Bible and, for example, the sermons of Archbishop Sandys lay not in the interpretation they shared but in the size of audience reached. Because of its popularity and of the great weight of scriptural authority it possessed, the Geneva Bible proved an excellent vehicle for the widespread dissemination of the apocalyptic tradition. It brought the message of Bale and Bullinger to generations of Bible readers from all levels of society. The notes helped to unlock the mystery of the prophecies of the Apocalypse for readers or listeners alike, but a concrete collection of stories illustrating the history of those prophecies awaited the hand of John Foxe.

Of all the interpreters discussed in this study, John Foxe ranked with his friend John Bale as one of a handful of important contributors to the apocalyptic tradition. Bale framed the first systematic chronological interpretation of Revelation based upon the idea of the two churches and Foxe brought his framework alive in an overwhelming mass of case studies. The 'Book of Martyrs' became a folk tradition in Foxe's own lifetime, still inspires many readers, and remains better known – if only in name – than any other work in the apocalyptic tradition. The *Actes and monuments* was not a mere hodge-podge of martyr stories. Foxe bound his stories together with a chronological apocalyptic framework, one clearly based on the Book of Revelation, not on Daniel like that of Joannes Sleidanus. In his reconstruction of the origins of the *Actes and monuments*, Haller pointed out that Bale, Edmund Grindal, Matthew Parker, and others helped and encouraged Foxe. Viggo Olsen and

Katherine Firth placed his work in the context of continental histories of the church published slightly earlier or at the same time. Aside from presumption, however, this information provides little evidence of the most important source of Foxe's organizational superstructure, *The image of bothe churches* by John Bale.[50] Although Bale's commentary failed to appear among the works cited in Foxe's *Eicasmi sev meditationes in sacram Apocalypsin*, a posthumously published analysis of the first seventeen chapters of Revelation, this omission need not trouble us. The *Eicasmi* contained Foxe's most mature apocalyptic reflections, but only the historically naïve could consider it a reliable guide to an interpretation composed at least twenty years earlier. Besides, Foxe cited no vernacular commentaries in the *Eicasmi* because he wrote it in Latin for an international scholarly audience.[51] The preface of the 1570 and consequent editions of the *Actes and monuments* contained a clue linking Foxe with Bale's commentary, a clue confirmed by other evidence in the 1563 and 1570 editions. In the preface Foxe explained that his history would illustrate the 'Image of both Churches,' explicitly quoting the title of Bale's book in the text and as a marginal note to underline the point. This was not merely fortuitous. At first, Foxe also followed Bale's chronology by dating the thousand-year binding of Satan from the ascension of Christ. He asserted this in his brief outline of the five ages of the history of the church in the 1563 and 1570 editions, although later in the text of the latter he dated this event to the time of Constantine. This break with Bale's chronology finally appeared in the brief outline at the beginning of the 1576 edition and continued in subsequent editions. As pointed out earlier, the very concept of the two churches as a key to Revelation and holy history was first applied by Bale.[52] John Bale's apocalyptic paradigm formed the basis of the framework of Foxe's great work, then, even if the younger man disagreed with some of the details of his friend's interpretation. The *Actes and monuments*, a long and complex work, firmly implanted Bale's approach as the mainstream apocalyptic tradition in England and carried it to a higher level of exactitude, demonstration, and popularity.

50 Haller, *Foxe's Book*, ch. 2 and 3, Bauckham, 'Prophecy,' Firth, 'Apocalyptic Tradition,' ch. 3, and Olsen, *John Foxe*, pp. 16–50; cf. Sleidanus, *A famouse cronicle* and *A briefe chronicle*

51 Foxe, *Eicasmi*, dedicated to Archbishop Whitgift; cf. Firth, 'Apocalyptic Tradition,' ch. 3, and Olsen, *John Foxe*, pp. 43–4

52 Foxe, *Actes and monuments* (1563), pp. 1–11 (1570), I, 'A protestation to the whole Church of England (unpaginated),' pp. 1, 139, 144, 137–44, and (1576), I, p. 1

Foxe combined the two views of God's instruments on earth emphasized by his predecessors – the imperial tradition and that of the oppressed and persecuted – into one viable synthetic whole. Praise of those godly princes who worked for the welfare of the true church echoed through the pages of the *Actes and monuments*. In the dedication which stood near the opening of the 1563 edition, Foxe showed this in his comparison of Elizabeth I with Constantine the Great. Both brought bloody ages of persecution to an end: 'At length the Lord sent this mild Constantinus, to cease blood, to stay persecution, to refresh his people. In much like manner what bitter blasts, what smarting storms have been felt in England during the space of certain years, till at last God's pitiful grace sent us your Majesty to quench firebrands, to assuage rage, to relieve innocents.' The Almighty worked through imperial instruments. Lest too honoured a position for Elizabeth be read into this comparison, it must be pointed out that Foxe dropped this dedication and its content in 1570, when he first dated the binding of Satan to the reign of Constantine. In the new dedication of the 1570 and later editions, Elizabeth played an important role, but not one with the cosmic impact of Constantine's new position. Foxe thanked her for setting the true church at liberty in England, an act that 'could not be contrived in any king's reign since the conquest, before these [h]alcyon days of yours.'[53] By comparing Elizabeth to the Constantine who bound Satan and by dating the opening of the last age of the earth to the beginning of her reign, later writers like Thomas Brightman transformed Foxe's international outlook into one more narrowly nationalistic – Haller's 'elect nation.' Foxe put forth no such scheme in the *Actes and monuments*. He believed that the true church was universal, 'bound to no one certain nation more than any other.'[54] In its struggle with the false church in the middle ages and in the reformation period, emperors, kings, and princes helped to lead the combat against the reviving power of Satan all over Europe.

Even before the thousand years elapsed, Satan began to break those bindings placed upon him in the reign of Constantine. This process was seen in the growing power and pretensions of the papacy. It came to a consummation in the pontificates of Gregory VII and Innocent III.

53 *Ibid.* (1563), dedication, and (1570), dedication
54 *Ibid.* (1570), I, p. I; cf. Haller, *Foxe's Book*, ch. 5 and 6, Firth, 'Apocalyptic Tradition,' pp. 151–2, Olsen, *John Foxe*, pp. 36–7, and Bauckham, 'Prophecy.' The latter three independently came to the conclusion that Foxe did not advocate the idea of England as an 'elect nation.' For Brightman, see chapter three below.

Thenceforth, as never before, the popish antichrist raged abroad spreading darkness and persecuting those who opposed his power. Crushing even his most mighty enemies, he reigned over church and state. Imperial instruments of the Lord led the resistance to papal pretensions until the redawning of light began with the preaching of the gospel in its simplicty and might by Wycliffe and Hus. Woodcuts illustrated this process, be they the series on Henry IV at Canossa or the series on King John of England – to pick out two dramatic sets. This cosmic conflict between popes and the secular rulers of Europe was but briefly traced in the 1563 edition. In the 1570 edition, however, it expanded from under a hundred to over five hundred pages! Because Foxe, like Bale, wrote for an English audience, it prominently featured the kings of England. When the reformation arrived, it entered under the auspices of Henry VIII – a fact underlined by Foxe by opening the second volume of the *Actes and monuments* with a woodcut of Henry VIII. In the 1570 and 1576 editions, Henry VIII and his council sat in state. From 1583 on, a woodcut of Henry VIII trampling upon Pope Clement, a much more apocalyptic image, replaced the earlier frontispiece. Godly bishop also joined godly prince – be it Eusebius and Constantine or Henry VIII and Cranmer – to bolster the authority of established power. The bishop martyrs played an important part in the persecutions of Mary's reign, sealing the Established Church with their blood. Of course, it was better when the authorities of church and state acted together to establish the true church. Were the wearer of the imperial crown of England to fail to lead the battle against Babylon, Foxe believed that such action should be viewed as a trial sent from the Lord, not as a justification for rebellion.[55] His typical mid-century compulsion for order and obedience buttressed his avowal of the imperial tradition. By using the imperial tradition as one of the main themes of his history, Foxe joined the ranks of Tyndale, Cranmer, Aylmer, Jewel, and Sandys. His positive portrayal of the Church of England and some of its most potent images – such as the bishop martyrs – provided a powerful defence of the Elizabethan settlement. Foxe forced later radicals who respected his authority to reinterpret this side of his holy history. Ironically, the other theme of the 'Book of Martyrs' provided them with the justification and documentary evidence necessary for such a task.

55 Haller, *Foxe's Book*, p. 154; see Olsen, *John Foxe*, ch. 1, Foxe, *Actes and monuments* (1570, 1576), II, page after titlepage, and (1583), II, page after titlepage. Haller illustrates the latter between pp. 176–7.

Foxe combined an explicit identification and illustration of the tradition of the oppressed and persecuted with his emphasis upon the imperial tradition – after all, his tome contained a treasury of martyr accounts. This was true especially of that portion on the Marian persecutions which dominated the 1563 edition and comprised most of the second volume in all subsequent editions. The title page of the *Actes and monuments* illustrated the descent of God's grace through the persecuted. No princes, kings, or emperors stood between Christ in glory sitting in judgment at the top of the page and the protestant preacher guiding his flock to worship the unpronounceable name of God at the bottom of the page. In the 1570 edition, Foxe deliberately synthesized the two traditions by emphasizing the oppressed and persecuted elect in his new introduction, by dating the binding of Satan to the reign of Constantine, and by greatly expanding the material on imperial resistance to the papacy in the middle ages. Foxe explained the purpose of his collection in this new preface:

Which history therefore I have here taken in hand, that as other story writers heretofore have employed their travail to magnify the church of Rome, so in this history might appear to all Christian readers the image of both churches, as well of the one as of the other: especially of the poor oppressed and persecuted church of Christ. Which persecuted church though it hath been of long season trodden under foot by enemies, neglected in the world, nor regarded in histories, and almost scarce visible or known to worldly eyes, yet hath it been the true church only of God, wherein he hath mightily wrought hitherto in preserving the same in all extreme distresses, continually stirring up from time to time faithful ministers, by whom always hath been kept some sparks of his true doctrine and religion.[56]

The latest and largest season of suppression in England raged in the reign of Queen Mary. From it sprang the largest number of Foxe's examples, although he also documented the cases of Henrician martyrs such as Robert Barnes, John Frith, and William Tyndale. Most of the non-clerical cases from the sixteenth century illustrated men and women of humble background standing fast against the wiles of Babylon. The chief agents of persecution – whether medieval or modern – were bishops, monks, or friars. Bishops Bonner and Gardiner featured prominently in the Marian period. The stories from the recent past tended to identify English bishops with persecution (and Babylon) and humble

56 Foxe, *Actes and monuments* (1570), I, 'A protestation'

protestants and ordinary preachers with the persecuted elect of God. Of course, inclusion of the histories of the great bishop martyrs balanced the account in theory. However, it was one thing to present a lively picture of Bishop Ridley debating with his equals and quite another to show William Hunter, a nineteen-year-old apprentice silk weaver, confuting the village summoner, vicar, and justice of the peace in turn, and holding his own with Bishop Bonner in argument. The impact of the latter proved greater because so unexpected. Only the Lord could inspire such a performance. The story of Hunter provides an excellent illustration of the vivid reality used by Foxe in his portrayal of the lowly and persecuted as God's instruments of reformation. It gave life to an image of a Marian martyr which could be taken up by those who became dissatisfied with the Elizabethan religious settlement, or with the Laudian régime.[57] Throughout the *Actes and monuments* the pope, bishops, and members of religious orders almost exclusively played the part of persecutors. People could see this in the illustrations as well as in the text. The woodcuts portrayed reformed bishops – degraded, of course, by the Marian authorities – without cope, mitre, or any other symbol of their office. It hardly seems surprising, then, that some of Foxe's readers jumped to the conclusion that even members of a reformed episcopacy who wore the trappings of hierarchy could become popish antichristian persecutors. Despite the glory of the bishop martyrs, a seed of suspicion toward the office remained. Foxe's pages on the oppressed and persecuted contained a rich storehouse of materials for potential nonconformists. Men like Henry Barrow and John Lilburne admittedly drew inspiration from the histories before becoming martyrs themselves. However, they accepted only a portion of Foxe's message.

Earlier writers emphasized either the imperial tradition or that of the oppressed and persecuted. Foxe juxtaposed the two traditions. He combined them into a synthesis that explicitly emphasized order and obedience but implicitly prompted the discontented into rebellious action. Foxe consciously supported the notion that God worked through established persons or institutions – such as godly prince, godly bishop, and godly preacher – to combat and overthrow the power of Babylon. His work deliberately buttressed order, condemned rebellion, and supported the reformed Church of England. Reformers committed to the Elizabethan settlement employed this imperial aspect to strengthen

---

57 *Ibid.* (1576), II, pp. 1462–5; cf. the brief version in (1563), pp. 1109–10. For Henry Barrow and John Lilburne, see chapters two and four below.

their position. However, Foxe also stressed the importance of the oppressed and persecuted as instruments of the Almighty. His pages illustrated this theme at least as vividly as the other. Those who abhorred what they called the halfway house of the Established Church used examples from the tradition of the persecuted and oppressed to temper their consciences for action. Like the sermons of Sandys, Foxe's 'Book of Martyrs' formed a *via media*, susceptible to distortion and attack by extremists from either side. Those imbued with a lesser store of moderation eventually tore the carefully constructed synthesis apart.

The erection of a reformed church in England, however much the reformers leaned on their Lord, took strenuous action by many people over more than one generation. Professional controversialists of great talent turned their literary resources – the word in the ear and the word in the eye – to the difficult task of redirecting the thought patterns of their contemporaries. In books, sermons, injunctions, acts of Parliament, and pamphlets – paintings and woodcuts as well – the reformers sought to transform men's minds, to bring people to the clarity of revealed truth. Shifts took place not only in formal doctrine, religious practices, and morals, but also in the interpretation of the past. They drilled a whole new history of the church into the minds of Englishmen. Its radically transformed emphasis turned the old orthodoxy upside-down in order to explain the contemporary situation. Such a precedent-minded society hardly could have accepted such a significant change in any other way. Visions of cosmic warfare transformed both past and present.

Each of the men discussed in this chapter developed or reflected an apocalyptic interpretation of the reformation. All employed apocalyptic imagery and believed in its veracity, even those, like Cranmer and Jewel, who clung to a medieval view of antichrist instead of accepting Bale's framework. The youngest was born in 1522. All participated in the Edwardian triumph. All but Ridley experienced exile in Mary's reign. Of those who lived to return to England, Bale stood out as an ancient among younger men. Jewel, Aylmer, Sandys, and Foxe belonged roughly to the same generation, one that shaped the Elizabethan church. As William Pierce said of that institution almost seventy years ago: 'There was not a bishop nor superior ecclesiastic in the reformed church to whom the Pope was not in very truth the Antichrist.'[58] A growing body of recent studies has confirmed Pierce's insight. One can

58 Pierce, *Historical Introduction*, p. viii

no longer claim that an apocalyptic interpretation of the reformation was confined to 'puritans' or 'extremists' – unless, that is, one wants to render these terms meaningless.

Holy history played a crucial role in the defence of the Church of England. Identifying Rome with Babylon, the pope or papacy with antichrist, English reformers joined St John's Revelation with historical evidence both to show how the church had become perverted during the middle ages and how the reformation represented a return to the purity of the early church.[59] After a period of competition that lasted into the first decade or two of Elizabeth's reign, Bale's chronological apocalyptic framework finally became the mainstream tradition in England. The notes of the Geneva Bible, sermons like those of Sandys, and, above all, Foxe's *Actes and monuments* assured its triumph as the standard approach. New streams developed from it, but the chronology of Bale or a variation on it remained the starting point for these accounts. Expectation moved in waves in reaction to contemporary events. When the times looked ripe, apocalyptic visions engendered a fever pitch of eschatological expectation with its corresponding call for prayer and physical action. No person or group maintained such high levels of feeling for any extended period, however. When things ran smoothly for the reformers, they seemed merely to mouth their apocalyptic visions, but when trouble threatened – as in the Marian reaction, the papal excommunication of Elizabeth, or the Spanish Armada – apocalyptic images flashed forth with full power and meaning again. The pope was always called antichrist, but St Paul's breastplate was not always firmly buckled on. Or was it for Elizabethans? Edwin Sandys thought so in the 1550s, 1560s, 1570s, and 1580s! The *Actes and monuments* preserved the context of heightened feelings and stressed the need for constant vigilance. It provided both the most popular lengthy version of the mainstream apocalyptic interpretation of the reformation and a mighty reservoir of explosive examples for the godly to follow whenever the beast of Babylon appeared to threaten God's chosen people in England.

59 See Rupp, *Six Makers*, pp. 70–1, Knappen, *Tudor Puritanism*, pp. 376–8, and Wiener, 'Beleaguered isle'

2

The parting of the stream

LORD CHANCELLOR: What is that man? (pointing to Canterbury).
BARROW: The Lord gave me the spirit of boldness, so that I answered: He is a
monster, a miserable compound, I know not what to make (call) him: he is
neither ecclesiastical nor civil, even that second beast spoken of in the Revelation.
LORD TREASURER: Where is that place, show it.
BARROW: So I turned to the thirteenth chapter and began at the eleventh verse,
and read a little ... But the beast arose for anger, gnashing his teeth, and said:
Will you suffer him, my lords? So I was plucked up by the warden's man from my
knees and taken away.

Henry Barrow, *Writings 1587–1590*, p. 188

The above confrontation between Henry Barrow, a young graduate of
Cambridge with good social connections, and Archbishop Whitgift, an
authority on the beasts of Revelation, dramatically illustrates the de-
velopment of a new stream of apocalyptic interpretation in England.
Ironically, Barrow's view sprang from the foundations of that upheld by
Archbishop Whitgift in his Oxford doctoral thesis. As we have seen,
England's earliest protestants explained the necessity of a break from
Rome in apocalyptic terms. When Queen Mary rebuilt the walls of
Babylon in the land, reformers drew upon that theory and combated the
cosmic foe with one accord. Foxe enshrined their deeds in the *Actes and
monuments*, lest posterity forget. At the same time, he both popularized
and demonstrated the veracity of Bale's chronological interpretation of
Revelation. For the rest of the century and beyond, few English protestant publicists quarrelled with the foundations of this mainstream trad-

ition – Rome had become Babylon, the papacy antichrist. However, when Elizabeth established a protestant Church of England, the ranks of the reformers divided on issues of church polity and practice. The debate over these issues took place within an historical apocalyptic context. If a particular ceremony, form of worship, or type of church polity first arose when antichrist ruled the church, could a reformed church retain it or did it not remain tainted by popery, an antichristian relic to be swept away? Questions of this sort found no easy answer. Elizabeth exacerbated the situation by demanding that the church continue to contain more traditional elements than desired by her spiritual advisers. After deeply searching their consciences, most reformers decided to work within the Elizabethan settlement. A vocal minority, however, took up their cause with prophetic criticism.

Historians have applied the term 'puritan' to all those who wanted further to reform the church. So defined, 'puritan' includes almost all Elizabethan bishops, as well as separatists like Henry Barrow. Such reformers divided over many issues. Tradition prevents the sensible solution of confining 'puritan' to that small group who worked within the Established Church for a presbyterian or congregational polity. Such persons, therefore, will be called 'radical puritans' in this book. It took some time to work out standard reactions to the Elizabethan settlement, but radical reformers, in attempting to reform the reformation, quickly took up the tools that earlier generations had employed against the unreformed church. When church and civil authorities attempted to silence them, such irrepressible critics answered by questioning the very nature of the Church of England. Was it a true church? Did it continue to reside in Babylon? Were its governors antichrists? Answers to these questions eventually came to mark the dividing line between radical puritan and separatist. Separatists forged a full condemnation of the Established Church. Puritans drew back from such a drastic step. Most radical puritans came to characterize it as Laodicea, after the lukewarm church warned by the apostles at the opening of the Apocalypse. Those of the 'root and branch' variety identified the English bishops with Babylon and demanded their immediate expulsion. Although a yawning gulf eventually divided separatist from radical puritan, both movements arose from the same beginnings – a deep reluctance to accept the Elizabethan settlement. While it took some time for the respective positions to jell, the gradual unfolding of events created three new branches of the mainstream apocalyptic tradition.

The first hesitant steps which would lead to separatism appeared in

London. People who secretly worshiped together during Mary's dark days remained so hostile to the Elizabethan settlement that they kept their conventicles in being or – at the very least – revived them during the vestiarian controversy of the 1560s. Only a glimmer of record survives to reconstruct their thought. In June 1567 the authorities arrested a group of men and women who had hired Plumbers' Hall for a religious meeting. When Bishop Grindal asked the leaders why they wanted to meet outside of the Established Church, one man replied that 'all our preachers were displaced by your law, that would not subscribe to your apparel and your law, so that we could not hear none of them ...'[1] He blamed the bishop for enforcing the prescribed vestments and depriving those who refused to conform. Grindal himself liked the vestments as little as these men, but felt obliged to enforce that ordered by the queen. William Nixon, another of the group, defended the decision of these laymen to desert their parish churches and form their own congregation: 'We do not refuse you for preaching the word of God, but because you have tied the ceremonies of antichrist to it, and set them before it, so that no man may preach or minister the sacraments without them. For before you compelled them by law all was quiet.' Like Elijah before Ahab, he claimed that the bishops started trouble by enforcing unholy ceremonies – those which had originated under antichrist had no place in a reformed church. However, Nixon still identified antichrist with the papacy, not with the Church of England or its hierarchy. His view gained support from Robert Hawkins, who claimed that the authorities 'have brought the gospel and sacraments into bondage to the ceremonies of antichrist, and you defend idolatry and papistry. There is no ordinance of Christ, but you have mingled your own inventions withal.' These laymen attacked the traditional elements in the Established Church as antichristian relics of popery, but they spoke boldly because they still hoped to change policy. The Elizabethan settlement was not called Babylon. Hawkins clearly implied a polarity between the true church and the Church of England when he retorted: 'It cannot be proved, that the ceremonies of antichrist, works of darkness, and the pope's canon law, may be clean to a true Christian; for the apostle saith, "There is no fellowship between Christ and Belial, light and darkness."'[2] He and his companions distinguished between the hierarchy

---

1 Porter, *Puritanism*, p. 52. For the vestiarian controversy, see Collinson, *Elizabethan Puritan*, part 2, Knappen, *Tudor Puritanism*, ch. 10, and Trinterud, *Elizabethan Puritanism*, part 1.
2 Porter, *Puritanism*, pp. 88, 86, 91

and themselves. They even tried to form their own congregation outside of the Established Church. However, they launched no explicit apocalyptic assault either on that institution or on the bishops that governed it in their interview with Grindal. The sources contain no account of what they said in private.

Grindal also interviewed the type of preacher that the Plumbers' Hall group wanted to hear. Master Pattenson, a deprived and unlicensed minister whose forename was not noted in the records, exemplified the spirit of the early separatist and radical puritan leaders. No social underling, he probably had graduated from university and certainly had been ordained earlier by Grindal. Pattenson feared God more than any man. When told that he needed a licence from the archbishop of Canterbury to continue his preaching, he justified his actions by appeal to a higher authority: 'But the Archbishop of archbishops hath not suspended me from preaching, but continueth His commandments to me still: and besides that ... He hath not decayed in me the gift of preaching, but rather increased it: and hath also given me a congregation that looketh that I should bestow it among them; and therefore I may not disobey Him to obey you.' Master Pattenson got into trouble not only for refusing to obey the law but also for the content of his unlicensed sermons. By 1567 he had applied the image of antichrist, hitherto reserved for Roman bishops, to at least one member of the reformed hierarchy. Grindal could rightly feel disturbed.

B[ishop]: Well, Sir, did you well, think you, to charge me in your sermons, and to send me word that I am an antichrist, and a traitor to God and my prince, and an heretic?
P[attenson]: I think I did not ill, so long as you show yourself to be such a one: but put away the cause, and I will cease from saying so.
B: Why, wherein can you prove me a traitor and an antichrist?
P: In that you use things accursed and abominable, whereby you yourself are made abominable before God also.[3]

Pattenson was a strong dissenter who challenged the authority of the episcopacy in word and action. His identification of Bishop Grindal as an antichrist went beyond the expressions of the Plumbers' Hall group in the direction of either the 'root and branch' or the separatist stream of apocalyptic interpretation. Even Pattenson, however, gave Grindal the

3 Dixon, History, vi, pp. 178–9n, prints the whole interview.

chance to change his status. At least in this interview he attacked the bishop for his actions, not for the nature of his jurisdiction. Pattenson said nothing about the nature of the Church of England. Dissatisfaction with the Established Church and its policies led the Plumbers' Hall group and Pattenson to work outside of the law and of that institution. The net of the law brought them before the bishop of London who showed remarkable tolerance in handling them. Even patient Grindal, however, could not allow such direct action in religion.

The ecclesiastical authorities arrested and imprisoned other groups and individuals of a similar sort. While causing some brethren to fall away, imprisonment also brought dissidents together and helped to strengthen some in their clandestine operations. One correspondent of John Knox in 1568, for example, wrote of his handling by the 'popish court' of the bishop of London: 'That persecution grew so fast as that it brought many a hundred to know one another that never knew before; and we joined all with one heart and mind to serve God with pure hearts and minds according to his Word.'[4] Thus, the underground movements spread! According to the Spanish ambassador at least one messianic leader had emerged in London by 1568. If true to type, he probably spouted apocalyptic messages. By 1570 some groups seem to have reached a position of separation from the Church of England. Bishop Cox showed clear signs of anxiety when he wrote to Rudolph Gualter at Zurich about the intransigence of those prophets

who by the vehemence of their harrangues have so maddened the wretched multitude, and driven some of them to that pitch of frenzy, that they now obstinately refuse to enter our churches, either to baptise their children or to partake of the Lord's supper, or to hear sermons. They are entirely separated both from us and from those good brethren of ours [i.e. the Puritan ministers]: they seek bye paths; they establish a private religion, and assemble in private houses, and there perform their sacred rites, as the Donatists of old, and the Anabaptists now.[5]

The letter of Bishop Cox cannot be dismissed as the overexaggerated worries of a hard pressed man. He pointed to the emergence of separatists and a split between them and puritans at a very early date. His judgment received confirmation from other evidence from the same

4 Lorimer, *John Knox*, p. 300
5 Peel, *First Churches*, pp. 20, 21–2 n. 3, the latter quoting *Zurich Letters*, I, pp. 234–8; the words in brackets are Peel's.

date. When driven to a 'pitch of frenzy' laymen indeed showed themselves unwilling to compromise with the Church of England – even with
its puritan preachers – but banded together in private groups outside of
the Established Church.

Even at this early stage these secret societies devised the initiation
right of an oath, the precursor of later church covenants. In order to join
one of these congregations the prospective member had to swear:

I have now joined myself to the church of Christ wherein I have yielded myself
subject to the discipline of God's word as I promised at my baptism, which if I
should now again forsake and join myself with the traditioners I should then
forsake the union wherein I am knit with the body of Christ and join myself to
the discipline of antichrist. For in the church of the traditioners there is none
other discipline, but that which hath been ordained by the antichristian popes
of Rome, whereby the church of God hath always been afflicted, and is to this
day, for which I refuse them.

This particular oath first appeared in one of the two treatises written by
'a simple unlearned man' around 1570; it surfaced among the papers
relating to Richard Fitz's congregation from about 1573 and again as late
as 1581. The author of it demonstrated a familiarity with Bale's historical struggle between the true and false churches which he probably
derived from the pages of Foxe. Since the 'church of the traditioners'
could only mean the Church of England, the oath provided a formal
mechanism for renouncing communion with that institution. The
anonymous author believed that the Established Church still formed a
part of Babylon: 'Antichrist, the pope of Rome, this name is banished out
of England, but his body, which be the bishops and other shavelings do
not only remain, but also his tail, which be his filthy traditions, wicked
laws, and beggarly ceremonies ... yea, and the whole body of his pes-
tiferous canon law.' All aspects of the Elizabethan settlement – ministry, government, ceremonies, and ecclesiastical discipline – reeked of
the corruption of antichrist. Therefore, those who wished to fight on the
side of Christ in the cosmic battle against Satan's supporters must
withdraw themselves from the Church of England. 'And, dearly beloved
in the Lord, you go to your parish church, and there stand up and say, I
believe in God, yet you do but mock with God so long as you walk in
those wicked laws of antichrist and maintain his knights and bishops
with such inordinate riches and unlawful authority, so long shall you

never banish the monstrous beast, the pope, out of England.'[6] Not content with forming the godly together in congregations of their own, bound by an oath in which they renounced the Established Church, this anonymous author asked the separated saints to denounce the Church of England in their old parish churches! The first separatist treatises contained no compromise.

The paucity of evidence about these early groups in London makes it virtually impossible to distinguish between separatist and radical puritan attempts at reform. With the possible exception of Richard Fitz's congregation, these conglomerations of the godly fluctuated in personnel and patterns of religious organization. Some, such as the Plumbers' Hall and St Martin's-in-the-Fields groups, or Master Pattenson, provide examples of what one historian has aptly called 'circumstantial separatism.' The godly attending such secret congregations could, without much difficulty, lapse into radical puritanism. Their service followed the book and order of Geneva and represented 'an improvised consequence of the failure of the Established Church to remodel itself in accordance with the principles of reformed worship.'[7] Mingled with such potential conformists were some true separatists. The group who administered the oath cited above fit into the latter category, for they made a deliberate, final break with the Church of England. A centre and testing ground for all sorts of vociferous criticism of the Elizabethan settlement sprang up in the constitutionally complex parishes of the Minories. Claiming freedom from visitation by the bishop of London, the congregation there held the right of presentation. The Minories forged a link between old, experienced hammers of popery, like Miles Coverdale, and clever, young organizers of further reform, like John Field. Pattenson preached there, as well. In the Minories, people could weigh the hidden teachings of separatist protest against those open attacks upon the Elizabethan settlement made by the radical puritans. In this atmosphere, Puritans and separatists must have fought some of their first battles for the allegiance of Englishmen. While holding the post of teacher in the Minories, John Field, the moving force behind the attempt to create a presbyterian organization within the Church of

---

6 Peel, *Seconde Parte*, I, pp. 56, 58, 56n, 57n. Both treatises remained in manuscript. For the separatists also see Burrage, *Early Dissenters*, passim, Hill, *Antichrist*, ch. 2, and White, *English Separatist*, passim.

7 Owen, 'A nursery,' p. 70; cf. Peel, *First Churches*, pp. 13–14

England, penned his first powerful plea, *An admonition to the Parliament*, in 1572.[8]

The admonition controversy was one of the most important theological disputes in the Elizabethan church. Both sides presented their arguments in print. One, therefore, can carefully assess them – an impossible task for the thoughts of the early separatists which have survived only in a few manuscripts. This religious wrangle revolved around the question of the nature of the reformed Church of England. Protagonists turned to holy history and its chronology to demonstrate their contentions. The scholarly disputations of Whitgift and Thomas Cartwright held centre stage in the debate, but it began with the blasts of the *Admonition*. When the scholars seemed exhausted, popular propagandists like Martin Marprelate and Martin junior moved the dispute into the realm of satire and lambast.

In *An admonition to the Parliament*, John Field and Thomas Wilcox cleverly employed the apocalyptic tradition to deride the episcopal government and some practices of the Church of England. Well timed to make a maximum impact, this explosive pamphlet appeared during the course of the parliamentary session of 1572.[9] Both authors had connections with the Minories and both became leaders in the puritan classical movement. Their argument both assumed and built upon audience acceptance of Bale's type of historical apocalyptic interpretation of the reformation. Their pamphlet made its points through systematic, crafty innuendo – tarring opponents with a brush that every good protestant could be presumed to abhor. Specifically, Field and Wilcox piled up similarities between the Church of England and that of Rome to create the impression that a link existed between the two churches. However, they never explicitly claimed that Rome and England shared the same church. This technique allowed the cosmic combat against Babylon to be identified with attempts to reform the Established Church without formally condemning the latter. Whitgift, by comparing the writers of the *Admonition* with the dreaded anabaptists, employed a similar method of innuendo against them.

The first *Admonition* began by comparing the state of the Church of England with the pure practices and presbyterian polity of the apostolic church. The authors viewed the early church of the New Testament

8 'A nursery,' p. 67. For Field, see Collinson, 'John Field and Elizabethan puritanism,' in Bindoff, *Elizabethan Government*.
9 Neale, *Parliaments, 1559–1581*, pp. 295–7. Collinson, Knappen, and Trinterud all discuss the admonition controversy.

through the filtering lens of Geneva. They attacked the offices that they could not find in scripture, such as 'the lordly lords, archbishops, bishops, suffragans, deans, doctors, archdeacons, chancellors, and the rest of that proud generation, whose kingdom must down, hold they never so hard: because their tyrannous lordship can not stand with Christ's kingdom. And it is the special mischief of our English church.' In his attack upon the unreformed church, Bale made an almost identical list of what he called the names of blasphemy written upon the head of the beast. In the days of the apostles, the *Admonition* continued, the leaders of the church were 'known by voice, learning and doctrine: now they must be discerned ... by popish and antichristian apparel ... And therefore titles, livings and offices of antichrist devised are given to them ...'[10] The hierarchical government of the Church of England could not be proper because it lacked scriptural sanction and originated during the period when the popish antichrist ruled the visible church. Field and Wilcox did not call the English bishops antichrists, but they marshalled apocalyptic innuendo against the hierarchy.

It rankled them that the government and clerical dress enforced by the Elizabethan settlement still smelled of popery, but, even worse, the preaching and teaching of the word remained corrupt as well. The *Admonition* pointed out that in the apostles' days nothing was 'taught but God's word, now prince's pleasures, men's devices, popish ceremonies, and antichristian rites in public pulpits defended.' The Book of Common Prayer, established by statute, came from the liturgy 'of antichrist, and therefore we have nothing to do with it.' The consecration ceremony of the Church of England 'is nothing else but a thing word for word drawn out of the pope's pontifical, wherein he sheweth himself to be antichrist most lively ... Canon law is antichristian and devilish, and contrary to the scriptures.' To complete the process of devastation of the Elizabethan settlement, Field and Wilcox turned the familiar phraseology of the fixed prayers of the Book of Common Prayer against the church courts: 'God deliver all Christians out of this antichristian tyranny, where the judges, advocates, and proctors for the most part are papists, and as for the scribes and notaries as greedy as cormorants, and if they all should perhaps see this writing, they would be as angry as wasps and sting like hornets. Three of them would be enough to sting a man to death, for why [that is, because] they are high commissioners.' The impertinent prose of this passage undoubtedly appealed to many

10 Frere and Douglas, *Puritan Manifestoes*, pp. 5, 11

contemporary laymen, especially those who disliked clerical pretensions or who had felt the stings of the church courts. According to the
Admonition, all of the flaws in the Church of England sprang from one
basic source, its unreformed polity, 'this antichristian hierarchy and
popish ordering of ministers, strange to the word of GOD, and the use of
all well reformed churches in the world.'[11]

For all their clever, biting innuendo, Field and Wilcox held back from
advocating separation. Vexed enough with the Elizabethan settlement
to take the bold step of making a public appeal to Parliament, they
wished to reform the Established Church, not to establish congregations
of gathered saints. Indeed, they fumed over the tainted relics from the
days when the popish antichrist ruled the church which still remained
in England and they advocated individual withdrawal from certain
established practices, but they did not claim that the Elizabethan settlement either retained or produced a false church. Radical puritans
groping for their own apocalyptic position, Field and Wilcox feared that
the Church of England, unless further reformed, might slip back into
Babylon. They best summed up this attitude in a statement from the
second edition of the *Admonition*: 'We strive for true religion and
government of the church, and shew you the right way to out antichrist
both head and tail, and that we will not so much communicate with the
tail of the beast: but they [the hierarchy] after they have thrust antichrist out by the head, go about to pull him in again by the tail ...'[12]
Although sharing many similarities with that of an anonymous
separatist quoted above, the imagery remained ambiguous. The head of
the beast could have represented the pope, the tail either hierarchy or all
unreformed practices still remaining. Field and Wilcox remained radical puritans who stood on the brink of separatism and drew back. They
accepted many of the arguments of the separatists and started from the
same premises – the same definition of popery – but they would not
follow through to a full condemnation of the Established Church.

During the course of 1572 that same Parliament discussed the fate of
Mary Queen of Scots at length. In a long forceful address to Elizabeth the
bishops of the Church of England urged that Mary's execution would
'abash and damp the minds of all the enemies of God and friends of
antichrist.'[13] It must have pained such men when the *Admonition*

---

11 *Ibid.*, pp. 12, 25, 30, 34
12 *Ibid.*, p. 36 n. 3
13 Neale, *Parliaments, 1559–1581*, p. 271, quoting BL (British Library), Cotton MSS. Titus
   F. I., fos. 172–86

placed them in this category. When their own imagery redounded against them, the bishops showed little charity in either their words or actions. Bishop Cooper preached against the *Admonition* at St Paul's Cross. The authorities apprehended Field and Wilcox and sent them to Newgate prison to ponder their programme at leisure. The removal of these leaders did not stop the cause, however. In the autumn of 1572 a second *Admonition* appeared. Once ascribed to Thomas Cartwright, the authorship of this tract remains in doubt. The second *Admonition* blamed the bishops for the 'great disquieting of this Church of Christ in England,' the ingenuous argument used against Bishop Grindal by the leaders of the Plumbers' Hall group. The author of the second *Admonition* took up Pattenson's critique of Grindal and applied it to the hierarchy as a whole: '... They are none other but a remnant of antichrist's brood, and God amend them and forgive them, for else they did battle to Christ and his church, and it must bid defiance to them till they yield.'[14] By placing the bishops in 'antichrist's brood' and advocating resistance to them, the author of the second *Admonition* went beyond the innuendo of Field and Wilcox to hint at what would become the 'root and branch' tradition. Taken as a whole, however, this second appeal lacked the impact of the first. The innuendo of Field and Wilcox begged for radical application. Its startling and appealing prose took simple words and applied them to a subtle message.

The first *Admonition* publicized elements of two emerging streams of the English apocalyptic tradition, points of view hitherto confined to secret writings or passed on by word of mouth. By attacking the polity, discipline, and liturgy of the Church of England and by implying that these endangered its status as a true church, Field and Wilcox both proclaimed a radical puritan vision and publicly opened a road to separation. A tradesman, an apprentice, or a literate yeoman could repeat the clever aspirations of the *Admonition* in a neighbourhood argument with direct and devastating effect; he could also borrow its vivid imagery and vision to bolster his own conclusions. The *Admonition*, printed several times, probably passed from hand to hand or from mouth to ear in many dissident circles and, thereby, gained an even greater circulation. In the process, no doubt, those careful distinctions that delighted educated clerics got diffused in the words of some less sophisticated supporters. This should surprise no one; even the historian

---

14 Frere and Douglas, *Puritan Manifestoes*, pp. 113, 111. For the authorship of the second *Admonition*, see Pearson, *Thomas Cartwright*, p. 73 ff.

of apocalyptic thought runs into difficulties when attempting to sort out all of the ambiguous usages of antichrist and antichristian. Composed in the borderland of the Minories, the *Admonition* reflected its environment by publishing those criticisms of the Established Church which formed the foundations of both the radical puritan and separatist attacks. Field and Wilcox viewed the rites, titles, and courts of the Church of England as antichristian remnants; others took them as signs that England still remained within the jurisdiction of Babylon. As we have seen, at least one separatist condemned the Established Church by following the latter argument in his manuscript treatises and oath. Were this 'simple unlearned man' unique, one could hardly explain the growth of the separatist movement.[15]

London, the centre from which Field and Wilcox launched their campaign of reformation, spawned the first visible separatists. By the 1570s puritan pastors who criticized the Elizabethan settlement in the provinces got pushed toward radical action by the godly in their congregations. One of these provincial groups showed a familiarity with the language of Patmos when, in 1580, it petitioned Elizabeth to finish the reformation: '... Your highness by the favour of God, have been the author of removing the doctrine of antichrist, and planting the doctrine of Christ ... so it might seem good to your highness to fulfil up your happy work, by removing the government of antichrist also, with all his archprelates ...' The men of Norwich who sent this supplication to the godly queen feared that the revenging hand of God would descend on England unless Elizabeth erected a proper church soon. Presbyterians at this stage, they asked for the creation of a 'holy eldership' and employed the apocalyptic language of the *Admonition*.[16] The fertile ground of Norwich soon produced the first separatist pamphlets, however. Seeking the godly, Robert Browne and Robert Harrison wandered from place to place before finding them in Norwich. Both of these men, after graduating from Cambridge, became teachers rather than accept a call in the corrupt Church of England. Each lost his post because of religious radicalism, even though the townsmen supported Browne, as he proudly pointed out. Like Foxe and the Geneva Bible, they sought to bring the results of their education to the people at large and did so with no small success. Until Browne persuaded him to cut his ties with the Established

15 See note 6 above.
16 Peel, *Seconde Parte*, I, pp. 157–8; for a continuation of the London movement, see items 99 and 100, pp. 148–53.

Church, Harrison was a radical puritan.[17] Browne arrived at his separatist position in an independent way, but co-operated with others in putting his ideas into print and action. These two intellectuals, at least one of whom sprang from gentry stock, interacted with their more lowly followers to work out the logical consequences of separation – a repudiation of the church and society which gave them birth and nourishment.[18] Together, Browne and Harrison articulated the reasons for separation, including an identification of the Established Church with Babylon, and put these into print. While these ideas did not originate with Browne and Harrison, they published them for the first time in a systematic way.

Three of Robert Harrison's works have survived; two of these broke into print during his lifetime. The manuscript 'A treatise of the church and kingdome of Christ' (c. 1580) and the pamphlet *A little treatise uppon the first verse of the 122 Psalm* contained the core of Harrison's apocalyptic vision. Early in his long career Robert Browne published five separatist works and he provided a narrative of his spiritual development in one of these, *A true and short declaration* (1584). Like the earlier, more obscure, separatists, Browne and Harrison defended their actions by applying their apocalyptic vision first against the bishops. Harrison characterized the Church of England as a body in which 'the chiefest and highest ecclesiastical authority is in the hands of antichrist,' while Browne portrayed the prelates with similar language: '... These blind guides ... which were never lawfully called ... sit in the seat of antichrist; for what is the seat of antichrist but that popish government and lordship in the communion of such Romish offices, and horrible abuses by them. And while they sit at the temple of God ... and exalt their traditions above God's, what are they but antichrist's?'[19] Browne and Harrison plunged forward at just that point where the authors of the first *Admonition* drew back. Both radical puritans and separatists

---

17 Browne, *True and short* in *Writings*, pp. 397–8, 408, 406–11. Citations will be to the edition of Peel and Carlson but will use the original title of the work cited. The introduction of this edition contains references to the standard studies of Harrison and Browne plus some corrections and additions.

18 Robert Browne was a distant kinsman of Lord Burghley. The fact that only nine of the 175 supplicants of 1580 appeared in the Norwich muster roll of that year indicates that most of the group came from humble social backgrounds, an impression strengthened by Browne's account. For a general discussion and a redating of the petition, see Peel, *Brownists*.

19 Harrison, 'Treatise,' p. 32, and Browne, *True and short*, p. 402; cf. Browne, *On 23rd Matthew*, p. 219

strongly felt that the hierarchy of the Established Church constituted an improper polity; radical puritans, however, said that episcopacy derived from when antichrist ruled the church, while separatists called the bishops antichrists.

According to Browne and Harrison, the government of the Established Church infused the whole body of its clergy with corruption. Any minister who remained within the Church of England necessarily received ordination and a licence to preach from the bishops. Browne refused to countenance such recognition of episcopal authority. Indeed, he 'abhorred such trash and pollutions as the marks and poisons of antichrist.' Harrison warned puritan preachers – men he long regarded with sympathy – that 'you have the mark of the beast ... for every antichrist is the beast, but you have received their waxen seals in your hands, and their handsfull of benisons on your heads, whom I before proved to be from antichrist [that is, from the bishops], and you do not repent or renounce it: therefore you have received the mark of the beast.'[20] No matter how pure their preaching, no matter how good their individual lives, the clergy of the Church of England remained a part of Babylon because they received their callings from bishops, not from gathered congregations. The descending derivation of their authority stamped all ministers in the Established Church with the mark of the beast of Revelation.

Browne went beyond his friend to assail the preachers in their stronghold. Both refused to accept the calling of English clerics, but Browne's levelling tendencies led him to sally forth against the worldly learning exhibited by the most accomplished puritans. Dangerous because it derived from pagan sources and because preachers used it for the verbal repression of unlearned men, university scholarship proved most perilous because it led its practitioners to draw false distinctions. The intelligent, educated preacher tried to compromise himself and his flock by glossing over the true nature of the Elizabethan settlement. '... They hide the wolf in the fold and say, here is Christ ... and say that antichrist is gone, he shall devour them no more. Thou art deceived O England, thou art gone from one destruction unto another: Thou hast escaped the snare, but art fallen into the pit.'[21] This was, of course, the bottomless pit of Revelation. Browne fired his volleys at the arts practised by those

20 Browne, *True and short*, p. 407, Harrison, 'Treatise,' p. 53, 39–40; see Harrison, *Little treatise*, pp. 119–20
21 Browne, *On 23rd Matthew*, p. 208, see 172–84

preachers in whom the puritans gloried. Although he fell into the trap of exploiting the same methods, he perceptively articulated a deep distrust of traditional modes of behaviour and of academic learning. Anything which acted to hide the false nature of the Church of England or which prevented the levelling proclivity of Browne's vision of the true church was grist to his mill.

Browne believed that the Elizabethan settlement perpetuated improper government, no vital discipline (the antichristian church courts), popish baptism, corrupt communion, and ministers who sought to hide the truth of the Lord with the trickery of their pagan learning. He intoned the voice of the Almighty to announce the inescapable conclusion! 'Therefore, thus saith the Lord: I feed not my flock at Paul's Cross in London, or in *Saint Mary's in Cambridge*, or in your English parishes. O ye my sheep, go not thither, as though they were my fold, and there I rested and fed my flock: for there be shepherds and flocks also that follow them, which are not of Christ, for they hold of antichrist.'[22] A more wholesale adverse judgment of the Church of England could not be made. Not only the bishops and the puritan preachers, but indeed the whole body of the nation attended parish churches – as law required – and therefore resided in Babylon. Perhaps the act of separation from a church whose boundaries included all in the nation demanded full condemnation – it certainly brought forth such a reaction.

Two alternative modes of reforming the church were presented by Browne and Harrison. The traditional protestant appeal to the godly magistrate appeared in their works. After listing all the chief abominations of the Church of England, Harrison finished with such a request: 'All these wormwood dregs of antichrist's cup, and whatsoever more, it appertaineth only to the office of the civil magistrate, to pour out and rinse even from the bottom. Which the Lord grant that it may soon be done.' This was rather wishful thinking. In reality, neither Browne nor Harrison believed that established authority would put their programme into operation. Disavowing God's imperial instrument, Browne's scathing language belittled the very idea of waiting for the magistrate to enforce public reform. Instead of reformation, a magisterial meddling with the church produced deformation: 'For we know that when magistrates have been most against the church and the authority thereof, the church hath most flourished. Woe to you, therefore, ye blind preachers and hypocrites; for ye spread a veil of darkness upon

22 *Ibid.*, p. 208, see 214; cf. Harrison, 'Treatise,' p. 37

the people, and bring upon them a cursed covering, because by your policy you hide them under the power of antichrist, and keep from their eyes the kingdom of Christ.'[23] By its very nature, an established or national church proved unacceptable to Browne. By accepting the authority of such an institution, puritan preachers turned themselves into despicable deceivers. Only the persecuted and oppressed could create another mode of organization and, thereby, sap the strength of Babylon.

Having rejected the godly prince, the bishops, and the puritan preachers as proper instruments of further reformation, Browne completed his repudiation of traditional forms by casting aside the parish – the smallest, most pliable element of the Established Church. Because even the parish reeked of corruption, he 'judged that the kingdom of God was not to be begun by whole parishes, but rather of the worthiest, were they never so few.' Only a small gathered group of saints freed from the insidious influence of the ungodly majority of men could put into practice Browne's vision of participatory religion. In such a body, 'every Christian having faith and knowledge' would speak the word of God to others, would preach. '... Preaching is not tied to the pulpit, nor to degrees, to person,' instead it should be 'that duty of speaking and teaching the truth, as it ought to be taught, and that in what place so ever.' The church of Christ included only those Christians who, after rejecting the world, covenanted together as saints. The *ad hoc* covenants or oaths of the early separatists now got transformed into both an ideological rejection of society and a formula for righteousness. Browne discarded the traditional hierarchical world and world view and substituted for it a levelled band of pilgrims. Only these godly truly followed their Saviour. All other men acted like those beasts of Babylon who might pretend to 'bow the knee before' Christ, but in reality cast 'dung on his face.'[24]

By identifying themselves and their followers as the persecuted saints of God, Browne and Harrison turned the tradition of the oppressed against the reformed Church of England. The persecutors included all persons who refused explicitly to reject the Established Church; everyone attending a parish church service remained in Babylon. Within that Christian dualism that characterized apocalyptic thought, the new categories of Browne and Harrison extended the ranks of evil to

23 Harrison, *Little treatise*, pp. 119–20, and Browne, *A treatise*, p. 167, see 169–70 and passim
24 Browne, *True and short*, pp. 404, 410, 421; cf. Walzer, *Revolution*, ch. 5. By excluding the separatists from his study, Walzer missed the origins of this mode of attack.

include all but a small handful of gathered saints. Such a theoretical position necessarily issued forth in action at the most basic local level; it cut the separatists off from most of their neighbours and helped to fulfil their prophecies of persecution. Browne told how he chose to leave the worldly comfort of his father's home to find spiritual solace with like-minded men. Even without formal harassment and imprisonment by the authorities, men and women who deemed it needful to disavow traditional modes of behaviour in such a customary society faced considerable pressure from their family, friends, and neighbours. Browne sought to ease the predictable tension that this produced by laying out new patterns of congregational procedure in which all members participated. He hoped, thereby, to increase group coherence and identity, to create something of a surrogate family. Of course, he drew upon past separatist experience. The binding link for the new society was the covenant – a frail cement. Eventually, Browne himself found contention, division, and finally expulsion his lot among the covenanted elect. This took place in Holland whence the congregation fled to practise its religion in freedom. Even before then, when persecution and harassment started, members fell away.[25] No wonder, then, that Browne and Harrison longed for the ultimate solution – the second coming of Christ.

Although neither of them left surviving writings which allow positive determination of the full extent of their apocalyptic visions, Browne and Harrison did have somewhat different attitudes. Harrison loathed cutting himself off from his puritan colleagues – in his heart he desired a national reformation, 'the full repairing of the walls of Jerusalem.' Only when hope for an elect nation expired did he withdraw. 'If there by any thing at all: I will promise and vow faithfully to tarry and wait with them also.' To wait, that is, with his puritan brethren for the magistrate. Even more than the company of men, especially of those who would not brave persecution, Harrison sought the company of Christ, 'Whose kingdom and glory we must seek both in wealth and woe, both in peace and persecution. His kingdom come with speed.' Harrison finished the pamphlet from which this passage is cited with a series of quotations from the Psalms – verses strung together to give hope to the persecuted, assuring them that they would triumph in the end. ' "Turn us again, O Lord God of hosts: Cause thy face to shine

25 *Ibid.*, p. 398 ff., 422–9; cf. Coolidge, *Pauline Renaissance*, pp. 62–9. For later manifestations of this type of behaviour, see Hobsbawm, *Primitive Rebels*, ch. 9, 'Ritual in Social Movements.'

and we shall be saved." *So be it.*'[26] Passive certitude provided the theme of Harrison's apocalyptic expectations, not active aggressiveness. It sounded a cry of tense resignation from the affairs of the world, not a call for battle by the saints. His world ended with a whimper, not a bang.

Robert Browne showed a more fierce commitment to separation than his friend. After all, he converted Harrison to the cause. Browne definitely thought that he lived in the last age of the earth. He even wrote a treatise on the Book of Revelation. If printed, it has not survived. He revealed the chronological basis of his apocalyptic vision, however, in a letter written on the last day of 1588.[27] The missing portion of this letter doubtless contained an unravelling of the complicated chronology of the events prophesied by St John. Browne thought that the last age of the world rapidly drew nigh, that most of the predictions of Revelation had been fulfilled. The raising up of 'fellow antichrists, that is the Turks, Saracens ... etc., to overrun the greatest part of the world ... is already come to pass, since the chief antichrist, that man of Rome, was exalted.' In addition the fall of antichrist, predicted in Revelation xi:16, verged on completion. Contemporary events represented the fifth of the seven degrees of the destruction of Babylon. 'This is that plague of antichrist which at this day is to be fulfilled, namely in speaking and preaching against their lordships' [the bishops'] great livings, and all their usurpings. For this is that vial poured out upon his throne ... the former are poured out already ...' By denouncing the bishops of the Church of England, Browne helped to fulfil the prophecies of Revela-

26 Harrison, *Little treatise,* pp. 121–3
27 Browne, *A book,* p. 225; the letter appears on pp. 517–29 as 'An answer to Mr Flowers letter.' Unfortunately, part of the original text is missing, probably a sheet of four pages. The editor's suggestion that the passage on the Book of Revelation is irrelevant to the rest of the letter seems mistaken. This passage fits into the logic of the opening section, which clearly states 'that antichrist is come already' and goes on to explain that interpreters have presented a confused chronology of antichrist (p. 517). The 'weighty matters' that Browne turned to next would be his own interpretation of the chronology of St John's prophecies. Hence, he mentioned that 'antichrist [did] climb up first, when ministers called first for names and titles of offices of those first Christian emperors' (p. 518). Then he discussed the apostolic church. The missing portion of the letter most probably dealt with the growing power of antichrist during the middle ages and the breaking forth of light with the first reformers. The material when the surviving portion takes up again would fit into this chronology (pp. 523–4). The jottings of the last section justify separation by answering specific objections raised by Mr Flower in his letter to Browne (pp. 525–9). Even the parts of Browne's chronology which do not need to be reconstructed only make sense within Bale's framework.

tion. His attacks upon the prelates – branding them antichrists – clearly fit into his apocalyptic vision. The pouring of the sixth vial was about to commence, so Browne warned his correspondent that compromise must by all means be avoided: 'This I write good uncle, that we may take heed how we justify and uphold that seat that must needs fall, I mean that pomp, glory, riches, power, etc. of the clergy lest we be taken in the sixth plague ... to defend this tottering state to our everlasting confusion.' By this Browne meant that the Anglican hierarchy must be abolished and the Elizabethan settlement brought into conformity with true Christian practice. The pouring of the sixth vial, or the sixth degree of the fall of Babylon, would commence a bloody battle between protestants and Roman catholics. The kings of the east, for Browne,

signify the princes of the protestants, and that they shall prosper in all their wars against the papists, even till Rome itself be burned, and then shall Gog that is antichrist of Rome, and Magog that is antichrist of the barbarians be joined in league and come up in battle array even into the plain of the earth, and when they shall have compassed in the poor church on all sides ready to devour it, Revelation xx:8,9, then shall Christ come with fire to judge all the wicked and so shall be the end or that full, last or everlasting plague of antichrist which is the seventh plague.[28]

With the final engagement imminent, Browne certainly wanted to range himself on the right side and persuade his correspondent to take the same course. More remarkable, Browne intertwined the spiritual strife against antichrist with physical warfare on earth. This represents one of the earliest examples of what became a standard argument in the English protestant apocalyptic tradition.

Browne wrote this letter during the year of the attempted Armada invasion of England, a year earlier singled out by the Lutheran reformer Philip Melanchthon as one that might mark the end of the world. No doubt, the threat of a Spanish attack induced Browne to prophesy an imminent pouring of the sixth vial in the form of actual warfare between catholic and protestant. The Armada year raised apocalyptic expectations in England and elicited a plea for an apocalyptic crusade against Spain by James VI of Scotland. Although Browne formally recanted his separation to the ecclesiastical authorities before 1588, the private thoughts revealed in his letter indicate that he still believed that

28 Browne, 'An answer,' pp. 526, 527

the Church of England stood in apocalyptic jeopardy. Without this letter, one could reconstruct only a small portion of Browne's detailed interpretation of Revelation. With it, one can see how his earlier attack upon the Established Church took place within the context of a systematic exegesis of the prophecies of St John, one based upon Bale's framework.

In the autumn of the Armada year a bombshell exploded upon the scene of respectable puritan activity when Martin Marprelate let fly his humorous but telling barrage at the bishops of the Church of England. 'Who Martin was we may never know,' writes the greatest living authority on Elizabethan puritans, 'but his publishers were familiar figures in the puritan movement ...' In October 1588 the first tract, *Oh read over D. John Bridges* (the epistle), appeared, to be followed in November by *Oh read over D. John Bridges* (the epitome). In February 1589 *Certaine minerall and metaphysicall schoolpoints* and in March *Hay any worke for Cooper* came off the press. Robert Waldegrave, the well-known presbyterian printer, printed these first four works. Three other pamphlets rounded out the corpus: *Theses Martinianae* (July 1589), *The just censure and reproffe of Martin junior* (July 1589) – both printed by J. Hodgkins – and *The protestatyon of Martin Marprelat* (September 1589) – printer unknown. A different author most probably wrote this last group.[29] Appearing within the space of a year, these tracts sought to sensitize all Englishmen to the evils of episcopacy. Instead, they brought forth that repression of the puritan movement engineered by Richard Bancroft.

To the authorities and to sober puritans alike one of the most exasperating things about the Marprelate tracts was the satirical appeal they made to public opinion. Whoever penned these pamphlets – a question still far from solution – he tried to stir up all men to discuss the legitimacy of the bishops. 'I saw the cause of Christ's government and of the bishops' antichristian dealing to be hidden. The most part of men could not be got to read anything written in the defence of the one and against the other. I bethought me therefore of a way whereby men might be drawn to do both, perceiving the humours of men in these times (especially of those that are in any place) to be given to mirth. I took that course.' John Field, who helped to write the first *Admonition* in 1572 and

---

29 Collinson, *Elizabethan Puritan*, p. 391, see pp. 391–6 and part 8. For the printer of the last three tracts, see Pierce, *Historical Introduction*, pp. 193–4. Despite the large literature on the Marprelate tracts, no scholar has yet made a systematic examination of their apocalyptic content.

who organized the attempt to establish a presbyterian movement within the Church of England, died before the loosing of Martin's stinging slings. Field's campaign to introduce further reformation through the agency of Parliament had failed. Pressed by the separatists, puritans began to despair of even changing the Established Church from within. In the last days of his life, Field was purported to have begun plotting more radical action – perhaps a revolutionary appeal to the common people. In the Star Chamber Thomas Edmunds reported that Field, near the end, had said that 'seeing we cannot compass these things by suit nor dispute, it is the multitude and people that must bring the Discipline to pass which we desire.'[30] The ghost of Field's threat, and maybe more, lived on in Martin Marprelate. Both Foxe's 'Book of Martyrs' and the Geneva Bible had reached a wide circulation by the time the Marprelate tracts appeared. Browne and Harrison had spread the cause of separation by their actions and writings. The pamphlets of Martin Marprelate soon joined these earlier works to help shape an apocalyptic interpretation of the reformation in the minds of a large number of rank-and-file Englishmen.

To appeal to the common man Martin combined personal invective of a lively type with a simplified presentation of the scholarly arguments of Thomas Cartwright, for he believed that Cartwright 'hath proved the calling [of the bishops] to be unlawful and antichristian.' Repeatedly he asserted that 'all the bishops in England, Wales, and Ireland, are petty popes and petty antichrists.'[31] Beside this wholesale condemnation of episcopacy, Martin used personal attacks against the actions of individual bishops with telling effect and used rhetorical devices to make people believe that Anglican prelates continued to manifest the worst characteristics of the popish hierarchy. He also sought to demonstrate that their callings came not from God, but that they were 'bishops of the devil.'[32] In the last of the Waldegrave tracts, Martin was unwilling to credit bishops with the ability to do any good thing. Even men of fine character, such as Cranmer, Ridley, or John Hooper, could not rise above the corruption of their calling. Purity of life made no difference: 'As though, you block you, every petty pope and petty antichrist were a

---

30 *Hay any worke*, p. 14 (sig. c 4v), and quoted in Collinson, *Elizabethan Puritan*, p. 390, cf. 394. Citations will be made to the original pagination of the pamphlets photographically reprinted in *Marprelate Tracts*.
31 *Oh read* (epistle), pp. 3, 4, see 7–8, 17–18; cf. *Hay any worke*, sig. b 1, pp. 1, 21
32 *Hay any worke*, pp. 26–8, cf. 13–14, 34; see *Oh read* (epistle), pp. 9, 26 ff., 34–5, 39, *Oh read* (epitome), sig. d 4r, and *Certaine schoolpoints*, pp. 39–40

reprobate.' Nor should one be deceived into condoning the actions of those bishops who did preach. 'Though our bishops be as evil as Judas, the false apostles, and Balaam, yet because they have sometimes brought unto us God's message, we must think no otherwise of them, than of God's messengers. For God will not suffer devilish and antichristian persons to be the chief restorers of the gospel.' Martin turned the apocalyptic tradition against the English bishops and cut them off from any role in the establishing of right religion. According to him, the only godly bishop was one who acted to abolish his office.

... Good John of Canterbury leave off thy popedom; good John of London, be no more a bishop of the devil; be no more a traitor to God and his word. And good sweet boys, all of you, become honest men; maim and deform the church no longer; sweet fathers now, make not a trade of persecuting; gentle fathers, keep the people in ignorance no longer; good gathers now, maintain the dumb ministry no longer. Be the destruction of the church no longer, good sweet babes now; leave your nonresidency, and your other sins, sweet popes now; and suffer truth to have free passage.

Such sarcastic prose aimed its blows at men who spent long years of toil trying to bring reformation to England. John of London was none other than John Aylmer, John of Canterbury John Whitgift. Martin abolished the imperial role which Foxe had given the hierarchy. If the bishops did not reform by eradicating their positions, Martin told them, then 'the magistrates ought to thrust you out of the commonwealth.'[33] The time to reform the Established Church from within had passed for this radical and it seemed that only a full-scale attack upon its leaders could bring real change. The clever crudity of Martin's prose assured the popularity of his pamphlets among the common people.

With the backing of Bullinger and other reformed continental divines, Elizabethan bishops justified their offices on the grounds that they received their calling as ministers from God and as bishops from the crown. Even Theodore Beza, who disliked the episcopal government of the Church of England, only argued that bishops could be of God, of man, or of the devil – not that all hierarchy was unacceptable. Martin put Beza's distinction to a cutting use. He would not allow members of the Anglican hierarchy to be bishops of God – his reading of the New Testament revealed no such creatures. He twisted the argument of John

33 *Hay any worke*, pp. 21–2, 31–2, 34, sig. B 1r

Bridges to show that they could not be bishops of man, for good measure claiming that Bridges committed 'flat treason in overthrowing her majesty's supremacy' in his attempt to establish a little *jure divino* for bishops.[34] Hence, Martin drew the inescapable conclusion that the English hierarchy received its calling from the devil. The denial of legitimacy to the bishops marked an important step, one previously taken only by separatists or dissidents like the deprived Master Patterson. The first four Marprelate tracts marked the real beginning of the 'root and branch' stream of the apocalyptic tradition. The characteristics of this category can be seen in Martin Marprelate's categorization of the bishops as antichrists, his denigration of the martyr bishops of Mary's reign, and his refusal to separate from the Church of England. This interpretation, taken up by Alexander Leighton in the 1620s, only became prominent with William Prynne and other radicals in 1641. Until then, few would dare to walk the thin edge between the radical puritan and separatist positions. Even Martin junior renounced the paternity of his father in this regard.

The last three Marprelate tracts carried the premise of the previous four to a different conclusion. Probably written by a different author, they also lacked the witty, biting prose which bestowed literary fame upon the earlier pamphlets. Martin junior began with the favourite target of the first set of tracts, the bishops. In *Theses Martinianae* he listed some one hundred and ten theses to demonstrate that episcopacy contradicted the true doctrine of the Church of England. The writings of earlier reformers, such as William Tyndale's *The practyce of prelates*, provided the basis for his points.

57 That by the doctrine of the Church of England, it is not possible, that naturally there can be any good lord bishop, Master Tyndale's, Practice for [sic] Prelates, pag. 374.

59 That by the doctrine of the Church of England, our bishops are none of the Lord's anointing, but servants of the beast.

63 That by the doctrine of the Church of England the places of archbishops and bishops are the seats of antichrist.

Tyndale, of course, wrote against the hierarchy of the unreformed church, not against that of the Elizabethan settlement. It must have been infuriating to the recipients of this invective that Tyndale was

34 *Ibid.*, pp. 29, 20. For a discussion of episcopal theory, see Sykes, *Old Priest*, ch. 1 and 2.

turned against protestant bishops, and that in the name of the Established Church. Martin junior, by implication, compared them to the
popish persecutors of the past. Explicitly, he denied that the polity of the
church was reformed. The earlier Marprelate tracts argued the same
position, albeit from a little different tack. Martin junior, however, also
condemned even those preaching clergy who recognized the jurisdiction
of the bishops. '79 That by the doctrine of the Church of England, to
have a bishop's licence to preach is the very work of the beast of
antichrist.' Since all preachers needed a licence, and non-preaching
ministers long had been anathema to the puritans, all the clergy of the
Church of England fell under the rubric of this classification. This
position led Martin junior to move beyond his predecessor and follow
Browne and Harrison. He demanded that the godly refuse to recognize
such a false church and therefore withdraw from it.[35]

The boldness of Martin junior was bolstered by his belief that once he
brought the chicanery of the authorities into the open they would lose
all support. Like Martin Marprelate before him and the young John
Lilburne later, he staked his life on overcoming them in public debate.
'... If in this encounter I overthrow them (as I make no question of it, if
they dare abide the push) then they to truss up and be packing to ROME,
and to trouble our church no longer.' This was rhetorical flourish,
although to Martin junior's troubled mind the fantasy of debating the
bishops out of the land may have seemed more than wishful thinking. In
reality, he expected another era of persecution for the English elect. He
believed '*That reformation cannot well come to our church without
blood.*' The bishops would be the 'butchers and horse leeches to draw it
out.' Equating them with the Marian persecutors and himself with the
Marian martyrs, Martin junior almost sought martyrdom to push the
cause of reformation forward.[36] The pages of Foxe contained many
variations on the same theme. Martin junior ripped the apocalyptic
tradition of the oppressed from Foxe's synthesis, however, and asserted
that the Lord would work through his persecuted saints to overthrow the
might of Babylon in England.

The last three Marprelate tracts transformed the disavowal of the
bishop martyrs of the earlier pamphlets into a new historical interpretation of the English reformation. Although Henry VIII and Elizabeth I
obtained a passing notice in this account, most of the bishops who

35 *Theses*, sig. B 2v–3v, B 4r, cf. 4v–D 1r; see *Just censure*, sig. C 1r
36 *Protestatyon*, pp. 10–11, 4, 5; the emphasis in the second passage was in larger type in
the original.

played an instrumental role in the establishment of protestantism in England received no mention. Instead, Martin junior magnified the part played by protestant critics of royal policy. For him, the doctrine of the Church of England had been framed by 'the writings of Mr Tyndale, Mr Frith, Mr Barnes, Mr Hooper, Mr Knox, Mr Lambert, etc., which were the first planters of the gospel amongst us ...' Later he extended this list to include the names of his contemporaries, Foxe, James Pilkington, Martin Marprelate, Dudley Fenner, Walter Travers, Anthony Gilby, and Cartwright. Only two bishops, Hooper and Pilkington, merited inclusion and they were hardly representative members of the hierarchy. Tyndale, Frith, Barnes, and John Lambert had been executed for heresy in the reign of Henry VIII. Tyndale, Frith, Barnes, and Hooper all fled to exile on the continent during that reign. John Hooper led the fight against traditional vestments before being consecrated as bishop of Gloucester in the reign of Edward VI. Probably the most radical of the Edwardian bishops, he acted as an ally of John Knox in opposition to kneeling at communion. James Pilkington, the only Elizabethan bishop in Martin junior's galaxy of reformers, suffered exile in Geneva and Frankfurt during Mary's reign and later sympathized with the opponents of official policy in the Elizabethan vestiarian controversy. Foxe's *Actes and monuments* provided a great deal of information on the earlier men, including some of their writings. All contemporary reformers listed took what Martin junior considered a proper position in the debate that sprang from the admonition controversy. Fenner, John Penry, Travers, Cartwright, and Gilby clearly proclaimed the truth, he argued, yet the hierarchy continued to maintain its 'thrice cursed popedom against such clear light.'[37] In one way or another, every one of Martin junior's heroes of the faith had suffered – through exile, martyrdom, deprivation, or imprisonment, and, for many, all four. Truly a constellation of the persecuted elect stood forth in these champions. God worked through individuals who spoke out boldly against the evils of the Established Church. Martin junior took the complex web of Foxe's history, lifted out favourable portions, and moulded these into a new genealogy of reform that used the tradition of the persecuted as its theme. Cranmer, Ridley, even Latimer – all heroes to Foxe – found no place in this historical reinterpretation. Making a clean break with the imperial tradition, Martin junior debunked the old and created a new image of the reformation in England.

37 *Theses*, sig. c4v, D 1, and *Protestatyon*, p. 12. Information on these people appears in Dickens, *English Reformation*, and Collinson, *Elizabethan Puritan*.

The Marprelate tracts succeeded in the aim of provoking both discussion and action. Many men read them in anger, others in mirth. Thomas Brightman, the great puritan commentator upon the Book of Revelation, thought that people should 'rather have cast those writings into the fire, than have worn them out with continual reading and handling of them.' All but a few puritan preachers appeared scandalized by these witty attacks upon the episcopacy. Most divines did not appreciate the direct appeal they made to popular opinion. One of the heroes of both sets of tracts, Thomas Cartwright, wrote to Lord Burghley that 'from the first beginning of Martin unto this day, I have continually upon any occasion testified both my dislike and sorrow for any such kind of disordered proceeding.'[38] The threat to order implicit in any attempt to sway the common man through biting propaganda against good reformed bishops disturbed many a puritan. When the 'root and branch' attack upon episcopacy of the first four Marprelate pamphlets became an explicit avowal of separation in the last three, however, puritans in general drew back in horror and disgust.

The Marprelate tracts, despite the scandal they created, never advocated as systematic and thorough a condemnation of the Established Church as Browne and Harrison. The latter were conspicuously absent from Martin junior's lists of heroes, a bit of evidence that underlined the circumstantial nature of his separatism. The Marprelate authors still wished for a national church and a presbyterian, not a congregational, polity. Their attack centred on the church hierarchy, even though Martin junior extended it to condemn all ministers in the Church of England. For all of their impertinence and popularity, these tracts seemed mild when compared with those written by Browne and Harrison. None the less, within the spectrum of English reformed opinion, both Marprelate authors passed beyond the apocalyptic views and the outspokenness of most radical puritans. Martin debunked the martyr bishops and called all English bishops antichrists. Martin junior placed all English ministers in Babylon and constructed a new, non-magisterial, genealogy of reformation. Together they opened the 'root and branch' assault upon episcopacy. Half a century would pass before this radical apocalyptic position found widespread favour among puritans and then only after a decade of Laudian conformity.

During the 1580s the threads of separatism lay scattered across the land. Robert Browne submitted to authority; the government con-

38 Both are quoted in Collinson, *Elizabethan Puritan*, p. 393.

demned by proclamation, hunted down, and either imprisoned or executed the men who spread his tracts. A few pamphlets circulating
among the alienated provided too little propagandistic impetus for
anything approaching a mass movement. Although Browne and Harrison drew a clear line between radical puritan and separatist, the second
group of Marprelate tracts seemed to pass over or blur some of their
distinctions. While Martin Marprelate pondered over the preparation of
his critique of the Elizabethan settlement, a far more dangerous critic
joined the separatist underground in London. A spokesman of great fire
and genius, Henry Barrow added clarity and seeming simplicity to the
separatist stream of the apocalyptic tradition.

A typical member of the Elizabethan élite in his background and
education, Barrow descended from a Norfolk squire related to the powerful Bacon family by marriage. He took a BA at Cambridge and read the
Common Law at Gray's Inn. As well educated and well connected as
Robert Browne, Barrow followed Browne's example by rejecting a normal career for the cause of radical religion – and he stuck to it. Active as
an important layman in the movement by 1587, he may have obtained
his separatist ideas in Norfolk, perhaps at Cambridge, or in attending
clandestine conventicles near London. He was arrested in November
1587 when visiting his friend John Greenwood at the Clink prison.
Barrow and Greenwood spent the rest of their lives in prison until being
executed for sedition in April 1593. While the authorities arduously
attempted to prevent Barrow from writing, he had his manuscripts
smuggled out of prison and printed in the Netherlands. The first appeared in print in 1589. His formidable spirit could not be stopped. In this
he resembled Latimer, Ridley, and other Marian martyrs before him,
and Bastwick, Burton, Prynne, and Lilburne later. Bred for leadership,
Henry Barrow rallied his more humble supporters in their offensive
against the church and the universities, the two most important intellectual bulwarks of established power.

Before Henry Barrow became a spokesman for the cause, separatist
attacks upon the Elizabethan settlement lacked focus. Authors either
concentrated on specific points or attempted to refute the arguments of
particular progagonists. The most compact platform listed nine reasons
for rejecting the Established Church. Henry Barrow's intellect cut
through layers of polemic to create a solid, lasting tool of separatist
analysis. In a brilliant contribution, he synthesized the core of the
separatist message into four main points. Each of these directly related
to the separatist apocalyptic vision.

Four principal and weighty causes why everyone that knoweth God and acknowledgeth the Lord Jesus ... ought speedily without delay to forsake those disordered and unholy synagogues and the false teachers of these times as they generally stand in England.

1 The false manner of worshipping the true God.
2 The profane and ungodly people received into and retained in the bosom and body of their churches.
3 The false and antichristian ministry imposed upon their churches.
4 The false and antichristian government wherewith their churches are ruled.

As early as 1587 this platform circulated among the brethren in manuscript. It provided an uncompromising condemnation of the Church of England. When Barrow repeated a variation of these four points at his examination of 18 March 1589, Lord Burghley and Sir Christopher Hatton reacted with great shock.

LORD TREASURER: Here is matter enough indeed: I perceive thou takest delight to be an author of this new religion.
The Lord Chancellor said he never heard such stuff before in all his life.[39]

What looked dangerously like a new religion to the queen's ministers, men very familiar with criticisms of the Church of England, put food in the mouths of those who forsook the Elizabethan settlement. Like all great propagandists, Barrow forged a slogan that would appeal to all orders of society. Simple enough for even the uneducated to understand and memorize, his model could pass by word of mouth among the illiterate. All of the evidence previously exploited by the separatists fitted into one of its compartments. In the course of dispute, one could expand each point infinitely just by adding supporting detail. When composing his more massive works, Barrow framed his extended argument by building on his four points – generations of separatists from Greenwood to Henry Burton followed his lead. This flexible formula gave Barrow's writings a simple, but deceptively expansive, consistency and organization that earlier separatist appeals conspicuously lacked. It also endowed most future separatist literature with a remarkable unity – and sameness to the historian who must read it. Barrow's four points

39 ENT, III, pp. 54, 179, cf. 120; references to scripture were deleted from the quotation. The writings of Barrow and Greenwood will be cited from the English Nonconformist Texts edition, either to the appropriate volume number or to the original title. Carlson provides a careful chronology of Barrow's life and works in ENT, III, IV, V, and VI.

significantly strengthened the form and the communicability of the separatists' apocalyptic assault upon the Church of England.[40]

Barrow deeply devoted his energies to unlocking the mysteries of the Apocalypse. The end of the world with its warfare between the forces of Christ and those of antichrist loomed imminent. God was 'ready to pour down his plagues ... as in the days of Noah and Sodom.' Reference to two of the most dramatic biblical examples of the Lord's judgments upon men illustrated the suddenness and finality of the expected return of Christ. In such times, each Christian had to distinguish the true from the false church and associate himself with the saints.

It behooveth us therefore, while yet God vouchsafeth us time, carefully by the light of God's word to examine our ways, and to ponder our estate, whether we be in that broad way that leadeth to destruction amongst those multitudes over whom the whore sitteth and reigneth or in the straight and narrow way which leadeth to everlasting life, with Christ's little flock ... whether we be in that great defection in that spiritual Babylon under antichrist and that beast, or whether we be in mount Sion, in the spiritual Jerusalem ...

This being known, all controversies shall forthwith cease; for then shall we either be guilty of our own destruction through our wilful obstinacy, or else shall we lay hold of eternal life, while yet it is offered, by forsaking our evil ways, and yielding obedience unto God's holy word.[41]

Barrow followed England's earliest protestants in his assumptions about the nature of truth – that the proclamation of the truth of the gospel would lead either to the direct acceptance of the message or to the condemnation of the obstinate who refused it. This point of view provided the basis of appeals for free debate constantly made by the radicals. No matter how the contest appeared to the eyes of the world, radicals knew that they would win. All persons, then, must be allowed to hear truth present its case at the very least, especially now that the day of judgment drew nigh. The end of verbal controversy would bring forth the beginning of open spiritual strife.

The Bible provided Barrow with the sole authority by which institutions could be judged or interpretations framed. Anything which deviated from its injunctions, for whatever reason, could not be accepted.

40 Numerous examples of the use of this structure could be cited; cf. Greenwood, *A briefe refutation*, ENT, VI, pp. 3–40, and [Burton], *Protestation*, sig. A 2v.
41 Barrow, *A briefe discoverie of the false church*, ENT, III, pp. 276, 278. Far from brief, this was Barrow's most important book.

Most protestants at least partially accepted the premise from which Barrow operated. They balked at his conclusions, however. The gulf between separatist and puritan on this point revealed itself in an interview between Barrow and a London minister who tried to persuade him to stay within the Established Church.

EGERTON: Though Christ hath left a perfect ministry, yet all things that are added unto it are not antichristian.
BARROW: Yes, all new ministries are antichristian and he of antichrist that executeth, standeth under, or justifieth them.

A distinct and easily discerned dividing line ran between the human followers of Christ and antichrist. No need to search the records of the first five hundred years of Christianity, as Whitgift and Cartwright had done.[42] No need to ponder – with most English protestants – to discern which traditional practices constituted *adiaphora* – things indifferent to salvation – and might be properly retained in a reformed church. Everything not clearly instituted by Christ would be swept away. Anyone who gave verbal or even implicit support to other practices upheld Babylon.

Judged by this rigorous standard, all aspects of the worship of the Church of England reeked of antichrist. Barrow confuted the very concept of an order of service, not just the form of the Book of Common Prayer. Indeed, the manner of pulpit preaching – so beloved of the puritans –fell short of his standards, as it had for Browne.

But here in these Babylonish synagogues one priest climbeth up into their pulpits for orations, and possesseth the place alone, where he declaimeth, delivereth his studied tale to the hourglass, which being run out, he must leave no place or time of addition, assent or dissent, to any other, all the people hasting away. In his pulpit, after he hath read his text, he may divide, teach or handle it, leave it or take it, corrupt, falsify, wrest or pervert it at his pleasure. In that privileged tub he may deliver what doctrines he list, be they never so corrupt, false, blasphemous.

Even the Laudians, who disliked puritan preachers for different reasons, could produce no more damning descriptions of long-winded reformed

---

42 ENT, IV, p. 212; cf. *A briefe discoverie*, p. 337 ff. Barrow followed Bale's chronological approach and argued that antichrist gradually extended his sway over the church; see ENT, VI, pp. 243–4.

pulpit style. But Barrow so cut himself off from tradition that he called English church buildings 'Babylonish synagogues,' not houses of God or even 'steeple houses,' the term later favoured by George Fox! A worship service dominated by the minister diverged from the pattern established by Christ. Anyone who performed or even participated in such feigned worship acted as an enemy of God. Although Christ instituted officers to preside over the congregation, each man who felt the spirit had a right to participate in church functions, providing he used discretion. Barrow firmly believed that all 'prophets (I mean such as are known to have the gift of interpretation of the scriptures) have all of them liberty to speak' no matter what their social standing. Only in the exercise of this type of Christian liberty could the purity of the church be maintained. 'For what part can be pure where the doctrine is not sound? Or what can be more miserable than to see with other men's eyes, to believe with other men's hearts, yea, to be brought into that slavery and subjection, that they must receive and believe whatsoever the prophets or ministers speak and agree upon, be it never so dissonant and repugnant to the word of God.'[43] With rich language still stirring to the reader, Barrow demanded that all people get an opportunity to come to their own understanding of truth – to see with their own eyes and believe with their own hearts. The priesthood of all believers represented a real goal for Barrow, not just an empty word in the mouth. He expanded the concept of Christian liberty to include participation of all members in the congregational service. Every potential saint, every individual, must enjoy the liberty to feel, to understand, and to express his or her own faith. Any other way introduced slavery. Only by a radical change to participatory services of this sort could the church in England break the bondage of Babylon.

The all-inclusive nature of the national church also came under the brunt of Barrow's uncompromising view. One could not presume to be a true Christian on the basis of being born in England and baptized as a child. Membership in the church could never coincide with the boundaries of the land, as many members of the Church of England believed. The contrast between Barrow's concept of church membership and that of a good Anglican like Archbishop Whitgift starkly but dramatically emerged in a brief exchange between the two men at Barrow's examination on 19 November 1587:

43 Barrow, *A plaine refutation*, ENT, V, pp. 250, 249; see *A briefe discoverie*, pp. 524–5, 365 ff., and, for a comment by Greenwood, ENT, IV, p. 210

A[rchbishop]: Of what occupation are you?
B[arrow]: A Christian.
A[rchbishop]: So are we all.
B[arrow]: I deny that.

England reeked of corruption, yet all the corrupt obtained automatic membership in the church. 'Neither hath all kind of sin and wickedness more universally reigned in any nation at any time, than here at this present in this land, where all are received into the church, all made members of Christ.' Divine history taught that only the church of antichrist opened its doors to all the inhabitants of a land. Even Calvin's warning that a visible church must contain both good and evil people drew an anathema from Barrow. Although admitting that 'the church here on earth shall never be without sin,' Barrow asserted that a true church must – as much as possible – consist of godly members. It must make a strong attempt to include only saints.[44] Since the Church of England did not separate the pure from the impure, Barrow castigated it for not fulfilling the commands of Christ.

Even those congregations in England which secretly tried to act as fellowships of the elect could not escape from the coming holocaust if they remained within the Established Church. Like some puritans, Barrow found a congregational system outlined in the pages of the New Testament. This particular polity demanded the election of pastors by the congregation, a plank in the platform of the second *Admonition to the Parliament*. This practice was not allowed generally within the Church of England. Barrow asked if any of its ministers could, then, have a true calling. Drawing material from Foxe's *Actes and monuments*, he argued that the parson of the Established Church merely continued the office of priest which sprang up under antichrist, not the position of pastor as described in scripture. 'If Mr Foxe say truly, the parson's office took beginning when the metropolitan bishop's sprang, and were as their bailiffs. But it is the same office that was and is executed in the Romish church. Therefore not the pastor's office.' New parson was merely old priest! When his puritan opponents tried to equivocate on the manner in which ministers were appointed, rather than elected, Barrow mercilessly exposed the fallacious felicity of their argument.

44 ENT, III, p. 97, and *A briefe discoverie*, pp. 283, 293

SPERIN: The patron's choice is the people's choice.
BARROW: How can you say the patron's choice is the people's, when they [the congregation] have neither privity, consent nor assent. ... Doth he [the patron] present, and the people must accept.[45]

Barrow would stand for no pretence – rightly so, for if the patron made no consultation with the people, but forced a parson on them from above, how could one claim truthfully that they exercised a choice? Participation by the congregation in all spiritual affairs constituted a *sine qua non* of the true church. Barrow would not allow Sperin's attempt to compromise with the traditional institutions of a hierarchically ordered world pass as the truth of Christ. Instead of seeking godly patrons like the puritans, Barrow railed at the system of presentation. The consistency of his logic cut across the grain of the society in which he lived.

In addition to the illegal imposition of ministers on congregations came their improper maintenance. Barrow pointed to a stark contrast between the teachings of Christ and the practices of the Church of England on this issue: 'For Christ having instituted an other maintenance for his ministry, namely, the free contribution and benevolence of his saints in these congregations whereunto they belong and administer. The Church of England, judging this all too base for her ministry, hath instituted or rather received of her mother of Rome lordly, yea, princely livings, courtly judicial sees, glebes and tithes, set and certain stipends.' Barrow fumed at the social superiority which the traditional system of support gave to ministers. All rectors and vicars of the Church of England obtained their livings from some form of stipend, be it glebe or tithe. Only some lecturers depended upon the free bounty of patrons or parishioners. Since almost all pastors were supported and presented in opposition to Barrow's interpretation of the declared word of God, all of them toiled in the vineyards of the whore of Babylon.

Thus now have we summarily perused all this rabble of the ministry of the Church of England, and have not found any one of them right ... But out of the smoke of the bottomless pit they came when that fallen star antichrist had the key thereof given him; to his body, his kingdom, the false church, they have always belonged, always served ... We see they bear not Christ's but antichrist's image, mark, life, power. What then should hinder this assertion, that they

45 ENT, IV, pp. 210, 246; see note 58 below for congregational polity

together with antichrist, their head, do grow, live, reign, stand and fall as the branches with the tree.[46]

Unless sweeping and fundamental change took place, the ministry of the Established Church stood and fell with that of Rome. Barrow could not compromise with time-honoured methods if he believed that they conflicted with the commands of Christ. By repudiating the legitimacy of presentation, temporalaties, and spiritualities, he denied validity to the organization of any national church and of the society with which it intertwined. He also refused to recognize that a reformation had occurred in England.

The hierarchy of the Church of England bore the brunt of responsibility for the corruption of that institution. Like the puritans, Barrow blamed the bishops for the unsatisfactory nature of the Elizabethan settlement. They held church and people in domination. Unto the prelates' 'bloody throne and antichristian power, and unto all the abominations proceeding from the same,' claimed Barrow, 'standeth all the land, both great and small, rich and poor, priest and people, in most servile subjection ...' He presupposed the validity of puritan arguments against episcopal government and, upon this base, lashed out at the office and its holders with bitter sarcasm. Martin Marprelate called members of the Anglican hierarchy 'bishops of the devil.' Barrow suggested that they inscribe their titles in the following form: 'John *by the permission of God and the power of the devil bishop of such a place ...*' Ironically, neither he nor Greenwood fully turned against the martyr bishops of Mary's reign. They attacked their office, but not their persons, by pointing out that the martyr bishops lived in an era when light had not yet become so clear. However, the advocates of episcopacy supported corruptions which antichrist introduced into the church. In their practices and arguments they 'most grossly draw all their water from that most filthy drain and poisoned sink of papistical corruption,' Barrow exclaimed, for 'the corrupt estate of this realm ... hath so long been made drunk with the whore's cup, that they can now taste or brook no other liquor.'[47] Even with the light of the gospel breaking through in the last age, the English church preferred to ignore the plans of Christ and continue to consort with the whore of Babylon.

46 Barrow, *A plaine*, pp. 258–9, 265–6
47 *A briefe discoverie*, pp. 285, 341, 560. For the bishop martyrs, see ENT, III, pp. 125–6, IV, pp. 4–6, V, pp. 280–2, VI, pp. 110–11, 141, 237. Chapters four and five below provide instances of the continuation of this contention into the seventeenth century.

Like most English dissidents, Barrow combined his denigration of the bishops with an attack upon the spiritual courts through which they exercised religious discipline. 'All these spiritual courts, officers, judgments, pleadings, customs, we find devilish and antichristian, and not to appertain to the church and kingdom of Christ, but to belong to the kingdom and throne of antichrist, and of the beast.' Like Browne, he abhorred these courts because 'their holy father the pope's canons' formed the basis of the system of law they enforced. As the capstone to the whole system of episcopal jurisdiction, the court of High Commission got singled out for special denunciation:

This monstrous court taketh utterly away the power and stoppeth the course of God's word, of his church, and of the godly laws of the land: prejudicial it is to the prerogative of the prince, to the jurisdiction of her royal courts, to the liberty of her free subjects, and to the Great Charter of England, as their practice evidently sheweth. How contrary it is unto God, and unto all the rules of his word ... will appear to all men that will bring them to light. So barbarous is their power, so odious their proceedings, as no apology can be made for them, unless by the same they will also justify the authority of the pope, and proceedings of the Spanish inquisition; both which ... they exceed.[48]

The High Commission drew special hatred because it acted as the instrument for suppressing dissenting religious movements in England. Barrow claimed that it broke the law of the land, the law of God, and the law of nations – so had the Marprelate tracts. With minor variations this threefold critique received tireless repetition by future religious radicals. Young John Lilburne applied it against the Star Chamber. Barrow's criticisms of the church courts also contained the levelling component of his vision of the true church: '... These their spider webs of their ecclesiastical laws and jurisdiction extend not but unto the smaller and common flies, the magistrates and greater personages are wholly exempt from them.'[49] Instead of proper congregational self-criticism and excommunication by the whole congregation, the Church of England practised a form of discipline established during the nadir of the history of the church.

Presbyterian government and discipline, on the other hand, merely gave new names to old tyrannous proceedings in order to continue social

48 *A plaine*, p. 257, and *A briefe discoverie*, pp. 341, 553–4; cf. Hill, *Society and Puritanism*, ch. 8–10
49 *A briefe discoverie*, p. 636; cf. *Theses*, sig B 4v (thesis 89), and *Protestatyon*, p. 22

repression, not to open Christian liberty. The presbyterians, Barrow predicted, 'would not molest or offend any of wealth or authority,' and he was probably not far off the mark. Mere substitution of new names would not change the mode of operation, 'as their pastors and elders for their parson and questman, their synods instead of their commissaries' courts, their high councils instead of the High Commission; let them never be afraid, for by that time they are acquainted with the new names, they shall not find the jurisdiction half so strange as it seems.' Just as he disavowed the social control implicit in the established form of worship and in the presentation and support of clergymen as anti-christian suppression of Christian liberty, so Barrow's assault upon modes of church government took the same form. He identified hierarchical social control with popery – with the slavery with which antichrist bound his followers and persecuted the saints. When this same type of control remained in force in the Church of England and in the presbyterian alternative, Barrow laid it bare in inspiring prose:

As for these new officers, these elders, they shall be but of the wealthiest honest simple men of the parish, that shall sit for ciphers dumb by their pastor and meddle with nothing, neither poor souls shall they know more than they say. As for the ordering of all things, that shall be in the pastor's hands only, especially in some chief men who shall be these presidents and rulers of synods and councils, and so the people be kept as far from the knowledge and performance of their duties as ever they were; for so long have the priests (for so still I call all false and antichristian ministers) usurped and detained the sole regiment of the church in their hands, as it will be a very hard matter for the people ever to recover their liberty again.[50]

This eloquent levelling passage expressed Barrow's belief that the common man need not merely follow the dictates of his social betters, but that he possessed a right to run things himself – especially if he belonged to the elect. Seriously accepting the priesthood of all believers, he attempted to work out a way to put it into practice. He identified it with 'liberty' and the ordinances of Christ. Barrow took the language of 'liberty' versus popish 'slavery,' employed so effectively by the early reformers against the unreformed church, and applied it to the Church of England and even to its puritan critics. Those who practised participatory congregationalism made up the party of saints, people with

50 A briefe discoverie, p. 561

freedom; all others lived under the socially repressive bondage and slavery of Babylon.

Barrow's alienation from traditional practices, combined with his vision of a truly new world, produced a rejection of the propriety of church buildings erected in the past. Like an Old Testament prophet, he countenanced nothing blighted by misuse and preached the destruction of all offending things:

But here peradventure it will be interjected that these synagogues may be purged, or (as our learned priests say) reformed, and so still used to the worship of God ...

Unto this I say: that idols cannot be cleansed with the blood of Christ, neither by his word which utterly condemneth them ... Again the idolatrous shape so cleaveth to every stone, as it by no means can be severed from them while there is a stone left standing upon a stone. So that neither they can be used to the worship of God, nor we have any civil use of them, seeing that they are execrable and devote[d] to destruction: so that they that use such execrable and unclean things cannot be clean, but must needs be defiled with the filthiness of these idols.[51]

On this very important practical issue, Barrow differed greatly from most English and continental reformers. Whereas almost all protestants continued to worship in the church buildings of the past, whether they stripped them of images and whitewashed the walls or not, Barrow would not pour his new wine into such old wineskins. Congregations could not perform Christian services in 'Babylonish synagogues.' Such language mocked the very idea of reform. Even in what most men might consider matters of little consequence, Barrow allowed no compromise with Babylon. He demanded the literal destruction of all old church buildings and advocated the lay annexation of all other church holdings, such as tithes and land. From the time of Henry VIII onward, English reformers had hoped and proposed that the crown employ the revenues of bishops and monasteries in support of education or charity. Henry Barrow saw the first of these as the worst of all possible alternatives, for he argued that the schools and universities of England comprised the very training grounds of the supporters of antichrist.

Like the practices, government, and ministry of the Church of England, the existing educational system arose during the middle ages, that

51 *Ibid.*, p. 478

period when the papacy ruled western Europe. 'The universities of Cambridge and Oxford have the same popish and idolatrous beginning that the colleges of monks, friars, nuns, and those vermin had, and still retain the same unsufferable and incurable abuses, *etc*. Therefore Queen Elizabeth hath, and ought by as good right to abolish them, as her progenitor did the abbeys.' These 'monkish dens' trained up clergymen in 'idolatry, superstition, and most filthy abominations' (of an unspecified nature) and by this process poisoned 'almost all estates of the land.'[52] Indeed, Barrow felt tempted to write a long treatise to demonstrate how these pernicious institutions undermined the spread of God's word – no idle threat from a man whose 'brief' treatise on the false church runs on for over four hundred pages in its modern edition! Without including all of the rich detail brought forth by Robert Browne, Barrow denounced the vain education that he had received. To purify the realm, one had to abolish the contemporary system of education. It exercised too horrendous an influence upon church and society to continue in existence. Godly separatists could not reconcile these old institutions of learning with the teachings of Christ, the carpenter's son. Barrow was adamant in his belief that English education

can by no means ... be made to accord to the gospel and kingdom of Christ, whereof these university divines have ever been the professed and most bitter enemies, furnishing antichrist's host in all rooms and places, even from the pope's chair, to the parish priest's pulpit or pew, with fresh servitors continually, corrupting the pure fountains, and perverting the text itself with their glosses, paraphrases, notes, figures, etc., fighting it with their school learning, vain arts, philosophy, rhetoric, and logic against the truth and servants of God, striving hereby to uphold antichrist's ruinous kingdom and abominable wares, which these merchantmen set to sale for gains as we by present experience see ... how these ... university clerks, rage and take on, and with their school learning seek to turn away the evident truth of God, to colour and plead for all the abomination and sin of the times, to heal the wound and uphold the throne of the beast ...

Of course, his own university training equipped Barrow to recognize and declaim the very faults in the scholarship that he despised. The arts that he deemed vain lost their lustre because university divines employed them to uphold the established order. The distinctions in which scholars delight became to Barrow equivocations of the pure simplicity of gospel

52 *Ibid.*, pp. 351, 349–50

truth. By upholding traditional learning and traditional interpretations of scripture, university teachers acted as physicians who would heal the wounded head of the beast (Rev. xiii:3) and, thereby, fulfilled one of the signs of the very last days. The important function played by the universities in providing arguments and trained personnel to uphold the status quo condemned them in Barrow's eyes: 'They have always been and still are the very hives and nurseries of these armed poisoned locusts and venomous scorpions, I mean either that false ministry of antichrist, even all the governing and teaching priests ... or those counterfeit religious hypocrites, monks, friars, nuns, clerks, or (as we now of late call them) scholars.'[53] Men with a programme to advance, like Barrow, often find little pleasure with the way in which scholars show that deceptively simple slogans actually contain many complexities. Barrow's attack upon the universities formed but one prong of his assault upon the divines of the Church of England who received their training there. He sought to identify the universities with the old religious orders because he knew that all good protestants disliked those corrupted offices. Barrow's criticisms reflected his dissatisfaction with traditional social institutions and with anything that helped to uphold the Established Church. Because the universities provided opposition to his revolutionary vision of the church and society, Barrow poured forth some of his most vituperous apocalyptic invective upon them.

The solution that Barrow proposed, although novel in some of its details and in its profoundly uncompromising quality, contained few new instruments of correction. Although he portrayed the Church of England as a part of Babylon, he still looked to the godly prince, acting as God's imperial administrator, as the source of authority for public reformation: 'Yet now if I be asked who ought to abolish this idolatry, to destroy these synagogues, to dissolve these fraternities, and to depose these antichristian priests: to that I answer, the prince, or state; and that it belongeth not to any private men: for we see they were set up and remained in Israel and Judah, until God raised up godly princes to pluck them down and destroy them; yea it were an intrusion unto the magistrate's office and seat, for any private man so far to intermeddle.' Not only did he absolutely forbid ordinary people to attempt public religious reformation through rebellion, Barrow even attempted to guide the magistrate by drawing up a programme of reform and presenting it to Lord Burghley, Elizabeth's chief councillor. The separatist press in

53 *A plaine*, p. 212, and *A briefe discoverie*, p. 540, cf. 548

Amsterdam printed this remarkable document in 1611 under the title *The first part of the platforme*. Because of Burghley's unfavourable reaction, Barrow started a second part, but it never saw the light of day. The printed platform listed specific steps for the queen to take in order to tumble the foundations of the Church of England. With expectation, Barrow proclaimed the joy which would follow upon Elizabeth's acting as the imperial instrument of the Almighty:

And lo, how the Lord inviteth and inciteth her highness hereunto, preferring and giving her the preeminence of this glorious work before all the kings of the world, as also how richly he rewardeth all that further this his service both by putting into their hands the rich spoil of this confused Babylon, and by bringing them to Sion the city of his solemn feasts. Oh what a joy, what a jubilee, what a happy day were this to the whole land ... to see our heavenly king, Christ Jesus, thus with one accord received and welcomed into his kingdom, his church: How should God's name and our queen's praise be celebrated for this by every mouth even with general applause and celeusma*? The sound whereof should not only fill this land, but be heard into all others to the giving them example and stirring them up unto the like extirpation of all idolatry, and unto the true practice of the gospel.[54]

Even in his alienation from existing religious practices, Barrow fondly wished that the Lord might single out England for special leadership in the coming cosmic strife. Like her father, Elizabeth easily could gain the material riches of Babylon by annexing the property of the church to the crown – a practical idea based upon precedent. However, Queen Elizabeth rejected Barrow's platform and he remained a prisoner until his execution. Under these circumstances – when the magistrate refused to hearken to the commands of the Lord – the saints had only the alternative of separating themselves from the ungodly. 'It is one thing to abolish public evils and another to abstain from public evils: only the magistrate may pull down the public monuments of idolatry; yet every private Christian both may, and upon pain of damnation ought to, refrain from public idolatry, or from any thing which is evil in God's eyes, though it be allowed and commanded by all the princes of the

54 *A briefe discoverie*, p. 481, and *First part*, ENT, III, p. 239. When his cell was searched and his papers seized in 1593, Barrow was composing a petition to Parliament. The fragment of it which remains is printed in ENT, VI, pp. 221–2. *celeusma: a watchword, battle cry, *OED*

world.'[55] As with most men of his persuasion, Barrow embraced separation only after other alternatives failed. When one considers the many things enforced by law in England which Barrow classed as 'evil in God's eyes,' the magnitude of this injunction begins to emerge; it grows when those things allowed by the prince fill up the list. Had large numbers of people refused to recognize the legitimacy of any aspect of the Church of England – from attendance at their parish church to the payment of tithes or the probate of wills and enforcement of morals in church courts – and had they withdrawn all support from the educational system as well, the effect on society would have been stupendous. Such action could have shaken these important institutions to the core. In reality, however, only a few brave people followed Barrow's programme and the authorities repressed them without much difficulty.

In the short era of apocalyptic time which remained before Christ came back to earth, separatist saints must prepare to suffer the pangs of persecution. Barrow's prediction of adversity for the godly contained all the characteristics of a self-fulfilling prophecy. Those who followed his advice and, thereby, broke the law certainly deserved punishment by imprisonment or worse. When theory and practice worked together in this case, Barrow dogmatically identified himself and his imprisoned followers with the elect:

ANDREWES: ... who be those saints you speak of, where are they?
BARROW: They are even those poor Christians whom you so blaspheme and persecute, and now most unjustly hold in your prison.

Although they might seem lowly and defeated to the world, the oppressed would triumph in the end by maintaining the true congregational church of Christ in the face of all adversity:

Thus, this holy army of saints is marshalled here on earth by these officers, under the conduct of their glorious emperor Christ, that victorious Michael. Thus it marcheth in this most heavenly order, and gracious array [that is, congregationalism], against all enemies both bodily and ghostly. Peaceable in itself as Jerusalem, terrible unto them as an army with banners, triumphing over their tyranny with patience, their cruelty with meekness, and over death itself with dying. Thus through the blood of that spotless lamb, and that word of their testimony, they are more than conquerors, bruising the head of the serpent: yea

55 A briefe discoverie, pp. 481–2, cf. 404–7, 672

through the power of his word, they have power to cast down upon Satan like lightning: to tread upon serpents and scorpions: to cast down strongholds, and everything that exalteth itself against God. The gates of hell and all the principalities and powers of the world, shall not prevail against it.[56]

One could hardly find a more militantly expressed martyr complex, or a more noble vision of change through the agency of passive resistance, against all of the odds of the world. Barrow portrayed the spread of the congregational church through persuasion, patience, and suffering. The strongholds which the saints would cast down existed in the winning of converts through the word. Despite the continued attempts to suppress it through repression, their cause survived into the days of freedom of the 1640s. Barrow believed that the elect must continue as an embattled remnant until the end of the world. The oppressed could spread the truth, but only Christ could win the final victory. However, the day of his coming was not far off. The Saviour would return soon 'to be glorified in his saints, and to be made marvellous in all them that believe.' At that time, the wicked supporters of the false church would reap a just reward for their beliefs and actions. Barrow fully expected all members of the Church of England to fall with the other brats of Babylon: '... They shall shortly give accompt to him that is coming with thousands of his saints.' Despite the militant tone of his language, Barrow remained a political quietist who awaited the imminent end of the world as a final solution to the cosmic warfare in which he was engaged. For him this remained primarily a struggle for men's minds – a spiritual battle between the true and false churches fought out with the word.[57]

Henry Barrow gathered together most of the strands of earlier separatist criticism of the Church of England and wove them into an intelligible pattern with powerful prose. In particular details he went further in his attacks upon the Established Church and upon traditional society than his predecessors – things such as his desire to destroy church buildings, to abolish the existing system of education, and his working out the theory of participatory congregationalism. Of vast importance, however, was the formidable tool for spreading separatism which he created in his four points. This formula made propagation of the cause an easier task among all levels of society. In polity, Barrow followed the congregational way and strongly denied the validity of both episcopal

56 ENT, IV, p. 143, and Barrow, A true description, p. 200; cf. A briefe discoverie, p. 564
57 A briefe discoverie, pp. 510, 533, see 553–4, 554 n. 1

and presbyterian government in the church.[58] This formed a part of his repudiation of the puritans – an attitude which he made into a fixed point of separatism. Barrow's significance as a separatist martyr must stand high among his achievements, especially since Robert Browne recanted and Robert Harrison died obscurely in the Netherlands. Barrow practised what he preached – despite many attempts made to get him to change his beliefs, he remained steadfast to the end and provided an example to his followers. His works guaranteed that the thin line between radical puritanism and separatism continued to constitute a yawning gulf by identifying the Church of England and all who remained within it with the forces of antichrist. In his conferences with puritan ministers – arranged by the authorities to persuade Barrow to moderate his views – the two sides agreed upon most matters, but their small difference on apocalyptic interpretation became a cosmic bifurcating force for Barrow. Puritans agreed that the Established Church contained antichristian elements, but for them it remained a true church.[59] For Barrow, anyone who would not follow the evidence to its logical conclusion and fully condemn the English church as false deserved a place on the side of perdition.

The call for withdrawal from the Established Church challenged the whole force of the emerging idea that England provided the chief bastion in the war against Babylon, an interpretation that jelled during and shortly after the Armada campaign. How could a corrupt, false church and nation lead the forces of Christ? An English role in sacred history could be read into Foxe, but the separatists, by denying validity to any national church, cut away any such notion and the united effort it supported. The rulers of society recognized the divisive thrust of separatist thought. They realized that if they allowed separation to spread freely, the already difficult task of governing the land would

58 For the development of congregational church polity, see Miller, *Orthodoxy*, Morgan, *Visible Saints*, and Coolidge, *Pauline Renaissance*, ch. 3. Morgan too readily extends the ideas of clerical radicals like Field and Wilcox to all puritans in his first chapter.
59 For the controversy between Barrow and Greenwood and George Gifford, see ENT, IV, 16–19, 30–92. 365–9, V, pp. 25–364, VI, pp. 1–73, 93–218. Conferences between these two separatist champions and conforming divines and the examinations of Barrow and Greenwood by the authorities appear in ENT, III, pp. 86–105, 170–207, IV, pp. 20–9, 117–213, VI, pp. 85–9, 223–9, 234–7. The evident hostility between puritan and separatist revealed in these sources provides a perfect example of what Freud once called 'the narcissism of small differences.' White and Coolidge both tend to paper over this dividing line.

become an even greater burden.[60] If the initiative for church reform slipped into the hands of the people, acting in opposition to or ignoring their magistrates, anarchy would doubtless result. Within the apocalyptic tradition, the separatist branch began as an offshoot of earlier thought, but it developed into an inflexible confrontation of the mainstream contention that the Elizabethan settlement created an image of the true church in England. It posed a real threat because it repudiated existing reformed religious ideology and practice – and that just at the time when most English protestants took pride in the progress made toward reforming the church and people. It defied the traditional hierarchical view of society and the social controls upholding it in a most dangerous way. The levelling thrust of the thought of Browne and Barrow, while limited to religious theory and practice, contained social implications which the authorities could not and did not overlook. If each man or woman who felt the spirit were free to speak out in church services – to challenge the interpretation of any preacher he disagreed with – how long would it take before that person used the same skills against landlords or magistrates? It was not mere coincidence that the later Leveller leaders – John Lilburne, Richard Overton, William Walwyn, and John Wildman – and Gerrard Winstanley, the leader of the Diggers, all sprang from the separatist tradition. Long before their day, the movement had established an alternative life style. By refusing to attend services at his parish church the separatist disobeyed the Act of Uniformity and thereby offered at least passive resistance to the magistrate. Barrow urged that this be extended to refusal to pay tithes, refusal to obey the laws requiring the eating of fish on certain days, refusal to swear any oath, refusal to participate in the educational system, and refusal to recognize the legitimacy of any aspect of the jurisdiction of the Established Church. Such actions, while minor individually, created a pattern of disobedience which could only be seen as an undermining of civil order. The authorities viewed it that way and therefore executed Barrow and Greenwood for sedition. Separatists employed the skills they learned in their congregations in the outside world. They did not 'mind their place' when addressing social or ecclesiastical superiors. Even then, the authorities exhibited remarkable patience with men like

60 ENT, II, pp. 532–7, VI, pp. 260–70, the abstracts made from the works of Browne and Harrison, from those of Barrow and Greenwood, and from the examinations of the latter. These formed much of the evidence of the sedition for which Barrow and Greenwood were executed.

Henry Barrow, Master Pattenson, and the members of the Plumbers' Hall congregation.

Because the separatist necessarily had to cut himself off – at least in a symbolic way – from the generality of human society, the first generations of men and women who took this path were made of strong stuff. They considered their interpretation of truth as more important than the conventions of society. Therefore, they propagated their ideas with what more traditionally minded people took to be impudence. Some reached a nearly antinomian conviction of their assurance of salvation. The voice of the Holy Spirit within man played a significant role in their theology. Compulsive in the certainty of their convictions, they believed they must be judged by the word, not by men.

BARROW: The spirit of the prophets must be subject to the prophets, yet must the prophets judge by the word of God. And for me I willingly submit my whole faith to be tried and judged by the word of God, of all men.

ANDREWES: All men cannot judge, who then shall judge of the word?

BARROW: The word, and let everyone that judgeth take heed that he judge aright thereby ...

ANDREWES: This savoureth of a private spirit.

...

BARROW: ... I have the spirit of the apostles.[61]

If not the spirit of the apostles, Barrow showed the toughness of an Old Testament prophet when it came to facing down authority. Separatists brought forth rage from contemporaries precisely because they questioned and explicitly rejected those values which most people felt must be accepted and conformed to by all for the good of society – every man in his place in church and state, the importance of formal education, the idea that everyone in the nation *ipso facto* belonged to the church. By singling themselves out as the elect, separatists publicly proclaimed their own religious superiority. Anyone who has experienced the passions unleashed in recent years by such issues as the civil rights movement in the United States or the immigration of 'coloured' people to Britain should have some empathic understanding of the furious reaction of contemporaries against the separatists – and of how such fury strengthened the resolve of activists like Henry Barrow or John Lilburne. Although led by gentlemen of no mean birth and standing, the rank and

61 ENT, IV, p. 141; see the remarkable encounter between Barrow and Archbishop Whitgift quoted at the opening of this chapter.

file of the movement came from the ranks of yeoman farmers, tradesmen, and craftsmen – independent men and women who stood on the
fringes of social and political power. With its levelling thrust,
separatism accentuated values that appealed to people who were successful in a small way and likely literate, people who had raised themselves above the masses, but had not reached a high enough position to
make full use of their talents or to express their deepest thoughts and
still remain in normal social channels.[62]

By 1590 a considerable body of separatist literature had appeared.
Some of it circulated in manuscript copies, the rest was printed abroad
and smuggled back into the country. During the next four decades the
quantity of separatist propaganda swelled, converts came in, and the
movement increased its membership – this despite continued efforts by
the authorities to stamp out both the movement and its appeals.
Separatists established working communities of exiles in the Netherlands and in New England. Although notoriously quarrelsome among
themselves on many issues, no separatist questioned the basic attitude
toward the Church of England taken by the founders of the movement.
They continued to place themselves among Christ's oppressed elect and
the Established Church in Babylon. In these same decades, radical and
'root and branch' puritans kept up their competition for the support of
putative dissidents and finally worked out more systematic statements
of their respective streams of apocalyptic thought.

62 Of the sixty-six imprisoned Barrowists listed by Carlson and Burrage whose social
status was given, an overwhelming proportion were tradesmen (71 per cent), while
gentlemen comprised the next largest group (20 per cent). Both figures represent a
much higher proportion than people of a corresponding status in the society as a whole.
Of those whose age was included – as of 1593 – over two-thirds ranged between the ages
of 21 and 34 (70 per cent) – that is, they were born after Elizabeth came to the throne
and were a fairly young group. Personal servants, as opposed to apprentices or jour-
neymen listed as servants, and some gentlemen deserted the movement when faced
with imprisonment, as did a small proportion of tradesmen. Such statistics, although
based on a small sample, confirm other evidence that the separatists came from the top
half of society, those with at least a minimum of social and economic independence.
Carlson, ed. ENT, IV, pp. 305–34, and Burrage, *Early Dissenters*, II, pp. 27–61. For
another Barrow-like gentleman, William Brewster, and his pilgrim followers, see
Marchant, *Puritans and the Church Courts*, ch. 8. For the social level of later sectarians, especially the Quakers, see Vann, *Social Development*.

3

The swelling of prophecy

Now, although in all ages ... there have not wanted witnesses pouring out their vials in some measure upon the throne of the beast ... yet we have with our eyes seen this fifth vial poured out ... most effectually, and apparently in the time of King *James* of happy memory. What a cloud of witnesses did that time produce ... proving and convincing by evident and invincible arguments, the pope to be ... that *man of sin*, that *son of perdition*, that *antichrist*, that *beast*? And was it a marvel to see such a cloud, when there was such a sun, whose influence might raise it up.

H[enry] B[urton], *The seven vials*, pp. 76–7

Even before the Spanish Armada threatened Britain's shores in 1588 to confirm their theory, English protestants knew that the reformation formed a part of the cosmic conflict of the latter days. The religious wars of the late sixteenth century added a new dimension by bringing spiritual strife into the temporal realm through the clash of armies and navies. Because men like Bale and Foxe so firmly fixed a chronological apocalyptic interpretation of the history of the Christian church, their framework gained wide acceptance and lay embodied at the presupposition level in works which concentrated on other issues. As long as their framework remained unrefuted, little occasion arose for explicit defence of it. However, the late sixteenth century witnessed a resort to offensive arms by catholics in the realm of the spirit as well as on land and sea. Direct challenge to protestant apocalyptic presuppositions came primarily from one source – the Jesuits. They attempted to undermine both the biblical commentaries and the historical compilations which buttressed protestant apocalyptic visions. The renowned Robert

Bellarmine led the attack by the Jesuit controversialists, but others, including Francisco Ribera and Cornelius of Lapide, contributed important works as well.[1] The intellectual challenge of the Jesuits coincided with the threat from Spain and from catholic missionaries sent to England. These challenges brought forth a flood of response.

To a man looking back from the vantage point of 1628, the preceding forty years produced a marvellous multiplication of apocalyptic treatises in Britain. From the year of the Armada to that in which Henry Burton published his commentary, over a hundred systematic expositions of the Roman antichrist appeared in English or by British authors, many in more than one edition.[2] The presses of England, Scotland, and Holland cranked out these refutations of Jesuit learning and counter-reformation aggression. Besides attempting to counter the common foe, these tomes also systematically exposed the division of the British apocalyptic interpretation into the main, the radical puritan, the 'root and branch,' and the separatist streams. Toward the close of the sixteenth century, a new element entered the apocalyptic tradition – the passion for chronological calculation of the future. By tracing a linear pattern of prophecy and its fulfilment in the past, the framework of Bale established an interpretation which begged to be extended along the same line into the future. It was – with mathematical and exegetical precision. Commentators not only refined the chronology of holy warfare in history, but they calculated the dates of the stages of the final struggle and even of the victory itself. Altogether, the apocalyptic tradition became not a more important part of the thought of reformers, but a crucial issue for explicit contention. Increasingly precise prediction of the future, combined with prophecy fulfilment by the religious wars of the sixteenth and seventeenth centuries, worked to heighten expectations and also to make disconfirmation likely by the end of the seventeenth century.

The winds of change blew down from the northern covenanted kingdom of Scotland. The scholarly James vi, later to be James i of England, wrote a learned interpretation of the Book of Revelation and applied his

1 Froom, *Prophetic Faith*, ii, pp. 484–509, Firth, 'Apocalyptic Tradition,' pp. 221–4, and Reeves, *Influence of Prophecy*, pp. 274–92
2 A quick survey of Pollard and Redgrave, *Short-Title Catalogue*, revealed over one hundred works of this type published between 1588 and 1628, as opposed to less than thirty between 1520 and 1587. Those discussed in this chapter represent dominant themes in the period. Cf. Bauckham, 'Prophecy,' passim, Ball, *Great Expectation*, ch. 1, and Hill, *Antichrist*, ch. 1 and 2

apocalyptic vision to current events. His two short works firmly placed this godly prince in the mainstream outlined above. In the anxious Armada year James published a short exhortation to his subjects based upon Revelation xx:7–10.[3] He had no doubt that 'The pope is antichrist and popery is the loosing of Satan, from whom proceedeth the false doctrine and the cruelty to subvert the kingdom of Christ.' He applied this insight to the activities of the Jesuits, to the religious wars on the continent, and to the expected war with Spain. These armies of Babylon threatened the existence of the saints. Like a good preacher, James showed the relevance of his interpretation of the biblical text to the lives and actions of his audience. The tract ended with a call for contemplation and, more importantly, for direct action:

It is all our duties in this isle at this time to do two things: one, to consider our estate, another to conform our actions according thereunto. Our estate is, we are threefold besieged. First, spiritually by the heresies of antichrist. Secondly, corporally and generally, as members of that church, the which in the whole they persecute. Thirdly, corporally and particularly by this present army. Our actions then conformed to our estate are these: first to call for help at God his hands; next, to assure us of the same, seeing we have a sufficient warrant, his constant promise expressed in his word. Thirdly, since with a good conscience we may, being in the tents of the saints, and beloved city, stand in our defence, encourage one another to use lawful resistance and concur or join one with another as warriors in one camp, and citizens of one beloved city, for maintenance of the good cause God had clad us with, and in defence of our liberties, native country, and lives. For since we see God hath promised not only in the world to come, but also in this world, to give us victory over them, let us in assurance hereof strongly trust in our God, cease to mistrust his promise, and fall through incredulity or unbelief, for then are we worthy of double punishment. For the stronger they wax and the nearer they come to their light, the faster approacheth their wrack, and the day of our delivery. For kind, and loving, true, and constant, careful, and watchful, mighty, and revenging is he that promiseth it; to whom be praise and glory for ever. AMEN

Any doubt that the reader of this passage might have had in his mind about the kind of action King James advocated was dispelled by the marginal note placed beside it. The king of Scotland, unlike most of the

---

3 James VI, *A fruitful meditation*, first published in 1588 and included in James I, *Workes*, which will be cited; see Willson, *King James*, ch. 13

men cited so far in this study, called for physical as well as spiritual warfare against the foe. 'All men should be lawfully armed spiritually and bodily to fight against antichrist and his upholders.'[4] The two churches of Bale or two armies of Knox prepared for bodily warfare. Victory would come on earth as well as in heaven, as the Lord of hosts led his reformed battalions into the final battle against Babylon. In the following decade James would not always seem so militant; however, his subjects would keep his early sentiments alive. The same argument James used against the Armada would be applied against his son by the supporters of Parliament on the outbreak of civil war in England. No matter how future generations employed his argument, James filled the role of a reforming godly prince who led his people against the foe at this time.

While sounding the trumpet call to arms James also prepared, at the same time, a more lengthy work, *A paraphrase upon the Revelation of the apostle S. John*. It first appeared in print in his *Workes* in 1616. It is more a paraphrase of the text of Revelation than a commentary upon it. In marginal notes and in the introductory argument of each chapter, however, James expounded a chronological interpretation of the Apocalypse which fit into the mainstream tradition. In these jottings meant to guide the reader, he traced the rise and decline of antichrist within the Christian church: '*Babylon the pope's empire is the outward part of the Temple; the true church is in Sancto Sanctorum, but under the persecution of these hypocrites for a certain space. Faithful pastors are sent from time to time to witness the truth. They are persecuted, condemned, and slain by antichrist. God raised up at the last stronger preachers, who shall describe the popedom, and fortell the destruction thereof. In the seventh trumpet is the day of judgment described.*' The framework of this history of the church tallied with that developed at great length by Bale and Foxe. The comparison of the visible church with parts of the Temple would be developed by future commentators. James had no need to fill in the details – his audience had heard them many times before. The Scottish king looked forward to the ultimate triumph of the reformed, as his summary of the argument of Revelation xix affirmed: '*The saints praise God for joy that the pope is destroyed. The glorious form of Christ's second coming set down at large. The pope*

---

4 James I, *Workes*, pp. 78 and m.n., 80 and m.n. Since Satan raged in the world, his thousand-year binding must have taken place in the past. For the two armies of Knox, see Firth, 'Apocalyptic Tradition,' pp. 173–4.

and his church is condemned for ever.'[5] Although James wrote these works as a young man, apocalyptic expectation continued to fascinate him in later years. He thought enough of these early writings to print them at the front of his collected *Workes* in 1616. He expressed belief in the identification of the papacy with antichrist in the preface of his last devotional tract, *A meditation upon the Lords prayer*, three years later.[6] With such a leader, no wonder his subjects turned with zest to unravel the mysteries of Revelation!

The first of a new breed of commentaries also came out of Scotland. John Napier, the wizard laird of Merchiston, not only invented logarithms but extended his professional interests to the number of the beast. He dedicated his book, *A plaine discovery of the whole Revelation of Saint John*, to James VI. It appeared first in Edinburgh in 1593, was reprinted in England and Scotland in 1594, and, by the time that new English and Scottish editions came out in 1611, was translated into Latin, Dutch, and French.[7] While James VI followed the old verse-by-verse format in his paraphrase, Napier framed his treatise with the latest techniques of Ramist logic. A chart at the front summed up the whole of his interpretation. The text began with an analytic section which specifically attempted to clarify the core of protestant polemics. This section – nearly a third of the work – consisted of a series of propositions which put forth Napier's chronology and his studied reading of the most controversial passages in Revelation. Part II, the bulk of the book, printed the text of St John's prophecy in one column, an analytic paraphrase in the second, and the history of the fulfilment of the text in the third. It went through Revelation chapter by chapter, verse by verse, and brought together text, paraphrase, and interpretation into one whole.

Although Napier followed the mainstream of English apocalyptic thought, he brought a passion for precision and clarity to his work. As a talented mathematician, he calculated the dates of historical events

---

5 *Ibid.*, pp 32, 60. Joseph Mede and Thomas Goodwin also identified parts of the Temple with various states of the visible church.

6 James I, *A meditation*, preface; cf. Willson, *King James*, pp. 81–2, 401. The Commons' committee investigating the works of Richard Montague in 1625 justly reported that Montague's denial that the pope was antichrist 'is contrary to that the king himself hath written to all Christian princes.' CJ, I, p. 805. John Pym chaired this committee.

7 (1611), 'To the reader.' Citations will be to this edition; however, an examination has been made of the first edition as well. Napier's treatise was translated into German later and abstracts of it appeared in 1610, 1623, 1641, 1643, and following. See Firth, 'Apocalyptic Tradition,' pp. 180–207, Clouse, 'John Napier,' and Ball, *Great Expectation*, pp. 59–60, 80–2.

prophesied by St John and assigned a chronology for the final fulfilment of the apostle's predictions. In the tenth proposition he asserted and attempted to demonstrate that: '*The last trumpet and vial beginneth anno Christi 1541 and should end in anno Christi 1786.*' He reckoned that the year 1786 set a *terminus ad quem*. The end would probably arrive sooner, 'because it is said, that for the elect's sake, the time shall be shortened ...' Even the day of the last judgment could be approximately, if not precisely, predicted: '*The day of God's judgment appears to fall betwixt the years of Christ 1688 and 1700.*'[8] His desire to equate particular prophecies of Revelation with past, present, and future events was perceptible in the commentary upon the thirteenth proposition – that which dealt with the three thundering angels of Revelation xiv. The first of these began

at the year of Christ 1541, who (verses 6 and 7) preached his everlasting evangel to the year of God 1590. Which year beginneth the second thundering angel (verse 8) and continueth proclaiming the final decay of *Babylon* to the year of Christ 1639. Which year, the third thundering angel beginneth who (verse 9) ... continueth exhorting and threatening these of the last dregs of antichrist to repentance to the year of Christ 1688. Where the fourth thundering angel, even Christ himself (verses 14 and 16) enters actually into his great harvest to gather up his elect ...[9]

This type of future projection of prophecies had not hitherto been common among apocalyptic visions printed in English. According to Napier, two of the three angels had already begun preaching against antichrist, the third would follow soon, and Christ himself would gather up his elect in less than a century. No wonder contemporaries became fascinated with the bold prognostications of this famous mathematician!

Napier pointed his finger directly at the enemy, stating that '*The pope is that only antichrist prophesied of in particular.*' The 1260-year rule of antichrist over all Christians, he calculated, terminated around the year 1560 when 'these papistical policies were destroyed in England, Scotland, and in some parts of Germany, France, and other countries ...' After that, the light of the Lord started to shine brightly once again, for 'the scriptures of God are lively and quickly interpreted and restored to their true estimation, and honour, and thousands converted daily from

8 Napier, *A plaine discovery*, pp. 14, 15, 19 (proposition 14)
9 *Ibid.*, pp. 18–19 (proposition 13, commentary)

their former papistry to the true fear of God.' The reformation not only represented a re-establishment of Christ's church on earth, it also held forth the promise of a better world to come. Napier looked forward to a progressive unfolding of light and understanding in the future. Eventually, such an awakening would lead to a *renovatio mundi*. The true church acted as the instrument of this enlightenment. Until the second coming of Christ finally fulfilled the Lord's plan, then, the reformed church must keep itself pure and undefiled. Such sentiments found expression in the concluding paragraph of Napier's work: 'Here end we also that interpretation thereof, which God by that selfsame grace hath made the faithful of these our latter days to understand, in discovery of God's enemies, and revealing of his truth, that his church being purged from antichristianism, may from henceforth abide pure and holy, and ready decked as a comely bride, waiting the sudden coming of her Lord and bridegroom, Christ Jesus.'[10]

By exposing Babylon in clear and polemic words, by employing his considerable mathematical skill in calculating the chronology of Revelation, and by extending the historical fulfilment of St John's prophecies into a measured and not too distant future, Napier heightened the sense of apocalyptic struggle against the supporters of Rome. A new trumpet would sound in 1639 to usher in the final stage of strife. By then, the godly would be able to see the enemy even more clearly because the Lord would have granted them further understanding. All Christians stood under an obligation to prepare themselves for the last battle and all ranks of people would participate in it. 'The Lord open the eyes of all men, and inspire the hearts of princes (as in the *Revelation* is promised) to destroy that idolatrous seat, and bring the antichristian kingdom thereof to an end.'[11] Napier favoured neither the godly prince nor the persecuted – he believed that both must co-operate to accomplish the task. A vociferous critic of those who questioned the mainstream apocalyptic tradition, he none the less replaced imprecise expectations of the second coming by a new progressively unfolding chronology of the future. Men in 1639 could and did wonder who represented the new angel and what new turn the assault against Babylon would take. The prophecies of Napier gave, to some at least, new cogency and expectancy to the prophecies of St John. The holy history of the past no longer merely helped to explain the present – it projected into a finite future.

10 *Ibid.*, pp. 53 (proposition 26), 87 (proposition 36), 185–6, 327. Firth, 'Apocalyptic Tradition,' pp. 200–4, discusses Napier and the *renovatio mundi*.
11 *Ibid.*, p. 65

John Napier joined his monarch in looking for a literal destruction of the armies of catholicism, but he went beyond James VI by producing a timetable for victory. The universal rule of the pope ended in 1560 with the establishment of protestantism in Britain – his ultimate ruin would be accomplished before 1700. In England, Thomas Brightman followed a more literary Ramist analytic method to reach a similar view and chronology. This Bedfordshire clergyman received his impetus to write about Revelation from catholic attacks upon the protestant tradition of interpretation. He felt compelled to refute what he considered to be the damnable apocalyptic heresies of the learned Jesuit polemicists, especially those of Bellarmine and Ribera. The fruition of Brightman's lonely contemplation, *Apocalypsis Apocalypseos*, or *A revelation of the Revelation*, came into being before the end of the sixteenth century, but was not published until 1609 – two years after the author's death.[12] Whereas Napier's relatively short treatise remained within the mainstream of protestant interpretation, Brightman's volume, millennial in length and in interpretation, accorded the radical puritan stream its first classic systematic exposition. Brightman also carried Napier's *renovatio mundi* a step further by projecting a literal reign of the saints on earth for a thousand years, thereby reviving in respectable circles the millennium pursued by the earliest Christians, by medieval heretics, and by sixteenth-century anabaptists. Many Englishmen perused this tome in its original Latin, in translation, or in popular summaries of key sections. It gave singular inspiration to the radicals of the early 1640s.

Brightman framed his commentary within the context of holy history established by his predecessors, but he gave it a more nationalistic thrust. Taking up the threads found in Ponet, Aylmer, and Sandys, Brightman became the first prominent commentator to forge a special role for England. The 'elect nation' stemmed from his work, not from that of Foxe. He agreed with Foxe, however, that Constantine bound Satan, that light broke through with Wycliffe – to whom he gave special emphasis – and his contemporaries, and that Luther initiated the first real reformation of the church. But Brightman added his own twist to the conceptual framework of Bale and Foxe. Believing that the scholar

12 Published in Latin in 1609 and 1612 and translated into English and printed in 1611, 1615, 1616, and 1644. Also see Brightman' *Workes*, and his *Antichristi pontificorum*. Three popular summaries of his interpretation appeared in 1641. On Brightman, see Ball, *Great Expectation*, pp. 82–4, 116–18, 168–9, 240–1, Clouse, 'Influence of Alsted,' pp. 41–60, Firth, 'Apocalyptic Tradition,' pp. 224–40, Gilsdorf, 'Puritan Apocalypse,' pp. 29–45, Toon, *Puritan Eschatology*, pp. 26–32, and Wilson, 'Studies,' pp. 148–57.

could closely correlate the visible church with the invisible kingdom of God, he applied the images of the seven churches of Asia Minor to the historical church. Hence the actual history of the Christian church in the world paralleled and embodied the working out of the prophetical warnings written by St John to these seven churches in the first three chapters of Revelation. With other radical puritans, Brightman believed that no deviation could be allowed from the one institutional pattern established by Christ: 'That first government of the church is common to all times and places, and ... it is not to be permitted to the arbitrament of men to follow what way they list, but that always in reforming a church, we must have recourse unto the first beginnings, to the which, as our only rule, we must call back whatsoever strayeth from it, and that they are not turned and tuned according to the crookedness and jarring sound of succeeding churches.' Brightman held up the reformed churches of France, Scotland, Switzerland, and Holland as examples of the fulfilment of this institutional injunction. These represented the church of Philadelphia, the parallel of Ephesus, and marked a return to the apostolic church.[13] Thus Brightman found apocalyptic verification in the opening chapters of the Apocalypse for establishing the pattern of Geneva upon all Christians.

Although the Lutheran church, seen as the image of Sardis, was 'the first reformed church, begun by the special providence of godly Martin Luther,' like its parallel Smyrna it was incompletely reformed and therefore lacked life. Having cast off the pope, it still clung to too many questionable doctrines and practices. 'The church of Sardis as it seemeth, did not admit the whole entire truth, but retained much of the heathenish superstition.'[14] While apologizing for the harshness of his verdict, Brightman deserted most of his colleagues to place Lutherans in limbo – he predicted that they would soon suffer reverses at the hands of catholics, a prediction which many believed had come true in the Thirty Years War. Unrelenting in the logic of his vision, Brightman also sorrowed over the state of the Church of England.

Although hostile to the barbed darts of Martin Marprelate against the Elizabethan settlement, Brightman showed strong dissatisfaction with the polity of the church in which he served. Through 'tear-filled eyes' he saw his native church as a 'mingle-mangle of the popish government

13 Brightman, *A revelation*, pp. 46, 109; for his reaction to the Jesuits, see 13, 622–770. Cf. Gilsdorf, 'Puritan Apocalypse,' pp. 31–40, and Firth, 'Apocalyptic Tradition,' pp. 227–31
14 *A revelation*, pp. 91, 99, see 91–9

with pure doctrine ...' Unlike the papists and the Lutherans, however, the Church of England preached sound doctrine. On the other hand, it lacked the proper government and discipline of the fully reformed churches. It fit the image of Laodicea – neither hot nor cold, but to be spewn out of the mouth of the Lord.

In our realm of England ... such a form of a church is established, which is neither cold, nor yet hot, but set in the midst between both, and compounded of both. It is not cold, in as much as it doth profess the sound, pure, and sincere doctrine of salvation, by which we have renounced the antichrist of Rome, and are risen out of that death as cold as ye were wherein we lay before. But hot it is not, as whose outward regiment is as yet for the greatest part antichristian and Romish. In the degrees of clergymen, in elections and ordinations, and the whole administration of the church censures. The which tempering of pure doctrine and Romish regiment, maketh this lukewarmness ...

Brightman's image of Laodicea, standing apart both from the separatist identification of the Church of England with antichrist and from the 'root and branch' branding of bishops as a part of Babylon, perfectly exemplified the apocalyptic position of most radical puritans. Although negative in warning, the image also held forth a potentially positive promise. A national church, like the other churches addressed by St John, Laodicea occupied a unique position, one without parallel. 'Laodicea stood for the potential church of England, which if she once fulfilled her destiny might parallel the first church of all, the Garden of Eden. This was the first reference to a special significance reserved for England based upon and delivered within the context of an interpretation of the Apocalypse.'[15] England alone possessed the capability of becoming an elect nation, one that might lead to a *renovatio mundi*.

England's full reformation, then, played a crucial role in Brightman's apocalyptic scheme. He dated the opening of the final fall of antichrist to the year 1558 when 'Christ sent our most gracious Elizabeth to be queen at the first blast of the seventh trumpet ...' The godly queen released large numbers of people from the tyranny and darkness of antichrist's bondage and helped to give birth to an eternal movement of cosmic victory:

15 *Ibid.*, pp. 125, 132, 137, and Firth, 'Apocalyptic Tradition,' p. 229. Brightman chided Martin Marprelate: 'It was notorious slander wherewith thou hast bleared the eyes of the princess [that is, Elizabeth] and brought thy brethren [that is, the puritans] into hatred with her' (p. 159).

... Elizabeth that most beautiful and comfortable star rose up, then was the Christian empire augmented with England, and Ireland, the next year after Scotland was added ... How notable an increase was this to be made more ample by the coming in of so populous nations: But the glory of this kingdom is so much greater, because it should be eternal. For so do the voices speak, and he shall reign for evermore. The former kingdoms of Christ did perish after some sort ... but from this beginning there should never want Christian princes, who should keep the truth safe and sound within their dominions. For now is that time begun when Christ shall reign in all the earth, having all his enemies round about subdued unto him and broken in pieces ...

Indeed, the Lord extended his bounty through England and offered a unique opportunity. So far, however, Laodicea responded with lukewarmness. England appeared indifferent to its special role in the last act of the unfolding apocalyptic drama. If its church remained impure, then the Almighty might abandon his Englishmen and choose unto himself another people. Brightman prayed for a different course:

And I hope that he who hath begun this everlasting kingdom will make our queen also to be the type of this his eternal kingdom [that is, bring full reformation to the Church of England]. There is no good man that doth not desire with all his heart that it may be so. Only we must take heed, lest that we suffer his truth to be corrupted, and his majesty to be wronged and offended by bringing in antichristian superstitions afresh again ... We have made Christ angry with us already, in that we are so far off from coming to a full and due reformation, but if we shall return again unto our vomit, with what fury will he burn against us? ... Howsoever that Christ hath now begun this eternal kingdom, yet hath he not tied it to certain countries. He will not want a kingdom, although he should translate his court and palace to some other place, which he is able to do at his pleasure.[16]

16 *A revelation*, pp. 388–9, 390, see 53–6, 388, 406, 587, 841, 611, Brightman believed that God employed imperial agents to establish his kingdom on earth, hence the stress upon Elizabeth. 'And yet this is no strange thing neither. He reigned thus in ancient times by means of Constantine, and other godly emperors' (p. 388). Lamont's view of Brightman as a leader in the renunciation of the concept of the 'godly prince' hangs upon Brightman's interpretation of Constantine, one that varied little from that of Foxe or Napier and that hardly seems negative unless read ironically. Just because bishops began to undermine the church shortly after the death of Constantine did not mean that the prince lost his imperial role. After all, bishops acted as wily enemies of monarchy and worked through stealth. As Lamont pointed out in his interpretation of Prynne's works of the 1630s, bishops could deceive even godly princes. Cf. Lamont, *Marginal Prynne*, ch. 3, and *Godly Rule*, pp. 49–51

While all of the godly had a duty to strive for a transformation of the Church of England, the real initiative lay with Queen Elizabeth. Brightman cast her in a leading imperial role. All Christians could act as a chorus by pressing for a completion of the reformation and by keeping a constant vigilance against any sign of backsliding. When the Arminians appeared to attempt to reverse the reformation in the 1630s by enforcing the ceremonies of the unreformed church, Brightman's followers took his advice. The imminence of triumph or defeat made surveillance into an utmost necessity.

The sounding of the seventh trumpet announced the imminent destruction of Babylon. Brightman believed that the saints initiated their reign of a thousand years on earth around the year 1300 when Satan broke loose from the shackles binding him since the reign of the godly emperor Constantine. From that time forth, the elect steadily increased their influence in the world. But the intensification of light also brought forth an increasingly ferocious reaction on the part of the forces of darkness. The blowing of the seventh trumpet in 1558, followed by the religious wars of the late sixteenth century, produced the evidence which convinced Brightman that the final battle between the elect of Christ and the battalions of Babylon drew near. Gathering armed forces together, 'The Turk and the pope shall conspire the utter desolation of the whole church,' Brightman predicted, '... but the rage of men shall turn to God's greater glory ...' Reformed armies literally would conquer Rome. After the fall of their capital, catholic troops in support of the pope would gather to assault Geneva. 'They shall come together to Armageddon, that holy city, that hill that is so fruitful with dainty and precious things, the angel whereof standeth in the sun ...' The victory of the saints, including temporal rule over those territories not fully reformed, would follow as a result of the great battle of Armageddon. It signified the destruction of antichrist in the west: 'That whole nation that was erewhile belonging to the pope's territory shall be subject after that to the government of the reformed church. Every country that shall live under the tutorage and schooling of that truth that is of the purer note, shall have a part of those dominions subdued unto them which were given to superstition before.'[17] In the east, the annihilation of the Turk by the converted Jews – now gathered together in their homeland again – completed the eradication of the forces of evil.

At first glance, Brightman seems less assured than Napier when map-

17 *A revelation*, pp. 392–3, 832, 835, see 829–32

ping out the full chronology of the future. He referred to the Scot when writing: 'But let us observe here how much they are deceived who are so venturous as to set down a certain year and day almost of the last judgment.' However, Brightman confidently prophesied that the saints would rule the world for another six hundred years and that a long but indeterminate reign of the converted Jews would follow after before the day of judgment arrived. Leaving the final end aside, he calculated approximate dates for the obliteration of the Turks, whose power would 'end at length at the year 1650,' and whose annihilation would be accomplished by 1695 or 1696.[18] 'And indeed we wait now every day while the antichrist of Rome and the Turk shall be utterly destroyed.' Wait indeed, his whole interpretation called for action! Satan had been limited to 390 years of tyranny when he broke his bonds in the year 1300, so the saints could expect to reign before the end of the seventeenth century.[19] Actually, Brightman showed as great a willingness as Napier to date the fall of antichrist; he merely thought that the last judgment would not follow immediately.

All apocalyptic writers who used the history of the Christian church as a help in understanding the Revelation of St John tended to fuse the world of the spirit with the world of flesh. Biblical precedents for such a task abounded, especially in the Old Testament. Brightman showed a painful awareness of the problems presented by the full application of the prophecies of St John to the past and the future. Therefore, he attempted to hedge his interpretation with qualifications. The thrust of his work, however, identified the saints with the reformed churches of Europe and with the potentiality of the Church of England. In the image of Philadelphia and the opportunity of Laodicea, he infused visible reality into the invisible kingdom of God. Except in its imagery, this interpretation deviated little from that of James VI or Napier. Brightman also felt that the reformed churches would obtain irreversible dominion over the western world in the course of the seventeenth century and that England possessed the capacity for leading this conquest of Babylon. Even this echoed the battle cry of James VI. However, Brightman dif-

18 *Ibid.*, p. 853, see 327, 851, 861 ff. Also see Brightman, *A most*, pp. 84–105, a work probably printed on the separatist press. The conversion of the Jews received a good deal of emphasis in late-sixteenth-century commentaries such as those of Brightman, William Perkins, and Hugh Broughton and in the seventeenth century; see Ball, *Great Expectation*, pp. 107–9, 146–56, Bauckham, 'Prophecy,' and Toon, *Puritan Eschatology*, appendix III.

19 *A revelation*, pp. 852, 843

fered by transforming this physical and spiritual victory of the reformed nations into a millennial rule of the saints on earth. '... *They shall reign upon the earth*, it is manifest that this company belongs to the militant church that reigneth upon the earth. For what should the saints in heaven, that have obtained heavenly glory, rejoice in an earthly dominion?' The Almighty upheld his elect, but the reformed accomplished their task of destruction and dominion without the second return of Christ. Armies of men, stirred by the spirit, would exterminate the power of antichrist, all who clung to him, and all who opposed the saints. Brightman moved far beyond a vague appeal for the imminent return of Christ as a solution to the troubles of his religious compatriots, beyond mere militant imagery even, to a millennial vision.[20] No English protestant took this step before him – few, at first, would follow. Radical puritans accepted his works because of the identification of the Church of England with Laodicea even when they rejected the pursuit of the millennium. Some radicals of the early 1640s accepted the millenarian vision, but placed the thousand-year rule of the saints entirely in the future on the authority of Joseph Mede. The prophetic authority of Brightman added to the appeal of his interpretation as time passed. When the clouds of the Thirty Years War spread across Europe and the Laudians gained power in Britain, Brightman's prophecies and warnings seemed to many to be coming true.

When James VI ascended to the English throne as James I, many members of the Church of England shared his interest in and interpretation of the Apocalypse, a phenomenon which continued unabated into the reign of his son. The very year in which James became king of England witnessed the publication of two apocalyptic treatises by men he later raised to the episcopal bench. The new king highly aproved of the refutation of Bellarmine, *Antichristi demonstratio*, written by Robert Abbot, the brother of the future archbishop of Canterbury. The same theme appeared in George Downame, *A treatise concerning antichrist proving the pope is antichrist*. The shock of the Gunpowder Plot shortly afterward added new evidence of the temporal battle raging between the godly and the forces of antichrist. It provided another example of the perfidity of the papists and of God's special mercy toward England. Sermons preached on the anniversary of the divine deliverance

20 *Ibid.*, p. 199. Contemporaries noticed Brightman's millenarianism and some, such as the Hiedelberg divine David Pareus, specifically rebutted this approach; see Pareus, *A commentary*, pp. 506–11, 514 ff., a work translated into English in 1644, but published in Latin more than two decades earlier.

of King James and his Parliament from the machinations of the warriors of Babylon would provide a significant key to the further dissemination of the apocalyptic tradition in the seventeenth century.[21] Apocalyptic treatises continually came off the presses in England, Scotland, and the Netherlands for the English reading market – not all of them written by future bishops by any means. Most followed the mainstream tradition. However, because they paved the way for the protesting works of the 1630s, those published by the separatist press in Amsterdam command considerable interest.[22] The views of the Apocalypse propounded in these works varied to a surprising degree. Only one of them advocated the separatist interpretation.

Just a year after the first edition of Brightman's magisterial study of Revelation appeared, Hugh Broughton, who earlier wrote a work stressing the apocalyptic importance of the conversion of the Jews to Christianity, saw the printing of his commentary, *A revelation of the holy Apocalyps*, on the separatist press in Amsterdam. He had petitioned James I (comparing the British king to Constantine) for the considerable sum of from £500 to £1000 per annum to sustain a project of translating the New Testament into Hebrew. Broughton also planned to write a treatise in Hebrew which would demonstrate that the coming of Christ fulfilled the prophecies of the Old Testament. Thinking that his commentary on Revelation would help in converting the Jews, he also presented *A petition to the king for authority to expound the Apocalyps in Hebrew and Greek to shew the Jews and gentiles that Rome in caesars and pope is therein still damned*. No separatist himself, Broughton debated the grounds of separation at length with Henry Ainsworth and tried to refute them.[23] It is rather surprising that the separatist press decided to print two of his works. Perhaps the apocalyptic importance of Broughton's mission to convert the Jews outweighed his lack of ideological purity. The commentary of Broughton deserves discussion because it gives a context to Brightman's stress on the converted Jews and

21 Cf. Taylor, *A mappe*, and Andrewes, *Works*, IV, pp. 203–405. The latter preached ten sermons on the Gunpower Plot without once giving it an apocalyptic interpretation. For the untypical nature of this approach, see Lamont, *Godly Rule*, ch. 2 and 3, and Hill, *Antichrist*, ch. 1.

22 Johnson, 'Exiled English,' and Wilson, 'Another look,' both discuss the separatist press and its publications.

23 Also see Broughton, *A most humble*, *A petition*, and *Certayne questions*. Ainsworth, his opponent in the last of these, was the pastor of the English separatist congregation in Amsterdam and its leading light until his death in 1622. Firth, 'Apocalyptic Tradition,' pp. 211–24, also discusses Broughton.

because it carries the calculation of the future to something approaching a *reductio ad absurdum*. It shows the line that apocalyptic thought could have taken in the seventeenth century.

Dedicated to James I, Broughton's commentary followed the mainstream of English protestant interpretation in many respects. He plotted the history of the rise of antichrist within the church and noted the beginning of his decline from the time of Wycliffe. He emphasized the application of the prophecies of St John to contemporary and future events, as well as to the past: 'The Apocalypse may be divided into speech unto the present age, and into prophecies for time to come.' Broughton explained that the preservation of Britain from the Armada and the Gunpowder Plot provided examples of '*How* Christ *helpeth his church by ruling* war and guile ...' However, he stressed that the Church of England, even though it had thrown off the pope, still remained in apocalyptic danger. Some of its bishops continued to war against the saints: 'Our greatest hindrance cometh by our bishops, that are void of loyalty and full of cruelty; I speak not against bishops, sage and learned, but bishops savage and unlearned. Waters of trouble, they help the dragon to cast from the mouth of his canons ...'[24] While he never equated episcopacy with Babylon, Broughton felt that some bishops acted in a dangerous way. For England to remain under the protection of the Lord, the godly prince must make some changes in the church.

Following Napier and Brightman, Broughton speculated on the chronology of future apocalyptic events. His timetable derived from an analysis of the past. Exhibiting due caution, he expected no imminent return of Christ: 'No man can tell when the world shall end, nor when the pope shall be utterly consumed by the spirit of Christ his mouth. But that many hundred years remain yet, we have many arguments of likelihood.' Such solicitude came close to destroying one of the components of apocalyptic thought. Broughton calculated that the pope would fall as he arose – by gradual steps over a long period of time and 'not all at once.'[25] Reckoning from creation, he figured that he wrote in the year 5537 (that is, the creation took place in 3926 BC and he penned this passage in 1608 AD). Until 6000 years elapsed after the creation, there would be no full overthrow of Babylon by the reformed countries. The jurisdiction of the pope would be sustained by Spain and Italy for another 463 years. Some cities and countries might fall in the cosmic

24 Broughton, *A revelation*, pp. 16, 98, 159
25 *Ibid.*, pp. 137, 36

struggle, but the final victory beckoned from far beyond the immediate future.[26]

The passion for chronology did not lead automatically to an interpretation of the Apocalypse which perceived the New Jerusalem just around the next corner. Broughton opened the possibility that the godly might be forced to wait a long time for their triumph – until the year 2072 AD, to be precise! He could still be right. Such an extended timetable tended to destroy a great deal of the thrust of apocalyptic thought by placing the end of the latter days into a future which still seems a long way off. Unlike the calculations of Napier and Brightman, those of Broughton could hardly be expected to heighten the expectations of seventeenth-century believers. Broughton's escape from the sense of imminence robbed people of their expectation that great events would happen soon. As a result, few followed his chronology.

Biblical scholars eagerly indulged in the passion for future chronology by the beginning of the seventeenth century, but it took longer to filter down to the ranks of the common man. At the popular level vague hopes of Christ's early arrival continued to be expressed. John Wilkinson's pamphlet, *An exposition of the 13. chapter of the Revelation of Jesus Christ*, slipped snugly into this mould. One of the followers of Henry Barrow, Wilkinson chose to suffer for his faith in England rather than flee to the continent. After his death in prison, friends assembled the commentary published under his name by the separatist press in Amsterdam from the papers Wilkinson left behind. As they explained: 'It was the purpose and desire of the author of this treatise to have published his judgment of the whole book of Revelation, but through the malice of the prelates who divers times spoiled him of his goods, and kept him many years in prison, he was prevented of his purpose. After his death some of his labours coming to the hands of his friends, in scattered and unperfect papers, they laboured with the help of others that heard him declare his judgment herein, to set forth this little treatise ...'[27] Although only a composite fragment of a projected larger work, this short commentary repeated many of the themes put forward by earlier separatist writers such as Browne, Harrison, Greenwood, and Barrow. The circumstances of its author robbed posterity of a huge separatist treatise on Revelation.

26 *Ibid.*, pp. 250, 36 ff. The above chronology has been created from the dates given by Broughton and makes allowance for the year of Christ's birth.
27 Wilkinson, *An exposition*, p. 2 (originally in italics). The little bit known about Wilkinson appears in Burrage, *Early Dissenters*, I, pp. 192–4, 370–5.

Wilkinson identified the first beast of the thirteenth chapter of the Apocalypse with the entire catholic church and its councils. The second beast represented the pope, who derived his power from the dragon – Satan. The image of the beast – set up and worshipped – referred to national councils or synods established by the pope. The convocations of the Church of England fell into this category, even though the jurisdiction of the papacy no longer ran there. The practices of the Established Church also continued to be those of antichrist. It collected tithes which formed a part of the 'worship of the beast.' It continued episcopal ordination and licensing of ministers and thereby extended the jurisdiction of antichrist into every parish in the land. Because the Church of England remained a false church, everyone who even attended its services – as required by law –faced perdition. Separation by the 'saints and servants of Christ' provided the only way of avoiding contamination.[28]

The ways mapped out by his Elizabethan predecessors led Wilkinson to his conclusions. Mere disavowal of Rome could not create a true church. Such an institution must be moulded in the congregational pattern of the New Testament. Since the churches established by the reformation of the sixteenth century did not, for the most part, consist of gathered groups of saints, they represented mere partitions of the power of Babylon. In fact, the reformation retained significance for Wilkinson only because it began the fall of Babylon by weakening the pre-eminence of the pope: 'Thus by the division of this great city, God's people may receive comfort and rejoice in assured hope, that the fall and destruction of Babylon is near, and that the Lord will shortly be avenged of their iniquities, which should teach us to *come out from amongst them, that we partake not of their sins* ...'[29] Wilkinson gave no probable date for this victory of the persecuted elect. He ignored the work of the scholarly chronologists or knew nothing about it.

However, millennial ideas like those of Brightman may lurk behind some hints dropped by this humble separatist martyr. His pamphlet did not avow an explicitly millenarian point of view, but it contained only a segment of his vision and one that lacked comment upon those portions of St John's prophecy most liable to millennial interpretation. Lacking the whole, we cannot know if Wilkinson really believed in a thousand-year reign on earth by the Lord's persecuted saints. In one passage a glimpse appeared: 'And I saw the souls of them that were

28 *An exposition*, pp. 7, 14, 19–20, 23, 29
29 *Ibid.*, pp. 20, 35, see 25

beheaded for the witness of Jesus, and for the word of God, and which had not worshipped the beast, neither his image, neither had received his mark upon their foreheads, or in their hands, and they lived and reigned with Christ a thousand years.'[30] This could hardly refer to the eternal rest of the elect in heaven. The passage stood at the end of the pamphlet. Read within the context of the suffering he endured, of his belief that he and his brethren formed a persecuted elect, and of his description of the separatists as gathered saints, Wilkinson seemed to suggest a millennial reward for the oppressed supporters of Christ. Not an original thinker for the most part, he mostly reflected the separatist tradition. However, Wilkinson may have introduced millennial concepts to those humble brethren who listened to him in prison and to those who prepared his papers for publication.

Milder puritan calls for changes joined the strident tones of separation sounded by Wilkinson in the publications of the Amsterdam press. One of these, *Sacrae heptades, or seaven problems concerning antichrist*, refuted catholic interpretations of the Revelation. Written by an anonymous educated layman, this work also advanced strong objections to the foreign policy of the Spanish match. Its clever editor claimed that he found the manuscript and acted as a midwife in its publication. Whether author and editor be equated or not, the preface and conclusion of the work warned about the dangers of alliance with papists, while the body of the text systematically sought to demonstrate the validity of identifying antichrist with the papacy.[31] *Sacrae heptades* did not take the form of a commentary. The author explained why in his ironic way: '... Being but a simple laic I dare not enterprise any part of scripture, but only to examine some parts thereof, which may seem pertinent to the matter in hand, and thereupon to propose some questions wherein I desire to be resolved.' Well read in commentaries and other pertinent works, he organized his treatise around seven problems concerning antichrist, a pattern similar to that used by Napier's part I, by Brightman's section attacking Bellarmine, and by Abbot's treatise:

30 *Ibid.*, p. 37 (quoting Rev. xx:4 in the second passage). Of course, Wilkinson did not say that this reign of the saints would take place on earth, but any other location would seem unlikely.
31 G.S., *Sacrae heptades*, preface, pp. 2, 100–1, 142. References to Charles I and Henrietta Maria indicate that the preface was written after the text which, from internal evidence, clearly was written before the death of James VI and I. Despite some stylistic differences between the text and the preface, it would be difficult to demonstrate that they came from different authors.

I   Concerning the place of antichrist, whether it be Rome Christian.
II Of the state or body politic of antichrist, whether it be the state or dominion of Rome.
III Of the names of antichrist.
IV Of the rising of antichrist.
V   Of the reign of antichrist.
VI Of the words and actions of antichrist.
VII Of the times of antich[rist] how they be fulfilled, and to what period they are come.[32]

For one weaned on the English protestant apocalyptic tradition, none of these questions posed an insoluble problem. But Jesuit writers challenged the presuppositions and evidence of this tradition, so our anonymous author joined the ranks of the mighty to respond with argument and scholarship. He mined the fathers and historians of the church for evidence to demonstrate his thesis and he also appealed to the tradition of Bale, Foxe, and the martyr bishops. Among contemporaries he cited the works of James VI and I, Napier, George Downame, and Robert Abbot – a group of respectable supporters.[33] Each of his chapters culminated in the time-honoured conclusion that antichrist must be identified with the papacy and ended with the injunction that knowledge of this fact was of crucial importance for the actions of Christians in this world. Neither the conclusions nor the proofs supporting it smacked of novelty. All propounders of apocalyptic visions believed that they could guide men to take the right side in the holy warfare raging abroad.[34] However, the preface and the conclusion presented this task in an unusual manner – one slightly subtle in form.

Permeating the pages of the *Sacrae heptades* was the view that the Almighty employed godly princes and magistrates to establish his re-

32 *Ibid.*, p. 2, and table of contents
33 *Ibid.*, pp. 2, 116, 120, 142–3, 154 and m.n. The learning and style of this pamphlet indicate that the author was well educated. His vigorous attacks upon clerical pretensions support the claim of lay authorship. Individual bishops receive both slighting and favourable references. It appears, then, that the author was an ordinary puritan gentleman.
34 *Ibid.*, preface and passim. For purposes of comparison reference will be made to two works printed in England in 1625. Cf. Beard, *Antichrist*, preface and p. 412, and Mayer, *An antidote*, sig. A 3r; both appear in the *Dictionary of National Biography* (*DNB*). Beard, the schoolmaster of Oliver Cromwell, dedicated his work to John Williams, lord keeper and bishop of Lincoln; Mayer, a prolific writer of biblical commentaries, dedicated his to James I. Both aimed at a wide audience.

formed church and to combat antichrist. Strongly steeped in the imperial tradition as well, the editor dedicated the treatise *'To all kings,
princes, and potentates, especially to King Charles defender of the faith,
and to the king and queen of Bohemia professing the faith, and therefore
persecuted. Also to all other Christians, whether reformed or Romish.'*
The contrast between Charles and his sister and brother-in-law should
be noted. In the preface he held up Henry VIII of England as an example
for the German emperor to emulate. The text also contained references
to apocalyptic struggles between princes and popes in the tradition of
Foxe.[35] The imperial tradition, however, started to sour somewhat in
the mouth of the puritan gentleman who wrote the preface. Even
though England became embroiled in war with Spain before he began
writing this section, the author feared for the spiritual safety of King
Charles. The fact that bishops continued to command the Church of
England and that the puritan preachers silenced under James remained
without employment in God's great work – he suggested that they be
sent to Ireland to convert the papists – caused anxiety enough. The
marriage of Charles added to this discomfort: '... This *Egyptian darkness*, which is in the land *of Goshen*, proceeds from his [antichrist's]
enchantments, to hold *Pharoah* still in hardness of heart ...'[36] The
metaphor is not too murky. Goshen represented England, Pharoah the
king. Antichrist acted through the king's new wife to deflect Charles I
from his role as a godly prince.

Apprehensive at the growth of catholic power and setbacks to the
protestant cause in the Thirty Years War, many Englishmen feared that
the marriage of the heir to their throne to a Spanish princess would bring
like dangers to England. When Charles finally married a papist French
bride, it did not allay these anxieties – this despite the fact that she was
the daughter of Henry IV, a king murdered by the supporters of Babylon.
'Our *queen's father Henry IV of renowned memory*, must not be forgotten; his blood is yet too fresh upon their fingers ...' If England wanted to

---

35 *Sacrae heptades* sig. *2r (an asterisk has been substituted for the more complicated
ornament used in the preface), pp. 88, 100–2, 124, 132, 142, 167, 190–1, 203–4. Cf.
Brightman, *A revelation*, p. 611, and Mayer, *An antidote*, dedication. While the
marriage of Elizabeth to the elector Palatine was very popular, a great deal of opposition arose in the press, the privy council, and Parliament to the Spanish match. See
Gardiner, *History*, IV, ch. 41–2, Willson, *King James*, ch. 21–2, and Breslow, *A Mirror*,
ch. 1, 3, 7

36 *Sacrae heptades* sig. *2r. This sort of metaphorical image, used several times in the
preface, contrasts with the blunt, forward statements made by radical puritans and
separatists.

retain its favour with the Lord, the prince must avoid all alliance with perfidious catholic states: 'Oh dear Christians, let us at length awake, and if God be God serve him, if Rome be Babylon, let us fly out of her, and if the pope be antichrist, let us utterly forsake him. For to follow both, serve both, cleave to both, or rely upon both, is absolutely impossible.' On this principle, every popish power deserved to be shunned. Our anonymous author based this judgment on the painful experiences of those Old Testament kings of Israel who fell from power by trusting in the mighty of the world, instead of in the Almighty. Such a policy became especially necessary at a time when Satan's might declined in a double manner: 'The one by the *preaching of the gospel*, the *other by the open falling away of peoples, nations, and countries from antichrist.*'[37] Alliance with catholic lands would reverse, or at least slow down, the defeat of antichrist and, therefore, it must be renounced. No truck with the armies of Babylon could be defended.

What applied to nations, applied also to individuals. According to the author, 'every papist is an antichrist,' an exceptionally wide extension of this term. The new queen of England had to lay aside her religion or else suffer the consequences. Unless she acted in this way, Charles I – and all of England with him – stood in grave danger of pernicious infiltration:

It cannot be denied, but *Jezebel* was once *young*, and *chaste* and *fair*, but this proves not that she is so now ... And we doubt not, but God will stir up some *Jehu* (zealous perhaps for his own interest, if not for God's) to cause her own *eunuchs*, those friars, monks, and other votaries, to throw her out of the window, that he may tread her under his horses' feet. And doubtless, as this shall in time come to pass by the *powerful preaching of* the word, which shall *waste him by degrees*, so, as an effect of the word preached, first, *the usurped authority of the papacy and Roman clergy over kings and princes* shall be broken and reformation shall begin, where *deformation* came first into the church.[38]

In this metaphorical passage Jezebel symbolized in general the whole church of Babylon and in particular Henrietta Maria, who arrived in England in 1625 with a train of friars, monks, and other papist spiritual advisers. The author seemed sceptical that Charles I would act the part

37 *Ibid.*, sig. ** 2v, pp. 211–12, 210, cf. 213–15
38 *Ibid.*, p. 211, sig. * 3v; cf. Brightman, *A revelation*, pp. 76–9, and Beard, *Antichrist*, p. 425.

of Jehu, either with his wife or with catholic countries. The sapping of his confidence in an imminent victory over antichrist stemmed from his disenchantment with princes – men who worked for their own interests instead of those of God. The cutting, ironic tone of the whole passage betrayed an unusual pessimism which contrasted with the buoyant confidence displayed by most apocalyptic writers. A similar dampening of spirit took place in the late autumn of 1641 when news of the Irish rebellion filtered into England, with similar results. Failure of a monarch to fulfil his proper imperial role provided one of the most powerful causes of apocalyptic militance.

A tentative turn toward the tradition of the persecuted crept into a parenthetical remark in the preface – '(for the faithful are but few, a very little flock, and not very rich in wool)' – but it ended with a rolling appeal to the King-in-Parliament which commended the continuation of a crusade against Spain. 'The Lord therefore join the hearts of our king, peers, clergy, and Commons in one, to finish this good work which they have begun, to the overthrow of antichrist, and bless this work to his full discovery, that kings, princes, priests, and people may learn to leave him.' If England did not follow the will of the Lord, it might suffer the fate of the churches of Asia Minor. These congregations – the very recipients of St John's prophecies – had disappeared from the face of the earth. Even in the depths of his pessimism, however, the author believed that the battle could be won if king, peers, and people joined together in the good fight. Unable to abandon the imperial tradition completely, like Bale he merely mistrusted his prince. The educated layman who brought this treatise to the press sounded like a man sorely troubled in conscience. By sending the manuscript and his preface to the separatist press, he trod on dangerous ground. No wonder he remained anonymous. This endeavour represented the first clear example of co-operation between conforming opposition English gentlemen and the Amsterdam separatists. Sir Simonds D'Ewes, referring to Thomas Scott's anti-Spanish Vox populi (1620), wrote that it was 'generally approved of, not only by the meaner sort that were zealous for the cause of religion, but also by all men of judgment that were loyally affected to the truth of the gospel, and the crown and throne.' By the former category he meant separatists, by the latter men like himself. The growth of the Arminian party within the Church of England added to the danger of the king's marriage to a papist and pushed puritan gentlemen like D'Ewes, John Pym, and the author of Sacrae heptades into a mood of constant vigilance by 1625.[39] Protest made strange bedfellows, as conservative gentlemen joined the radicals in their militance.

The lines and strategy of worldly conflict accentuated in the *Sacrae heptades* were transformed into an explicit demand for holy warfare in another work printed on the separatist press in Amsterdam in the previous year. Its author, Alexander Leighton, eventually became a martyr to Laudian oppression. In his two treatises, the irascible Scot not only advocated an aggressive foreign and domestic policy for Britain, he also carried forward the 'root and branch' apocalyptic tradition forged by Martin Marprelate. The biting tone of his language reflected that of his predecessor. Leighton acted as a key link between the militance of the most radical puritans of the Elizabethan era and the 'root and branch' opponents of episcopacy in the early 1640s. For his efforts, he received the brutal punishment which would transform Bastwick, Burton, and Prynne into puritan martyrs in the late 1630s. Being too radical for most puritans of the 1620s, however, he never gained their popularity. Scorned and abandoned, Leighton none the less foreshadowed the militance which most puritans acquired only after a decade of Laudian rule.

Alexander Leighton dedicated his earlier book, *Speculum bellisaeri: or the looking-glasse of the holy war*, to a trinity of powers he felt would uphold the church of Christ in the world. The king and queen of Bohemia, persecuted protestants pushed from their throne by the battalions of Babylon, received the primary dedication. The second was to 'the prince his highness Charles, the hope of Great Britain.' The intensity of his confidence in this godly prince rang out in a rhetorical question: '*Charles* the great made Rome great; and may not a greater *Charles* raze Rome's greatness?' Great expectations, soon to be dashed! Although he gave primary place to royalty, Leighton made a third dedication of his treatise to Parliament. He advised that body to 'Do what you should, and let God do what he list.'[40] In the excitement of the return of Prince Charles and Buckingham from Spain, Leighton rejoiced and he added his vigorous support to the consequent war policy which these two pushed through Parliament against the wishes of James vi and i.

Like many raised on the stories of the Armada and the Gunpowder Plot, Leighton looked on Britain as the key in the struggle against antichrist. He feared the growing power of the papists abroad and the

39 *Ibid.*, sig. * 3v, ** 4v, cf. 170 ff., and D'Ewes, *Autobiography*, i, p. 159. See Gardiner, *History*, v, pp. 351–64, Lamont, *Godly Rule*, pp. 65–7.
40 Leighton, *Speculum*, sig. B iv, 3v. The classic account of Leighton's thought and punishment is in Gardiner, *History*, vii, pp. 143–52.

subtlety of their infiltration into positions of power in England: 'These fellows *have more cunning then Archimedes*; they would move the whole *earth, if they had but England to stand on*. It is to be feared that they have got too much footing, and that we have more *legions of those evil spirits* amongst us then we *are aware of*.'[41] Impelled by his interpretation of Revelation and by his reading of contemporary events, he sought systematically to break down objections to holy warfare and to encourage an aggressive foreign policy. The stakes were high.

War, for Leighton, was justified both by the law of nature or nations and by the absolute command of God. Nature allowed a person to defend himself or his confederates, while the Almighty ordered revenge upon his enemies and deliverance of his friends. After having defended the concept of warfare, Leighton, using a plethora of classical, biblical, and historical examples, proceeded to show how best to carry it out. He laid great stress upon such things as discipline, the virtue of the soldier, and especially upon good advice and pointed out that proper religion buttressed all of these things. A belief that they fought the battles of the Lord strengthened soldiers for temporal warfare. Military men played an important role in working out the plan of the Almighty. 'As the spiritual warfare of a Christian is the matter of greatest moment under heaven; so next unto it, in my judgment, is the bodily war.'[42]

Leighton's counsel involved more than the preparation of actual fighting men; it also included an appeal to the prince to take proper advice. He listed examples of princes who were misled by evil sycophants and the judgments executed upon them by providence. The word of God provided the best grounds of guidance, ministers the most trustworthy guides to the truth of the Lord. Left to the dissimulations of the great ones of the realm alone, the king was apt to be misled. '... My purpose is to point out the remedy, and the physician; namely, that *plain-dealing word*, from the mouth of the *man of God* ... I know no better physician then a good minister.' To illustrate his interpretation, Leighton referred to the examples of the Old Testament prophets Elijah and Amos – not the most comforting men to recommend to princes! Leighton gave such advice in more than an abstract way. He sounded a

---

41 *Speculum*, sig. B 4v
42 *Ibid.*, pp. 58, 77, see 5–20. By distinguishing so clearly between spiritual and bodily warfare, Leighton showed that he did not equate the two in principle. Drawing upon the somewhat atypical sources of sermons to militia musters and Leighton's works, Walzer overdraws the pre–civil war puritan view of warfare, but makes some good points about the apocalyptic tradition, in *Revolution*, ch. 8.

note of warning specifically to the rulers of England and of the Netherlands with the imagery of Brightman, pointing out that 'except the
deadness of Sardis, and the lukewarmness of Laodicea be really repented
of, the Lord will pull them out of the cliff of that rock.' By this rock, he
meant the stone made without hands of Daniel ii:34–5, a symbol of the
true church which would destroy the power of evil in the world. Popery
seemed to him to be reviving even in that paragon of the true reformation, Scotland, 'where there was not so much as one hoof of the beast
left.' Like Elijah, Leighton feared that the sons of Baal would rob the
land of its heavenly protection. Gondomar, the Spanish ambassador,
and other papists worked to strip the land of its strength in the Lord:

We have hugged the gods of *Rome* too long, and kept in the *strange fire* of their
sacrifice so carefully, that we are become, as some call us, a nation of devils, for
[t]reasons and conspiracies; by this means many are infected, others grown
lukewarm, the most part key cold, for which the Lord hath increased the hatred
of foreign and of our homebred *Egyptians* against us, and sharpeneth their wit
that they may *deal craftily with us*; not that God is the author of the evil of sin,
but of the action, as it is a just plague and punishment to us. With their craft
they have undermined our wit, they have undermined our state, and which is
worst of all, the[y] have undermined, yea and almost blown up, the power of our
religion; they have made *Israel naked, and Judah contemptible and bare* ...[43]

Even for an apocalyptic thinker, Leighton displayed an inordinate pen-
chant toward plot theory. The subversion of reformed nations came as a
punishment for their failure to finish God's reformation.

England jeopardized its special role as God's elect nation and peculiar
people in this world struggle by its imperfectly reformed church. Drawing on Brightman's image again, Leighton predicted that doleful consequences would follow if England failed to adopt the presbyterian
programme *in toto*. '... Our *Laodicean conceit* shall be so far from
sheltering us, that thereby we provoke God, that he can bear no longer,
but that he must needs *spew us out of his mouth*; which if he do, it is *to
be feared we are such a loathsome thing, that he will never take us up
again, but make a new people to himself*.' From these premises he called
upon the prince and the magistrates to purify the Church of England and
prevent such a conclusion. He also warned Prince Charles not to become
entangled in a Spanish marriage. And he advised the bishops of the

43 *Speculum*, pp. 107, 120, 153

Established Church to 'let your train fall. Away with the little beast with two horns ...' The task of purging idolatry out of England, however, rested squarely upon the shoulders of the magistrates – theirs was the power and the glory. Leighton commanded them to root out England's national sins: stage plays, sabbath breaking, scoffing at preciseness, petty oaths, abuse of animals, and usury – mostly things that Prynne would attack in the 1630s. Leighton warned that if these evils be not abolished, judgment awaited the nation; if magistrates carried out the necessary changes, however, victory beckoned:

What your enemies are, and what attempts they shall make, and how certainly and suddenly they shall fall, it is clear in the Revelations. It is true indeed you have monstrous enemies unparalleled by any other; namely, the devil, the imperial force giving the *devil* or *dragon* for his arms, and the *pope* or antichrist ... whose chief instruments be these hellish furies, *the Jesuits*; these shall gather together all the waters of the whore on which she sitteth; but the sunshine of the Lord's wrath shall dry them up ... her wound shall not be cured, she shall be burned with fire, she goeth to utter destruction.

With rousing words he called prince and Parliament to go forth to fight the holy war. Even though outnumbered by the physical strength of those powers – led by the German emperor – supporting Rome, the godly could grasp the victory by resolute action combined with the help of the Lord. If the magistrates failed to enforce the will of God, England would fail. 'Great Britain had best look to her vine.'[44] Much dead wood needed pruning.

Leighton's *Speculum belli* represented almost too perfect an example of militant radical puritan apocalyptic thought. Its plain talking, prophetic warnings, appeal to the fulfilment of Revelation in contemporary events, and call for an offensive holy war took up themes hesitatingly enunciated by earlier writers and expressed them with forceful determination. Leighton composed it for the occasion of war with Spain. Clearly displeased with elements of the practice and government of the Church of England, he employed Brightman's image of Laodicea to characterize that institution. He also sounded ringing appeals to the godly prince, asking him to purge the church and to initiate physical and spiritual warfare against the catholic powers. Although firm in the belief that he lived in the latter days, Leighton made no attempt to

44 *Ibid.*, pp. 192–3, 195, 305, 316, see 231 ff., 267 ff.

calculate a chronology of future events. Like his hero Elijah, he delivered his prophecy and waited for Ahab to act.

According to the title page, Leighton's next book, *An appeal to the Parliament, or Sions plea against the prelacy*, was 'Printed in the year and month wherein *Rochell* was lost [that is, October 1628].' The dolorous predictions he made earlier seemed to be coming true. This time, he bypassed the royal family and dedicated his work to Parliament. Conditions had moved to such desperate straits that Leighton no longer trusted in the unaided prince. He implored the assembled worthies to come to the rescue of their land: 'Be you eyes, ears, and hands to our sovereign, as you[r] place authorizeth; and he by you shall scatter the wicked, and bring the wheel over them. The fire of God's wrath is already broke in upon us, and if the fuel of ... national sin be not removed, the wrath of God will never cease till it hath consumed us from being a nation to himself.' Leighton believed that England's military defeat at the hands of France showed that the Almighty had begun to withdraw his support. Therefore, Parliament must take up the imperial apocalyptic mission, seize the initiative from the hands of the king's evil advisers, and purge offending members from the body politic. Anglican bishops formed the worst group of wrongdoers: 'These bishops be the knobs and wens and bunchy popish flesh which beareth down, deformeth, and deadeth the body of the church that there is no cure (as we conceive) but cutting off.'[45]

Like Martin Marprelate before him, Leighton reached into the apocalyptic armoury of the separatists to select one of their weapons for making a 'root and branch' assault upon episcopacy. He concentrated upon the derivation of episcopal authority: '... *The calling* of the *hierarchy*, their dependent offices and *ceremonies*, whereby they subsist are all unlawful and *antichristian*.' Like Martin junior, Leighton cited a string of witnesses to prove his point – Wycliffe, Luther, Bullinger, Hooper, John Lambert, John Bradford, and Bale – all of whom condemned the prelates of the unreformed church. He also followed his Elizabethan predecessor in constructing a clever syllogism to demonstrate the false nature of church hierarchy:

These governors are justly called antichristian who are assistant to the pope in his universal government.

45 Leighton, *Sions plea*, dedication, p. 11

But the bishops, archbishops, chancellors, etc., are assistants to the pope in his universal government.

Therefore bishops, archbishops, chancellors, etc., are justly called antichristian.

The relatively recent claim that reformed bishops derived their episcopal authority *jure divino* added fresh fuel to his fire and gave his argument a credence lacking in that of the Elizabethans.[46]

Bishops occupied an unlawful calling and, to make things worse, they also exercised their jurisdiction in an improper way. The church courts endured as antichristian remnants, rending the provisions of Magna Carta! Like all religious radicals, Leighton thought that the *ex officio* oath of the High Commission sinned 'against all laws of heaven and earth.' He cited Fuller and Bacon against the oath and compared it unfavourably to the procedure pagans followed when dealing with the apostle Paul. '*Heaven and earth is against it*; it is against the law of God, the law of nature, the common law, the canon law, councils, and imperial statutes.' The unlawful calling and illegal jurisdiction of the hierarchy made it impossible for a good subject to retain his loyalty to the king and obey the bishops at the same time. Because they obtained their power from a foreign source, the hierarchy deserved punishment for breach of Praemunire. 'Now that they derive their authority from the pope, carry themselves as popelings, have all the power (if not more then they had under the pope), exercise a full popish power over subjects in their means, persons, and consciences, and plead for the derivation of their episcopal authority in print from the *pope*. It is as clear as the light.'[47] This may seem a rather thorough condemnation of the bishops. To cap it off, however, Leighton traced all corruptions in the Church of England through the ages to their explicit or covert actions and espied an episcopal plot to undermine royal authority in all of their actions. The circularity of the argument no doubt reinforced its effectiveness.

Evil first enterered the English church with the arrival of St Augustine, the missionary sent from Rome. Through episcopal agents, the power of antichrist increased during the following centuries. King John challenged it, but proved unequal to the task. 'Undermining *prelates*

46 *Ibid.*, pp. 3, 11–12, see 12–28, 31
47 *Ibid.*, pp. 32, 47, 38, see 24–8. Most of these criticisms were made previously by Henry Barrow and would be repeated by John Lilburne.

and domineering favourites have cast our bravest kings into many cold sweats.' Edward vi wanted to root out the hierarchy because he was 'desirous not to leave a hoof of the Romish beast in his kingdom,' but unfortunately he lacked godly supporters and 'he was mightily opposed in all his good designs, especially by the prelates,' so his good intentions came to nought. Queen Elizabeth established reformation in the land, but the guile of the prelates subverted it both in her reign and in that of James vi and i. Instead of leading the church, they persecuted the saints. The cup of their wrath turned all men to call for the downfall of the hierarchy:

... Sion's plea against them hath ever been maintained since the beginning of the reformation, witness both the doings and the sufferings of the saints in that behalf, but now their tyranny and treachery in betraying the truth to popery and Arminianism, together with the profaneness of them and theirs, unveileth more full to men of all ranks (as nobility magistracy, ministry, gentry, and commonalty) the iniquity of their place, and the ruin thence ensuing, which maketh them to cry with one voice, *down with the Babel of prelacy* ...[48]

Not until 1641 would men of all ranks actually make this cry in any great numbers. However, long before then, others took up Leighton's argument that the Arminians dethroned the godly prince by claiming *jure divino* derivation for episcopacy. Unwilling to stop there, Leighton's logic led him on to place the bishops in the camp of Babylon.

Having isolated the cancer, Leighton advocated several methods of cutting it out. Responsibility for this operation lay with the '*magistrate* and *minister*, according to their several places and stations.' Ministers must use the 'sword of the spirit (namely the word),' to condemn the evils of episcopacy. Parliament, as the great council of the state, inherited the imperial mantle from the corrupted crown. While it had a duty to tell the plain truth to all men, for 'we stand all in need from the king to the beggar to be awaked, and made sensible of the necessity of this work to be done,' Parliament had the special role of counselling the king. 'Make it plain that their antichristian authority, the beauty of Christ's church, and the glory of his crown, and the good of his people cannot subsist together.' After proclaiming the truth for all to see, ministers and magistrates acquired a second duty, that of separating

48 *Ibid.*, pp. 210, 69, 70, 180, see 70–81. Like that of Martin Marprelate in the 1580s, Leighton's unpopularity in the 1620s stemmed from the fact that he was far too radical even for radical puritans.

themselves from the evils of the Church of England and its antichristian governors:

If we look to prosper, you must resolve and draw others on to *abandon all the abominations from our eyes wherewith we have defiled ourselves ...*

Thus we separate not from the churches, but from the evils of them and also from obedience to antichristians, lords over them ... How shall ye ever deliver the land, or Christ himself, of them and their burdens, if ye obey them?[49]

Notice the distinction made between his position and that of the separatists. Realizing full well that kings expect subjects to comply with their commands, Leighton called upon the leaders of society to obey God rather than man and warned that obedience to unlawful power could lead to national disaster as well as individual damnation. The calling of a national synod of divines formed the third means of removing the bishops. The fourth consisted of self-reformation as a prelude of national reformation – here he cited the example of Scotland. Fifth was the abolition of the wealth of the bishops by annexation of their lands to the crown. 'The 6th and last mean[s] of removal is the continuance of a Parliament till the tenants of the hierarchy be tried by *God* and the *country*, that is, by the laws of God and the land.' Ironically, Leighton's programme contravened those very laws of England, and Charles I dissolved this Parliament before it could meddle in religious matters. The six means of removing the episcopacy put forth by Leighton added up to a platform with significant political thrust. Put into effect, it would have created a massive campaign of civil disobedience. Books, pamphlets, and sermons repeated one or more of his proposals in the following years until they entered the realm of action during the civil war period. Other English protestants perceived the late 1620s, when England warred with France and Spain and catholic imperial armies triumphed on the continent, as a time of threatening trouble. To put it into contemporary perspective, in 1628 *Sion's plea* advocated actions no more radical than those of the men who held the speaker in his chair to prevent immediate dissolution and pushed the Eliot resolutions through the House of Commons in 1629. All acted in a resolute way to prevent the spread of popery and Arminianism.[50]

Although bursting with militance, Leighton ignored the millenarian

49 *Ibid.*, pp. 197, 269, 273, 281–2
50 *Ibid.*, p. 337, see 299–301, 330–6

ideas of Brightman. Believing that contemporary events fulfilled the prophecies of St John, that the final fall of antichrist had begun, Leighton wanted to guarantee a place for Britain on the triumphant side of Christ. Anxious over England's military humiliation by the catholic countries of France and Spain – a partial fulfilment of his earlier predictions, Leighton strained to remedy the root cause of that disaster by probing at its source and pushing for reform. Victory in the field would follow from the removel of the cancer of hierarchy at home. Parliament must insure that England remained with Christ and did not slide into the camp of Rome. '... We are confident, if all that love the Lord (especially men of place) will do their part, we shall have our king as an *angel of God* in this particular, though Rome must fall by the sword, yet the word must both instruct princes that Babel can no otherwise be healed, and also inarm them for her ruin.'[51] Leighton always remained within the imperial apocalyptic tradition. He continued to appeal to crown and Parliament, not to the oppressed and persecuted. Although clearly believing that he lived in the very last days, he neither calculated the chronology of the remaining time nor called for the imminent return of Christ as a solution for the problems of the godly. Leighton fretted more about preparing England for Christ's return than about trying to predict the date of that event. He aimed his 'root and branch' appeal at the military and political activities of men, not at the direct intervention of the Lord of hosts. Time enough remained for England to change.

The international tensions which engendered the bellicose books of Leighton heightened the anxieties of many Englishmen. In his isolation from the world as a fellow of Christ's College, Cambridge, Joseph Mede zealously watched the events of the Thirty Years War and corresponded with a wide circle of friends on the subject. A man of encyclopaedic interests and profound scholarship, Mede published his erudite Latin exegesis of Revelation in the interval between the printing of Leighton's two tempestuous tomes. This shy, retiring scholar who stuttered in conversation made a stark contrast to the assertive Scot in personality and style. Leighton, for all of his bravery and outspokenness, gained no acknowledged followers. Mild Mede, exercising his philological skills and announcing his discoveries in an understated way, founded a school of English millennial thought which continues to the present day. In the 1640s, when Leighton lay long forgotten, Mede's vision inspired the most fervent radicals! The willow proved more lasting than the oak.

51 *Ibid.*, sig. A 3v

Joseph Mede applied an enormous range of humanist linguistic training and historical knowledge and a firm grasp of Ramist logic to the
mysteries of the Apocalypse.[52] After positing a series of 'synchronisms'
which related the various prophecies of St John to each other in a
rational and sequential way, Mede proceeded to unlock the meaning of
the text and link each portion of it to holy history.[53] The first six seals
covered pagan Rome from the death of Christ to the conversion of
Constantine, who overthrew the 'devilish government of the Roman
empire' and seemingly made Christianity secure. Out of the seventh seal
arose the trumpets which represented the judgments of God upon the
Roman empire. They began with the incursions of the barbarians and
the division of the empire into eastern and western portions in 395 and
ended with the overthrow of Satan. The seventh trumpet was cotermin-
ous with a thousand-year rule of Christ and his saints on earth.[54] While
the trumpets dealt with temporal affairs, Mede synchronized them with
the internal history of the Christian church which he found predicted in
the second half of the Book of Revelation.

Simultaneous with the sounding of the first trumpet came the
triumph of antichristian apostasy within the institutional church – a
deformation which would continue for 1260 years.[55] Mede interpreted
this as a revival of heathenism and it was portrayed by the outer court of
the Temple, the inner court being the primitive church which continued
to survive in a hidden and scattered way. Throughout the ascendancy of
antichrist the elect kept up their witness to the truth.[56] The ten-horned
beast, a synchronism with the ten kingdoms that succeeded the Roman

52 [Mede], *Clavis*. First published in 1627, an enlarged edition appeared in 1632; reprinted
   in 1642, it was translated into English by Richard More and published in 1643 as Mede,
   Key. Also see Mede, *Apostasy*, and successive editions of his *Works*. See Ball, *Great
   Expectation*, pp. 59–60, 85–7, 136–7, 173–7, Clouse, 'The rebirth of millenarianism,' in
   Toon, *Puritan Eschatology*, pp. 55–65, Firth, 'Apocalyptic Tradition,' pp. 288–306,
   Gilsdorf, 'Puritan Apocalypse,' pp. 64–70, Tuveson, *Millennium and Utopia*, pp. 76–85,
   and Wilson, 'Studied,' pp. 146–7, 157–69.
53 See the chart between pp. 26–7 of *Key* and the compendium at the end of *Key* for a guide
   to Mede's synchronisms. The works listed in note 52 have ably discussed and outlined
   Mede's method.
54 Mede, *Key*, I, p. 56, see 80–121
55 *Ibid.*, II, pp. 80–5; see *Apostasy*, p. 145. If the 1260 years began in 395 AD, the fall of
   antichrist would be completed in 1655.
56 *Ibid.*, II, pp. 2–15; see *Apostasy*, p. 62. For the courts of the Temple, see Revelation
   xi:1–2. The worship of saints and images, the celibacy of the priesthood, and other
   practices and ceremonies provided Mede with evidence of the revival of heathenism
   within the Christian church.

empire in the west at the blowing of the second trumpet, represented the secular power of the pope. His spiritual ascendancy shone forth in another of St John's images: 'The *two horned beast* or *false prophet* is the bishop of Rome with his clergy; having horns like a *lamb*, of whose authority of binding and loosing he braggeth that he hath a deputation, but speaking idolatry and slaughtering of the saints as the *dragon*.'[57] In these ways, Mede strongly buttressed the identification of the papacy with antichrist.

The pouring of the vials synchronized with the sixth trumpet (the invasions of the Turks) and measured the stages of antichrist's defeat. The first vial saw light dawn again in the teachings of such medieval heretics as the Waldensians, the Albigensians, Wycliffe, and Hus. With the second vial, whole nations followed the lead of Luther and left the jurisdiction of antichrist. The third vial denoted the killing of papists by reforming princes; Mede used the defeat of the Armada and the enforcement of laws against catholic priests by Elizabeth I as prime examples of its effects. While these prophecies had found fulfilment by the time that Mede wrote, the last four vials depicted future events. These would bring destruction upon the holy Roman empire, upon Rome and the papacy, upon the Turks, and upon the whole power of Satan respectively. The last vial would pour suppression upon 'all enemies of our Lord Christ in what country soever.' Indeed, constant combat between the forces of Babylon and the elect characterized the entire era of the vials. 'After this war upon the *Waldenses* and *Albigenses*, cruelly did the beast rage divers ways, as well against other remnants of them in other places, as also against others their companions of the same pure religion in what place soever, till at length, nevertheless, after the year 1500 whole kingdoms, principalities, commonwealths, the churches being reformed, fell away from the domination of the *beast* to the party of the saints. Against whom afterward war is waged, and continueth at this day, neither shall it be ended, until the ruin of the beast.'[58] Until the pouring of the seventh vial, synchronized with the seventh trumpet, the godly could expect continual opposition from the powers of darkness.

Truth would triumph in the end, but until that day trials remained. Notes of warning broke the calm surface of Mede's basically optimistic reading of providential history. He reckoned that the dominion of the saints started its progressive advance in the fourteenth century and

57 *Ibid.*, II, pp. 64–5
58 *Ibid.*, II, pp. 120, 61–2, see 114–21 for his interpretation of the vials.

could be expected to wax supreme before the end of the seventeenth century. Mede made no clear chart of the chronology of future events, but one could easily be derived from his works. He pointed out that the 1260-year span of antichrist's apostasy began late in the fourth century. Contemporaries could expect it to end within a quarter of a century from the time when Mede first published his work in Latin, within fifteen years from the time that it came out in English. Mede, himself, tried to temper the buoyancy arising from such expectations. Trials probably awaited the godly before their ultimate triumph. The killing of the two witnesses of Revelation xi:8, Mede believed, portrayed a resurrection of antichrist's power within reformed churches:

The killing, therefore, of the witnesses ... will seem to be a molestation and dejection of them from the office and place which they, a little while, had got in the reformed church by the efficacy of their preaching ... Whereby it must needs likewise come to pass that the pillars thereof being taken away, and false prophets of the beast being again brought in instead of the prophets of Christ, the whole polity of the reformed church, as far as this shall happen, shall go to the ground, which whether it shall happen sooner or later, only he knoweth, in whose hands are times and opportunities.[59]

This passage provides a typical example of the cautious, contingent style of expression employed by Mede. Later writers applied the interpretation it put forth to the state of the Church of England under Laud. Other parts of Mede's interpretation also gained wide currency in the 1640s.

Upon Mede's shoulders must rest the primary responsibility for the revival of millennial thought in England. Whereas Brightman pointed out that the rule of the saints already had been in existence in the world for three hundred years, Mede placed the millennium in the future and thus made possible visions which would stress a radical discontinuity between the past and the future millennium. Mede added his considerable authority to that of the continental theologian and encyclopaedist, Johann Heinrich Alsted, to make pursuit of the millennium respectable in scholarly circles. English translations of their works brought these ideas within the grasp of the common man. Mede reached his conclusions after a careful study of the eschatological portions of scripture and

59 *Ibid.*, II, p. 15. Mede himself showed no hostility toward the ceremonialism of the Laudians.

of the early fathers of the church – especially Justin Martyr – and he tested it in his correspondence with interested divines and laymen. So far was he from passionate partisanship, however, that he included in his works the views of early fathers who opposed the idea that the saints would have a temporal reign. In fact, Mede acted as such an un-perspicuous advocate that a hurried reader could easily overlook his millennial ideas.[60] Many contemporaries discovered his stunning con-clusions, however. William Twisse, later the prolocutor of the Westminster Assembly, recorded his initial reaction – hardly a favoura-ble one, for he was not a man given to novelty. He had heard a rumour of Mede's belief in 'the glorious kingdom of Christ here on earth, which many hundred years ago was cried down as the error of the *millenaries* ... And it seemed wondrous strange to us, that such an opinion should, after so many hundred years, be revived ...'[61] Strange indeed, for Mede lent his weight to an idea linked by contemporaries to the abominable anabaptists. After corresponding with Mede and reading his works, Twisse became so converted to Mede's interpretation that he wrote prefaces for the English translations of those works which appeared in 1641 and 1643. No longer would the rule of the saints only be sublimated into spiritual interpretations as heaven or as the visible or invisible church of Christ.

Although no radical himself, Joseph Mede proved capable of inspiring revolutionary fervour by his writings. Both princes and persecuted played important roles in Mede's interpretation. He buttressed the mainstream of English apocalyptic thought in devising new means of linking the papacy with antichrist and in resifting the chronology of the past. But his delineation of the apostasy of antichrist as a revival of heathen practices within the church found easy application to the Arminian movement in the Church of England by those who opposed the policy of Laud. By dating the acceleration of antichrist's rise to the period shortly after Constantine, Mede gave his weight to a strand of interpretation found in Foxe and Brightman. One of his students would shift this chronology slightly backwards into the reign of Constantine

60 *Ibid.*, II, 121–35. The prefaces to the posthumous English editions of Mede's works made certain that the reader would not miss his millennial vision. In a sense, Mede was the father of Utopian and revolutionary millennial visions in his revival of millennial thought, but he had more moderate followers, as well; see Ball, *Great Expectation*, ch. 5. Clouse and Firth discuss Alsted at length.
61 Mede, *Apostasy*, preface, sig. A 2v. Firth, 'Apocalyptic Tradition,' pp. 288–95, 299–306, discusses Mede's correspondence.

and, thereby, discover the key for dethroning the godly prince. Mede's revival of millenarian thought fathered the Fifth Monarchists and Gerrard Winstanley. Like Brightman, the other great commentator of this period, he would have been shocked by many of the future manifestations produced by his interpretation of the Apocalypse. 'Certainly Mead's work, and very likely Brightman's, were not intended as trumpet calls to action in the name of a fore-ordained cause. But they could be transformed into such instruments of party purposes with relative ease.'[62] The last chapter of this study will provide some glimpses at that facility. Once in print, the works of Mede – like those of Foxe and Brightman – became common property. Readers could and did interpret them as they wished, ignoring some parts and giving added emphasis to others. By the time that Mede died in 1638, the age of illustrious exegesis had drawn to a close and that of protesting propaganda had dawned.

A bewildering variety of views resulted from these attempts to combat the counter-reformation mission and to refute Jesuit attacks upon the core of the protestant apocalyptic tradition. Bishop, scholar, puritan, and separatist jointly defended the necessity of an apocalyptic break from Rome. Although agreeing that Rome represented Babylon, they differed strongly in placing protestant churches on one side or the other in the cosmic conflict of the latter days. All expressed concern that Englishmen stand in the ranks of Christ and cited victories – such as the Armada and the Gunpowder Plot – as examples of what would happen if England played its proper role. However, each author employed his apocalyptic vision to support his view of the form which the Church of England should take. Separatists withdrew from the Established Church because of its abominations and predicted that it would fall with the rest of Babylon. Anxious radical puritans pushed strongly for further reform of Laodicea, 'root and branchers' for the abolition of hierarchy as a part of Babylon, and pointed to the military defeat of protestants on the continent as an example of the judgment of the Lord upon those who renounced Rome but held back from a full reformation. Providential history merged with contemporary politics.

Unlike their predecessors, quite a number of the authors of this era tried to predict the future with as precise a chronology as they worked out for the past. Napier, Brightman, and Mede expected Christ and his followers to annihilate Babylon before the end of the seventeenth century. Broughton stretched this to the twenty-first century. Some of their

62 Wilson, 'Studies,' p. 169

prophecies about the stages of future development seemed to contemporaries to come true. The apparent veracity of Brightman's predictions about the protestant churches in Germany, Mede's belief that the preachers of the reformed churches would be deprived by the forces of Babylon, Napier's prognostication that a new trumpeter would begin to sound forth in 1639, added the weight of empirical confirmation to their chronology of the future. In her analysis, Dr Firth noted that 'Mede was transformed from scholar into prophet. He was not alone: Brightman had gone that way before him; and Napier, Alsted, and even Ussher were to follow.' By substituting detailed plans of the future for the vague hopes expressed in previous generations, the scholarly chronologers transformed themselves into prophets. Even though some reformers refused to countenance such precise forecasts, none could halt the art of calculation. Readers could and did pick, choose, and debate about the number of the beast.[63]

Brightman's millenarianism introduced a new, potentially explosive element into English apocalyptic visions. By linking the reformation of the church with a thousand-year rule of the saints on earth, he paved the way for a new political outpouring of the spirit. Joseph Mede made such possibilities probable by placing the millennium entirely in the future – a prize which the saints could win through their own actions. A New Jerusalem would come on earth through the agency of human warfare, through the shaking of old social, political, and religious foundations. Other authors warned against the dangers which could come from the millenarian interpretation.[64] These warnings went unheeded by those radicals of the 1640s who relished the thought that King Jesus would rule the earth through his saints.

Although some sixteenth-century writers stressed the role of the persecuted and oppressed as apocalyptic instruments, the separatists

63 Firth, 'Apocalyptic Tradition,' p. 340. For an attack upon Brightman's chronology, upon millenarianism in general, and for a prediction that the final fall of antichrist would begin around 1860, see Mayer, Ecclesiastica, pp. 419, 401. Mayer's compendium drew upon scores of commentaries, most of them by contemporaries, and represented the type of debate which must have taken place in other surroundings. In the three-hundred-page section of the Ecclesiastica dealing with Revelation, he made the following marginal references: David Pareus (120), Thomas Brightman (111), Heinrich Bullinger (97), John Foxe (46), Patrick Forbes (45), and John Napier (30). 'Mayer's life was spent digesting the work of former commentators on the Bible and adding notes of his own.' DNB, xiii, p. 148
64 For post-Brightman, but pre-Mede, warnings, see Mayer, Ecclesiastica, p. 311, and Forbes, An exquisite, p. 225. Forbes was a Scottish bishop; DNB .

stood almost alone in consistently pressing this view in the early decades of the seventeenth century. Without forgetting the heroic deeds of the martyrs, commentators concentrated on creating change through established channels and emphasized the unique role cut out for England, if properly reformed. Even Brightman and Leighton, the codifiers of the radical puritan and 'root and branch' streams of interpretation, stressed the role of the godly prince and thereby showed their strong desire to work through respectable agents. Honour for God's imperial instrument seemed overwhelming, but distrust of Charles I had begun to grow. What if he refused to play the role assigned to him by the Almighty? Would England then lose its special status, its potentiality of becoming an 'elect nation'? All fingers pointed in this dangerous direction. Not all men could forgive seventy times seven as Christ recommended. The seventeenth-century owner of Brightman's *Revelation of the Revelation* wrote inside the cover of his copy: 'A man of words and not of deeds is like a garden full of weeds.'[65] When the tares began to choke out the good corn, the time for propaganda, protest, and punishment arrived. New martyrs stepped forth.

65 Brightman, *A revelation*, inside cover of the copy in the Bodleian

4

The soldiers of anti-Laud

I hope these arrogant lofty prelates will not be offended with me, if I make it apparent to them (and others) by their fruits and works, that they are so far from being the sons or successors of Christ and his apostles, or of divine institution, that they are of their father the devil (for his works and lusts they do), the successors from the Jewish high priests who crucified our Saviour, persecuted, silenced, imprisoned, excommunicated his apostles, and so, of diabolical ordination, not divine.

[William Prynne], *A looking-glasse for all lordly prelates*, p. 1

Although 'dark corners of the land' still existed in England and Wales in the 1630s, protestant writers and preachers had illuminated the history of strife between God's saints and the satanic power of the papacy for over a century. A chronological apocalyptic interpretation of the reformation lay embedded in the presuppositions of the clergy of the Church of England. At the highest level, Archbishops Bancroft and Abbot carried on the tradition of Archbishop Whitgift by defending the break from Rome as a separation of the true church from one which had become Babylon. Below them stood ranks of scholars, both lay and cleric, who taught, preached, and published their interpretations of this epic cosmic struggle. Bishop Jewel may have exaggerated when he wrote that 'There is none, neither old nor young, neither learned nor unlearned, but he hath heard of antichrist.' In the half century after his judgment appeared, however, the people heard of antichrist time and time again. The widespread distribution of the inexpensive and popular Geneva Bible, of Foxe's *Actes and monuments*, of more than a hundred treatises and commentaries, of numerous popular pamphlets, and the preaching of innumerable sermons insured that the people would identify anti-

christ with the papacy. The historian will never know what the uneducated and illiterate lower half of the population thought. Separatists
and the tub preachers of the 1640s, whenever one can trace their social
standing, sprang from the upper half of society, albeit often from the
lower reaches of that range. Just as in the Established Church itself,
gentlemen, yeomen, tradesmen, and artisans provided the leadership
and the rank and file of such movements. Indeed, the levelling thrust of
sectarian practice rarely extended beyond those who had attained some
social and economic 'independence.' Even bearing such reservations in
mind, it would be far easier to underestimate than to overestimate the
appeal of the apocalyptic vision of the reformation within all social
orders.[1] Entwined in myth with great English national and protestant
acts of the past such as the Marian persecutions and the Armada,
apocalyptic visions incorporated a puissant potential of springing to life
upon the stage of action. Ironically, just when defences seemed most
secure because this plank of the Anglican platform stood recently buttressed against attacks from without, doubts arose from within.

Initially a tiny minority, a brotherhood of divines who questioned
the mainstream traditions of the protestant past and probed to the point
of insecurity some basic assumptions of most articulate Englishmen
sprang up within the Church of England. Although the one term arose
among their enemies and the other overstresses the importance of the
archbishop of Canterbury, they shall be called the 'Arminian' or 'Laudian' element in this book. While no terminology used to characterize
this group will please every scholar, these terms at least avoid the
anachronism of 'High Church' or 'Anglo-Catholic.' During the reign of
Charles I, the Arminians got a powerful grip on the government of the
Established Church.[2] The new trend first became evident when the Duke

1 Jewel, *Works*, II, p. 902; see [Bancroft], *Daungerous positions*, pp. 1–2, Abbot, *The
   reasons*, pp. 4–5, 9–10, 18, 21, 24–5, 30–2, 35, 38, 52, 63–4, 83, 89, 271–2, 283, 429,
   [Abbot], *A treatise*, sig. A 3r, pp. 17–20, 29, 34, 74–5, 94–8, 114–16. Since the apocalyptic
   tradition formed part of the intellectual baggage of both educated protestant divines
   and tub preachers who both spread it widely through word of mouth and print, it seems
   safe to say that most people in Gregory King's upper half of society who took religion
   seriously had accepted this framework by the 1630s.
2 Cf. Porter, *Reformation and Reaction*, and Nicholas Tyacke, 'Puritanism, Arminianism and counter-revolution,' in Russell, *Origins*, ch. 4. While Porter de-
   monstrates that 'Arminian' theology existed at Cambridge in the late sixteenth century and stimulated the writings of Arminius, he strains this evidence by trying to
   inflate it into a mainstream tradition of the Church of England. Arrived at independently, my interpretation reinforces that of Tyacke. Tyacke's thesis, 'Arminianism in
   England,' was not available for consultation.

of Buckingham, abandoning his earlier relationship with John Preston, sided with the Laudians at the York House conference of 1626. Strengthened by the systematic isolation of George Abbot, the archbishop of Canterbury, Arminian control over the hierarchy became secure with the elevation of William Laud to that see in 1633.[3] The members of this loose party disputed some of the key concepts of the past in their writings and actions. By deliberately resurrecting and enforcing ceremonies and practices abolished in most parts of England since the reformation and using these as tests for conformity, they seemed to many to be sliding backwards toward the unreformed church – to be flirting with the whore of Babylon. Revived ritualism moved many upholders of the 'old ways' into print and protest. The Arminians gave them further cause by questioning, if not completely denying, the identification of the papacy with antichrist. Some merely shed scepticism on the sufficiency of scripture as a means of establishing such an affirmation. Although they shared this doubt with Calvin, it flew in the face of a classification virtually unquestioned by English protestants since the break with Rome! Others, including Laud himself, asserted that the Roman confession remained a true church.[4] The willingness of some Arminians to engage in friendly debate with Jesuits galled many who clung to the faith of their protestant forefathers.

The Laudians also sapped the basic secular thrust of the apocalyptic tradition – the stress upon magistrates or the oppressed and persecuted as God's instruments on earth. Most English protestants gloried in assigning to kings and magistrates a role as initiators of reform and as protectors of the true church. Glad for the protection of Charles I, the Arminians diverted the imperial stream into episcopal channels. 'The Christian Emperor was being dethroned – with Charles I's smiling pleasure.' Grasping the lead from laymen formed an integral part of the clerical

3 Hill, Puritanism and Revolution, ch. 8, Maclear, 'Puritan relations,' and Cosin, Works, II, pp. 17–81
4 Laud, A relation. John Calvin stood aloof from the apocalyptic concerns of other reformers, as did Richard Hooker who blunted at the thrust of the identification of Babylon with Rome in the early 1580s, while Lancelot Andrewes ignored the apocalyptic tradition early in the seventeenth century. Some Arminians followed either Hooker or Andrewes, but others moved into outright opposition. See chapter three above, note 21, Tuveson, Millennium and Utopia, p. 226 n. 1, and Hooker, Of the Laws, I, pp 32, 54, 70. One must not jumble together rejection of apocalyptic thought and of predestination theology with acceptance of episcopal polity, as if they made up a package. Some Laudians took this view, but individuals like John Whitgift and John Goodwin saw no contradiction in holding one of these positions and not the other two.

movement of deriving the institution of episcopacy from apostolic times – the claim of *jure divino*. Of course, Beza and Andrew Melville had done much the same thing in their doctrine of the two kingdoms, but *jure divino* presbyterianism of their sort never gained a strong following in England. Bale, Foxe, Brightman, and others placed a strong stress upon the role of preachers (Foxe even of bishops), but a different tone infused their works. It boiled down to a matter of initiative. In a real sense, the Laudians substituted the 'elect bishop' presiding over a 'godly church' for the 'godly prince' leading his potentially 'elect nation.' This clerically centred interpretation shunted aside the whole impulse of the imperial tradition, considered that of the oppressed as too base to mention, and thereby undermined the thrust of hosts of apologists for the Church of England.[5] In short, the Arminians refused to call the pope antichrist and also appeared to depose the magisterial protectors of the people of the Lord. To contemporaries, these two innovations weakened England's defences against catholicism at the very time when sages prophesied that the last battles would begin! The shock would have been great enough at any time, but acceptance of the chronologies of Napier, Brightman, and Mede strengthened its force.

Many Englishmen grew restive and angry at the uniform enforcement of practices and ceremonies which smelled to them of popery, but not all prepared themselves for internecine spiritual warfare. Some fled abroad to the sanctuary of the Netherlands to pray for change and practise their freedom in faith, as had the earlier separatists.[6] Others sailed off to build a New Jerusalem and a New England on the shores of North America.[7] Still more remained at home, hiding their real thoughts and waiting for the day of deliverance, unless finally forced to escape.[8] A very distinguished historian has said of Laud that 'his primary interest was the attainment of unity and not the pursuit of truth.'[9] His opponents prized truth above unity. A fearless band of the godly – including laymen as well as preachers – launched a relentless campaign to stem the tide of

5 Lamont, *Godly Rule*, p. 67; see Sykes, *Old Priest*, ch. 1–4, and Pearson, *Church and State*

6 See Sprunger, *Learned Doctor*, especially part III, and the works cited therein.

7 See Rutman, *American Puritanism*, and his bibliography for a start on the vast literature of this topic.

8 Thomas Goodwin and Jeremiah Burroughs published licensed works in the 1630s which had an essentially devotional character and contained no hint of their congregationalism; see STC, 4127–30, 12037–44.

9 Jordan, *Religious Toleration*, II, p. 130

what they took to be innovations. Their writings and speeches helped to popularize the dissatisfaction that many of their countrymen felt – felt but dared not breathe. In Parliament, pulpit, and pamphlet the war raged to counteract the Arminian, Laudian, backsliders to Babylon. Parliament fell silent in 1629 to the echo of the Eliot resolution against innovation in the Church of England, passed in the Commons while young aristocrats held down the speaker to prevent an immediate dissolution. Eleven years passed before it met again. A systematic campaign to abolish lectureships and to deprive ministers who refused to conform to the 'new' practices muzzled puritan pulpits.[10] Stricter clerical control stifled the press. Authorities refused to license any works censorious of the aims or practices of the Arminian programme. At the same time, they permitted the printing of books of dubious orthodoxy, as hitherto defined in the Established Church, if written by men who supported Laudian ideals.[11] Of course, their opponents advocated the suppression of Arminian books and clergymen. Cut off from normal means of expression, the upholders of the 'old ways' spread unlicensed works across the land. Laud lashed back with a vicious scourge of punishment for men who repeatedly broke the law. Like many a man of fixed principles (including his leading opponents), he lumped all of his critics together into the same camp and thereby helped them to form a united front.

The most renowned blow fell upon three adopted Londoners who would not be intimidated by threats of imprisonment – Bastwick, Burton, and Prynne. This triumvirate of martyrs helped to mould as well as to symbolize protest against the growth of the Arminian movement.

---

10 Cf. Seaver, *Puritan Lectureships*, ch. 8, Shipps, 'Lay Patronage,' and King, 'Bishop Wren.' King seems to ignore the fact that Wren's one new article was framed deliberately to provoke puritans.

11 Greg, *Some Aspects*, ch. 1 and 3, Siebert, *Freedom*, ch. 5 and 6. Cf. Williams, 'Laudian imprimatur,' and *Index of Dedications*, pp. 237–8, and Bennett, *English Books*, ch. 3 and 8, who challenge the idea of a rigid Laudian censorship. Williams notes that 14 per cent of the licit books published in 1634 and 35 per cent in 1640 bore an imprimatur. Clearly, 1640 was not the year of tightest control by the Laudians. These statistics take no account of those authors who held back controversial works or those who felt compelled to resort to illicit modes of publication. The words of Richard Montague to John Cosin, written in 1624 before either came to power, reflect the attitude of at least one Laudian toward the press: 'Before God it will never be well till we have our Inquisition. Jos[eph] Hall to commend thus! Were it *rei mei juris* he should lose all promotions he hath for it, as he hath licensed it.' Quoted by Lamont, 'Episcopacy,' p. 83 n. 3. In this passage, Montague was attacking Bishop Hall for licensing a book that he found disagreeable; presumably Montague wanted an Index, as well as an Inquisition.

Their cruel and unusual punishment in 1637 was a key catalyst in transforming dislike of the Laudians into hatred and in precipitating resistance to Laud's programme of unity.[12] They became symbols of popular protest against the religious policies of Charles I in the way that ship money became the focus of constitutional opposition in Hampden's case, or that fury against the prayer book in Scotland in St Giles church in Edinburgh led the way to the national covenant in Scotland. Although he did not grasp the full implications of this event, even Laud recognized its crucial importance.[13] Bastwick, Burton, and Prynne were all gentlemen – a doctor, a minister, and a lawyer. Each protested his innocence and bore the loss of his ears and the pain of the stocks with impressive endurance. To many onlookers the pages of Foxe – with their persecuting popish bishops and steadfast martyrs – sprang to life again in these events.

Even before the Star Chamber decree of 1637 increased the regulation of printing in England, vociferous critics of either the Arminian movement or the Established Church found it mandatory to turn to unlicensed printers at home or in the Netherlands to put their works before the public. Prynne and Burton employed English printers of good standing at first; however, after 1636 they had to have their writings published mainly in Amsterdam. The government also took strenuous measures against those who peddled illegal publications. The most famous of these placed his case before the public eye in a series of pamphlets and petitions, in the process learning arts which proved useful when he later became one of the leaders of the Levellers. The young John Lilburne was arrested for having some of Bastwick's pamphlets printed abroad and for smuggling them into England. Cruelly whipped through the streets of London, strapped in the stocks, and finally chained in the most loathsome part of the Fleet prison, Lilburne also became a symbol of popular protest. However, contemporaries paid less attention to him at first than to the more renowned triumvirate.[14] A lesser light in the 1630s, Lilburne

12 A contemporary pamphlet published by the separatist Richt Right press, *A briefe relation*, described their trial and punishment. Cf. Fuller, *Church History*, III, pp. 383–8, Clarendon, *History*, I, pp. 125–6, 264–9, Gardiner, *History*, VIII, pp. 226–34, and Haller, *Rise of Puritanism*, ch. 7

13 Laud, *A speech*, and Wentworth, *Strafforde's Letters*, II, pp. 99–102. This letter which Laud wrote in August 1637 also refers to an earlier unprinted one on the same subject. His speech went through three printings in 1637 alone.

14 Without Lilburne's pamphlets, next to nothing would be known about him or his activities in the 1630s. The only entry in the *Calendar of State Papers, Domestic* which refers to Lilburne is Wharton's petition and it does not do so by name; *CSPD*, 1637–8, p. 569.

none the less provides a key example of the shift made by some radical puritans to separatism in reaction to Laudian uniformity and of the process of that shift.

The apocalyptic tradition constituted a crucial part of the world view through which all of these men scrutinized the politics of church and state. It supplied much of the imagery for the ferocious language with which they flayed the Arminians. It animated the anxiety which made them feel that decisive action was demanded – no matter what the personal costs. It strengthened the martyr complex which lurked within each of them and provided vivid examples of how martyrs behaved. As the frustration of seeming defeat thrust itself upon their bodies and minds, they changed their interpretations of institutions and events. Their language recorded such shifts. These outspoken, irrepressible men made increasingly radical attacks first upon the Arminians and then upon the bishops. Contemporaries recognized the apocalyptic framework and the force of their arguments. Persecution not only promoted their propaganda, it drove them from defence of the Church of England to a call for demolition of its governing structure.[15] Each man moved to the path of dissent at his own pace.

An outspoken defender of the imperial crown of England at this stage in his career, Henry Burton differed from the other members of the triumvirate in having had some personal familiarity with Charles I. Before turning to the pulpit of St Matthew's Friday Street in London in 1625, Burton took an MA at Cambridge in 1602, acted as tutor to two sons of Sir Robert Carey (later created Earl of Monmouth), and served as clerk of the closet to Prince Henry and Prince Charles. When the latter became king in 1625, Burton lost his position at court. Ever since, his detractors have used this incident to explain his alienation from the Arminians. Militant protestantism, however, lay firmly embedded in his Yorkshire soul and any explanation which ignores this fact tells more about the shallowness of those who propound it than about the character of Burton.[16] Although no blood of Marian martyrs flowed in his veins, Burton's mother treasured an English copy of the New Testament preserved by her mother during Queen Mary's times and she

---

15 Notestein and Relf, Commons Debates for 1629, pp. 12–13. The apocalyptic content of the attack upon Arminianism and popery made throughout this Parliament got stated explicitly in this speech.
16 See Fuller, Church History, III, pp. 383–4, Heylyn, A briefe answer, and Cosin, A Collection, pp. xxxvi–vii. For Burton's life and thought, see Burton, A narration, and Hughes, 'Henry Burton.'

encouraged him to read it to the family. Early in his career, Burton wrote a Latin treatise on antichrist for Prince Henry. About the age of thirty (c. 1618), he resolved to enter the ministry. In 1623, before his dismissal from court, the authorities refused to license a book he wrote against Mr Fisher the Jesuit. Burton strongly believed that God had chosen him to defend the Church of England from the intrusion of impurities. Often calling himself a 'watchman of Israel,' he sensed the Lord had endowed him with a 'special *mission*, and *commission* as the prophets had.'[17] This belief gave him the strength and courage to engage his adversaries with tenacity of will, for he knew that reserves of divine support would always uphold him.

Between 1624 and 1639 Burton wrote at least fifteen works. Most of these contained unlicensed assaults upon the Arminians. Only three were of pamphlet length. Brought before the court of High Commission in 1626, the Privy Council in 1627 (for his book *The baiting of the popes bull*), he emerged unscathed and unquenchable. Temporarily suspended from his benefice in 1629 for his book *Babel no Bethel*, he spent a short time in the Fleet prison. When finally charged in the ecclesiastical courts for two sermons preached on 5 November 1636 (later published as *For God and the king*), he refused to countenance the right of clerical courts to try him for that offence and barricaded himself within his house behind a strong, stout door. In February 1637 the authorities finally forced his entrance and led Burton off to the Fleet again. The Star Chamber condemned him in June 1637 to be degraded from office, to lose his ears, and to be imprisoned for life. Only a committed and dedicated man could have ignored the threat of severe punishment so often expressed.

Like Prynne and Bastwick, Burton began his authorship in firm devotion to the imperial tradition of English apocalyptic thought. He dedicated eight of the fourteen works he published during this period to Charles I and two additional ones to the King-in-Parliament.[18] The

17 [Burton], *A replie*, p. 16. In B[urton], *Baiting*, secondary dedication to the duke of Buckingham, Burton first described himself as a 'watchman of Israel,' a title he repeated many times in the following years.

18 Of the sixteen works by Burton published before 1641 which appear in the bibliography below, seven were dedicated to Charles I and two additional ones to the King-in-Parliament. Cf. Williams, *Index of Dedications*, pp. 37–8. Many of these works appeared as by 'H.B., rector of St Matthew's Friday Street' on the title page. Since Burton often signed his name at the end of the epistle to the reader in these works, it would seem pedantic to treat them as anonymous.

image of England's godly prince leading the forces of Christ to final victory over the Roman Babylon blazed through almost all of Burton's early writings. 'The Lord (I say) forever keep our noble king's heart upright to Christ, that ... he may become the royal standard bearer of Christ against antichrist, utterly to demolish that kingdom of the beast, whose throne was so darkened with his royal father's pen.' If only Charles would carry on where his father left off! Even in his most radical expressions of this period, Burton still relied upon established lay power – the crown and Parliament – to purge the Church of England of its iniquities and to exercise primary initiative in the ongoing cosmic struggle. But he feared that Charles, misled by his Arminian advisers, might neglect his momentous role and act as a weak reed in the days of decision.[19]

The culmination of the prophecies of St John rapidly approached and each side was mustering its forces for the showdown. The Almighty had already poured out six of the vials of Revelation, the fourth symbolized by the religious settlement enacted under Elizabeth and the fifth by the 'cloud of witnesses' who wrote against antichrist during the reign of the royal standard bearer James VI and I. When referring to these commentators, Burton waxed rhapsodic: 'Was it a wonder to see so many brave champions marching in the field, bidding battle, and laying battery to the beast's throne, when they had such a royal general, to lead them, as it were, to give the first and bravest onset?' The light ignited by Luther swelled into a powerful sun during the reigns of Elizabeth and James and scorched the papists. If contemporaries would only open their eyes, they would clearly see the pouring of the sixth vial in the Thirty Years War on the continent, the increased activity of the Jesuits in England, and the growth of the Laudian faction in the Established Church.[20] 'Now is *antichrist* come to his full height; he will now adventure his kingdom in one main battle; now is the time in all appearance, for the fulfilling of that prophecy of Revelation xvii ... The preparation unto this war ... is set down in the former chapter upon the *pouring* out of the vial of the 6th

---

19 Burton, *Seven vials*, p. 102, cf. 77, 104, [Burton], *A replie*, sig. c3v, pp. 44, 86–7, Burton, *Censure*, dedication, pp. 127–8, *Baiting*, dedication to Charles I, pp. 21, 50, *Israels fast*, sig. A3–4v, p. 10, *Truths triumph*, dedication, *God and king*, sig. (a) 4r, pp. 40–5, 75–7, 85–7, and *An apology*, dedication. Many of Burton's dedications are unpaginated. Visual representation of Charles I as the imperial leader of the forces of Christ was presented in the woodcut title page of *Baiting*, which carried the tradition of sixteenth-century English anti-papal iconography into a new era.

20 *Seven vials*, p. 77, see 88–9, 95–102, 104, 109–10

angel ... Lo here this fulfilled before our eyes this day; when were there more swarms of Jesuits ... and that, as to be doubted, in *England* where this battle is mainly intended to be fought, then at this day?' Brightman made a mistake – the battle of Armageddon would not centre around Geneva, but in England! The mission of God's elect nation and its anointed head took on overwhelming significance in Burton's mind. The seventh vial, which signified the complete destruction of Babylon, was opened 'but as yet not poured out.'[21] All signs pointed to the imminence of the time of deliverance – the saints would soon triumph over the forces of darkness.

More than ever before, an imperative invited all who wished to help their Saviour to prepare themselves for the holy crusade. God had proclaimed 'a sufficient warning to awaken us out of our sweet slumber, and to buckle on our armour, to defend our religion, country, lives, liberty, the noble England, against this proud *antichrist* and all his confederates.' In the din of the clash of arms, Burton stressed the ultimate importance of the necessity for the Established Church to remain a pure spouse of Christ unspotted by any tarnish of Rome. Hence the 'watchman of Israel' warned Charles and Parliament – repeatedly sounded his alarm so that they might listen – that the Church of England was being transformed by the corruptions of the Arminians. Their odious actions imperilled all England. Burton blasted his trumpet against the Laudians first in 1626, refuting Montague's *Appello Caesarem* in a dialogue in which Orthodoxus (the Elizabethan Anglican tradition) refuted the follies and blasphemies of Babylonius (Roman catholicism), and Asotus (Arminianism). As the Arminians became increasingly powerful within the Established Church and they pushed their policy of uniformity, Burton's anxiety expanded and the breadth and ferocity of his attacks upon them grew in each succeeding work. In 1628 he listed them with the Jesuits among the 'Achans' who were troubling 'Israel.' These *'popish Arminians, or Arminian papists,'* he wrote, 'under the seemly veil and matron-like habit of the *Church of England'* laboured with might 'to bring in that old *Babylonish* strumpet hoodwinked, that we should all reacknowledge her for our mother.'[22] This continued to be the

---

21 *Baiting*, pp. 37–8, *Seven vials*, p. 146, see 132–4

22 *Baiting*, p. 44, *Israels fast*, sig. B 2v, cf. p. 32. For the anger that Montague's book stirred up in Burton, see *A plea*, sig. A 3r. Achan brought punishment upon the children of Israel by hiding a Babylonian garment. In the 1630s he became a symbol of the dangers of the ceremonialism of the Laudians, an image which remained popular well into the 1640s.

basic charge of Burton and his colleagues against the Laudians. They repeatedly asserted that the Arminians endeavoured to bring the Established Church into conformity with Rome – to undermine the reformation.

In the 1620s Burton conceived of himself as being a defender of the Church of England – and in actual fact he was. He referred to the Established Church as 'Israel' or 'Zion' in the works he had published during that decade, not as Laodicea with Brightman. Unlike the radical puritans from the *Admonition* onward, Burton never discussed or even referred to any impurities in the Church of England, except those innovations introduced by the Arminians. He accused the Laudians of turning England's church into the halfway house of Laodicea, 'halting between two with prevaricating feet, having on the *Linsey-Wolsey* garment, neither hot, nor cold, and the like. What have these to do with the great day of God Almighty?' He believed that if they were successful that the Established Church would become lukewarm, not that it already stood in danger of being spewn out of the mouth of the Lord. The perilous position of being undermined from within – of *'destruction by deceit'* – faced the church and land.[23] Like Leighton, but in a far less radical way, Burton became convinced in 1629 that only Parliament commanded enough power to stop the plot of the Arminians to subvert the stronghold of the Almighty.

So little hope is there of curing this creeping gangrene, or fretting cancer, if this sacred senate [that is, Parliament] take not the surer order to prevent their overspeading of the most noble church and state in the world.

For the antichristian apostasy, the Romish synagogue is maintained tooth and nail to be a true visible church ... And it should seem (I crave pardon, if I mistake) as though there were some secret plot ... for the reducing of popery into *England*, or *England* to popery, or at least reconciling us together upon some indifferent terms.

Following his protestant predecessors, Burton justified the reformation break from Rome in apocalyptic terms. The sympathy which the Arminians felt and showed toward catholicism seemed to him and to many

---

23 *Seven vials*, pp. 129, 132, see 63–81, 109–10, *Israels fast*, sig. B 4r, pp. 10, 32, *A tryall*, sig. A 3v–4r, D 3r, F 2r, H, *Truths triumph*, dedication. These publications provide more significant evidence for working out Burton's attitude toward the Church of England at this time than his later claim that he had been a radical from the start; cf. *A narration*, pp. 1–8.

contemporaries to threaten this accepted tradition and the break it symbolized. Burton's belief that those pure pockets of doctrine remaining in the Roman church before the reformation were completely polluted by the Council of Trent heightened his anxiety. No wonder he grasped every means at hand to combat any attempt at reconciliation. He especially opposed the assertion that Rome remained a true church – a proposition never held before by even the most 'vexed' reformed writers – because it made nonsense of the identification of Rome with Babylon.[24] If Rome could not be equated with Babylon, all English reformers had made a mistake, the most important justification worked out for renouncing the papacy proved invalid.

In the years following the dissolution of Parliament in 1629, the Laudians gained control of the government of the Church of England and enforced conformity to their programme. These activities made Burton feel that the time of decision had arrived. On the anniversary of the Gunpowder Plot he returned to the text on the title page of *The baiting of the popes bull* and preached two sermons which baited the governors of the Established Church. At last, events had driven him to a more radical stance and he set out upon the path that would lead him to separation. The Arminian plot to transform the Church of England that he espied earlier, now appeared to him as a re-enactment of the growth of antichrist within the Christian church. Step by step, degree by degree, as apocalyptic writers told of the early church, the Church of England met its betrayal from within. 'And in tracing their footsteps, and gradual proceedings, we shall observe how they have kept the same order, for the re-erecting of the throne of the beast in this our land, which hath been observed by the founders and builders of the spiritual Babylon in former ages ... As of old, the mystery of iniquity could not be produced in one day, but ... was many years a hatching, before it came to any perfection, so our new refounders of popery could not accomplish their work in one day ...'[25] Contemporary readers of this passage knew about the rise of the papal antichrist within the church in the middle ages. To establish his point, therefore, Burton needed only to work out a

24 Burton, *Babel*, dedication, see p. 121: 'Again, what one sound protestant doth say, that the church of Rome is a *true church*? A church some say, but not a *true church*. No not Junius, the most vexed and quoted author about this point.' On this point, also see *Truths triumph*, passim, and *Seven vials*, p. 20. In the latter, Burton referred to the commentaries of Beza, Brightman, Bullinger, Forbes, Foxe, James VI and I, and Whitaker.

25 Burton, *God and king*, pp. 103–5, cf. 32–3

parallel scheme for the Arminian movement and show that it moved in the same direction.

Drawing from the works and actions of individuals who sometimes held differing points of view on issues (when observed objectively), Burton gathered the innovations of the Laudians into a unified programme of eight general points, all of which moved England closer toward Babylon. The innovators had partially accomplished their aim and would soon complete it. The revivers of Rome 'do every day get ground,' he warned, 'and their building goes on a main, with incredible celerity.' Since Arminians held most of the bishoprics in England, Burton felt that 'nothing can now stay them, but they will either break all in pieces or their own necks' and he actively promoted the latter alternative.[26] As early as 1629 Burton showed little faith in contemporary Anglican bishops. Comparing them unfavourably with their martyr predecessors of Mary's reign, he perhaps revealed his true feelings toward the hierarchy. In another work of the same year he began to question any exercise of spiritual primacy by the prelates. His claim that no orthodox books could pass the censor, while Arminian publications faced no hurdle of that sort, formed an implicit critique of episcopal policy, even if it contained a great deal of truth. In 1636 a direct attack upon the actions of the Laudian bishops appeared in his anonymous work, A divine tragedie: 'What havoc is made in our church by sundry of the hierarchy in suspending godly ministers ... against all laws of God and man ...? What could the pope have done more, than some of our prelates have done in this kind, for the darkening of the glory of Christ's kingdom, and for the setting up of antichrist's throne again in this land?'[27] This sounds like old-fashioned radical puritan innuendo. The Arminians acted like the papacy, but they could not yet be identified as antichrists themselves. However, because they suspended divines who refused to countenance the Laudian ceremonies, Burton more than suspected that some bishops would not rest content with transforming

26 Ibid., p. 32, 164; the eight topics appear on pp. 111–66
27 Truths triumph, dedication, Babel, pp. 54–5 (55 misnumbered as 29), A divine tragedie, pp. 32–3 (my emphasis). All evidence points to the composition and publication of A divine tragedie prior to the sermons that Burton preached on 5 November 1636. The secondary dedication of Babel to Francis White, bishop of Ely, contained transparent barbs directed at White, one of the 'orthodox' bishops. In this, Burton was more radical than Prynne who started his attack upon moderate bishops in 1641. However, because of his position at court, Burton was in a position to have known about White's role at the York House conference and, therefore, more likely to have been suspicious.

the Established Church into Laodicea. When these suspicions seemed to gain confirmation during the course of 1636, he reacted with vigour.

The ire of Burton first raged forth against the derivation of episcopacy *jure divino*. Such a justification broke all precedent within the reformed Church of England. It made Anglican bishops identical to 'the pope and his prelates, as all holding by that title, and not from the authority of kings and princes.' By adducing a divine origin for the existing government of the church, Burton argued, members of the hierarchy erred against the proclamation issued by Charles I in 1629 that specifically upheld Elizabethan practice and condemned all innovations. Bastwick and Prynne also cited this proclamation to demonstrate the illegality of *jure divino* pretensions. It offered them an expedient wedge for dissociating the imperial crown of England from those diabolical advisers who acted under the king. Best of all, the proclamation demonstrated that those bishops who enforced new ceremonies constituted the real lawbreakers, not their critics. In fact, the true followers of Christ in England took the lead in resisting Laudian uniformity. By battling Arminian innovations, they not only upheld the law of the land, but they pressed forward the spiritual warfare of the Amighty:

> ... God ... hath not left himself without witness, but hath raised up many zealous and courageous champions of his truth, I mean faithful ministers of his word, who choose rather to lose all they have, than to submit and prostitute themselves to the wicked, unjust, and base commands of usurping antichristian mushrumps [that is, the Laudian bishops] ... Yea, their very not yielding in this battle, is a present victory ... And surely this shall be the certain issue of that main battle, that is now a fighting between the beast, and Christ, between the dragon and the Lamb ... Antichrist with all his ... confederates, for all their malice, power, policies, and machinations ... must all down to the ground, and then it shall not repent those, that have been *faithful unto death, who shall receive a crown of life*.[28]

Resistance to the Laudians formed one of the engagements in the warfare of the latter days. Because the Arminians had captured most of the

---

28 *God and king*, pp. 48, 83–4; the mushrooms represented newly arisen Arminians, men unknown to the Elizabethan church, see Hill, *Antichrist*, p. 70 n. 5. The text of the 'proclamation' against innovation in the church appears in Gardiner, *Constitutional Documents*, pp. 83–99, the relevant passage being on pp. 88–90. Burton correctly argued that Elizabethan bishops derived their calling from the prince, not directly from God.

Anglican bishoprics, they jeopardized the whole Church of England and caused Burton to turn in reaction against the very concept of church hierarchy.

Throughout his sermons of 5 November 1636 Burton revealed his growing alienation from episcopacy as such by criticizing 'the prelates' instead of merely 'some and sundry prelates,' the category employed in the book he published earlier in the year. He began to identify all bishops with the party of Babylon and to view all who resisted Laudian uniformity as the elect of God. Urging the saints to persevere in the paths of the Lord, he condemned those who conformed. Ministers in particular must not dissemble and yield to the 'prevailing power' of the Arminians, for in so doing they would forfeit their rank as officers in the holy army – 'their captain *Christ* will never trust to such captains again.' Christians must obey God rather than man by refusing to 'meddle or partake' with the bishops to the extent of withdrawing from the bishops' 'bondage'–that is, dissociating themselves from all forms of episcopal jurisdiction. The Arminians had pushed their popish plot so far that the English bishops had been transformed into 'the very limbs of the pope, and so our *church* [made] a member of that synagogue of *Rome*.'[29] England was reunited to Babylon! Between 1624 and 1636 Burton moved from being a conforming puritan or an Anglican (if this term can be used to describe those belonging to the concensus tradition of the Church of England under Elizabeth I and James I), to becoming a nascent separatist. It took him several years to realize the full implications of his new position.

In a pamphlet written in prison before his final trial and punishment, Burton continued to rail against his episcopal enemies. He claimed that their actions reached 'The very height of antichristian tyranny, sedition, and rebellion.' Curiously, his speech on the pillory contained little apocalyptic content. While in Lancaster castle he fought to keep alive and had no energy for writing. However, he managed to write several works during his exile on Guernsey – despite being denied pen and paper by the authorities. One of these was his reply to Laud's account of his conference with Fisher the Jesuit.[30] In this work Burton adopted the

29 *God and king*, pp. 32, 99, 69, see 16–17, 66–7
30 *An apology*, p. 30; see *A briefe relation*, pp. 23–9, for his speech on the pillory, and *A narration*, pp. 21–2. Burton's attack on Laud, *A replie*, was completed on 26 June 1639, but not published until 1640 (p. 405). Another work written on Guernsey was [Burton], *Lord bishops*, finished after the calling of the Short Parliament, but before news of the dissolution of that body reached Guernsey (that is, in April or May 1640); *Lord bishops*, dedication, sig. K 4v–L 1, 2v, and Lamont, 'Prynne, Burton,' pp. 103–13. The authorities knew that *A replie* was being printed and, without success, tried to track down the illegal press; see *CSPD*, 1640–1, p. 40.

separatist apocalyptic tradition and paved the way for his later defence of gathered churches. While tasting the pangs of prolonged imprisonment, like John at Patmos, Burton finally joined the ranks of truly radical protest.

The former 'watchman of Israel' now transformed his attack upon the Arminians into a repudiation of episcopacy and of the Church of England. Burton clearly enunciated the first part of his new position in the dedication of his lengthy treatise on Laud's conference: '... All prelates, even as they are prelates, are by their profession and practice, so many *antichrists, adversaries* to CHRIST, who (as the great *antichrist*) sit as gods in the temple of GOD, lording over the faith, soul, and conscience of GOD's people, thrusting CHRIST out of his throne ...' Any differentiation between good and bad bishop disappeared as Burton spoke out against the office and not the men who held it. Like Martin Marprelate, he demanded that the bishops lay down their offices. '*Cast away your rochet and mitre*; divest yourself of all *episcopal ornaments* and *titles*; utterly renounce and relinquish your *hierarchy* ...' Only by abandoning all pretence to rule in the church could prelates justify their claim to ministry. As the '*mystery of iniquity*, which Satan began to brood and hatch even in the apostles' days,' prelacy could not exist in the church of Christ.[31] It constituted one of the marks of the beast of Babylon. Any church ruled by such an evil government clearly stood in grave jeopardy. Burton extended his analysis by condemning the Church of England: '... The *Church of England*, being a prelatical and hierarchical church ... is justly condemned of *antichristianism*.' He went on to demand, with the separatists, that Christians cut themselves off from its communion. A memory of former love for his mother church – his belief that it represented Zion or Israel – flitted through when Burton condemned Laud for corrupting it completely. 'Now before your time,' he upbraided the archbishop, 'the Church of England, though in many things it symbolized *Rome*,' a criticism not found in his earlier works, 'yet still it renounced all *communion* with her, as being ... that *great whore*, whose husband is the *great antichrist*.'[32] All of this had changed, however. Despite the warnings of prophetic voices, the Laudians joined England with Rome.

Partially conscious of the important break he was making, Burton groped toward the implications of his new position. In an earlier work,

---

31 [Burton], *A replie*, sig. B 4v, pp. 32, 53, see sig. B 2v, pp. 61, 107, 289–90, and *Lord bishops*, sig. A 2r, 3v–4, B 4v, E 1, G 4r, K 3v–4

32 *A replie*, pp. 61, 175. Marginal notes attacking the bishops reinforced this opinion; see pp. 88, 102, 144, 189, 203.

he wrote unfavourably about 'the fanatical Brownists and anabaptists ... who renounce society with us' and scourged his Arminian opponents for giving 'too much advantage to such separatists' by bringing in scandalous innovations. Ten years later, however, Burton explicitly repudiated his earlier stand and justified separation in a rhetorical question posed to Laud: 'Hath not then the separatist (as you call him) just cause and ground to charge your *Church of England* with antichristianism, whose *church-government*, and *discipline* is such as the apostles never approved, but expressly reproved and condemned, and practised to the *contrary?*' Of course, Laud used the term separatist to cover a very wide spectrum which included all persons who refused to conform to his programme of uniformity. Burton agreed with this widening of the term. He pointed out that the archbishop branded many 'godly and zealous ministers' with separation and placed in this category 'all good men, whom you hunt after, and prosecute continually in all your courts ...' Laudian persecution drove many puritans out of the Church of England, or out of the country – godly geople who conformed in the more comprehensive days of Elizabeth and James. In addition to the actual separatists, such saints as the preachers patronized by the Earl of Warwick or the non-separating congregationalists who settled in Massachusetts Bay bore the cross of Arminian conformity. Burton sometimes used the designation of separatist with a bit of latitude. However, he differed from most deprived divines by actually accepting separation. He believed that *'England's half reformation* [was] *now made a whole deformation.'*[33]

With his conversion to separatism, Burton came to emphasize the oppressed and persecuted as the instruments of the Almighty and to denigrate the very notion of a national church. The Laudians had totally corrupted the Church of England, but a true church none the less existed *in* England. For Burton, however, the church now became a gathered group of persecuted saints, not a national organization. 'For those that belong to Christ, are a sort of poor snakes despised in the world, and always *persecuted* and *oppressed* by your *hierarchy*, so as they can hardly find so much as a little *corner* anywhere in the *world* ... where they may hide their *heads*, or live in *peace*.' Only the elect remained as the true spouse of the Saviour in England, or anywhere else in the world. Gathered together under the mixed monarchy of congregational polity with Christ as their king, they withdrew themselves from

33 *Babel* (1629), p. 73, and *A replie*, pp. 55, 63, 262 m.n.

any recognition of the Established Church, including parish services and the church courts. Although persecuted for the present, the day of deliverance – when all the powers of the world would prove unable to repress the saints – drew nigh.[34]

Despite the dedication of *A replie to a relation* to Charles I, Burton's faith in the godly prince suffered a serious erosion. Requesting the king to make peace with God in England, he suggested application of the method used in Scotland, 'the calling of a *Parliament* for the redressing and removing of the main cause of the disorders and enormities in the church and state,' the bishops. Burton plainly indicated that he no longer trusted in the unaided strength of the king by warning Archbishop Laud that, 'in putting forth this your book under the king's patronage, you lay a greater *burden* upon his *shoulders*, than he is able to *bear*; and should he undertake it, it would *break* his *back.*'[35] The conditional nature of these ominous words evaporates when one remembers that Burton once served Charles and knew that the king personally patronized men like Laud. After all, Burton was forced to relinquish his post at court to make a place for Richard Neile, the well-known Arminian who eventually rose to the archbishopric of York. In effect, Burton now implicated Charles in the designs of the Laudians and warned him of the consequences. That it took fifteen years of considerable harassment before Burton could issue such a public statement indicates the remarkable strength of his faith in the imperial tradition. By supporting Laud Charles threatened to bring condemnation upon himself. At last, England's monarch no longer looked like the triumphing champion of Christ portrayed in Burton's earlier works.

Drawing from the arguments of Bishop Bilson, Burton cautioned that nobles and commoners could take up arms in defence of their accustomed liberties without the stain of rebellion when the king became a tyrant. By their actions in the 'Bishops' Wars,' the Scots provided Englishmen with an example of the just defence of religion and liberties

---

34 *A replie*, p. 284, see 75–6, 286, 300, 330, sig. A 2v. Warnings about the irrepressible power of the saints appeared in the preface in a consultation between a mother (the true church) and her daughters (faith, hope, charity, etc.). Although Burton often referred to his 'mother Church of England' in earlier works, he gave no indication that he intended that institution here. Cf. Hughes, 'Henry Burton,' pp. 185–96, and Wilson, 'Studies,' p. 230. The former dated Burton's break with the Established Church to 1639, the latter to 1629; neither noticed a major shift in 1636.

35 *A replie* sig. C 4v, p. 2

through arms.[36] Appealing to the lesser magistrates to overrule their superiors if necessary, Burton claimed that 'there is a *necessity* of duty lying upon all *Christian magistrates*, to *exterminate* and *extirpate* the whole *hierarchy* and *prelacy*, as *antichristian enemies of Jesus Christ* ...' If the bishops continued their blind resistance, spiritual warfare would have to be transformed into temporal. Burton sounded a clear warning. Religious strife already raged between the saints and the forces of Babylon. Temporal opposition mounted against the illegalities of the personal rule of Charles I. The situation could easily result in the outbreak of civil war. Burton admonished the authorities, 'maintain not still open war against the spiritual kingdom of *Jesus Christ*, lest he destroy thy temporal' kingdom.[37] In reality, Burton became an advocate of apocalyptic rebellion. If lesser magistrates meeting in Parliament or exercising their power in their local communities refused to do the work of the Lord, the common people would have to grasp the initiative and exercise their right of defence. God would employ the oppressed and persecuted saints to extirpate the powers of darkness. The 'watchman of Israel' transformed himself into a prophet of popular revolt!

Anyone reading only those works published by Burton after he changed his position in 1636 would come to the correct conclusion that he was a religious radical of separatist inclinations. However, he reached this position only in late 1636 – one must not read it back into his earlier works. Burton still displayed dregs of his earlier beliefs, however, in the appeals that he wrote in prison. Even in his most radical publication of the 1630s he continued to praise the bishops martyred in Mary's reign (Cranmer, Latimer, Hooper, and Ridley) and to commend Bishop Jewel, the defender of the Elizabethan settlement.[38] His earlier love for the Established Church still blossomed forth. In this, and in his dampened desire to work through the dominant social orders, Burton remained less radical than a more typical fiery separatist like John Lilburne, who focused full attention on the poor oppressed saints as agents of the Almighty. None the less, Burton's continuous contention

36 *Ibid.*, p. 296, sig. B 2v, C 4v, pp. 86, 87. Burton referred to Bilson, *True difference*, p. 520. An Elizabethan bishop, Bilson wrote to justify the Dutch rebels and, with Ponet, provided a classical argument for rebellion. See Hughes, 'Henry Burton,' pp. 152–71, and Lamont, 'Rise and fall.'
37 *A replie* pp. 302, 87; see *Lord bishops*, sig. K 4v, L 2v. In the latter, Burton outlined an eleven-point programme of protest, thus moving over into political radicalism.
38 *A replie*, pp. 33, 134. This element was absent from *Lord bishops*, his first work of the 1640s.

with the Laudians led him from stalwart support of the Church of England to separatist severance from it.

If Henry Burton began his career of conflict as a man who desired to preserve the comprehensive Church of England which existed before the reign of Charles I, his co-sufferer William Prynne represented almost a perfect type of the conservative, precedent-oriented 'common law mind.' Both launched a quantitative assault upon innovation. Prynne began his authorship in much the same way that Burton started his – by condemning the Arminian faction. Unlike Burton – or Bastwick for that matter – Prynne remained firmly entrenched in his traditionalism in the 1630s and did not join the radicals until 1641. Nor were Prynne's publications as apocalyptic as Burton's books.[39] For all of the belaboured repetition they contained, Burton's works were fluid in style compared to the strings of quotations from vast quantities of historical sources that Prynne tried to pass off as writing. Attempting to correct the foibles of laymen as well as criticizing clerics, the pedantic lawyer, however, ranged more widely in his efforts to create a godly society than did the misconstrued divine.

The youngest of the triumvirate, William Prynne was also the least experienced in the ways of the world. Whereas Bastwick sojourned abroad and Burton served at court for over a decade, Prynne pursued a scholar's career – not a bad introduction at that to the world of polemics. Born in 1600 (the same year as Charles I), he received his BA from Oxford in 1621, continued his education at Lincoln's Inn, and was called to the bar in 1628. While learning the intricacies of the English common law, Prynne brought out his first book – a treatise defending orthodox Calvinist doctrine suitably dedicated to George Abbot, the archbishop of Canterbury. Prynne claimed to uphold 'a principle and ground of that religion, which hath been long established and settled in our church, till some factious and novelizing spirits (if not worse) were so bold and impudent of late for to disturb it.' Supporting the Church of England against new and dangerous doctrines, Prynne admonished Abbot to use his power and suppress the innovations of the Arminians before that nefarious party grew strong enough to wreak havoc in the land. Otherwise they would 'quell, at least ... cloud that glorious truth and gospel' brought by the reformation to England, for they were 'schismatical,

---

39 Prynne's conservatism is stressed by Lamont, *Marginal Prynne*, ch. 1–4, which provides a firm base for my slight additions. For the 'common law mind,' see Pocock, *Ancient Constitution*, ch. 2 and 3.

factious, and antichristian spirits.' If Abbot put down the Arminians before they obtained a more secure foothold in the Church of England, his action would represent a strong step toward 'the subversion of the kingdom of *Satan* and *antichrist*.'[40] By linking the Arminians with the forces of Babylon in his initial work, Prynne pursued a more pungent course than had Burton in his beginnings.

When Parliament met in 1628 Prynne joined Burton in bombarding John Cosin's *A collection of private devotions* – a particularly galling example, to them and others, of Laudian formalism. Whereas Burton dedicated his retort to the Church of England, Prynne took the more political path of devoting his to the House of Commons. Both men believed that enemies at home – infiltrators who 'vent the adulterous drugs and poisonous doctrines of the *whore of Rome* under the veil and colour of DEVOTION' – threatened England's victories abroad, such as those expected by Buckingham at Rhé. Cosin's book seemed doubly dangerous because it pretended to be protestant, but actually came closer to catholic practice than anything else printed in England since the Elizabethan settlement. It embodied one phase of the plot to lead England gradually back to Rome.[41] The discerning could tell this from the first page alone, for 'the frontispiece proclaims the book itself, and him that pen'd it, to be merely popish. It hath the very *mark, and seal of the beast upon its forehead*; therefore, it must needs be his.' Since the church courts failed in their duty to punish such men, Prynne saw no alternative to parliamentary censure of them. To keep England free from apocalyptic anxiety, established authority must discipline such deceivers.[42]

In the same year Prynne also brought forth his first antagonistic assessment of contemporary morals. He feared that God would truly pour out his wrath upon England unless the people repented of their wicked follies. In addition he launched a substantial missile against the

40 Prynne, *Perpetuitie*, dedication (unpaginated), passim. The same theme later appeared in his *God no imposter*. Thomas Fuller called the former a 'useful and orthodox book' in his *Church History*, III, p. 383.
41 Prynne, *A briefe survay*, pp. 2, 39. He also attacked Cosin's book because it gave such undesirable types as '*papists, Brownists, anabaptists, separatists, and nonconformists*' reason to censure the Church of England (p. 82). Prynne knew that Burton had written a book on the same subject and that he too could not obtain a licence to publish it (sig. ¶¶ 1r).
42 *Ibid.*, p. 4, see the dedication and p. 104. Prynne referred to Cosin's use of symbols on the frontispiece, images hitherto adorning only Roman catholic books – especially the IHS which Prynne thought Jesuitical.

Arminians while Parliament remained in session, a treatise which doubled in size at the appearance of its second edition, *Anti-Arminianism*, in the next year. Dedicating this work first to Parliament and second to the archbishops and bishops, Prynne stressed the primacy of laymen in settling religion in the realm as his main theme, for 'such were all the ancient and modern reformers of the church, that ever I could read of.' He had read widely indeed – essentially this book contained a mine of quotations! Prynne entreated all English bishops to follow in the footsteps of their predecessors and '*take courage, zeal, and resolution to yourselves, as some of you to their* honour *have already done) and now rescue us from those Jesuitical, Romish ravening wolves, those Arminian thieves, and wily foxes, who seek to make our church their prey.*' He hoped that the mass of evidence he arraigned would bring the Laudians to see the light and join with orthodox bishops in defence of the light of the gospel. After citing the thirty-nine articles, the Book of Common Prayer, the catechism of Edward VI, selections from official homilies, and some two hundred pages of quotations and references to a host of authors who refuted the Arminians, Prynne concluded that his position represented the mainstream of Anglican thought.[43] Whatever the drawbacks in style for continuous reading, *Anti-Arminianism* provided a storehouse of source material for anyone who wished to argue with the pretensions of the Laudians. As a compilation, it impressed even those who disagreed with Prynne's conclusions.

Prynne argued that maintenance of orthodox doctrine protected England in the past from 'all the policies and powers of hell,' such as the Armada and the Gunpower Plot. Now, however, the 'antichristian complotments of foreign enemies, or domestic *traitors*' began to dismantle this canopy of transcendent security and, thereby, to place all Englishmen in jeopardy. Already the unity of the Established Church began to crack asunder from the pressure applied by these plotters. The popish scheme to capture the Church of England manifested itself in the practice of bowing at the name of Jesus during the service, a ceremony that represented '*the very spawn, the relics of the whore and popes of Rome,*' thought Prynne. He presumed that open revelation of the veiled schemes of the Arminians would render 'their bloody antichristian religion, which hath secretly crept in upon us by degrees, forever execrable to all

---

43 Prynne, *Anti-Arminianism*, sig. A 3r, ¶¶¶ 3v, see p. 271. This was the expanded version of *Church of Englands old antithesis*. Prynne had a great deal of difficulty getting this work published. Also see Prynne, *Unlovelinesse*, p. 104, and *Healthes*; the former attacked current hair styles, the latter the drinking of healths.

English hearts.'[44] As for those who engaged in such nefarious designs, the health of the Established Church would best be served if the authorities severed them from its body 'root and branch' so that no portion of their disease remained to cause future illness.[45]

Despite his blows against the Arminians, Prynne's monumental scourge of stage plays became the vehicle for his first taste of degradation and punishment – and this for one of his few licensed books! He began work on *Histrio-mastix* in 1624, got it approved by the censor in 1630, and finally saw this bulky tome into print in late 1632. The authorities clearly fabricated their charge of libel against Prynne for the things he wrote in this treatise. They tore sentences out of context and twisted them into incredible meanings to attempt to prove Prynne's guilt. One need not be conspiracy-minded to suspect that the animosity of William Laud lay behind the severe sentence passed on Prynne. The pedantic lawyer was stripped of his degrees, deprived of his ears in the pillory, and imprisoned in the Tower. Prynne himself openly blamed the new archbishop of Canterbury, thus beginning in earnest that contest between them which would end with Prynne as the victor under very different circumstances.[46] Henceforth until his release in 1641, Prynne had to smuggle his productions out of prison – he also took the precaution of having them printed anonymously.

Prynne's punishment helped him to feel a kinship with the martyrs of the past and an animosity toward his persecutors. He began to see that the troubles of the Church of England – which multiplied with the extension of Laudian uniformity – stemmed from one source, the haughty, wicked bishops who misgoverned the church. He replied to their actions with fury, denouncing prelates whose pride made them the scourge of the saints throughout history and linking them with the evil which had ruled in the world since the fall of Adam:

There is and hath been from the fall of *Adam*, to this present, a bitter, perpetual, implacable enmity and war, between the old serpent (the devil) and his seed, and Christ the seed of the woman, his church and her seed, the elect and

44 *Anti-Arminianism*, pp. 277, 279, and Prynne, *Lame Giles*, pp. 48, 279, cf. [Prynne], *Certain quaeries*, passim
45 *Ibid.*, sig. B 2r. Prynne applied this 'root and branch' recommendation against the Arminians on numerous occasions.
46 Gardiner, *Proceedings against Prynne*, pp. 1–28, 32–56 (Prynne's letter to Laud of 11 June 1634). For information of the publication of *Histrio-mastix*, see *CSPD*, 1631–3, pp. xx–xxi, 3, 1633–4, pp. 135–6, 188.

regenerate saints of God ... So hath there been between the lordly prelates, their officers, spawn, and generation, and Christ and his true spiritual seed and faithful members, even from their first original, till this present; witness the desperate enmity, the implacable malice, and horrid cruelty of the ancient lordly *Arian* court-bishops towards the orthodox Christians of old; of the popes and popish prelates to the true ministers, professors of the gospel, and protestants; and of the ceremonious, pompous, lordly English lord prelates toward the puritans, and precisions (as they nickname them) the powerful, painful, zealous, godly preachers, ministers, and Christians since; of all which, our books of martyrs, with other ecclesiastical histories, and late treatises give ample testimony, which present experience cannot but subscribe to.[47]

Bad bishops were not symbolic manifestations but living examples of the luciferian pride of antichrist, for Prynne, as he linked them with their horrid colleagues of the past. Proud prelates were and always had been forces of cosmic corruption in the church. Despite such stinging language which gave the impression of being an attack upon episcopacy, Prynne granted that some past and present bishops stood in the ranks of the godly. A strong reluctance to disclaim church hierarchy as such persisted, as Prynne saved up his wrath for those bishops who claimed their office *jure divino*. The domineering presence of these lordly mutations of the species caused untold trouble and disorder in the church: 'what innumerable schisms, treatises (which the undoubted parity of ministers and bishops *jure divino* had prevented) have the prelates' pretended superiority by divine institution, over presbyters and their fellow ministers, produced in all ages, churches, especially in our own (which from the first glimmerings of the gospel in John Wycliffe's days till now, hath been more or less disquieted with this unhappy controversy?) ...'[48] Once again, Prynne applied his general principle to English experience. Turning to the past, he showed that generations of English reformers opposed the *jure divino* derivation of episcopacy. Ministers, doctors of divinity, and bishops – specifically such authorities as Bishops Hooper, Jewel, William Alley, Pilkington, Whitgift, and John Bridges – provided strong support for his argument. In 1636 Prynne's programme was milder than some of his language seemed to imply. It consisted of requesting the bishops to renounce their *jure divino* claims, to recognize explicitly that they received their offices from the king,

---

47 [Prynne], *A looking-glasse*, pp. 31–2; see Lamont, *Marginal Prynne*, p. 69
48 *A looking-glasse* p. 49, see sig. A 2r, and *Unbishoping*, pp. 3–4

and, by these means, to restore peace and unity to England's troubled church. By pointing out that the contrary to 'No Bishop, No King' could come true, Prynne began to move toward that radical position he would adopt in 1641.[49]

Prynne's last works of the 1630s applied violent imagery to some individual bishops and against the Laudians in particular, but his underlying point of view remained essentially the same. He appealed to Charles to use his imperial power for curbing these usurping '*popes of this our lesser world* ... before they grow so headstrong as wholly to usurp your royal diadem,' for the actions and *jure divino* claims of the Laudians moved in that direction. Added to the age-old layman's complaint against clerical power came a new anxiety that the Arminians would attempt to supplant the godly prince as the instrument of the Almighty by the godly bishop. To stop this, Prynne in 1637 took up the old separatist cry that clerics should hold no secular offices: '*Godly emperors were ... far from employing bishops and clergymen in temporal state affairs*'; Charles should put their precedent into effect in England. Far more pressing at this time, however, was the way in which contemporary bishops exercised their jurisdiction in spiritual affairs. The enforcement of Laudian conformity – especially when done through writs which omitted the royal name – confirmed the nature of the Arminian plot. Matthew Wren, bishop of Norwich and one of the most forward Laudians when it came to weeding out puritans and enforcing ceremonial uniformity, appeared to Prynne as 'a plain antichristian pope and tyrant' who persecuted the godly. In the court of High Commission bishops now proved themselves '*as bad or worse than any in the Spanish or Roman Inquisition, from whence they are derived,*' a charge made by the separatists for many years, 'and more exorbitant, than any of our popish bishops' proceedings heretofore against our martyrs, recorded by *Master* Foxe ...' Were bishop Latimer alive again, he would be martyred a second time![50] The situation had degenerated so far that Prynne felt obliged to list the names of the subverters of his 'mother Church of England.' Their next act, he predicted, would be to join England explicitly to Rome. Despite his disgust the obvious anxiety over the theories and actions of the Laudians, Prynne made no assault yet upon the office of bishop. Cantankerous and suspicious of episcopacy

49 *Unbishoping*, pp. 3–4, 20–1, 165, 173 (misnumbered as 165); cf. *A looking-glasse*, pp. 2–3
50 [Prynne], *A breviate*, pp. 14, 66, 84, 159, 41; see *A quench-coale*, pp. 3–4, 35, 61–2, 65, 67, 193

indeed, he held back from joining either Burton and the separatists or those who called for 'root and branch' extirpation of prelacy.

Following the practice of Burton, Prynne dedicated both *A quench-coale* and *A breviate of the prelates intollerable usurpations* to Charles I. Ostensibly Prynne wrote these works to inform his imperial majesty of the true state of the church and kingdom, to open the king's eyes and ears to things which evil courtiers and prelates kept hidden from him. In both books Prynne admonished Charles to take matters into his own hands and make the necessary reforms while time still remained. Unwilling to rely wholly upon the godly prince, however, Prynne believed that the illegalities of the Laudians had grown to be so pressing that 'every faithful subject ... is obliged to resist, to the uttermost of his skill and power,' to overcome these tyrants. To encourage such action he composed a series of instructions to churchwardens, showing them how to counter the illegal visitations of bishops. This handbook proved effective enough to cause consternation to the authorities. Particularly galling to Prynne were the oaths used by some prelates to elicit information: 'These visitation oaths [they use] ... purposely to ensnare men in the bishops' traps, for the advancing of their own usurped antichristian jurisdiction ... no good Christian or subject can or ought to take them, but utterly to withstand and refuse them as illegal ...' In his counsel of passive resistance to the jurisdiction of the hierarchy, the lawyer advocated seditious practices. He and his fellow sufferers exemplified effective modes of opposition in their own actions as well as bloody reminders of the costs that could ensue. Whereas Burton later fantasized a strong speech from the pillory, Prynne actually exhorted onlookers to stand firm in the cause of Christ 'to the shedding of your dearest blood, otherwise you will bring yourselves, and all your posterities into perpetual bondage and slavery.'[51] Antichrist in all his forms must be annihilated. Only the resolute would know the sweet taste of the Lord's victory. All Englishmen shared an involvement in the raging confrontation, but they must take the right side. Liberty and reformation beckoned like precious jewels bought at a great price.

During the 1630s William Prynne never left his espousal of the true traditions of the Established Church. He limited his often pungent

51 *A breviate*, pp. 121, 242, *A briefe relation*, p. 21. A copy of Prynne's handbook is annexed to *A breviate*; it represented an overt appeal over the heads of the political governors of the nation to those of lesser social standing and asked churchwardens to take direct action. For the confiscation of the original printing, see *CSPD*, 1637, pp. 174–5.

attack upon the bishops to their illegal actions and their claim of *jure divino*. While Prynne demanded 'root and branch' removal of the Arminians and displayed a growing scepticism toward prelacy, his language never even suggested real separation from the Church of England, unlike that of Burton. Nor did he share the radical 'root and branch' views of Bastwick. Prynne joined with the other two members of the triumvirate, however, by carrying the fight against the Arminians to the common people and by his example of fortitude in suffering. The common law lawyer even drew up a manual of resistance for churchwardens and thereby increased the effectiveness of popular protest in a practical way.

Although united with his co-sufferers in strategy, John Bastwick differed from them in important ways. Unlike the sober-sided Prynne and Burton – almost caricatures of the common image of puritans – Bastwick's strongly developed sense of irony and humour shone brightly in his colourful prose. He never wrote as many works as the other two – certainly no lengthy English treatises stuffed with quotations came from his pen. A capable stylist in both Latin and English, Bastwick gained fame as a master of the pungent pamphlet. More experienced in the ways of the world and more fluid in his way with words than either Burton or Prynne, Bastwick probably was guilty of the hidden meanings ferreted out of his works by Laud's assistants. Born in Essex in 1593, he spent some time at Cambridge before journeying abroad to expand his experience. After fighting in continental wars as a soldier – apparently in the Dutch army – he went to visit Italy and ended up taking an MD at the University of Padua. He returned to England in 1623 and established a successful medical practice in London. A parishioner in Henry Burton's church, Bastwick took religion seriously enough to pen two Latin tomes, *Elenchus papisticae religionis* and *Flagellum pontificis* (the latter containing an appendix and supplementary epilogue written by Prynne), which ostensibly refuted the claims of the Roman hierarchy but in reality assailed any derivation of episcopacy *jure divino*. When the authorities tried to stop his pen, Bastwick would not be faced down. In 1634 he not only refused to post bond and sureties for good behaviour, but flattered his judges by 'saying he stood before them as Paul before Nero.' Hauled before the High Commission in 1636 for his *Flagellum pontificus*, he became so angry over his treatment that he wrote a third Latin tome, Πραξεις τῶγ επισκπωγ, *sive apoligeticus ad praesules Anglicanos*, which attacked the jurisdiction of that court. For his second work and for radical words reported to the court by a reliable witness, Bastwick received a fine of £1000 and imprisonment to last until he repented.[52] While in prison he heard that further punishment, including the loss of his ears, lay in store for him as a result of his Latin attack upon the High Commission. The radicalism attributed to him by witnesses soon broke into print.

Among the visitors Bastwick entertained in his affliction was John Wharton, an old, much persecuted nonconformist who urged his host to write something in English, 'for the people (saith he) understands not Latin, and therefore can reap no benefit by your labours, neither will you ever be known unto them.' Bastwick responded with the first of his works in the vernacular, the unsubtle humour of which greatly amused Wharton. Manuscript copies were written out for others and soon Bastwick's lodgings became a meeting ground for those who disliked bishops, including the young John Lilburne. By the spring of 1637 several of Bastwick's short polemical pamphlets appeared in print in London.[53] Ironically, by punishing the physician Laud forced him to bring his confrontation with the English hierarchy out into the open – and that in the most effective and popular anti-episcopal parody since Martin Marprelate.

In accord with traditional Anglican thought, John Bastwick held an exalted view of England's imperial crown, claiming that he was resolved 'though left alone, ever to say, LET THE KING LIVE FOREVER.' To him, as to his colleagues, the claim of *jure divino* episcopacy worked to dethrone the godly prince – to fly in the face of that divine right monarchy which buttressed England against papal pretensions. The Arminians 'challenge their authority *jure divino*, and say, that Jesus Christ made them bishops, and the Holy Ghost consecrated them, and that they were before kings, and held the crowns of kings upon their heads,

---

52 *CSPD*, 1634–5, p. 269, see 547–9. There are numerous entries on Bastwick's trial, but these are the most important.
53 Quoted in Haller, *Rise of Puritanism*, p. 252; cf. Bastwick, *Answer to Bancks*, p. 28. Bastwick published four out of a projected seven parts of his 'letany.' From the general format and the peculiarities of typography (especially an elided 'sh' and a 'w' with long points), it is certain that all of Bastwick's vernacular pamphlets from the 1630s came off the same press. So did Bastwick, *Confession*, a work that merely repeated the arguments of his earlier tracts and shall not be discussed. Matthew Symons, Laud's agent who made a trip to the Netherlands to find the presses publishing illegal English books, claimed that Bastwick's pamphlets were printed by James Moxon of Rotterdam, formerly of Delft; *CSPD*, 1637–8, p. 365. They were not published by the Richt Right press or that of J.F. Stam, both of Amsterdam. I would like to thank Dr W. Craig Fergusson for a good deal of help on presses and printing.

and the popes say no more.'[54] By refusing to accept their offices from the crown, the bishops claimed that power used in the middle ages by popes to justify the deposition of kings and emperors. Readers of Foxe would be familiar with this theme – some of the finest woodcuts in the *Actes and monuments* illustrated it. Since it raised those who claimed it above God's true lieutenants on earth, this type of authority was that of antichrist. Bastwick averred that he had not opposed proper bishops who claimed their jurisdiction from the crown in his earlier works. In his pamphlets, however, he ventured on many fronts to make their jurisdiction appear onerous and unnecessary. Contrasting the Anglican hierarchy with the disciples of Christ, he noted the pomp and state of those who claimed to be the successors of the humble apostles – a form of bishop baiting which had a long history. In a long, colourful passage which described a prelate coming down a crowded London street, Bastwick added an apocalyptic sting to his tale. A serving man, pushing people aside, was quoted as saying: 'Sirs, I say you common people, you laymen stand back there, give room for my Lord Bang-whore, stand back I say, you women there a plague of God on you, what make you here among the clergy?' The layman's hatred of clerical pretensions, evident in other parts of Bastwick's pamphlets, sprang back to life in this sort of racy description.[55] Some people who read this passage and others like it obtained the message that only the poor and oppressed could be the true servants of Christ, although that was not what the author intended.

Bastwick focused attention upon the persecuting activities of the Laudians and attempted to link them with the Marian hierarchy. They seemed to him to desire a return to the fires of Smithfield. By examining the actions of bishops throughout the ages, Bastwick came to the conclusion that blood-thirstiness was an inseparable characteristic of the office. Contemporary Anglican prelates proved that they were antichrists by their wholesale deprivation of godly ministers. These Arminians fulfilled the prophecies of the twelfth chapter of Revelation by

54 Bastwick, *Letany* [1], p. 21, *Answer to Bancks*, p. 20, see 1–2, 6, 12, 21, 29; also see Bastwick, *Answer to exceptions* [2], pp. 4, 8, 26–7, *Vanity* [3], pp. 16–8, *A more full answer* [4], p. 3, and *A briefe relation*, p. 9. Although Bastwick's English works had no dedications, he was very fond of quoting and favourably referring to James vi and i, as was Burton.
55 *Letany* [1], p. 7, *A more full answer* [4], pp. 3–4. Besides punning on the bishop of Bangor, Bastwick implied that the hierarchy had carnal relations with the whore of Babylon – that is, that they were papists. Haller discusses Bastwick's prose style and its popular appeal in *Rise of Puritanism*, pp. 256–8. For anti-clerical feeling, cf. [Prynne], *A breviate*, p. 244.

their actions. 'Now *the prelates are the tail of the beast*. And is not this I pray you true, in our horizon? Are not all the good, painful, and laborious preachers silenced by them? Are not all our shining lights smothered by their power and authority?'[56] By bringing the cries of the persecuted and oppressed to life on the pages of his pamphlets, Bastwick presumed that these would finally reach the ears of the king, who would immediately remedy the situation. However, he never went as far as Burton in identifying the oppressed with the elect. He certainly believed that persecutors exemplified *'the very practice of antichrist'* and therefore concluded that the English bishops were 'the very *offspring of antichrist*.' He cried out against the whole government of the Church of England, from its archbishops 'WILLIAM the DRAGON' and the 'ABBEYLUBBER OF YORK' to all the 'bishops, priests and deacons, those little toes of antichrist.' Bastwick launched a 'root and branch' campaign against any form of hierarchy in the offices of the church. He turned to 1 Timothy vi:13 – the classic text cited by all presbyterians and congregationalists to justify their views of church polity – and pointed out that 'it is blasphemy to say, that the word of God laid down no rule of government ... and to prefer antichrist's government before Christ's; and antichrist's service before Christ's service, and antichrist['s] discipline before Christ's discipline; and antichrist's ornaments and pomp before the simplicity of Christ and his apostles.'[57] This passage contains the germ of a whole programme of reform for the Church of England. It extended far beyond mere removal of the hierarchy to include many other aspects of church government and worship. Pushing for a 'full reformation,' Bastwick did not begin his career as a conservative defender of the Established Church like the other two members of the triumvirate.

Bastwick clarified his position in a vehement attack upon the Laudians in which he branded them 'a *generation of vipers*, whose employment is nothing else, but to maintain the *superstition* already retained, to *usher in more*, and popery itself upon the first occasion ...' While sharing the popish plot interpretation of the Laudians put forth by Burton and Prynne, Bastwick started from a different point. The Arminians represented an even greater danger for him because they aggravated a situation already far from perfect – or even acceptable. Any episcopacy came from the forces of darkness and placed the church it

56 *Letany* [1], p. 13, see 5; see *A more full answer* [4], p. 2, and *Answer to Bancks*, p. 22
57 *Answer to exceptions* [2], pp. 10–11, *Vanity* [3], p. 24; see *A more full answer* [4], pp. 4–6

governed in danger. '... The hierarchy is not of God, but of the devil, that is the cause of all disorder and ignorance.' More than an echo of Martin Marprelate sounded in this conclusion. Bastwick, like the separatists, went beyond the bishops to include all English church officers in his condemnation. Anyone ordained by a bishop – as required by law in England – got corrupted by that very act.[58] Later in his life Bastwick claimed that he supported presbyterianism in his early works.[59] He may have stretched the point for his first two Latin works. However, in his English pamphlets a radical 'root and branch' puritan position rang out true and clear – one which matched the style of Martin Marprelate, the ferocity of Leighton.

Although John Bastwick employed arguments similar to those of his fellow sufferers, he differed from them in his attitude toward the Church of England. Never did he describe it with favourable imagery. Never did he join with Burton to call it 'Israel' or 'Zion,' nor with Burton and Prynne to refer to his 'blessed mother Church of England.' The unending citation of predecessors arraigned by Burton and Prynne to prove that they upheld orthodoxy against innovation found no place in Bastwick's pamphlets. In fact, the only occasion on which Bastwick posed as an upholder of traditional English protestant thought came when he contradicted Laud's contention that Rome remained a true church. With a flourish, Bastwick then appealed to the writings of King James VI and I to demonstrate the identification of Rome with Babylon beyond doubt, adding that 'THIS IS ORTHODOX ENGLISH.'[60] Clearly, at the time be began his vernacular authorship and probably before, Bastwick had reached a more radical position toward reformation than had either Burton or Prynne at the same date.

The radical puritan streak in his writings appeared not only in his denigration of episcopacy and in differences of language in general, it received confirmation in Bastwick's attitude toward the Book of Common Prayer. Both Burton and Prynne disavowed the changes made by the Arminians in the prayer book, but neither questioned the validity of the form of worship it prescribed. Bastwick, on the other hand, proscribed the book itself as being 'taken out of the filthy dunghill of Babylon and the abomination of the beast,' that is, as an English translation of the old, unreformed, and therefore corrupt, Latin service. At

58 Answer to exceptions [2], p. 19, Answer to Bancks, pp. 19–20, and Letany [1], p. 9
59 See Lamont, Marginal Prynne, pp. 36–7.
60 Letany [1], p. 20, and Answer to Bancks, p. 20

best, the prayer book bore the mark of Laodicea and therefore deserved rejection. In a subtle deprecation of the English episcopal martyrs of Mary's time, Bastwick pointed out that they had accepted such forms because they lived in an era in which 'darkness universal ... had over-spread the world and especially this kingdom. So they rejoiced at the least beginning of reformation ...' Clouded by popish mists since dispelled by the spread of the light of the gospel, the sixteenth-century reformers could not have established doctrine and practice in a definitive way. Were they still alive, he thought, and able to avail themselves of the light now shining, they would petition the king to exterminate such a corrupt form of worship. Like previous radicals Bastwick judged that the prayer book inculcated evil ways and brought destruction upon those who used it – 'indeed this SERVICE BOOK alone, sends more souls to hell and the devil, than all the profaneness and debauchedness in the kingdom, and more and more upholdeth superstition and popery, than all other policy could ever have done' – an evaluation opposite to that of Prynne.[61] The struggle for reformation remained fiery so long as such baggage of antichrist as the service book and hierarchy continued to corrupt the Church of England. Until the complete removal of these things, Englishmen would continue to labour under the threat of God's judgment.

It is not surprising that Bastwick viewed himself as one of the warriors of Christ in the battle against Satan. In opposing the bishops he nourished high hopes of being 'as formidable to them as ever DRAKE was to the Spaniards.' Drawing upon his martial experience, he held up the living models of himself and old John Wharton to guide his readers in the art of spiritual warfare against the enemy, proclaiming bravely: 'I will stand to; for I am resolved never to leave the field by flying, but to join battle, and fight against the GREAT DRAGON, FATHER ANTICHRIST, and against GOG AND MAGOG, as long as I can stand on my legs.' Since the final battle drew nigh, all men must prepare themselves to stand on the proper side.[62] For all of his spleen and all of his military imagery, Bastwick strongly disclaimed temporal warfare. Properly horrified at any desire to incite rebellion against the king, he drew upon the writings of his beloved James VI and I to denounce insurrection as a viable

---

61 Vanity [3], pp. 6–7. Barrow and Greenwood had used this argument to preserve the sanctity of the bishop martyrs and yet attack their position on reform; John Lilburne would take it up.
62 Letany [1], pp. 13, 12, see 10, 18–19, and Vanity [3], p. 25

solution to England's woes: '... This is a remedy worse than the disease, and more displeasing to God, and dishonourable to the subject; and deserves a greater yoke of servitude; but we must continue our humble petitions to the king and tell his majesty how the matter stands.'[63] Desperately or ironically believing that King Charles, if only informed of the true estate of the realm, would send his evil advisers away, Bastwick explicitly refrained from joining his companions in advocating resistance to established authority.

Implicitly, however, his writings and example promoted such action. He denied the legitimacy of the court of High Commission and argued that its *ex officio* oath stood in opposition to the law of God, the law of nations, the law of the land, and the canon law. He claimed that bishops were worse than devils and implied that even the smallest recognition of their authority polluted an individual. He justified the right of the meanest man to proclaim in public the illegal practices of the prelates. He requested his readers to use his 'Letany' in their daily devotions, to pray '*from plague, pestilence and famine, from bishops, priests, and deacons good Lord deliver us.*'[64] Mocking the prayer book he so detested with this formula, Bastwick created a watchword of protest – one easily memorized and passed on by word of mouth, humorous and devastating, and bound to be popular with all Englishmen rankled by the clerical pretensions of the Laudian movement. Bastwick did not need to advocate resistance in an explicit way. The spiritual warfare he engaged in and the very structure of his language inculcated such action. His apocalyptic imagery underlined the urgency of the cause. His humorously ironic mind must have delighted in the progeny produced by his pamphlets.

Paradoxically, Bastwick, by aiming his tracts directly at a popular audience and arming them with a serious wit akin to that of Martin Marprelate, displayed a more radical approach than either Burton and Prynne. In a real sense, he attacked the Church of England on a far broader front than did Prynne in the 1630s or Burton before 1639. Like other 'root and branch' puritans, Bastwick straddled the thin line which divided the separatists from radical puritans. Although he adopted the separatist identification of episcopacy with antichrist and condemned, by implication, all ministers in the Established Church, Bastwick stop-

---

63 *Answer to exceptions* [2], p. 27
64 *Answer to Bancks*, p.28, *Letany* [1], pp. 3, 9, and *A more full answer* [4], p. 4. The mock prayer or 'letany' first appeared in his *Letany* [1], p. 10, and was repeated in all of the subsequent pamphlets.

ped short of the demand that all Christians withdraw from that institution and gather themselves together into congregations of the elect. He also shared the puritan belief in the viability of a national church – if properly reformed. Like Martin junior, Bastwick took up much of the imagery of the separatists, but in substance he remained a 'root and branch' presbyterian like Leighton and Martin Marprelate, his outspoken predecessors.

Contemporary critics thought that Bastwick, Burton, and Prynne acted as co-conspirators in a unified attack upon the Church of England. Peter Heylyn went so far as to call Burton 'the general *superintendent* of all the churches, the forlorn hope, the sentinel perdue of the whole brotherhood,' but his vicious attacks upon the triumvirate hardly qualify as a judicious source.[65] On the other hand, these three men did quote and borrow from one another's books. Prynne wrote a postscript for one of Bastwick's tomes and Burton probably composed a postscript for Prynne's *A quench-coale*. The three men knew each other personally, Bastwick being one of Burton's parishioners to boot. Bastwick, however, denied explicitly being part of any plot with the other two men just prior to their joint punishment, saying that 'their familiarity hath been ever very little, they having not by the 4 or 5 years together neither seen nor heard one of another ...' With typical puritan casuistry, this statement concealed more than it revealed.[66] In the 1640s they quarrelled vociferously among themselves, but by then the intellectual and political climate had greatly changed. None the less, Burton and Prynne probably carried on more than a casual friendship during the 1630s. Their thought and writing style contained so many similarities that several of Burton's works have been attributed to Prynne. Until the two sermons of 5 November 1636 which marked the public beginning of the shift in Burton's ideas from their Anglican roots toward the congregational way, the thought of these two men had more in common than differences of detail and emphasis might indicate.[67] They shared more than ideas.

65 Heylyn, *A briefe*, sig. b 4r; see Laud, *A speech*, passim, and Dow, *Innovations*, passim. Despite its title, Heylyn's work was neither brief nor moderate.

66 *Answer to Bancks*, p. 5; see [Prynne], *A quench-coale*, pp. 333–55 ('Written by a judicious divine'). This section not only resembles Burton's style, but fits his thought of the time; see pp. 348, 354–5.

67 Burton wrote two anonymous works attributed to Prynne in the stc; *A divine tragedie* (1636) was reprinted as his in 1641 and Lamont has attributed *Lord bishops* (1640) to him. Lamont, however, argued that Burton and Prynne were closer in their ideas in 1640 than ever before or after. Neither he nor Hughes noticed the shift in Burton's interpretation of the Church of England that took place in 1636. Cf. Lamont, 'Prynne, Burton,' p. 111, and Hughes, 'Henry Burton,' ch. 6–7

Either the printer William Jones or the formidable puritan stationer Michael Sparke published almost all of the earlier works of both Burton and Prynne.[68] In 1636, when it became too dangerous to use established English presses, they sent their writings to foreign presses. With some slight exceptions, this process continued until the collapse of Laudian uniformity in late 1640 made it no longer necessary. Prynne, of course, lived in the Tower from 1633 to 1637, but a witness claimed that Burton, presumably before his own arrest in February 1637, often visited the Tower to converse with Prynne.[69] More than talk must have passed between the two men, for most of their works published in 1636 and 1637 came off the same press – that of J.F. Stam in Amsterdam.[70] This was hardly a fortuitous coincidence. The weight of this hitherto unnoticed evidence leads to the conclusion that Burton and Prynne co-operated in a joint attempt to discredit the Laudian régime. The precise involvement of Bastwick cannot be ascertained with the same degree of certitude.[71] One should not leap to the conclusion that the type of conspi-

---

68 *CSPD*, 1628–9, pp. 228, 364, 472, 525, 538, 541, 569, 1629–31, pp. 166, 485, 510, 1631–3, pp. xx–xxi. 3, 35, 39, 321, 426, 524, 1633–4, pp. 135–6, 188, addenda 1625–49, pp. 299–300; see Siebert, *Freedom*, pp. 140–1, 154–5, and Rostenberg, *Literary*, I, pp. 161–202. One can understand the frustration and anger felt by those who tried to stop unlicensed printing when one reads Burton's caustic reply to the High Commission in 1628 or the even more obstreperous answer of Sparke on 5 May 1629. In and out of prison for ten years because of his publishing activities, Sparke was a clever and determined supporter of the anti-Arminian spokesmen. He helped Prynne get *Histrio-mastix* past the nose of the censor. See 1628–9, pp. 364, 538, 1631–3, pp. xx–xxi, 3, 1633–4, pp. 135–6, 188, addenda 1625–49, pp. 299–300.

69 *Historical Manuscripts Commission (HMC)*, 4th report, p. 233

70 Johnson, 'J.F. Stam,' pp. 185–93, lists the following works published by Stam's press in Amsterdam: Burton, *An apology* (1636), *A divine tragedie* (1636), and *God and king* (1636); [Prynne], *Certaine quaeries* (1636), *Lords day* (1636), *Unbishoping* (1636), *A breviate* (1637), *XVI new quaeres* (1637). The second of Burton's and all of Prynne's works appeared anonymously. Stam also printed *A briefe relation*, which described the trial and punishment of the triumvirate. The successor of the separatist press, John Canne's Richt Right press, reprinted both *A briefe relation* and [Prynne], *A quench-coale* (1637). Some connection may have existed between Stam and Canne. Johnson also noted that a London edition of *A divine tragedie* and of *God and king* was printed. Prynne managed to get one of his works, *Instructions to churchwardens*, printed in England during the late 1630s, but the authorities discovered the press and seized all of the copies. Prynne's servant, Nathaniel Wickins, made the arrangements for this and brought to the printers an unusual capital 'c' that Prynne had obtained from Holland; *CSPD*, 1637, pp. 174–5, 543–4.

71 Anthony Marshall claimed that John Bastwick often 'had consultation with Burton at

racy projected by Peter Heylyn existed among these three men. They did not need to write collaborative works, or even consult each other before publishing, to have formed a loose federation for fighting the Arminians. Although the exact nexus binding Bastwick, Burton, and Prynne together still remains hidden, one can say without hesitation that they acted as confederates before being linked together by Laud at their joint trial and punishment.

This triumvirate of putative martyrs provided only the most famous victims of the campaign to suppress unlicensed attacks on the Arminians. Alexander Leighton lay in prison, forgotten by most and remembered mainly by those who feared him.[72] From the relative safety of the Netherlands, others continued to publish pamphlets and treatises critical of the Church of England or of its hierarchy, to smuggle these back into the realm, and to spread them across the countryside through networks of distributors. As the authorities grew fearful, the risks of such operations increased. In May 1637 William Hawkins, the London agent of the Earl of Leicester, reported that 'Many pamphlets and angry books are daily dispersed, which are not to be seen with safety.' Later in that same year, however, two clerical clients of the Earl of Warwick, William Greenhill and Jeremiah Burroughs, smuggled 'several barrel loads of seditious books into England' from the Netherlands. Disguising themselves as 'soldiers returning from the battle for Breda,' they landed their goods in East Anglia.[73] Although the evidence is very obscure, complicated, and open to various interpretations, a systematic study of the press campaign against the Laudians during the late 1620s and the 1630s would form an important contribution toward our understanding of the growth of opposition to the government of Charles I. Only occasionally do the printed sources yield information on the lesser men

his house in Friday street about printing' his works, Πραξεις and *Newes from Ipswich* [*sic*]. Unable to attribute White [pseudonym], *Newes*, I see no compelling reason why it could not have come from East Anglia. Bastwick's 'letany' tracts were not printed on any of the presses used by Burton and Prynne. In 1634, however, Burton preached 'a seditious sermon' for Bastwick's brother-in-law, Thomas Cotton, at Cotton's private church and another sermon in nearby Colchester on the same visit; *CSPD*, 1634–5, pp. 252–3.

72 Leighton never became a popular hero like Bastwick, Burton, and Prynne. Although one newsletter of 1637 reported that 'the common people are extremely compassionate toward them,' the same was never noted of Leighton; *CSPD*, 1637, p. 311.

73 *HMC*, De L'Isle and Dudley, VI, p. 108, Shipps, 'Lay Patronage,' p. 178; cf. the publications of the Richt Right press listed by Wilson, 'John Canne,' pp. 34–48

involved in this type of activity.[74] One of these men, however, although cruelly punished by the authorities as an example, fought back by producing pamphlets and petitions and, thereby, brought his case before the public. As a young apprentice in London, John Lilburne refused to remain silent and to fall back into the obscurity from which he sprang.

The pamphlets in which Lilburne argued the justice of his case provide an extended insight into the trade in illegal pamphlets and they also show how young puritans of his type, driven by Laudian uniformity, took the plunge into separatism. The son of a minor Durham gentleman of ancient family, John Lilburne was apprenticed to a London merchant – a not uncommon means of providing for younger sons at this time. He remained sensitively aware of the social status of his birth, something that set him apart from many other London apprentices.[75] During these formative years Lilburne often listened to the sermons of the puritan preachers who adorned the pulpits of London. He also vociferously devoured their writings. His visits to Dr Bastwick in prison made him a marked man in the eyes of the authorities. Their inquiries forced him to leave his master in June or July 1637, probably after the public punishment of Bastwick, Burton, and Prynne. Seeking both to establish himself and to help the cause of the Lord, he sailed off to the Netherlands to become involved in the trade in unlicensed books. Before leaving England, he probably made some sort of business arrangement with old John Wharton, the man who had encouraged Bastwick to write pamphlets in the vernacular.[76] During his stay abroad, Lilburne proba-

74 At the trial of the triumvirate sixteen other persons were cited as accessories to the publication and distribution of their unlicensed works. A search of the CSPD for the years 1628–41 yielded further information on four of these printers, booksellers, and distributors. Only one of them, Edmund Chillington or Chillenden, emerges from the shadows. An apprentice and sectary, Chillington became an agitator in the New Model Army, a captain, and a fifth monarchist. In the 1630s he probably smuggled illegal publications into the country as well as distributing them. Arrested for peddling copies of Newes from Ipswich, his evidence led to the arrest of John Lilburne in late 1637. See CSPD, 1635–6, p. 49, 1636–7, pp. 427, 487, 1640, p. 148, Capp, Fifth Monarchy, p. 245, and note 78 below.

75 Lilburne, A worke, pp. 20–1, Christian mans, pp. 1–2, 7, Coppy and Apprentizes in Innocency and truth, pp. 4–5 and unpaginated respectively. Lilburne wore a sword – that mark of gentle status – at the time of his arrest, gloves when called before the Star Chamber, and employed a physician to treat the wounds which resulted from his whipping. See Gregg, Free-born John, ch. 1–6, Haller, Rise of Puritanism, ch. 7, Robertson, Religious Foundations, ch. 2, and appendix 1 below.

76 An eighty-five-year-old bookseller, Wharton had appeared before the High Commission seven or eight times for dealing in unlicensed works. He may well have arranged

bly attended his first separatist service in one of the Amsterdam exile congregations. He must have established contact with the Richt Right press as well.[77] Lilburne's activities in the Netherlands coincided with those of Matthew Symmons, an agent sent over by Laud to collect information on the printing of unlicensed English works. When Lilburne returned to England near the end of 1637, he was arrested and imprisoned for smuggling illegal pamphlets into the country. The authorities obtained information on his operation and whereabouts from John Chilliburne, a servant of Wharton, and Edmund Chillington (or Chillenden), a former book smuggler who turned state's witness to make his own punishment lighter. At this time, Chillington plied the trade of button seller and lived near Wharton's house.[78] Too many nets had been set for Lilburne to escape. According to Lilburne's account of his own trial, the archbishop of Canterbury took great delight in capturing Lilburne and Wharton: 'Well my lords, said the great prelate, this fellow (meaning me) hath been one of the notoriousest disperser[s] of libellous books that is in the kingdom, and that is the father of them all (pointing to old Mr. Wharton).' Although the web of Lilburne's testimony about his printing activities is impossible to untangle, Laud may have been correct in his assessment! If Lilburne did, in fact, arrange for the publication of the works he was accused of smuggling, he would have had to contact at least two presses in the Netherlands, that of J.F. Stam in Amsterdam and that which published Bastwick's pamphlets. If the presses of J.F. Stam

---

for the publication of the works of Burton and Prynne in Amsterdam – certainly he talked Bastwick into writing in English and probably got his pamphlets published. Probably a separatist, Wharton was arrested this time for contracting with Lilburne to publish Prynne's *A breviate* and *XVI new quaeres*, both of which were printed by J.F. Stam of Amsterdam. *CSPD*, 1637–8, p. 2, Lilburne, *A worke*, pp. 4, 11, *Christian mans*, pp. 2, 10, 14–16

77 Lilburne, *An answer*, p. 23, asserts that he heard only one separatist sermon before his arrest. The Richt Right press printed all three of Lilburne's pamphlets which survive in editions from the 1630s. *A briefe relation*, which Lilburne may have compiled, was printed by J.F. Stam and by the Richt Right press. The epilogue of this work reads like Lilburne and the body of the text consists of a style of reporter martyrology similar to his acknowledged works. If Lilburne left London shortly after the punishment of the triumvirate, as seems probable, it would explain why no account of their triumphant departures appeared in this pamphlet.

78 Lilburne, *Christian mans*, passim, and *A worke*, pp. 10–11; see note 74 above and Haller, *Rise of Puritanism*, pp. 272–8. Symmons' report is summarized in *CSPD*, 1637–8, pp. 365–6.

and John Canne were actually different establishments, a third press would have to be added.[79] A real conspiratorial network existed.

Before their public punishment, Wharton and Lilburne shared a chamber in the Fleet prison. The young man later confessed that he learned much from the ancient enemy of episcopacy. Wharton probably nursed the seeds of separation planted in Lilburne's mind. The first fruits ripened under the lash while Lilburne was being whipped for more than a mile on his bloody journey from the Fleet to Westminster. Because the Lord strengthened him to bear such pain and agony with no outward show of suffering, Lilburne's punishment confirmed him in the assurance of his election: 'And this I counted my wedding day in which I was married to the Lord Jesus Christ; for now I know he loves me in that he bestowed so rich apparel this day upon me, and counted me worthy to suffer for his sake.'[80] As all of his works testify, Lilburne's soul was ravished by his spiritual experiences at his punishment and in prison afterward. Henceforth, he turned his back upon his puritan past, repudiated the Church of England, and found comfort in the experiential religion of the spirit.[81] Separatists gained from the polarization of religious opinion in England created by the Laudians. A movement of many branches because of its underground and congregational nature, it picked up adherents in the 1620s and 1630s, a portent of the explosion of sects in the 1640s. Lilburne provides a graphic illustration of this trend.[82] If Henry Burton became slowly transformed into a separatist – as it were,

79 *Christian mans*, p. 8. If Lilburne arranged for the publication of the works he was accused of smuggling, he would have had to contact at least two presses in the Netherlands. Accused of desiring to print *The unmasking of the mystery of iniquity*, he replied that he could not get a true copy of it. This probably was Burton's *The baiting of the popes bull, or an unmasking of the mystery of iniquity*, originally printed in 1627. I have found no other contemporary work with this title.

80 Lilburne, *A worke*, p. 8, see 4, and *Christian mans*, pp. 14–16. For similar imagery, see the speeches of Burton at his punishment in *A briefe relation*, pp. 23–9, and Burton, *A narration*, pp. 13, 25, 34–7.

81 Haller, *Rise of Puritanism*, pp. 272–87, and Robertson, *Religious Foundations*, ch. 2, deal with Lilburne's separatism. From the time of Henry Barrow onward, separatists laid a strong emphasis upon the Holy Spirit working within the believer, giving him an experienced assurance of his election.

82 See Haller, *Rise of Puritanism*, ch. 5 and 7, Jordan, *Religious Toleration*, II, pp. 223–31, and Huehns, *Antinomianism*, ch. 1–2. Prynne blamed the Arminians for promoting separatism as well as popery by their actions and ideas; *A briefe survay*, p. 82, *A breviate*, p. 122, and *A quench-coale*, pp. 35–7. Adding that Laudian uniformity obviously represented the triumph of antichrist within the Established Church, John Canne urged puritans to follow their ideas to a 'logical conclusion' and separate from the Church of England; *Necessitie* (1634) and *A stay* (1639), both printed by his Richt Right press. Burton accepted this argument by 1639.

against his will – John Lilburne, with zealous flamboyance, took to their doctrines and their apocalyptic vision with astounding agility and speed.

On his way to the pillory, Henry Burton stopped to tell a friend that 'I shall this day preach down antichrist in the pillory,' or so he later claimed. If the account in *A briefe relation* is accurate, and we have no good reason for doubting its veracity, Burton did not keep his promise. When arriving at the same place after a longer and more painful walk, John Lilburne harangued his persecutors as antichrists until they stopped his first speech to the people by gagging his mouth. In the typical style of his new-found position, he sought to demonstrate that the English hierarchy formed a segment of the forces of cosmic evil. His listeners need not take his word alone for this; they could find verification in their Bibles:

But my brethren, for your satisfaction read the 9 and 13. *chapters* of the *Revelation*, and there you shall see, that there came *locust[s]* out of the *bottomless pit*, part of whom they [the English prelates] are, and they are lively described. Also you shall there find, that the *beast* (which is the *pope*, or Roman state and government) hath given to him by the *dragon* (the *devil*) his power ... so that the *pope's* authority comes from the devil, and the prelates and their creatures do challenge their authority, jurisdiction, and power ... is from Rome.

Lilburne arrived at an inescapable conclusion. If the English hierarchy – in its own books – derived its power through the pope, and the pope obtained his from the devil, Anglican bishops also received their calling from Satan. The bishops ordained and licensed all preachers in the Established Church and thereby infected them. The Church of England, therefore, formed part of the false church. Like all separatists, Lilburne advised his listeners, and later his readers, to 'withdraw yourselves from that antichristian power and slavery that you are now under, even as God himself hath commanded and enjoined you in Revelation xvii:4.'[83] Old John Wharton, who stood in the neighbouring pillory, must have wondered if he listened to Henry Barrow resurrected!

In his speech, his actions, and his writings, John Lilburne acted like a soldier of Christ who was fighting the good fight against the nefarious power of antichrist in England. He shouted to the crowds around the pillory:

Oh repent ... and for the time to come, put on courageous resolutions like valiant

83 Burton, *A narration*, p. 13, Lilburne, *A worke*, p. 18, see 14–17

soldiers of *Jesus Christ*, and fight manfully in this his spiritual battle, in which some of his soldiers have already lost part of their blood, and withall; study this book of *Revelation*, and there you shall find the mystery of iniquity fully unfolded and explained; and also you shall see what great spiritual battles have been fought betwixt the lamb and his servants, and the *dragon* (the *devil*) and his vassals, and some are yet to fight.

Like the martyrs of old, Lilburne stood in the fore of the raging strife and tried to rally troops around him. Although he often referred to the Book of Revelation, his apocalyptic vision had other roots as well. He was steeped in the important popular writings of the past. Having read 'a great part of the Book of *Martyrs*,' he knew how to interpret the prophecies of St John by applying them to the history of the church. In the stories of young apprentices like William Hunter, he found one sort of model for his actions – another came from contemporaries like Bastwick, Burton, and Prynne who had 'already lost part of their blood' in the struggle.[84] And Lilburne's martyrs also included separatist saints like Henry Barrow and John Greenwood, who were among 'those famous worthies and martyrs in Queen *Elizabeth's* time, who for the point of total separation from the antichristian Church ... of England, lost their lives ...'[85] Lilburne not only extended Foxe's list in time, he also questioned the veracity of the beliefs of some of Foxe's martyrs. Like Barrow and Bastwick, he explained away the shortcomings of the bishop martyrs of Mary's reign by means of a theory of the progressive unfolding of religious light. They lived during the dawning of the first full light of the gospel. With their eyes still partially blinded by the darkness of popery, they could not possibly have arrived at the full truth. Hence, he could attack some of the beliefs of these men and still keep them as heroes of the faith. The pages of Foxe continued to influence Lilburne, but separatists made up his true galaxy of saints.

Firmly convinced of the imminence of the end, Lilburne stressed the need for each person to act soon or else lose all hope of obtaining salvation. Abundant signs pointed to the fact that the spiritual warfare of the saints and the brats of Babylon drew to a close. The fifth trumpet had sounded, blasting out its warning for all who would merely open their eyes to see. The third angel had proclaimed in a loud voice that Babylon was falling. As Burton had prophesied, the Almighty presently

---

84 Lilburne, *A worke*, p. 18, *The poore*, p. 5
85 Lilburne, *Coppy*, p. 14; see *An answer*, pp. 33–4

was pouring out the sixth vial of his wrath.[86] With the end rapidly approaching, the vassals of antichrist – trying to shore up their tottering tower of Babel – increased their persecution of the saints. Despite the worldly might of Babylon, it would fall soon to the hosts of the Lord. God now turned to the same type of instruments as those who gathered around Christ during his life on earth – the ignorant, the poor, the persecuted, and the oppressed. Again he employed things 'which are not, to bring to nought things that are ... he by the least instrument is able to bring to pass the greatest things.' Lilburne showed little faith in the godly prince and thought the very concept of 'godly bishop' anathema. People of rank and quality, of established social and political power, almost always fought for evil.[87] He paid allegiance to Charles as his secular ruler, but left the imperial tradition far behind. To him, the idea of an elect nation or of a national church contravened the teachings of Christ.[88] Lilburne parted company with Bastwick, Burton, and Prynne on these points – not one of his works contained an appeal to Charles I to reform the church! Lilburne firmly differentiated between secular and spiritual. Far more alienated from society than the triumvirate, he placed himself in that company of 'fools, idiots, base and contemptible poor men and women in the esteem of the world' whom the Lord elected to usher in the culmination of providential history, the separatists. The very frailty of these instruments would ensure that all the glory of their accomplishments would go to magnify the Almighty. Leaving his family behind, Lilburne buckled on his armour and marched off in the company of gathered saints to confound the mighty and to build Zion.[89]

Lilburne's espousal of the principal points of the separatist position does not seem to tally with his claim that he had little contact with them before his trial and punishment. Both Robertson and Haller doubt the veracity of his claim. They base their scepticism upon the fact that

86 Lilburne, *Come out*, pp. 15–16, *An answer*, p. 34, and *Coppy*, p. 16. Cf. Bastwick, *Vanity* [3], pp. 13–14. According to Napier, the third angel would start to thunder in 1639 and continue to 1688 when the fourth angel (Christ) would return to gather up his saints.

87 Lilburne, *A worke*, p. 19; see *Come out*, p. 20, *Coppy*, pp. 14–15. Even the publisher of Lilburne's pamphlets exhibited more confidence in the godly prince; see *The poore*, pp. 6 m.n. (b), 12 m.n. (b).

88 *Come out*, p. 4, *An answer*, pp. 15–16, 24, 33, 37–8

89 *Coppy*, p. 14, cf. 3; see *Christian mans*, pp. 6–7, *A worke*, pp. 19, 21, 24, and *Come out*, p. 34. Like many separatists, Lilburne fit into the pattern of familial behaviour posed by Walzer, *Revolution*, ch. 5. Of course, his family deserted him first.

three of his early works display a full knowledge of the separatist programme. In these writings, he refuted puritan objections to separation
and encouraged repudiation of the Established Church. Separatist
apocalyptic images also form the basis for the titles of two of his early
pamphlets.[90] However, Lilburne probably told the truth. All of the
knowledge of the separatist position displayed in his early works could
have been obtained from the sources listed in these same pamphlets.[91]
Add to them the sermon he heard before being arrested and his conversa-
tions with Wharton in prison and we probably have the sum total of the
separatist sources of Lilburne's early thought. He did not compose the
titles of his first three pamphlets – John Canne, his publisher, or someone
else at the Richt Right press did this, for Lilburne showed his ignorance
of these titles. The prefaces of all of Lilburne's early tracts and the
marginal notes of *The poore mans cry* reveal that his editor, most
probably Canne, was a mature separatist full of apocalyptic expectations.[92]

90 *Coppy*, pp. 15–16, *An answer*, p. 23, *A cry* in *A picture*, p. 23; see Haller, *Rise of Puritanism*, pp. 275–6, and Robertson, *Religious Foundations*, p. 25. *A worke* attri-buted Lilburne's punishment to the beast of Revelation, while *Come out* admonished readers to separate themselves from the whore of Babylon – that is, the Church of England. *Come out*, *Coppy*, and *An answer* were specifically separatist polemics.

91 The following sources include all of the information needed to provide Lilburne with the separatist ideas that he put forward in his early works. Internal evidence shows that he consulted the works listed: (1) Henry Barrow, *First part of the platform* (1611) – see *Coppy*, pp. 14–15. Since this pamphlet was never reprinted, Lilburne probably got a copy of it from Wharton. (2) *A licht for the ignorant* (1638) – see *An answer*, p. 29, and – under its subtitle – *The poore*, p. 14. Printed by the Richt Right press, this tract presented a masterly, simplified version of the separatist point of view in a highly apocalyptic manner. It was reprinted in 1641 with a portrait of Lilburne by W. Hollar as the frontispiece. (3) Bastwick's pamphlets – see *Christian mans*, pp. 2, 7, 9, 10, *A worke*, pp. 12, 14–16, 26–7, and *Come out*, pp. 13, 33. (4) *The beast is wounded or information from Scotland* – see *The poore*, p. 14, *Come out*, p. 13, and *An answer*, p. 25. This may have been *The Scots dispute*; I was unable to find a contemporary pamphlet with a more similar title. The marginal notes of this publication of the Richt Right press, being full of apocalyptic imagery, resemble those of Lilburne's *The poore* in content. (5) Lilburne heard one separatist sermon, probably in the Netherlands – see *An answer*, p. 23. (6) He conversed extensively with Wharton who most likely was a separatist and who probably supplied Lilburne with separatist works to read.

92 In the spring of 1639 Lilburne knew that three of his pamphlets had been printed; however, he could not have seen them since he gave them the wrong titles; *A cry*, p. 22. *Christian mans*, *A worke*, and *The poore* were those in print; so was *Come out*, but Lilburne wrote it as a letter and did not know that it had been turned into a pamphlet. It seems safe to assume that the publisher entitled all of these tracts.

The experience of his punishment and the short pamphlet *A licht for the ignorant* played a more important part in making John Lilburne into a separatist, and thereby in precipitating his ideas, than all but two other books which he read, the Bible and Foxe's *Actes and monuments*. His quick conversion exemplified the effectiveness of separatist propaganda and the religious polarization which became increasingly characteristic of England in the 1630s. This religious polarization preceded that in the political realm and helped to turn disagreement into confrontation and conflict. Lilburne provides a model of those who, having little formal education, none the less studiously read puritan treatises and tracts and seriously listened to puritan sermons. Like many of his contemporaries, he had deeply imbibed the English protestant apocalyptic tradition from the works of Foxe and others. But when put under the pressure of persecution, Lilburne deserted Foxe's imperial interpretation for a separatist vision which seemed more relevant to his situation.[93] He threw himself into the covenanted army of God's oppressed and persecuted saints with abandon just as he would later command his troop of dragoons in Lord Brooke's regiment with the same spirit.

Lilburne's identification of the Church of England with Babylon and his actions in the Star Chamber had political as well as religious ramifications. When he demanded that all Christians withdraw from the Established Church, refuse even to listen to its preachers, withhold payment of tithes, and reject the jurisdiction of the church courts, he followed a well-worn trail of separatist civil disobedience that stretched back at least as far as to Henry Barrow. By refusing to take the *ex officio* oath of the Star Chamber, however, Lilburne broke new ground. For years religious radicals had refused the *ex officio* oath of the High Commission, but they carefully dissociated it from that of the Star Chamber. Lilburne defended his action by turning Nicholas Fuller's classic arguments against the Star Chamber oath, thus breaking a long-standing taboo. He added to it by asserting that this *ex officio* oath

---

93 Haller, *Rise of Puritanism*, p. 274, and Robertson, *Religious Foundations*, appendix, pp. 125–32, list the sources of Lilburne's thought, but both overlook the publications of the Richt Right press stressed in this account. The ease of Lilburne's full-scale conversion to separation stands as a tribute to the effectiveness of separatist popular propaganda, of works like *A licht* and *A guide unto Sion*. The latter gave a brief outline of the positive programme of the separatists. Reading and believing in these two pamphlets, any literate person could become an 'instant separatist' fully capably of defending his beliefs.

was 'expressly against the Petition of Right.' Even Nathaniel Wickins, a servant of Prynne imprisoned for printing and distributing illegal pamphlets, expressed shock! Wickins retained the normal distinction between the *ex officio* oath of the High Commission and that of the Star Chamber – that is, that the former broke the law of God, nature, nations, and the common and canon laws, while the latter did not.[94] It took revolutionary zeal to apply arguments designed to attack the church courts against the judicial procedure of the Privy Council. Lilburne also blamed the Lord Keeper and Laud for his unjust punishment – not just the ecclesiastical authorities, as had Burton and Prynne. For a mind which rigidly compartmentalized religious and secular power and for a man who continually claimed that he would never disobey his prince, such steps were radical indeed. Despite all of his pretence of fighting only spiritual battles, Lilburne fundamentally dissented from aspects of purely civil government when they affected his well-being.[95] He had already transformed his religious radicalism into political radicalism.

The early thought of Lilburne took place within a highly apocalyptic, but not yet millenarian, framework. He had not yet integrated civil authority into this vision, however. The kingdom of antichrist included the Church of England, but not the government of Charles I. When he rejected the godly prince as God's instrument and joined himself to the oppressed and persecuted, Lilburne potentially became a social radical. Already radical in his religion, he rejected the very concept of a national church and worked outside official channels to abolish the Established Church. By 1645 Lilburne had developed into a political and social revolutionary. He also had joined the ranks of the millenarians and longingly awaited the day when King Jesus would return to rule the earth with his saints for a thousand years. By that time, the godly had started to revenge themselves upon the persecuting of Charles I by dashing his power in pieces. In Lilburne's mind, the civil government of Charles I and of the English monarchs who preceded him formed part of the host of antichrist. Monarchy, as such, must be destroyed. Sometime

94 Lilburne, *A worke*, pp. 12–13, Wickins, *Wood-street*, p. 31; see *Come out*, passim, Fuller, *The argument of*, and Hill, *Society and Puritanism*, ch. 9. Since Wharton also refused the Star Chamber oath at the same time as Lilburne, one cannot know exactly which one of them made the ideological breakthrough.

95 Lilburne, *Apprentizes* (unpaginated), and *A cry*, p. 24. In the first he correctly referred to Conventry as Lord Keeper, while in the second he gave this office to old Sir Henry Vane. Cf. *A worke*, p. 19, and *Come out*, pp. 14–15, where Lilburne stated that he would submit to temporal authorities because their calling, unlike that of the bishops, came directly from God.

between 1640 and 1645 Lilburne came to apply his apocalyptic vision to secular power with revolutionary consequences. Unfortunately, only one bit of evidence survives from this crucial period of his development, a letter from his captivity at Oxford, and it gives no hint of the change taking place in his thought.[96] Unless Lilburne proves an exception, however, he probably took up millenarianism and turned it against the royal antichrist sometime after the outbreak of civil war in England in 1642.

The pages of Foxe came to life again as the great tragedians turned the pillory platform into both a stage and a pulpit and, through the noble demeanour with which they bore their cruel punishments and degrading stance, well won the applause that they received. By pitching their appeals to the level of the crowds who came to watch, they followed the technique of the martyrs of Mary's reign and gained the sympathy and support of the curious both for their cause and for themselves. The committed already stood on their side. More than ten years later a royal martyr would repeat the same stage manner when faced with a more severe sentence. Such behaviour deeply impressed contemporaries. Bastwick, Burton, and Prynne became public heroes. The story of their sufferings and of their defence spread through the countryside in newsletters. A more lengthy report appeared in pamphlet form to augment the first brief notices.[97] Lilburne played his role to the hilt as well and became his own publicist, but his great popularity with the people lay in the future. Thronged by crowds as the authorities moved them out of London, the triumvirate also received homage in country towns and cities as they moved off to their isolated prisons. As we shall see, they would receive even more exalted expressions of popularity when they returned to London after years of exile.

Bastwick, Burton, and Prynne transformed themselves into important symbols of protest against the oppressive nature of the Laudian régime. All three united to condemn the Arminians by identifying them with the ranks of antichrist. By linking their confrontation of the Laudian bishops with the cosmic warfare raging in the world, the triumvirate charged their cause with transcendent significance. The Arminian programme created a collective identity crisis – if one can talk of such things – among English protestants by challenging those symbols by

96 Lilburne, *A letter to Prinne* and *A letter sent*; cf. Gregg, *Free-born John*, ch. 8–10
97 *CSPD*, 1637, pp. 252, 287, 311, cf. 332, 433–4, 492. Even William Hawkins, no sympathizer to their cause, was impressed by the undaunted way in which the triumvirate bore their sufferings; *HMC* De L'Isle and Dudley, VI, pp. 87, 105, 114–15.

which the Church of England had been differentiated from other forms of Christianity in the popular mind – and especially from Rome. In identifying this challenge and pointing out its consequences, Burton and Prynne (and Bastwick to a lesser degree) truly upheld the traditional doctrine and practice of the Established Church. To stave off this new, innovating enemy burrowing within the fabric of English life, they turned to the apocalyptic armoury and took up those weapons wielded by their ancestors in justifying the reformation from its beginning. As the authorities choked off argument, both sides increasingly engaged in confrontation tactics – the Laudians by enforcing their own form of uniformity from their positions of power, their opponents by making more and more radical attacks upon the Arminians in pulpit and press. As debate gave way to direct action, the prophecies of both sides became self-fulfilling. The Laudians became more vicious in their suppressions, turning into persecuting beasts as their opponents predicted. The opponents turned into seditious rabble-rousers, from a government point of view, as Laud always said they really were. Bastwick, Burton, and Prynne demand our attention not only as popular sufferers, but their careers and publications illustrate the way in which even moderate puritans became increasingly radical in thought and action in reaction to the Laudian régime. At the start of their careers Burton and Prynne stood closer to a moderate Anglican like Thomas Fuller than Fuller did to Laud. Laud pushed them into strident strains. Except in its implications and in some specific actions recommended, the radicalism of the triumvirate remained in the religious sphere in the 1630s. They became effective propagandists for their side of the struggle partly because the authorities made them into putative martyrs, but also because, drawing upon a century-old tradition, they touched the depths of the English protestant soul in their apocalyptic appeal. Their most important asset sprang from this source – they upheld the English myth of national warfare against Babylon and suffered as a consequence like the martyrs portrayed by Foxe. Their opponents, disavowing this vision, therefore disavowed such earth-shaking psychological victories as the Armada and the Gunpowder Plot. Charles I, by clinging to the Arminians, would finally draw down upon the realm and upon his head that punishment predicted by Henry Burton in the dedication of *For God and the king* to the holder of England's imperial crown.

5

From expectation to militance

Antichrist shall never prevail again as he hath done: God *will give*, yea, *he hath given* such a spirit to his saints, as they will never be brought to bow their backs again ...

Jeremiah Burroughs, Sions joy, p. 57

The soldiers of 'anti-Laud' lost their battle against the Arminians in the 1630s. Bastwick, Burton, Prynne, Lilburne, and a host of others could not persuade King Charles to withdraw his support from Archbishop Laud. No Parliament met to strengthen the appeal of reformers. The hold of the Laudians upon the Church of England seemed strengthened with each preacher silenced, each opponent punished and imprisoned. The apogee came with the canons of 1640, especially in the '*et cetera*' oath which enforced support of episcopacy upon all pastors and most educated men.[1] However, the summer in which the Convocation of the clergy passed these canons also witnessed the collapse of the personal rule of Charles I. The king and his bishops initiated the start of their own destruction by attempting to force a new prayer book upon Scotland in 1637. The Scots, urged on by the apocalyptic visions of their ministers, took up defensive arms to maintain the liberties and religion of their kingdom.[2] In the years which followed, Scotland's covenanted army twice triumphed over the divided English in the 'Bishops' Wars,'

---

1 Kenyon, *Stuart Constitution*, pp. 166–71; cf. Baxter, *Reliquiae*, pp. 15–16. I wish to thank Dr Caroline Hibbard for directing my attention to this passage in Baxter.
2 See especially Burrell, 'Apocalyptic vision' and 'The covenant'; cf. Williamson, 'Antichrist's Career'.

occupied the northern parts of England, and forced Charles to call his second Parliament of 1640 to mend the troubles of his realms.

The elections in the autumn of 1640 returned a House of Commons that lacked confidence in the royal policies of the previous eleven years. During the first year of the Long Parliament, a large majority of the members followed the lead of those in both Lords and Commons who wished to enact a programme of reform. Parliament abolished the institutions which made possible the period of personal rule, removed the crown's evil ministers, and started to reform the church. The execution of the Earl of Strafford on 12 May 1641 both symbolized and consummated the passing of the old order, as did the crowds who helped to force his condemnation. Less than a fortnight earlier, Parliament pledged its desire to create a new order by passing the Protestation and commanding each member of both houses to take its oath. Later urged upon all men by the Commons, the Protestation acted as England's first national covenant against popery and arbitrary government.[3] Throughout the first year of the Long Parliament – that year of expectation – reformers turned the tables not only in parish churches but in the highest places in the realm.

The tone for this policy of sweeping change rang out in John Pym's powerful speech in the Commons of 7 November 1640. In the policies of the previous decade, Pym espied a popish plot to subvert the religion and government of England, a pernicious conspiracy that endangered the kingdom, and he demanded a deliverance from the policy of 'thorough' in church and state.[4] This speech endowed the warnings that brought Bastwick, Burton, and Prynne to the pillory in 1637 with *post facto* respectability. On the same day, Pym brought the cases of these martyrs before the Commons and the House began its efforts to redress the misrule of the past by issuing orders for the release of the persecuted. United again, Burton and Prynne sailed together to Southampton from their respective prisons in the Channel Isles and, celebrated by rich and poor, made a joint triumphal march into London:

The people were so extraordinarily joyful of their return, that they rang the bells in most places they passed, for joy; ran to salute and shake them by the hands, crying out with one unanimous shout, *welcome home, welcome home, God bless you; God be thanked for your return*, and the like; yea, they strewed the

3 Gardiner, *Constitutional Documents*, pp. 155–6
4 Kenyon, *Stuart Constitution*, pp. 203–5

ways where they rode with herbs and flowers, and running to their gardens, brought *rosemary* [for remembrance] and *bays* [for victory] thence, which they gave to them and the company that rode with them into London; who were estimated to be about a 100 coaches (many of them with six horses apiece) and at least 2000 horse, those on foot being innumerable. The day they came from Egham into London, the sun arose most gloriously upon them soon after they came out of their inn, without any cloud, (which they both observed) and so continued shining all the day, without interposition of any obstacle to eclipse its rays, so as heaven and earth conspired together to smile upon them, and to congratulate their safe returns from their bonds and exiles.[5]

The welcome extended to these prophets expressed the hopes and long-ings of all levels of society that Parliament would finally redress their grievances.

If Prynne detected divine favour in the sun streaming down upon the returned captives, his companion read even greater providential sig-nificance into the same events. Burton believed that his triumphal return signalled an end to episcopacy in England and a fulfilment of his earlier prophecy that the bishops would one day 'gnash their teeth' in impotent humiliation for persecuting the saints. Savouring the sweet-ness of revenge, Burton fancied himself as one of the two witnesses of Revelation xi, killed by antichrist and resurrected after three and a half days. His punishment and life imprisonment had started three and a half years before – a year obviously symbolized a day.[6] Since this event fell in the very last days, the second coming of Christ approached rapidly. Burton looked forward with great expectation to welcoming his Saviour soon! Another preacher, John de la March, picked out Burton as one of the two witnesses in a sermon delivered on the Isle of Guernsey in February 1639. He now claimed that Burton's honourable welcome to London fulfilled the prophecy of Revelation xix:1, the rejoicing of the saints at the final fall of Babylon. In a similar mood, Robert Woodford, the steward of Northampton, recorded his reaction to these events, which he witnessed, in his diary: 'My heart rejoiceth in the Lord for this day; it is even like the return of the captivity from Babylon.' Slightly

5 [Prynne], *A new discovery*, part II, *A briefe survay*, pp. 114–15; cf. Burton, *A narration*, pp. 29–43, Clarendon, *History*, I, pp. 264, 268–9, *HMC*, De L'Isle and Dudley, VI, p. 346, and *HMC*, 9th report, II, p. 499 (the diary of Robert Woodford, steward of North-ampton). Burton and Clarendon believed that most of the people came from London; however, since Parliament was sitting, the city was packed with countrymen.

6 Burton, *The sounding*, pp. 51–75, see 75 m.n.

later, Bastwick received the same sort of joyous reception.[7] The rehabilitation of Bastwick, Burton, and Prynne – those persecuted prisoners – seemed miraculous to contemporaries, especially to those who followed the main actors and viewed it through apocalyptic spectacles. In less dramatic ways, many other men who later attained prominence came back to England from exile with a similar feeling in their hearts. From the Netherlands and from New England the victims of Laudian uniformity returned, unprodigal sons, to build a New Jerusalem in the land from which the Arminians had driven them.[8]

Some miraculous prophecies remained unfulfilled, even in the year of expectation. Richard Farnham and John Bull, two artisan prophets who said that they would rise from the dead to rule the world as God's instruments, remained in the grave.[9] Not content to rely solely upon the direct intervention of the Almighty, other people took to the streets, pulpit, and press to interpret, advise, and agitate. By the end of 1641 the London bookseller George Thomason collected over seven hundred pamphlets, evidence of the collapse of censorship and of the momentous impact that events made upon the minds of his contemporaries. In the next year alone he amassed nearly two thousand more. Thumbing through these tracts, one soon discovers that many Englishmen turned to the apocalyptic traditions of their past in order to understand and to influence the startling changes taking place from November 1640 onward.[10] The visions of St John helped to give coherence to the trials experienced by the reformers in the 1630s and to the deliverance wrought by the Long Parliament. Layman and cleric alike expressed their joys, fears, and hopes for reformation in church and state. Contemporaries could not ignore their clamour, although some relished it more than others.

The Parliament men who controlled England's destiny sought and

---

7 De la March, *A complaint*, sig. A 1–2v, p. 49, *HMC*, 9th report, II, p. 499, and *CSPD*, 1640–1, p. 323. Woodford referred to the return of the Jews from ancient Babylon, a type of the prophecies of St John.

8 Sachse, 'Migration.' At least six of the thirty-four men who preached to Parliament in 1640–2 returned from exile.

9 H[eywood], *A true discourse* and *False prophets*. After their deaths in prison, a faithful group of female followers awaited their resurrection.

10 Fortescue, *Catalogue*, I, pp. xx–xxi, and Spencer, 'Politics' and 'Professional connexions.' In my research for this chapter, I examined all items published in 1640 through 1 November 1642 in the Thomason collection, plus all other works in the British Library for the same period where the author could be discerned.

obtained spiritual counsel to help them meet the momentous responsibilities they faced. In initiating this remarkable project, John Pym extended a formal invitation and thanks to Cornelius Burges, as did Sir Robert Harley to Stephen Marshall, on behalf of the Commons. On 17 November 1640, members of the Commons turned aside from their business for a day of fasting and listened to the words of Burges and Marshall in St Margaret's Chapel, Westminster. More than meets the eye may hide behind this move, for Marshall lodged in the Earl of Warwick's stable of puritan preachers. After a period of *ad hoc* trial, the Commons adopted an official programme of monthly fast sermons on 23 February 1642 and the Lords followed suit in the autumn of 1644.[11] Sermons delivered before members of Parliament made such an impact upon those that heard them that the Commons got them printed to influence the population at large. Constituting a unique body of comment upon the events of the 1640s and 1650s, they provide a framework for understanding contemporary interpretations of the first two years of the Long Parliament.

I ASSESSMENTS OF THE PAST

During the first year of the Long Parliament, most articulate Englishmen thought they knew what they did not want. No matter how much their reasons differed, they desired to dismantle the engines of personal rule. Interpretations of the immediate past strongly influenced their approaches to current decisions, however. In the early 1640s few upheld the Arminian party. Of those who preached to Parliament, only Thomas Cheshire spoke favourably of 'the former years of the peaceable reign of our present gracious sovereign.' As early as 1641 the actions of religious radicals caused Cheshire to fear that '*Babel* were now building, rather then the house of God' in England.[12] Except in his anxiety over division, Cheshire spoke for few men. Even the future restoration bishops, John Gauden and Edward Reynolds, deplored the 'corruptions' imposed by

---

11 Wilson, *Pulpit*, pp. 60–3, 102–6, Christianson, 'From expectation' and the works cited therein. The semi-official nature of parliamentary fast sermons increases their importance as a source for the analysis of apocalyptic thought.

12 Cheshire, *A sermon* (29 June 1642), p. 15, and *A sermon preached*, p. 14. The date on which a fast sermon was preached will be included in its first citation. Like that of George Morley, delivered on 29 November 1640, Cheshire's fast sermon was not authorized for publication by a committee of the Commons. He got it printed himself, 'because none other would,' as Thomason wrote on the title page of his copy.

the Laudians.[13] Like other moderate Anglicans they attempted to heal the wounds opened in the Church of England in the 1630s by glorying in the bishop martyrs of Mary's reign, by reasserting the validity of the Elizabethan settlement, and by resurrecting the apocalyptic synthesis of John Foxe.[14]

Peacemakers, however blessed, formed a small minority of those who wrote in the early 1640s. The experience of puritans in the 1630s and the apocalyptic filter through which they perceived the lessons of Laudian uniformity, in large part generated the militance with which they pushed for reform in the 1640s.[15] Reformers believed that the hierarchy of the Established Church, or its leading members, nearly succeeded in an attempt to bring England back under the yoke of the popish antichrist. This interpretation represented the consensus view in parliamentary fast sermons.[16] Its more radical variations and corollaries gained widespread circulation in the press. Because they felt that the Almighty had rescued Britain from the brink of Babylon only by a last-minute intervention in events, puritans strained their resources to prevent such a situation from ever developing again. Only further reformation could insure that England would never return to Rome again.

On the anniversary of the accession of Queen Elizabeth I, 17 November 1640, Cornelius Burges and Stephen Marshall tentatively announced this theme in the parliamentary pulpit. Although not dipping as deeply into the apocalyptic armoury as his colleague, Burges employed images that more than hinted at the vision underlying his assessment of the contemporary situation. He attempted to persuade the Commons to form a national covenant with God as a pledge that they would carry the English reformation to its fruition. No radical, Burges explicitly praised sixteenth-century bishops for initiating a protestant

13 Gauden, Love of truth (29 Nov. 1640), and Reynolds, Israels petition (27 July 1642): see the DNB
14 Lamont, Marginal Prynne, ch. 4; cf. Reynolds, Eugenia's teares, p. 25, and Sclater, Papisto-mastix, pp. 10–13, 41, 58. A prebend of the Cathedral Church of Exeter, Sclater defended Bishop Hall in 1642 for his attacks on Rome.
15 Cf. George, 'Puritanism as history,' Lamont, 'Puritanism,' and Capp, 'Godly Rule' and 'The millennium'
16 Of the nineteen sermons preached to the Commons between November 1640 and January 1642, only three failed to present a variation on this apocalyptic interpretation of the 1630s: Gauden, Love of truth, presumably that by Morley, and F[ord?], Reformation (15 June 1641). Ford and Gauden deprecated the Laudian régime in more vague terms. Morley's sermon was not printed. Ussher, Vox Hibernae (Lords, 22 Dec. 1641), contained nothing on this point.

settlement. Gradually, the land had cast off the deleterious effects of its popish past until the Laudians moved to reverse this process. They pushed the Established Church into a precarious position, 'not only to coast anew upon the brinks of *Babylon*, from whence we were happily delivered, but even to launch out into her deepest lakes of superstition and idolatry, under the pretence of some extraordinary *piety of the times*, and some *good work in hand*.'[17] Like most English protestants, Burges believed that the reformation represented the delivery of England from Babylon. The Arminians, by reviving ceremonies and casting doubt upon the identification of the pope with antichrist, seemed to question the very truth of England's protestant settlement and, thereby, endangered both church and nation.

Stephen Marshall, soon to become the preacher politician par excellence, reinforced these sentiments by calling upon Parliament to repair that breach battered through the protective walls of the Church of England in the 1630s.[18] Specifically, he attacked the doctrine and worship of Arminians and concluded that 'little differences is [*sic*] to be found betwixt their practice, and the superstitions and idolatries of the Church of *Rome*.' Marshall reminded his audience that 'throughout all the time of antichrist's apostasy,' that is, in the middle ages, 'the true *church of Christ* ... were never guilty of the spiritual pollution of that apostatical church of *Rome*.' The need to retain purity pressed even more firmly at the present, for the final battle approached rapidly and the foe stepped up his activity. 'Satan knows his time is short, he stirs up all his instruments, as if one spirit possessed them all. And is it not a shame, that the Lord's friends should be more backward in his cause, than the vassals of Satan are in their master's?' Marshall placed the Laudians among these active instruments of the devil. Sometimes oblique in casting them in this role, he presented his message clearly enough in print, however, so that the reader did not need to hear the ironic tone of his voice to spell it out. As one branch of the cosmic conspiracy to overthrow the true church, the near success of English Arminians threatened Britain with the devastation of war, the punish-

---

17 Burges, *First sermon* (17 Nov. 1640), p. 54, see 35–8, 49, 53–5. His text related to the delivery of the children of Israel out of their captivity in Babylon (Jeremiah 1:5). Burges remained a moderate; see the *DNB* and Neale, 'November the 17th,' in his *Essays*.

18 Marshall, *A sermon* (17 Nov. 1640), p. 36. Preachers used this image *ad infinitum* in the following years. Marshall was a client of the Earl of Warwick; for his life and thought, see Hazelip, 'Stephen Marshall.'

ment suffered by Germany for similar sins. Dangerous times still awaited: 'And GOD knows whose lot is next. Little quiet I fear is to be expected in Christendom, till the beast his kingdom be ruined.'[19] The pernicious power of the Laudians merited full destruction precisely because of this precarious situation. After all, they fomented the 'Bishops' Wars' with Scotland and might strike again. According to both Marshall and Burges, then, the Arminians plotted to reverse the reformation in England, their triumph in the 1630s promoted a backsliding of the Church of England which moved it to the very gates of Rome, and only divine intervention, through the Scots, prevented the restoration of Babylon in Britain.

The second pair of parliamentary preachers expounded on the same theme. Samuel Fairclough compared the Arminians to Achan (who brought the wrath of God upon the Israelites by keeping a hidden Babylonian garment) and implored his audience to rid the land of this dangerous faction. As his third doctrine, he defended the proposition: 'That the divine policy and heavenly remedy to recover a commonwealth and church by *Achans* endangered is that those that have authority under God do totally abolish and extirpate all the cursed things whereby it was destroyed.' If Parliament applied this advice to England, its actions would both placate the wrath of the Lord for the relapse of the Laudians and hasten the ruin of Rome, the mystical Babylon.[20] Unreformed Achan represented an Old Testament type of the Arminians, his Babylonian garment a type of their love for the ways of Rome. Like other preachers, Fairclough mingled the imagery of the Old Testament with the prophecies of St John to produce a powerful and militant mixture.

Thomas Wilson, who shared St Margaret's pulpit that day, produced a more specifically apocalyptic, less prophetic, sermon than Fairclough, but it contained a similar analysis of the 1630s. Employing Brightman's image for the Church of England, Wilson berated the lukewarmness of Laodicea and compared the troubles of England in 1639 and 1640 with the near triumphs of antichrist in 1588 and 1605. While Fairclough breathed revenge upon the offenders of the past decade, Wilson only touched upon this theme as an introduction to his demand for a thorough reformation in England. The destruction of Babylon led into the other great task which God called upon the Long Parliament to

19 *A sermon*, pp. 34, 28, 43–4, see 33–4, 46
20 Fairclough, *The troublers* (4 April 1641), p. 24, see 50. A client of the puritan patriarch of Suffolk, Sir Nathaniel Barnardiston, Fairclough had been cited to appear before the ecclesiastical authorities several times; see the *DNB* and Shipps, 'Lay Patronage,' ch. 2.

accomplish, the building of Zion. '*Your happiness,*' Wilson told the assembled worthies, 'shall be great in pleading thoroughly for Zion and against Babylon, as it was prophesied, Oh daughter of Babylon who art to be destroyed, happy shall be he that rewardeth thee as thou hast served us ...'[21] Since Babylon, whether papist or Arminian, persecuted and oppressed the saints, Wilson demanded retribution as a joyful preliminary to reformation.

The interpretation enunciated by these four men obtained considerable support in the parliamentary pulpit.[22] With various degrees of intensity and explicitness, other people representing a wide range of status and opinion converged to condemn the Laudians in similar tones. Even outside of St Margaret's pulpit, preachers aimed their advice at the locus of power by dedicating printed versions of their sermons to Parliament. Pamphleteers, on the other hand, aimed missiles at all literate people and even beyond, guaranteeing that their message would reach the illiterate by using woodcut title pages and illustrations and including in their tracts catch slogans which anyone could memorize. In 1641 a pamphlet reported that 'each schoolboy's mouth is filled with a *Give a little Laud to the devil.*' The same anonymous author claimed that he desired 'to divulge his [Laud's] infamy in print, for every rural fellow to scoff and jeer at,' no idle threat from the wit who tossed off over twenty scurrilous jibes, mostly at the bishops, in 1641 alone.[23] While not all of this criticism employed apocalyptic imagery or assumed an apocalyptic framework, a significant portion fell into this category.

For men of a moderate nature, like Richard Ward, the '*innovations* and *altar*ations' introduced by the Laudians unhinged the Elizabethan settlement and, thereby, threatened England. In these changes, he discerned an Arminian conspiracy 'to draw us back into some antiquated and demolished vanities of old used by the papists, and disused in

---

21 Wilson, *Davids zeal* (4 April 1641), p. 45, see 16, 37–8, 41–2. The rector of Otham, Kent, Wilson had his petition against Laud presented to the Commons on 10 November 1640 by Sir Edward Dering, who made a fiery speech on the occasion; see Shaw, *English Church*, I, p. 13, and S[winnock], *Life of Wilson*. Lamont demonstrated the importance of Thomas Brightman for the radicals of 1641 in *Marginal Prynne*, pp. 59–62, while Wilson distinguished between prophetic and apocalyptic eschatologies in *Pulpit*, ch. 7. The latter often mingled with one another in practice.

22 Christianson, 'From expectation,' p. 229 n. 4 (note the shift of Milton since)

23 [Overton], *Canterburys will*, p. 3, and *Mercuries message defended*, p. 5. Despite the fact that the latter phrase appeared in the middle of an objection, it obviously reflected the author's true intent. I accept the attributions in Wolfe, 'Unsigned pamphlets,' and thank John K. Graham for calling this article to my attention.

reformed churches, as altars, crosses, tapers, images, pictures in walls, windows, garments, and the like; because these being once admitted, will serve as so many gradual steps to re-advance that Babylonish strumpet to that seat of supreme and spiritual monarchy from whence, by our forefathers, she was justly dismounted.'[24] The introduction of ceremonies and symbols into the worship of the Established Church represented but one aspect of the attempt to bring Rome back by degrees. Doctrinal innovation and persecution of the godly rounded out the popish plot of the 1630s. Only a wind from the north – the 'Bishops' Wars' – turned back this dangerous stream of deviation. Parliament had a duty to save the English church and state by continuing in the proper direction. When they rectified the ills of the previous decade, 'the blessing of the Lord shall be upon you, and ye shall go on and prosper, maugre the malice of all the devil's and antichrist's instruments.' Ward honestly opposed all novelty, whether it sprang from the Laudians or from the sects, and he directed attention to the martyr bishops of Mary's reign, to Bishops Jewel and Thomas Morton, and to other divines of a similar sort as guides to reformation. For him, all Christians must be of one mind. Each man, within his station and calling, also shared a duty to restore a proper balance and order to church and commonwealth.[25] A return to the good old ways of the Elizabethan and Jacobean Church of England struck Ward as the solution to the problem of religious dispute.

John Taylor, whose strong desire to uphold a hierarchical universe eventually led him into the role of a royalist propagandist, specifically aimed a similar message at the common people. An experienced pamphleteer already, Taylor employed the medium of the anonymous, satirical tract, not the sermon. To illustrate his belief that the Laudians tried to turn England into Babylon, Taylor purported to report the correspondence which took place between Laud and the pope. In reply to the archbishop's request for a remission of sins, the pope wrote that 'no petition or request of yours, nor any such loyal subject to us, as your grace has been, should suffer repulse,' and granted him full pardon, free of charge. He congratulated Laud for his good work in the 1630s, '(for

24 Ward, Principall duty, pp. 14–15, 59. A minister in Essex, Ward held an MA from Cambridge.
25 Ibid., pp. 20–1, see 11, 15, 19, 24–9, 61–3, 66; see [Bernard], The anatomy, pp. 5, 23–4, 56, 82, Geree, The down-fall, sig. c 2v–d iv, Price, A sermon, pp. 12, 26, 32, 34 (misnumbered 43), and Smectymnuus, An answer, pp. 19–20, 31–2, 55–6, 76, 90, 92, and A vindication, pp. 47, 89, 167, 183, 196, 213. Both Bernard and the authors of Smectymnuus exhibited more radical attitudes than Ward and the others.

you had almost reduced great part of the island) to be conformable to our holy rites, ceremonies, and customs (which the ignorant call superstitious, and committing adulteries with the whore of *Babylon*) ...'[26] An afterpiece woodcut of three men kneeling at the foot of the pope asking 'Oh pardon us!' and receiving his benediction reinforced the image of Arminians grovelling before their spiritual father. On the titlepage, a woodcut showed the British unicorn thrusting off the pope's tiara with its horn, forcing him to drop the symbols of his power, his staff, and the keys of St Peter. Drawing upon a host of popular protestant prejudices, Taylor presented a persuasive interpretation of the 1630s. Although not reconciled to the Arminians, he soon ignored them in full pursuit of the sects as the major force upsetting the natural order of the kingdom in the 1640s.[27]

In contrast to these more conservative writers, Richard Overton – the future Leveller leader – launched cutting attacks which displayed little anxiety over upsetting established authority. He cleverly identified Laud with the beast of Revelation by adding up the numerical value of the letters of the archbishop's name to the sum of 666. In the sudden collapse of Arminian power, Overton detected the beginning of the fall of Babylon. 'Proud Nimrod thus and's troop,/ Of late have lost their power,/For *Babel* 'gins to stoop.'[28] In another pamphlet, Laud purported to repent and finally admitted in his last will and testament that the pope was antichrist. Overton also portrayed the pope, riding on his seven-headed beast, as holding a fair at Lambeth to raise money for ransoming the English bishops from the Tower.[29] In a rhetorical question, he spelled out the connexion between Rome and Canterbury in the 1630s: 'Did the pope's great favourite *William à Canterbury* painfully labour to supress the true worship of Jesus Christ, and in the place thereof zealously endeavour to erect a new fardel of superstitious ceremonies, devised by a pack of deluding Jesuits, and preferred to his Grace by the whore of Babylon; with what facility will a company of indifferent Jack à bothsides, lukewarm Laodiceans, either for hope of prefer-

---

26 [Taylor], *The popes*, pp. 1–2. Taylor, the water poet, produced over forty tracts in 1641–2, most of which attacked the sects. Few men, if any, knew the common people of England as well as Taylor; see the *DNB* and Notestein, *Four Worthies*, ch. 3.

27 Taylor, *A delicate*, sig. A 2–4r, *A plea*, p. 3, and [Taylor], *Divisions*, sig. A 2v, *Hellish*, p. 3, and *Religions lotterie*, sig. A 2v. One of his early attacks on the sects, *A swarme*, appeared in June 1641.

28 [Overton], *Mercuries message*, sig. A 4v, see A 1v

29 [Overton], *Canterburys will*, p. 6, and Overton, *New Lambeth*, sig. A 2v

ment, or fear of imprisonment embrace and allow these his stinking traditions?' The answer came as no surprise. Overton compared Laud to Achan and his supporters to the followers of Baal, Old Testament types of the corrupters of pure worship. His attacks upon the Laudians almost moved over into an assault on episcopacy itself and some of his stinging satire bordered on making light of apocalyptic visions.[30] None the less, although more vicious than most of his colleagues, even Overton started his career as a publicist in the mainstream apocalyptic tradition.

The interpretation disseminated by these people placed the Arminians in the camp of antichrist, but held back from condemning all English bishops. While its expositors either refused to spell out or disagreed upon the future form of the Church of England, they shared a common explanation of the events of the 1630s which demanded the removal of Laud and his supporters as a minimum reform. So long as Arminians retained any semblance of power, they argued, the threat of destruction towered over Britain.

More radical reformers discerned an extensive contingent of antichrist's cohorts within the Established Church, one extending beyond the ranks of the Laudians. The ideas and actions of the Arminian bishops in the 1630s, combined with the *jure divino* defence of episcopacy in 1641, caused a sizeable group to turn against the office as such and demand its 'root and branch' abolition. The position taken by Martin Marprelate and Alexander Leighton at last swelled into a stream of apocalyptic interpretation in the popular press. One pamphleteer, placing his ideas in the unlikely mouth of Calvin, denounced the English hierarchy in no uncertain terms: 'These horned beasts of the popedom have still usurped the title of prelates and bishops, and will needs be worshipped under the pretence of church government, but it is a stark lie, they are not set up by God, but have thrust themselves into this order.' He derived the calling of bishops from the pope and, ultimately, from the devil. Another anonymous writer took up the theme of *Mer-*

---

30 [Overton], *Mercuries message defended*, pp. 1–2, 8; cf. *New Lambeth*, passim. Other tracts identifying the Laudians with the forces of antichrist include T.B., *Newes*, sig. A 3v–4, Bond, *King Charles*, pp. 2–3, B[rome], *A Canterbury tale*, sig. A 2–4, *Canterburies pilgrimage*, sig. A 2v–3, 4r, *A copie of a letter from Rome*, pp. 1–2, *A divine paternoster*, Du Perron, *The copy*, pp. 3–5, *Englands petition* (an engraving with a text), *Great Brittans ruine*, pp. 4–5, 9–10, 22, 25, J.H., *King Charles*, pp. 5–6, J.L., *Englands doxologie*, pp. 1–2, 4, 5–7, 11, *Organs funerall*, sig. 4v, R.P., *The bishop's*, pp. 1, 4–5, *The papists petition*, pp. 3–4, 6, 7–8, *A plea*, pp. 8–9, 11–12, *Wrens anatomy*, pp. 3–4, 7, 10, 12. Most of these appeared in late 1641 or early 1642 as part of the campaign to remove bishops from the House of Lords.

curies message, the identification of Laud with the beast of Revelation, and applied it to all members of the hierarchy through the medium of a supposed recantation by the English primate. After admitting that he and his subordinates tried to return England to Rome and that episcopacy formed a part of Babylon, Archbishop Laud purportedly requested all English bishops to renounce their calling: 'And if ye will not forsake your ways, lay down your antichristian offices at the foot of the church, which ye have so miserably torn ... wrath shall come and fall upon your necks as thunder from the clouds ...'[31] Only this radical change in government could drive the 'man of sin' out of the Church of England. Short pamphlets of this sort, however, rarely did more than promote established interpretations in vivid imagery, pithy prose, and mangled verse. They reflected the concerns of more weighty 'root and branch' writers. In 1641, laymen of status, fame, and learning seriously challenged the veracity of the Elizabethan settlement, worked to dethrone godly bishop and godly prince as the leaders of England's reformation, and led the 'root and branch' assault upon episcopacy. For once, the demand of 'no bishop' eventually produced that for 'no king,' but not until after a bloody civil war broke out in England.

William Prynne joined the radicals at last in 1641, especially in his lengthy treatise, *The antipathie of the English lordly prelacie both to regal monarchy and civil unity*. As William Lamont demonstrated, the precedent-oriented lawyer compiled this work to justify the changes in his thought brought on by a decade of Laudian uniformity and by the *jure divino* arguments of Bishop Hall. Partisan Prynne catalogued the injuries to both church and state caused by the prelates by constructing a biography of evils for each English bishop from Augustine through Laud. The assembled evidence led him to denounce the latter, both in actions and in theoretical claims, as the worst primate in the history of the English church. With circular reasoning, Prynne argued that the behaviour of bishops demonstrated their false calling, while the improper nature of their jurisdiction necessarily made them act in an evil way.[32]

---

31 *Englands glory*, sig. A 2r, see B IV, D, and *The recantation*, p. 41, see 4–5, 7–8, 14, 17, 20, 22–3, 24–6, 27–8, 31, 37. Other anonymous tracts expressing a similar interpretation include *The bishops manifest*, pp. 2–3, 5 (misnumbered 7), 6, E.E., *The bishops*, pp. 1–2, 4–5 (not by Edmund Elys), *The envie*, pp. 1–3, 6, *A most sad*, pp. 12–14. [Overton], *Vox borealis*, sig. A 2v, 3v, 4v, D 1, *The prentices*, pp. 1–5, *Questions*, sig. A 2v, 3v–4, *Reasons why*, p. 2, *A strange prophecie*, sig. A 2v, 3v, 4, *The times*, sig. A 2v–3, 4v, B 2r, *Triple episcopacie*, pp. 7–9. Most appeared in late 1641 or early 1642.

32 Prynne, *Antipathie*, two parts, I, pp. 157–8, II, p. 310, and see Lamont, *Marginal Prynne*, ch. 4

In his earlier works, Prynne had employed this type of polemic against the Arminians, but now he gave up hope in episcopacy itself.

Prynne's radicalism in 1641 stemmed, in large part, from his new view of the apocalyptic tradition. The pope remained the 'Great Antichrist,' but church hierarchy, as such, represented the whore of Babylon. Bishops, then, became lesser antichrists. Like other 'root and branch' advocates, he asserted that 'the calling of lordly prelates is neither divine nor apostolical; but rather antichristian and diabolical.' However, Prynne refused to follow Burton, his fellow martyr, into the ranks of the separatists. He wished to detach the bishops from the Church of England, instead of demanding that Christians withdraw from that body.

What then remains but that the king, Parliament, and people (having such a just cause and fair opportunity) should all join cordially together, utterly to subvert this chair of pestilence, and with *great violence to throw down this our English* Babylon, *and in one hour to make her so desolate as she may be found no more at all*; so the people beholding her long expected and much desired overthrow, *may cry mightily with a strong and joyful voice*, with the *angel* in the Apocalypse, *Babylon* (Canterbury) *the great is fallen, is fallen; which hath been the habitation of devils, and the hold of every foul spirit, and a cage of every unclean bird, and in her was found the blood of prophets, and of saints, and of all that were slain upon the earth.*[33]

The very act of overthrowing the ungodly bishops would unify king, Parliament, and people into one mighty arm of the Almighty.

A shift in Prynne's attitude toward monarchy followed from this transformation of his earlier attack upon the Arminians into an outright denunciation of episcopacy. By denigrating the role of Constantine, Prynne renounced that reliance upon the unaided prince as God's imperial instrument which infused his works of the 1630s. Continuing his recent appeal to the common people, he also hearkened back to that solicitation of Parliament which characterized his earliest publications. Into the vacuum created by his damning verdict on prelacy and his debunking of the godly prince, Prynne elevated Parliament and the people. This new synthesis of radical materials prepared the way for his later attempts to prove that the crown was responsible to the common-

33 *Ibid.*, II, ch. 8, p. 308, cf. 310, and I, p. 177 (misnumbered 176)

wealth and its institutions.[34] While Prynne's 'root and branch' assault upon episcopacy remained a religious programme, it necessitated a reinterpretation of the holy history of Foxe and a disavowal of the Elizabethan settlement. Both contained political implications.

Swept up in the necessity of the radicals to see the past in a new light, John Milton pressed home a similar historical reappraisal with a vengeance in his early antiprelatical tracts. No writer in 1641 more ferociously deflated the image of Constantine and, thereby, the concept of the godly prince. Milton portrayed the emperor who established Christianity as a superstitious believer in relics who corrupted the church by giving it wealth. Ignoring the fact that their criticisms hinged upon the spurious 'donation of Constantine,' Milton unfairly quoted Dante, Petrarch, Aristo, and other humanists to buttress his position.[35] Instead of binding Satan for a thousand years, as proclaimed by Foxe and Brightman, Milton argued that '*Constantine* marr'd all in the church.' It would be difficult to imagine a more radical transformation of the symbol of the imperial instrument of the Lord used by generations of English protestants. A decay in the purity of the church crept in during the reign of Constantine, but even worse were the 'effects that followed; his son *Constantius* proved a flat *Arian*, and his nephew *Julian* an apostate, and there his race ended; the church that before by insensible degrees welked and impaired, now with large steps went down hill decaying, and at this time *antichrist* began first to put forth his horn ...'[36] The fact that prelates praised Constantine proved his wickedness to Milton. The taint engendered by bishops extended at last to the emperor and, by implication, to the very notion of a godly prince.

In order to demonstrate the impropriety of episcopacy, Milton traced the decay of this office from its apostolic purity – when bishop meant presbyter – down to the diocesan prelates of antichrist. Hence, he distinguished between true bishops and false prelates on the grounds of func-

---

34 [Prynne], *A soveraigne* and *A vindication*. Thomason dated the first to 18 August and the second to 6 December 1642. Prynne's important works of 1643 lie outside the scope of this study; see Lamont, *Marginal Prynne*, ch. 5.

35 [Milton], *Of reformation* in *Complete Prose*, I, pp. 556–8, 576–7, cf. 553–79. Reference will be to the Yale edition, but will cite the original title of each pamphlet. All but one of these tracts appeared anonymously. See Fixler, *Milton*, and Hill, *Antichrist*, for Milton's apocalyptic thought. Mede, Milton's tutor, unwittingly paved the way for his pupil's attack upon Constantine by placing the binding of Satan in the future.

36 *Of reformation* p. 557

tion and jurisdiction. The governors of the Church of England, who troubled the land by attempting to slide it back to Rome in the previous decade, fit firmly into the latter category: 'They are not *bishops*, GOD and all *good men* know they are not, that have filled this land with late confusion and violence, but a tyrannical crew and corporation of im- posters, that have blinded and abused the world so long under that name.' They drew their calling from the devil, for 'it is God that makes a bishop, and the devil that makes him to take a prelatical bishopric.'[37] Just as the pope, antichrist, arose out of the institution of diocesan episcopacy, so now that same jurisdiction transformed its holders into 'true merchants of Babylon,' whether or not they pretended to be re- formed. In a statement tinged with hyperbole, Milton left no doubt about his evaluation of the English hierarchy: 'I cannot think but that it is the absolute voice of truth and all her children to pronounce this prelatry, and these her dark deeds in the midst of this great light wherein we live, to be more antichristian than antichrist himself.'[38]

This denunciation of prelacy led Milton to pour derision upon the religious leadership of the bishop martyrs and to elevate the villified and oppressed, from Wycliffe to those called puritans, into the true initiators of reformation. The bishops persecuted the godly, but could not eradi- cate their work. Once again 'Britain's God' turned to his special people to give a lead in reforming the church; commanded by Parliament this time, they should fulfil their Protestation oath by abolishing episcopacy 'root and branch.'[39]

And if our princes and knights will imitate the fame of that old champion, as by their order of knighthood solemnly taken they vow, far be it that they should uphold and side with this English dragon; but rather to do as indeed their oath binds them, they should make it their knightly adventure to pursue and van- quish this mighty sail-winged monster that menaces to swallow up the land, unless her bottomless gorge may be satisfied with the blood of the king's daugh- ter the church; and may, as she was wont, fill her dark and infamous den with the bones of the saints.[40]

37 *Ibid.*, p. 537, see 526, 590, 602, 614, 617; see [Milton], *Animadversions*, pp. 671, 704, 724
38 Milton, *The reasons*, pp. 581, 580, cf. 582; see *Of reformation*, pp. 614, 617, and *Animadversions*, p. 716
39 *Animadversions*, p. 704, cf 727–8; see *Of reformation*, pp. 525, 531–5, 580–5, 603–4, and *The Reasons*, p. 788
40 *The reasons*, p. 857, see p. 861. For royal symbolism under Charles I, see Strong, *Van Dyck*.

Apocalyptic thought rarely throbbed with such baroque splendour. Milton compared Parliament to St George, the oath of the Protestation to the vow of a Knight of the Garter, and the dragon to the beast from the bottomless pit – representing prelacy, in this case. If members of Parliament did not keep their oath by eradicating episcopacy, he predicted, a new period of persecution would engulf England and reverse the reformation. Milton must have chosen this rich, cutting symbolism deliberately. Charles I displayed a repeated fondness for the image of St George and often employed it to represent his imperial power and his role as a godly prince. By denigrating Constantine and shifting the content of St George to Parliament, Milton transformed two key symbols of English royalty. One could no longer tarry for the chief magistrate. The Almighty was arousing his people to begin the final fall of Babylon. The 'high and stately tragedy' of St John's Apocalypse moved relentlessly into the final acts.[41] Unless they wished to endanger the realm, the 'princes and knights' of Parliament must forward this great design of the Lord by removing the government of antichrist from the Established Church. The imperial tradition shifted its weight to the shoulders of the Lords and Commons.

At least one of these exalted instruments avowed a similar interpretation of the situation. Robert Greville, Lord Brooke, stood out as a conspicuous noble opponent of the personal rule of Charles I. In 1639 he joined Viscount Say and Sele in refusing to take the military oath at York, and in 1641 he took the remarkable step of becoming a pamphleteer. Lord Brooke, although unexperienced in this sphere, emerged as one of the most effective 'root and branch' adversaries of church hierarchy. Like the others, he denigrated episcopacy by illustrating the rebellious nature of the order in affairs of state (including even those who derived their office *jure humano*), by emphasizing the flaws of the bishop martyrs, and by characterizing the Elizabethan and Jacobean prelates as persecutors, not as protestant champions. This rewriting of history attempted, through innuendo, to equate the English and Roman hierarchy. Lord Brooke clearly wished to 'prove that popery properly taken, is the same *in re*, with our episcopacy; or at least that *this* is but a piece and part of that mystery of iniquity,' that is, the governors of the Church of England lodged in the tents of Babylon.[42]

41 *The reasons*, pp. 760–1, 815, and *Animadversions*, pp. 706–7 (where the saints are compared to the many waters of Revelation xix:6).
42 Greville, *A discourse*, p. 58, cf. 33–43. An earlier version appeared in 1641; see Haller, *Rise of Puritanism*, pp. 331–8, and Schwarz, 'Aristocratic protest.'

The essence of popery consisted both in accepting a jurisdiction dependent upon the pope and in acting like him to usurp the kingly office of Christ. English prelates followed the deviations of the papacy from the doctrine and discipline laid down in the scripture. Although accepting the separatist argument that the office of English bishops had a diabolical derivation 'for, our bishops' first power came from the pope,' Lord Brooke observed the flaws in this historical approach and attempted to strengthen it. He reasoned that even if these officers derived neither their traditions nor authority from Rome, whether directly or indirectly, their actions alone made them into antichrists.

So that a bishop's wearing a surplice, cope, mitre; using the cross, bowing to the altar, and many such things (though they may be errors, yet all these, or one of these) makes him not a pope, a popeling, or properly antichristian; but receiving these from the pope's dictates, doing them because he commands, acknowledging his power in commanding, this makes a *papist*; and commanding them, pressing them on others, in such despotical power, makes a true *pope*, a *real antichrist* ... I care not whether we call him a *pope, papist, Romanist*, or any other name; I call him antichrist; and if you will call *antichrist* by the name of *pope*, I call such an imperious commander among us, (though he have no shadow of dependence on Rome, or Romish pope) an English *pope*, I mean an English antichrist.[43]

This definition, of course, applied quite nicely to the enforced uniformity of the previous decade, a point rubbed in by Lord Brooke: 'In our gracious king's reign they have come to cutting off ears, cheeks, and have yet struck deeper, and essayed many *soul-schisms*, not only in the hearts and consciences of thousands of good men, but whole states also and kingdoms, as much as in them lay.' His chain of logic forced an inescapable conclusion – antichrists sat in the sees of England, Scotland, and Ireland. 'Their mad outrage in all the three kingdoms of late hath so incensed the common people, that in all men's eyes they are become most vile: and while all men reflect on their constant trade of mischievous practices, the wisest begin to conclude, the very calling hurts the men, as much as these disgrace the calling.'[44] The 'wisest' finally grasped and embraced that characterization of episcopacy incessantly repeated by separatists in treatises, pamphlets, and sermons for more than half a century.

43 *A discourse*, pp. 51, 73, 58–9, see 54–9
44 *Ibid.*, pp. 93–4, 95

With aristocratic generosity, Lord Brooke acknowledged the source of his apocalyptic castigation of church hierarchy and also marched beyond the call of duty to advance at least a lawyer's case for the whole separatist programme. By stressing the proper outrage of the common people, he displayed a willingness – found in few peers – to condone popular direct action. His call for a favourable reception of the despised tub preachers indicated a sensitivity to the idea that the utterances of the lower orders might express religious truth.[45] Since the days of Browne and Barrow, men of authority rushed forward to despise, imprison, and persecute the separatists. Puritan preachers applauded and added their chorus of derision. In this context, Lord Brooke's suggestion that the separatists be accorded serious public consideration must have produced a powerful impact. No man of such high rank dared do even this before.

By calling the English bishops antichrists, the 'root and branch' writers joined Martin Marprelate and Alexander Leighton on the thin border between the radical puritan and the separatist positions. What first appeared as an isolated phenomenon finally emerged as a stream of apocalyptic interpretation – one especially advocated by laymen.[46] Not professed in a parliamentary fast sermon until 1642, it remained a distinct minority point of view there and in other pulpits.[47] Among pamphleteers, however, a host of more obscure and anonymous lights seconded such outstanding spokesmen as Prynne, Milton, Lord Brooke, and John Vicars. Although they accepted the separatist condemnation

45 *Ibid.*, pp. 95–107. Lord Brooke does not marshal his arguments like a converted separatist. The oft-quoted statement on page 107 that he was 'speaking their words, not my own' probably was true. Although most scholars have treated this claim with scepticism, few of them have read much separatist literature.

46 In addition to the works cited above, see Brinklow, *The true coppy*, [Fenwick], *The downfall*, sig. A 2v–3r, pp. 2, 8–11, 19, 21–2, 28, 35, Franklin, *An epistle*, sig. A 3r, 4v, [Leighton], *A decade*, sig. A 3r, 4r, Loveday, *An answer*, pp. 5–6, Robinson, *Petitioners*, pp. 6–7, 23, 27, 32, 34–5, 50, Vicars, *Jehovah-Jireh*, pp. 3, 6, 14, 16, 20, 23–5, 44–5, 70, 79, 81, and Ward, *An encouragement*, pp. 1–2, 9–10, 13–14.

47 Only two parliamentary preachers espoused this interpretation, Sedgwick, *Zions deliverance* (29 June 1642), p. 26, and Wilson, *Jerichoes down-fall* (29 Sept. 1642), pp. 6, 14–16. For the works of other divines, see [Bernard], *A short view*, pp. 1–2, 30, 34–5, Byfield, *The power*, sig. *** 3, A 1, pp. 4, 16–18, Case, *Gods waiting*, pp. 23, 66, 87, 106, 128–9, Hughes, *Certaine*, pp. 23, 27–9, 32, 40–1, Mocket, *The churches*, pp. 40–1, 57, 65, [Walker], *A true copie*, sig. A 2r, 3r, [Woodward], *The churches*, sig. b 3v, c 1r, pp. 47–9, 83–4. The London 'root and branch' petition to the Commons put forth the same reform programme, but did not identify the bishops as antichrists; Gardiner, *Constitutional Documents*, pp. 137–44.

of episcopacy, these interpreters did not believe that the Church of England suffered complete corruption at the hands of its governors. Reformation, however imperfect, still reigned in England. Once one removed the prelates 'root and branch,' Parliament, preachers, and people could join hands to finish the task started by their predecessors in the sixteenth century. The men who shared this vision, then, remained radical puritans who continued to stress the viability of a national church. Even if they debunked two traditional symbols of the English reformation, the godly prince and the bishop martyrs, they held back from a call to gather congregations of visible saints without tarrying for the magistrate. The Established Church, despite its bishops, still stood outside the gates of Babylon.

Those radicals who treasured the logic of logical conclusions could not stop at the half-way house of 'root and branch' and continued to press for inclusion of the whole Established Church in Babylon. After agitating in the wilderness for generations, the separatists at last approached the promised land. Although their message changed little since the days of Henry Barrow, it struck people as increasingly cogent in the 1630s. Laudian bishops drove quite large numbers of the godly over that gulf which had always divided radical puritans from separatists and, thereby, fulfilled the prophecies of men like Prynne and Burton.[48] Growing numbers deserted the Church of England for the sanctity of the sects. There 'are so many sects and schisms lately sprung up here in this kingdom, that they (like the plagues of Egypt) have overrun the land; but the Brownists, the brothers of the separation, bear the greatest sway,' groaned one frightened pamphleteer.[49] A host of like-minded people joined in this chorus of complaint. Traditionalists reacted with horror, especially when tub preachers left their places of hiding and

48 The Richt Right press in Amsterdam continued its spate of cleverly composed pamphlets with C[anne], The informer and Syons prerogative. Separatist works also came off English presses in some quantity, an unprecedented development. See An answer to Oxford, Chidley, The justification, Coachman, The cry, A discovery of the archwhore, A discovery of the great fantasie, Hunt, A plaine, The spirituall, and These spirituall, Quintine, A brief treatise, R[itor], A treatise, and The untrussing. 'Prophet' Hunt provides an excellent example of a real tub preacher. Most civil war sects sprang from separatist roots, not from those of the clerical non-separating congregationalists who came to be called 'independents.'

49 The brothers, sig. A 2r. Similar statements appeared in the host of pamphlets that attacked the sects from 1641 onward. Among these, one must distinguish between those presenting stock anti-puritan satire and those containing valuable information; see Holden, Anti-Puritan Satire, and Morton, World of the Ranters, ch. 2.

beamed forth their light for all to see. Convinced that the fall of Babylon rapidly approached, other separatists screwed up the courage to attack the remaining visual vestiges of antichrist's power in England through direct action. Most disturbing of all, educated and respected divines began to preach in separatist tones. Freedom of the press assured an audience for all.

Among the returning exiled victims of Laudian uniformity stood three Cambridge MAs who now avowed a separatist condemnation of the Established Church. Symbolically, Samuel Eaton came back from New England, Henry Burton from prison, and Jeremiah Burroughs from the Netherlands. All previously held benefices. Before leaving for the new world with his brother in 1634, Eaton preached in Cheshire, as had his father before him. As early as January 1641 he publicly proclaimed the separatist programme in his old county at St John's Church, Chester, and at Knutsford. Unfortunately, no full texts of his sermons survive, but accounts of them contained in hostile sources ring true. Although brief and lacking in detail, they provide the skeleton of what clearly amounted to a full separatist condemnation of the Church of England. In the tradition of Henry Barrow, Eaton – by pointing out that 'the very names parsons and vicars were antichristian' – went beyond a 'root and branch' attack upon bishops to place all conforming ministers in the camp of perdition. By stressing that gathered congregations of saints constituted the only true Christian polity and by denying validity to any national, provincial, or diocesan church, he firmly underlined the separatist rejection of the very notion of an Established Church.[50] To judge from the reaction of Sir Thomas Aston, these sermons caused a good deal of shock in Eaton's old community. Few would have expected a former beneficed clergyman to launch such a full-scale assault upon the Church of England. Eaton sparked off the Cheshire petition to Parliament in favour of episcopacy and he received some national notoriety in the accounts of Aston and Taylor. None the less, he operated in an area far remote from London, while his colleagues, Burton and Burroughs, agitated in the capital and preached a similar message to members of Parliament.

As a decorated hero in the fight against Laudian uniformity and a plausible prophet of the new order, Henry Burton reached the height of

50 [Taylor], *Brownists*, p. 3 (misnumbered as 5), and Aston, *A remonstrance*, pp. 5–6. Eaton's father was vicar of Great Budworth in Cheshire, while he himself held the benefice of West Kirby in the same country before leaving for New England; *DNB* and Richardson, *Puritanism*, pp. 40, 137.

influence and popularity in 1641. While Prynne forcefully joined the ranks of the radicals in that year, Burton hesitantly worked out the theoretical and practical consequences of his earlier conversion to separatism in a paradoxical atmosphere. Just after he decided not to tarry for the magistrate, the Long Parliament first freed him from prison and then invited him to preach a fast sermon to the Commons. While none of his previous love for the Church of England remained, enough of Burton's almost excessive devotion to the imperial tradition surged up to blunt aspects of his commitment to the separatist cause. As a result, Burton either hesitated to express or masked his true religious feelings in public until 1643. The full separatist programme, therefore, appeared more openly in his anonymous *The protestation protested* than in his parliamentary fast sermon. In the latter, Burton stressed the evils of the previous decade by contrasting the pulpit at St Margaret's with the pillory from which he preached just four years previously. After thanking the 'worthies of our kingdom for scattering' the swarms of perfidious papists and Arminians who had polluted the land, he reminded members of the Commons that England still lay under 'an antichristian Babylonian, Egyptian bondage.'[51] Although the tyrants of the recent past – the Laudians with their Babylonian captivity – lay scattered, Parliament had removed only the most flagrant oppressors, not oppression itself. Pointing out that the English episcopacy represented a 'limb' of antichrist, Burton implored Parliament to 'break off all the yokes from the necks of God's people' by abolishing all means of enforcing false doctrines. To the uninitiated, this sermon sounded much like the normal call for reformation. Burton, however, aimed at liberating the saints from statutory restraints, not at the impossible task of reforming a national church. Even his trust in the godly magistrate became conditional. 'The children of God,' he warned emphatically, 'have not yet deliverance, but they shall have it.'[52] The Almighty demanded immediate reformation – without Parliament if necessary, but not necessarily without Parliament.

If Burton somewhat veiled his true feelings in front of the assembled Commons, he explicitly exhibited them in his anonymous tract. There he outlined the nature of England's bondage to the pope in a scheme that applied equally to Roman catholicism and to the Elizabethan settlement: 'We hold communion with popery so long as we do publicly retain

51 Burton, *Englands bondage* (20 June 1641), pp. 20–1, cf. 10; cf. [Burton], *The protestation*
52 *Englands bondage*, pp. 24–5, 26, 32, 11, see 7–10; see *The protestation*, sig. B 3–C 3V

and maintain any of the doctrines of popery. And the doctrines of popery we retain and maintain are these. First, the imposition of the liturgy. Secondly, the discipline. Thirdly, the government. Fourthly, the cere-monies.'[53] This variation on Henry Barrow's four points provided the explicit organizational structure for Burton's tract and an implicit framework for his parliamentary sermon. In the anonymous work he went beyond a condemnation of episcopacy to denounce the liturgy, discipline, and ceremonies of the Established Church as 'popery and antichristian' as well. Expressing his real ideas more bluntly here, Burton positively pressed the separatist solution upon all Christians: 'Surely God's people must be separatists from the world, and from false churches, to become a pure and holy people unto the Lord.'[54] Since the Church of England still stood in the bondage of Babylon, this injunction applied there if no sweeping reform occurred soon. Two years later, Burton took his own advice and gathered a congregation of saints in London. Until then, he remained a separatist in word, if not in deed.

Jeremiah Burroughs, the only other parliamentary preacher who reflected the separatist apocalyptic vision, appeared too captured by the euphoria of the year of expectation to challenge the leadership of Par-liament. Burroughs, using the image of Jerusalem to represent the Church of England, poetically portrayed the sufferings of the saints under Laudian uniformity: 'Jerusalem was not long since as a woman forsaken, her children went about mourning in the streets, they saw *Jerusalem* even turned into *Babylon*, they saw that havoc was made of the saints, of faithful *ministers*, of *truths*, *ordinances* ... The adversaries of *Jerusalem* were great, and her enemies prospered, and for this her children sighed, and wept, and lamented one to another, their hearts were even turned within them: they mourned like doves, looking for judgment, but there was none.'[55] He spoke like a psalmist and the beauty of Burrough's biblical language served to heighten the effect of his proclamation. Laud, forcing a regression of the Church of England to its pre-reformation state, turned Jerusalem into Babylon. The experience

53 *The protestation*, sig. A 2v. Various contemporaries discerned and attempted to refute this separatist position; see Geree, *Vindiciae voti*, and [Hall], bishop of Exeter, *A survay*.

54 *The protestation*. sig. A 3v-4, B 3v

55 Burroughs, *Sions joy* (7 Sept. 1641), pp. 8-9. A client of the Earl of Warwick, Burroughs became a prominent pastor in the 1640s and was one of the congregational 'dissenting brethren' in the Westminster Assembly. Even Warwick could not protect him from exile in the 1630s. See the *DNB*, Shipps, 'Lay Patronage,' and Nuttall, *Visible Saints*, pp. 11-12.

of the 1630s, when he at least tacitly supported the Scots in the 'Bishops' Wars' and when Bishop Wren drove him into exile, caused Burroughs to condemn the Established Church with separatist imagery.

For Burroughs, however, recent events showed that the saints no longer lay in the depths of their misery, nor would they ever again: 'Antichrist shall never prevail again as he hath done: God *will give*, yea, he *hath given* such a spirit to his saints, as they will never be brought to bow their backs again ...' The judgments of Providence toppled the Arminians just when they seemed to reach the height of their power. The Scots humbled this 'antichristian party' in two bloodless wars, a sure sign of God's favour to the godly. After that, the Lord raised up the Long Parliament to crush 'those Babylonish brats of innovation' in an orderly way.[56] The persecuted and oppressed first led the way to further reformation, but now God's imperial instruments in Parliament carried the task to fruition. As a result, Christians need not break the laws of England through direct action. Close ties with the Earl of Warwick, no doubt, reinforced Burrough's trust in the godly magistrate. Despite his full condemnation of the Established Church and his belief in congregational polity, then, he refrained from immediate separation.

Eaton, Burton, and Burroughs believed that Laud's domination of the Church of England in the 1630s recreated Babylon in Britain. None of them condemned the Established Church in such terms before the enforcement of Laudian uniformity. Burton disavowed his earlier reliance upon the godly prince, abandoned the imperial apocalyptic tradition altogether, and asserted that the elect must covenant toether in independent congregations.[57] When preaching before the Commons he still gave lip service to the importance of the magistrate, something one could hardly avoid in such a setting, but he limited even this to an appeal that Parliament destroy the Arminians and free the saints from the bondage of a national church. While Burroughs held back from separation, Eaton plunged ahead at a more reckless pace than Burton. Standing on the fringe of the sects, these three respectable divines represented degrees of the most far-reaching radicalization in the puritan brotherhood wrought by the experience of the 1630s. For the next

56 *Ibid.*, pp. 57, 24, 43
57 Burton, who took up separation by 1639, was not typical of the puritan brotherhood in the 1630s, nor did he become so in the early 1640s; cf. Lamont, 'Puritanism,' pp. 140–3. Eaton probably became a separatist at Salem and was hardly representative of the New England divines. Most of the educated pastors who took up sectarian positions in the 1640s were younger men.

decade, like-minded colleagues joined them to ride a putative wave of the future.

In front of this trio of univeristy-educated intellectuals stood a phalanx of men and women of more humble status – cobblers, feltmakers, tinkers, weavers, leather sellers, husbandmen, and artisans.[58] Hardened by years of derision and persecution for their beliefs, these experienced lay preachers and organizers now strained to finish the final destruction of Babylon. Except for the occasional renegade minister who also cut himself off from ordinary society, those of small but independent means – not the leaders or intellectuals of England's hierarchical society – maintained the separatist tradition into the 1640s. With their leaders driven into exile, imprisoned, or executed, it took considerable skill by common people to keep these groups of gathered saints in existence from the time of Browne and Barrow to the outbreak of the English civil war. They managed, however, and learned the exhilarating lessons of self help. Educated pastors who thought to tame and control such congregations found the task less than easy.

Only brave persons openly joined separatist groups before the civil war began. Even the new freedom created by the Long Parliament remained precarious for them. In the midst of the anti-episcopal campaign, for example, apprentices savagely attacked a conventicle at Praise-God Barebone's dwelling in London. Only the timely arrival of constables and a guard to arrest the separatists prevented the crowd from smashing up the house and its flock. According to a hostile source, while some of the saints fled from the scene the apprentices 'catcht one of them alone, but they kicked him so vehemently, as if they meant to beat him into a jelly. It is ambiguous whether they have killed him or no, but for a certainty they did knock him, as if they meant to pull him in pieces, I confess, it had been no matter, if they had beaten the whole tribe in the like manner.'[59] Not all apprentices followed the example of young John Lilburne, nor did religious disputes follow the lines of social cleavage in the seventeenth century. John Taylor, the lyrical water poet who took pride in his humble status and origin, provided the vicious account and commentary quoted above. Like many other people of all ranks and degrees, he feared that the separatists would destroy not only the divine order of the Established Church, but the divine hierarchy of

---

58 These occupations derive from those attributed to 'tub preachers' by numerous pamphlets attacking the sects in 1641–2.

59 [Taylor], *The discovery*, sig. A 2–3r. This incident took place in December 1641. No wonder that separatists joined the parliamentary armies.

society as well. The troopers of the New Model Army did not prove him wrong.

For social as well as religious reasons, then, moderate members of the puritan brotherhood and their supporters quaked at the understanding extended by Lord Brooke to such lowly nonconformists and trembled when three respected colleagues took up a separatist condemnation of the Church of England. The narcissism of small differences still formed an unbridged gap between puritan and separatist, although some congregationalists now dared to extend their hands, or to leap, across it. In the hour of opportunity the reformers remained apart in their apocalyptic assessments of the past – even in interpreting the nature and significance of the Laudian decade. While all condemned the Arminians, growing and militant minorities rushed beyond the consensus to abandon all hope either in episcopacy or in an Established Church. Lacking complete agreement on how far beyond Rome the borders of Babylon stretched, the reformers hardly reached unanimity when attempting to delineate the New Jerusalem.

II   VISIONS OF A NEW JERUSALEM

The opening of the Long Parliament ushered in a great wave of expectation – a fervent feeling that, at last, all things remiss would soon get corrected. The shift of initiative, however, moved so quickly that it caught the reformers with an undeveloped ecclesiology. Granted that leading presbyterian and congregational divines at first agreed to keep their disputes over polity from the eyes of the public, this hardly seems sufficient explanation of the fact that only a small minority of those who preached before the Commons during the first year of the Long Parliament felt impelled to lay out particular plans for a new church settlement. For various reasons, most of the brotherhood came unprepared. Moderates stressed the need to root out Arminians and to restore something like the Elizabethan settlement, perhaps with a less powerful church hierarchy.[60] Both Mede and Brightman, the most learned apocalyptic chronologers, provided precedents for this moderate episcopalian position. Almost all parliamentary preachers called for the establishment of a university-educated ministry in all corners of the

---

60 Kirby, 'Sermons,' stressed this theme to such an extent that she tended to lose sight of the differences among preachers. Her contention that these fast sermons were 'Erastian' was ably refuted in Lamont, 'Episcopacy.'

land, some as a means of outflanking the sects.[61] Scottish presbyterians and Amsterdam separatists pressed for their tried and true programmes of reform. Few Englishmen, however, had experienced these alternative forms of church polity and most, therefore, hesitated to give them whole-hearted support. Henry Burton put forth no positive programme of reform because he believed, in an old-fashioned way, that Christ would return in the immediate future, judge the quick and the dead, and initiate a heavenly New Jerusalem.[62] Even strongly committed laymen like James 'Prophet' Hunt, the Kentish farmer, and John Fenwick, the persecuted Newcastle merchant, placed little detailed content in their plea to establish Jesus Christ on his throne, that he might rule in England. Soon this image would denote a millennial rule of the saints, but neither Hunt nor Fenwick advocated much beyond the abolition of episcopacy in 1641[63] One group of divines, however, presented a discernible, unified, radical platform of reform in a series of sermons to the Commons. Reflecting the excitement and expectation of the year of deliverance, these men employed the parliamentary pulpit to espouse a recognizable congregational New Jerusalem.

Although some previous preachers clearly indicated that they no longer accepted a Church of England ruled by bishops and with an enforced liturgical service, Joseph Symonds led the way in presenting some sort of formulated alternative. With contemporaries he believed that recent events in England linked into the final fall of the beast:

It's like now the set time of God is come for the fall of Babel, and the reformation and deliverance and enlargement of the churches of Christ. In the xii of *Daniel* we have a prophecy of the deliverance of *Israel*; the time of it is in verse 11. *From the time that the daily sacrifice shall be taken away, and the abomination that maketh desolate set up, there shall be a* 1290 days, that is years. This seems to be in *Julian* the Apostate's time ... There is no time so like to the time which Daniel meant ... And so with this way of account Master Brightman and others also do accord; for it you add 1290 to 360, in which time the abomination of desolation

---

61 Haller stressed the call for a preaching ministry in *Rise of Puritanism*, ch. 9, and *Liberty and Reformation*, ch. 1.

62 Burton, *Englands bondage*, passim, and *The sounding*, sig. A 4, pp. 1, 12–19, 28, 40–4, 62, 70–5, 85, 87, 89, 90–3. Certainly, he held no millennial view in 1641, as Capp, *Fifth Monarchy*, p. 47, asserted. Scots, separatists, and New England congregationalists put forward their programmes in England with vigour.

63 [Fenwick], *The downfall*, and Hunt, *The sermon and prophecie*. Contrast these with their later works.

was, it casts the beginning of the accomplishment of this prophecy upon the 1650 year, so that the time of their deliverance is not far off. But *Rome* must fall before that. Therefore, I conclude that this is an hopeful season. Take heed of delays.[64]

The collapse of the Arminians in Britain helped to prepare the way for the fall of the Roman Babylon in the mid-seventeenth century and, thus, to fulfill beloved Brightman's chronological interpretation of Daniel and Revelation.

Breaking down the walls of the enemy cleared the ground for erecting a new city, the visible church of Christ 'built for himself and the saints, that in it they might enjoy each other.' Directly denying the Anglican concept of *adiaphora*, Symonds maintained that the institutional church must base itself upon the pattern laid down in the New Testament: 'Matters of worship are never left to man's liberty. God only appoints the manner and means of his worship.' In this proposition, of course, he merely reasserted one of the basic foundations of puritan criticism of the Established Church, albeit in an unusually uncompromising way. The pattern revealed by the word of God differed from the presbyterian systems of Cartwright and the Scots. Instead, Symonds espied that polity asserted by both separating and non-separating congregationalists. When he spoke of the time growing ripe for the 'reformation and deliverance and enlargement of the churches of Christ,' Symonds deliberately used the plural because the true visible church consisted of gathered congregations of saints.[65] While more than hinting at this polity, Symonds either decided to hide it somewhat from the eyes of the uninitiated or to leave a full exposition of it for his colleague, Nathaniel Holmes.

Making only perfunctory remarks on the downfall of the Laudians and the defeat of antichrist, Holmes specifically displayed a blueprint for erecting the new church. He started by rehearsing various interpretations of the 'new heavens and a new earth' mentioned in his text (2 Peter iii:13). In turn, Holmes rejected the 'spiritual' reading (advocated by

64 Symonds, *A sermon* (30 May 1641), sig. E IV–2. Before returning from exile, Symonds was associated with Sidrach Simpson's gathered church in Rotterdam. Later he became provost of Eton; see Nuttall, *Visible Saints*, pp. 11–12 n. 8. Other 'root and branch' calls for reformation that contained hints of the congregational ideal included Fairclough, *The troubles*, Wilson, *Davids zeal*, Case, *Two sermons*, and Bridge, *Babylons downfall*, all preached in 1641.

65 *A sermon*, sig. C 2v, B 2v, C 2v–3r. Symonds clearly meant congregational churches in the last of the quoted passages.

Burton at this time) that these words referred to the 'heaven of heavens, and the eternal glory of the saints there,' and the fantasies of the millenarians. 'Other divines commonly called the chiliasts, or millenaries, would (as their names import) understand this text of the martyrs reigning a thousand years on earth in a particular heaven on earth, peculiar to them, before they be taken up, soul and body, into heaven above. But these are as wide on the other side ...' Having spurned the two extremes of exegesis, Holmes preferred to 'fly in the middle region' instead, a place soon populated densely by those of congregational persuasion. 'We, therefore, by new heavens and a new earth understand *a new form of worship*, religion in the expression thereof reformed, brought more close to the rule of the gospel, made more spiritual and *heavenlike*, and earthly men made new, changed, turned into new creatures by the power of religion so reformed.'[66] According to this vision, the new world fit into the normal operations of God's grace as observed by generations of puritan physicians of the soul. It symbolized the conversion of people to a new reformation that would carry that of the sixteenth century to its logical conclusion.

Holmes drew upon the perfected practice and theory of English congregationalism to paint his picture of the new world. Despite its vicissitudes in England, the Netherlands, and New England, the congregational way had emerged as a fairly fixed form of polity in the early seventeenth century. This 'new church' contained no false doctrine, discipline, or government, for it derived all of these elements 'immediately from God,' that is, from scripture. It consisted of congregations, each existing as a 'particular corporation' of gathered saints. 'They neither admit nor permit (if after admission degenerated) him that is unworthy, neither officer nor member of the assembly, congregation, or particular church.' The godly could join only after undergoing a careful examination. Having demonstrated their spiritual insights, all members could teach each other. This careful screening, participatory service, and proper polity made the reformed churches of Geneva and the Low Countries (and presumably of Scotland) seem 'much fuller of dust than a new one.'[67] While these national Calvinist churches served

---

66 Ho[l]mes, *The new world* (27 July 1641), pp. 3, 4, 7. Holmes received his DD from Oxford in 1637; see the *DNB*. Interpretations of this sort competed with frankly millennial visions among the non-separating congregationalists of New England and the Netherlands during the late 1630s. For the former, see Gilsdorf, 'Puritan Apocalypse,' ch. 3–5, and Maclear, 'New England.'

67 *The new world*, pp. 53, 54, 45, 55, see 43–50

as the first model of reformation , they did not stand as a pattern for all time. God now turned to his Englishmen and offered them the opportunity to be the first nation that would reform the reformation itself. Presented with this unique blessing, England could usher in the new heavens and a new earth.

The land, the time, and the people all seemed ripe for this culmination of holy history. England formed one of the ten horns of St John's beast, one of those kingdoms 'that having once hated and opposed the whore of *Babylon*, shall never be reconciled to her till she be burnt with fire.' The calculations of the most careful commentators converged to agree that the appointed end of antichrist's reign of 1260 years would soon arrive. Napier and others had prophesied that 'the time of antichrist's fall should begin to good purpose in 1639,' Holmes reminded members of the Commons. 'And what God hath done from that year and so on, you have eyes and ears to inform yourselves, perhaps better than I.' With conspicuous understatement, he led his audience to see that the victories of the Scots and the fall of the Laudians fit into the timetable of the apocalyptic chronologers. Events in England took on an awful meaning. Not willing to rest, Holmes admonished these worthy magistrates to grasp the opportunity proffered by the Almighty: '... For ought I can see, *you are the promised people*, you the Parliament and Parliaments of his majesty's three kingdoms to be leaders and examples to the Christian world to pull down that of antichrist that is yet standing.'[68] Responsibility for the overthrow of Babylon rested squarely upon the shoulders of those listening to Holmes' sermon.

The Lord charged Parliament with an additional duty, that of building the New Jerusalem. Only such a gathering of men, duly constituted, met the revealed qualifications for those who would establish the new church as outlined in Revelation xxi:17. If England discharged its chosen role, then, a new world of congregational churches could commence on that small island and expand from this base to encompass the whole world.[69] The beginning of the end promised great things. While Holmes explicitly asked Parliament to erect the visible church of Christ, he also warned that the Lord of hosts would turn to other instruments if necessary. God could replace the mighty by his persecuted elect. Nations and individuals who wished to find their names enrolled in the legions of Christ must conform to his commands of a *jure divino* congregational polity. Such combinations of warning and opportunity frequently rang

68 *Ibid.*, pp. 35, 37, see 35–57
69 *Ibid.*, pp. 38–40

out from the parliamentary pulpit, but normally they indicated only a lack of ultimate reliance upon imperial instruments. Despite some similarities, then, Holmes differed significantly from impatient Burton in 1641 by definitely preferring a magisterial reformation.[70]

Apart from some bold New Englanders, few congregational divines spelled out their model of Zion with such force and detail at this time. Strangely enough, Holmes – who remained in England during the 1630s – probably had less practical experience in this form of church government than those many colleagues who tasted the bitterness of separation from their homeland. Nor did all congregationalists agree with the thrust of Holmes' apocalyptic vision, especially with his explicit disavowal of millenarianism.[71] Ironically, congregational exiles – particularly those in the Netherlands – took the lead in bringing the millennium to the people. Influenced by Thomas Brightman, Johannes Alsted, and Joseph Mede, they bounced between apocalyptic and millennial expectations in the late 1630s. Although differing in detail and application, a number of these university-educated pastors tentatively agreed that Christ and his saints would rule the earth for a thousand years. At least two powerful pamphlets, probably pirated notes of sermons preached in the Netherlands, broke into print in the year of expectation and gave Englishmen their first public vernacular glimpse at the pursuit of the millennium.[72]

70 *Ibid.*, pp. 23–4. Holmes believed that God intervened in the elections to the Long Parliament by having the people reject ungodly court candidates; *The peasants*, p. 65. By 1643, however, Holmes could no longer wait for Parliament, so he joined Burton to form a gathered church in London. Sometime during the civil war, he left the middle way and became a millenarian; see Ball, *Great Expectation*, pp. 95, 178–80, passim, and Clouse, 'Influence of Alsted,' pp. 223–45.

71 Among the ten men who preached to the Commons during the first year of the Long Parliament, four – Burroughs, Burton, Simpson, and Symonds – had experienced exile during the 1630s. In the summer of 1641 two colleagues preached an interpretation similar to that of Holmes; see Sedgwick, *Scripture* (n.d.), passim, and Simpson, *A sermon* (n.d.), pp. 3, 16–17, 26–7, 38. Sedgwick's sermon had little apocalyptic content. Henry Burton, who also preached his fast sermon in the summer of 1641, did not identify the New Jerusalem with a reformed church; he felt that Revelation xx was an obscure chapter; see *The sounding*, p. 93.

72 Archer, *The personall*, and [Burroughs], *A glimpse*. Thomason collected his copy of the former in January 1642 and of the latter in November 1641. Archer's pamphlet first appeared in 1641 and was reprinted three times. Also see the millennial I.E., *The land*. According to the son who edited his works, Thomas Goodwin preached his millennial sermons gathered under the title 'An exposition of the Book of Revelation' in 1639. They only appeared posthumously; Goodwin, *Works*, III, p. 15, 155, 200. For the attribution of *A glimpse*, see pp. 217–19 and appendix II. For a discussion of millenarianism in the 1630s and 1640s, see Ball, *Great Expectation*, ch. 5.

The author of *The personall raigne of Christ upon earth*, John (or Henry) Archer, lectured at All Hallows, Lombard Street in London. Forced to relinquish this post by the authorities, he joined Thomas Goodwin and his associates at Arnheim. Apparently, Archer did not live to see the opening of the Long Parliament, but died abroad. In his only surviving work he argued that Christ would rule the world through three types of kingship: providential, spiritual, and monarchical. The first two had existed for a long time. Since the fall, Christ acted as the sacred governor of all things and also had plied his prerogative over some people – especially the elect – through the word and spirit. The erection of his monarchical state, which differed considerably, appeared imminent. '... When he entereth upon it, he will govern as earthly monarchs have done, that is, universally over the world ... and in a worldly visible earthly glory; not by tyranny, oppression, and sensually, but with honour, peace, riches, and whatsoever in and of the world is not sinful, having all nations and kingdoms doing homage to him, as the great monarchies of the world had.' Archer called this universal kingdom the 'fifth monarchy,' a term derived from his exegesis of the second chapter of Daniel. The prophet called it the 'stone cut out of the mountains without hands' (Daniel ii:45). Mede, Brightman, and congregationalists like Holmes interpreted this image as a symbol for the triumph of the true church through more ordinary channels. When he transformed it into a prophecy for an imperial political reign of the elect, Archer broke with a long-standing tradition.[73]

Christ planned to return to earth, chain Satan, defeat the armies of the wicked, and resurrect dead martyrs and chosen ones to help preside over the future. No need for apocalyptic instruments here, the personal intervention of the Almighty assured a victory. After reorganizing the world in forty days, Christ would return to heaven, leaving a government of saints – headed by the resurrected apostles – to rule the world for a thousand years. Converted at last, the Jews played an important role in this millennium.[74] For the chosen ones, this new order promised a fulness of all 'temporal blessings, as peace, safety, riches, health, long life, and whatsoever else was enjoyed under any *monarchy*, or can be had in this world ...' After a thousand years of bounty for the saints and

73 Archer, *The personall*, pp. 2–3, 7–8; cf. Mede, *Apostasy*, pp. 69–70. For the little known about Archer and for his thought, see Ball, *Great Expectation*, pp. 127, 165, 220–1, Clouse, 'Influence of Alsted,' pp. 95–105, and Seaver, *Puritan Lectureships*, pp. 172–3, 250–1.

74 *The personall*, pp. 15–16, 20–1, 25–6

their offspring, Archer expected the wicked – slaves, so far, of the elect – to rise up in revolt. Satan, broken free from his bonds, would command this conspiracy, but the Saviour would shortly return again to begin the day of judgment. The separation of the sheep from the goats, with its reward of bliss for the saved and eternal damnation for the rest, might last another thousand years.[75]

The fall of Roman Babylon and the conversion of the Jews preceded the inception of the millennium and signalled its imminence. Drawing upon the prominent authorities of the previous generation – Brightman, Patrick Forbes, Alsted, and Mede among others – Archer established a firm chronology for these all-important future events. He dated the coming in of the Jews to 1650 or 1656, the start of the collapse of antichrist's 1260-year reign to 1666, and the commencement of the millennium to around 1700.[76] Pessimistically inclined in the short run like many exiles, Archer predicted a dramatic increase in the power of Rome just previous to its annihilation. The woe of 'popery shall again overrun *Europe*, and bring back under papal power every king in *Europe*, and ... suppress all opposers in every kingdom by papal power,' he groaned. To see the fulfilment of this prophecy, contemporaries had only to observe those reverses suffered by reformed religion in Germany during the Thirty Years War or in England during the persecution of the Laudian era. Retaliation against the revival of Roman rule, the pouring of the fifth vial, recommenced in 'one *of the ten cities of Europe which were under Rome's papal power, in whom witnesses were slain*' and the tables at last turned '*by an earthquake, that is, by a commotion of the people*' who would 'revolt from Romish religion and reform' the church again.[77] A new, more perfect, form of church sprang up as a result, this time to last and spread across the world.

No wonder Archer's pamphlet commanded enough attention in England to justify five printings in 1641 and 1642. To those who heard about or read this arresting vision, it must have presented a cogent explanation of those commotions that contemporaries experienced in the recent past, as well as a novel and exciting elucidation of the future. Even the uninitiated could easily equate the defeat of the Laudians in Scotland and England with the revolt of the tenth part of the beast's kingdom.

---

75 *Ibid.*, p. 29, see 32–4, 39
76 *Ibid.*, pp. 46–50. Archer actually pointed out that by dropping the first numeral from the year 1666 that it became the number of the beast.
77 *Ibid.*, pp. 51, 46. Christ won the final victory, but the persecuted elect – by revolting from popery – triggered the last campaign.

True believers longed to witness even greater marvels – the conversion of the Jews, promised in less than ten years, and the inception of the suppression of Rome in fifteen years. Although few of these early converts could expect to live long enough to help Christ inaugurate his millennial kingdom, members of the elect could rest assured of a place in it because of the first resurrection. Archer's criterion for delineating the elect was not a rigid one: 'all they who are to enjoy the privileges of this kingdom of Christ are described, *by not being infected with popery*, Revelation xiv:2 and x:4.'[78] External actions like renouncing popery in all its works and all its ways met this test. Zeal for the spiritual and temporal benefits of the millennium provided a powerful force that encouraged people to promote the events which prepared the way for the return of their Saviour.

Atypical of the English apocalyptic canon, Archer's treatise made almost no attempt to relate the predictions of Revelation to either history or current events. Full of doctrine, of scriptural interpretation, it devoted small space to the use or application of its dogma to the lives and actions of its audience. The prophecy that the common people would lead the way to the overthrow of Babylon provided one of the very few exceptions. In a real sense, this made Archer's vision even more capable of radical construction in the hands of uneducated readers who could infuse their own relevance into his potent ideology.[79]

While Archer mapped out the future in detail and remained nearly silent about the present, the author of another millennial message coming out of the Netherlands concentrated on instilling contemporary events with cosmic meaning. Derived from the same tradition and preached by a friend of Archer, *A glimpse of Sions glory* explored the expectation that the prophecies of St John were unfolding in England. In this anonymously printed sermon based upon Revelation xix:6, Jeremiah Burroughs proclaimed that the actions of the Long Parliament at last initiated the collapse of Babylon and the rise of Zion.

Burroughs proposed 'to shew unto you, how upon the destruction of Babylon, Christ shall reign gloriously, and how we are to further it.' Leading up to the climax, the Thirty Years War represented the pouring of the fourth vial upon the sun '(namely upon the emperor and that

---

78 *Ibid.*, p. 31
79 On the last two pages, Archer advised the quietist policy of waiting for the millennium. At least one of his followers did not; see note 130 below. Application of the doctrines derived from a biblical text to the contemporary situation formed the 'uses' of a Ramist sermon; see Wilson, *Pulpit*, ch. 5.

house of Austria).' In the course of the accomplishment of this prophecy, the next stage concomitantly commenced: 'God is beginning the pouring forth of the fifth vial, namely upon the throne of the beast, upon Babylon; this is the work that is in hand; as soon as ever this is done, that antichrist is down, Babylon fallen, then comes in Jesus Christ reigning gloriously; then comes, in this Hallelujah, the Lord God omnipotent reigneth.' The last line of this quotation came from Revelation xx:6 and presented the paean of the saints at the pouring of the sixth vial upon Babylon. Although some of the prophecies of Revelation still awaited consummation, Burroughs urged the godly 'by faith to speak of things as if they were done' and by action to make events come to pass.[80]

Christ already ruled in the hidden, persecuted elect who formed themselves into gathered congregations. As in the past, the message of destruction and salvation received its first articulation from them: 'First, it is in the voice of the waters, the voice of Jesus Christ reigning in his church, comes first from the multitude, the common people, the voice is heard from them first, before it is heard from any others ... as when Christ came at first, the poor receive the gospel ... so in the reformation of religion, after antichrist began to be discovered, it was the common people that first came to look after Christ.' Like John Lilburne and other separatists, Burroughs transformed the apocalyptic tradition of the persecuted and oppressed into a social analysis which placed the poor and lowly in the vanguard of religious reformation. Pointing out that the Lord of hosts often acted in this way, he referred to the Scottish rebellion as an example of the common people taking the lead in upholding Christ's truth. Now the multitude moved to inaugurate the reign of Christ and pointed out its direction, 'yet it is not for them to bring it to perfection; that which they do commonly is mixed with much confusion and a great deal of disorder.' The perfection of the insights of the lower orders in an ordered and lasting way necessarily called forth the use of more mighty instruments: 'God moves the hearts of the great ones, of noble, of learned ones, and they come to the work, and their voice is the voice of mighty thundering, a voice that strikes terror, and hath a majesty in it to prevail.'[81] Well did this client of the

---

80 [Burroughs], A glimpse, pp. 2, 3; in other words, Mede's interpretation had started coming true.
81 Ibid., pp. 5, 6. Most scholars have overlooked this stress upon the completion of the reformation by the ruling orders of society; cf. Haller, Rise of Puritanism, pp. 270–2, Wolfe, introduction to Milton, Complete Prose, I, pp. 149–51, and, for a careful analysis that takes account of this point, Liu, Discord in Zion, pp. 1–7.

Earl of Warwick know. No potential Leveller, Burroughs demonstrated from the words of St John that the voices of both the waters – the common people – and the thunder – the upper orders – played an indispensable role in establishing the kingdom of Christ. Appealing to all levels of society, but especially to the common people who would lead the way, he synthesized the imperial tradition with that of the oppressed in a unique manner.

The elusive image of the reign or kingdom of Christ received several definitions in *A glimpse of Sions glory*. Burroughs often employed it to mean a true visible church – gathered congregations of saints – that revived the polity of the apostles. To such a group he proclaimed that 'if the kingdom of *Christ had* been kept in congregations, in that way that we and some other *churches* are in, it had been impossible that antichrist should have got head.' On the other hand, Christ's kingdom also encompassed the notion of a thousand-year monarchy of the elect on earth. This millennial vision sprang primarily from Revelation xx, where the favourite disciple reported that the saints would reign with Christ for a thousand years: '... Now the reigning with *Christ* a thousand years is not meant reigning with him in heaven, for after these thousand years, there shall be many enemies raised against the church, GOG and MAGOG shall gather themselves together; if it were meant of heaven, that could not be; and therefore it must be meant of Jesus Christ coming and reigning here gloriously for a thousand years. And although this may seem to be strange, yet heretofore it hath not been accounted so; it hath been a truth received in the primitive times.'[82] Even in the Netherlands, the millennium seemed an admittedly novel doctrine.

After quoting and unfolding other parts of scripture to bolster this new vision, Burroughs delineated the glories of the millennium in a series of thirteen points. Unlike Archer, he dealt almost entirely with spiritual, not temporal, blessings for the saints. The outline included union among protestant churches, the resurrection of former martyrs, the binding of Satan, the conversion of the Jews, and a clearer revelation of the will of God. Point twelve mentioned the abundance of outward prosperity which followed from a 'resurrection of the creatures of the world' to a more pure state. Point eight showed how the rule of the godly might commence without bursting the bounds of normal modes of political action. It contrasted the position of the saints under persecu-

---

82 *A glimpse*, pp. 11, 14–15. Millenarianism still seemed controversial among the exiles in the Netherlands.

tion – their normal lot – with the way they would flourish in the future. Once more, Burroughs showed few of the characteristics of a social revolutionary.

... Though the governors of *Judah* have counted them factious and schismatics and puritans, there is a time coming when the governors of *Judah* shall be convinced of the excellency of God's people ... that the inhabitants of *Jerusalem*, that is, the saints of God gathered together in a church, are the best commonwealth's men ... they shall be countenanced by them as the strength of a kingdom, as those that will be most useful in a kingdom ... Religion shall be honoured in the world one day, and not only at the day of judgment, but here.[83]

This prediction, of course, fit into the pattern of pleas made by reformers since the early sixteenth century, the contention that godly men made the best magistrates, but Burroughs now placed fulfilment of it into the context of the coming millennium. Identifying the saints with congregationalists, he predicted that they would soon come into positions of power in England. Perhaps his connection with the Earl of Warwick gave him a special insight into political affairs.

Deriving his chronology from Brightman, Burroughs dated the destruction of Babylon to around 1650. Brightman's prophecies about Sardia (Germany), alas, already had come true and at last the work of the Lord reached fruition in Britain:

We hear the voice of the multitude in our own country, as the voice of many waters, they cry up the kingdom of *Christ*, and cry down the kingdom of *antichrist*, cry down *Babylon* and the *prelacy*; but this doth seem to be the voice of many waters, that the adversaries derided it, scorned it ... But blessed be God, we begin to hear the voice from the thunderings too, in a more terrible way; God begins to work upon the great ones of the land, the worthies of the land that are drawn together in that ASSEMBLY ... This is the work of the day, for us to lift up our voice to heaven, that it might be mighty to bring forth more and more the voice of our PARLIAMENT as a voice of thunder, a terrible voice to the antichristian party ...

Soon the Commons would invite Burroughs to lift up his own voice before them. The dawn of this new era delivered the saints from persecution and derision. To help topple the kingdom of the beast, they must

83 *Ibid.*, pp. 28, 26, see 21–31

'testify against *antichrist and antichristianism*,' that is, publicly denounce the hierarchical Church of England. Since little time remained,
the godly had to gather themselves in congregations in preparation for
the New Jerusalem that Christ would found at his coming.[84] All of the
elect must put aside the divisions of the past so that confusion could not
hinder the promise of the future.

Although both preached millennial messages, a noticeably stark contrast in tone and emphasis separated *A glimpse of Sions glory* from *The
personall raigne of Christ upon earth*. Whereas Archer announced that
Christ would return from heaven to launch the thousand-year reign of
the saints by fiat, Burroughs emphasized the vigorous participation of
the people in preparing the way for their Saviour's arrival. Archer was a
quietist, Burroughs an activist. Burroughs stressed those typical aspects
of the English apocalyptic tradition, curiously ignored by Archer, by
finding fulfilment of specific prophecies in contemporary events and by
affirming that the Almighty worked through human instruments. Laying out particular tasks of broad scope, *A glimpse of Sions glory* asked all
sections of society to fight the spiritual battles of the Lord in this world.
In practical terms, this signified breaking apart the episcopal Church of
England and erecting a congregational structure to replace it. Archer's
vision of the millennium really demanded the destruction of society as
it then existed, but Burroughs believed that God would work through
existing institutions to implement his ends. In one sense, the rule of the
saints began for Burroughs when congregationalists gained political
office, or when the mighty of the land took up their cause. Now that
Parliament sat, such developments hardly seemed unlikely to a client of
the Earl of Warwick. Although lacking in application to events and
seemingly apolitical, Archer's treatise cried out for revolutionary interpretation. Burroughs' pamphlet, on the other hand, often sounded
revolutionary, but actually it pressed for reform. In a virtuoso performance, Burroughs managed to combine workable religious and political
goals with the pursuit of the millennium. He synthesized the apocalyptic tradition of the oppressed with the imperial tradition – minus the
godly prince – into a powerful combination that placed the initiative for
reform in the hands of the lower orders, its completion in the care of the
élite. Moreover, his pamphlet contained that type of reference to contemporary events that makes for instant relevance.

John Archer never sailed back to England; probably he died before the
collapse of Laudian uniformity made such a trip feasible. One wonders if

84 *Ibid.*, pp. 7, 33, see 32–3

he would have stuck to his millennial weapons in England, for most of his colleagues did not – at least in public. For whatever reason, members of the congregational brotherhood – with one exception who only dropped broad hints – held back from a pursuit of the millennium prior to the outbreak of the civil war. Jeremiah Burroughs proved no exception to this rule. Cautiously postponing his homecoming until 1641, he preached before the Commons on 5 September of that year. This sermon contained many of the expressions and interpretations found in *A glimpse of Sions glory*, too many for mere coincidence, but avoided even a peek at the millennium. Flushed with expectation, Burroughs addressed the assembled worthies as special apocalyptic instruments of the Almighty: 'My subject is joy, and this eases the work much; you right honourable, are the *anointed of the Lord*, I mean, set apart from your brethren to the great work of the Lord that He is doing in this latter age of the world.'[85] The 'anointed of the Lord' usually symbolized the charismatic priestly nature of divine kingship, so Burroughs explicitly shifted the imperial mantle from king to Parliament – more openly and cogently, one might add, than any other preacher or pamphleteer at the time.

Silenced and forced into exile, Burroughs now rejoiced that the elect at last dared 'openly profess the name, the truths of God, the purity of his worship' in England, instead of having to gather in hidden conventicles or to flee the land for refuge. The common people, the meaner sort, forged the way by finding and practising congregationalism, the true policy commanded by Christ.[86] In the past, the powerful despised and persecuted them for this, but suddenly the Lord began to speak through Parliament to swell the voice of the lower orders: 'We hear *a noise now* not only as from many waters, but from thunder, saying, *Hallelujah, the Lord God omnipotent reigneth*, Apocalypse xix:6. The voice from *the many waters* was from the *people*, but that was despised, condemned; but the voice from *the thunder* is from those in *places of dignity* and power, and this voice is terrible to the adversaries.'[87] This repeated the interpretation put forth in *A glimpse of Sions glory*. The language,

---

85 Burroughs, *Sions joy*, p. 2, see sig. A 3, pp. 24–5, 51–8. William Sedgwick broke ranks to hint at the millennium in the parliamentary pulpit.
86 *Ibid.*, pp. 3–4, cf. 32–3
87 *Ibid.*, p. 44; cf. *A glimpse*, pp. 5–7 (quoted above). The parallel between these passages is so great that Burroughs certainly must have attended the earlier sermon, not yet published in May 1641, and most probably preached it. The Hallelujah found an echo in [Burroughs], *The petition*, sig. A 2, while the text and interpretation got repeated in [Burroughs], *The glorious*, pp. 145–6. I know of no other author in 1640–2 who employed Revelation xix:6 as a text so frequently or who gave this interpretation to it repeatedly.

biblical text, imagery, interpretation, and stress upon both imperial and oppressed instruments all told the same message. Previously he preached before the many waters – now he addressed the thunderers.

By the time that Burroughs spoke to Parliament one of the aspects of the millennium unfolded in the anonymous pamphlet already had come to pass. Honoured by the rulers of England as 'loyal subjects and brethren,' the godly saw their enemies scattered like chaff before the wind. 'The greatest blow that ever was given to *antichristian government* is that which now it hath had; *Babylon is* fallen, it is fallen, as it shall never rise again in power.' Significantly, he preached in honour of the peace with Scotland, a country that had recently abolished episcopacy. Although stating that Babylon had fallen, Burroughs also reminded his listeners that enemies still existed who would attempt to stop the saints. If England's magistrates, he admonished, 'take courage in setting yourselves against the *antichristian party*, in all those ways that God calls you unto, the issue will certainly be glorious.'[88] So long as enmity continued to exist, one could only speak of the destruction of Babylon as accomplished in faith.

All signs pointed in the same direction – the commencement, now in Britain, of the culmination of history. Before the eyes of Burrough's contemporaries flashed the fruition of the last prophecies in the timetable of St John, events like the resurrection of the two witnesses and the destruction of the 'Babylonish brats of innovation.' The seven seals were opened (understood) and the process of their implementation rushed on. The time for final decisions approached. Just as Burroughs earlier urged his humble saints in the Netherlands to exert great effort in the Lord's battle, so now he admonished Parliament to crush the residue of antichrist's power in England and to complete the architecture of a congregationalist Zion. God had first revealed the reformation in England and he called on his Englishmen to pioneer its perfection: 'that which God hath begun to do amongst us, we hope is the beginning of that great work that he intends to do in this latter age of the world, to raise up *Jerusalem as the praise of the whole earth.*'[89] While not spelling out the details of this New Jerusalem with the rich explicitness of Holmes, Burroughs more than hinted at its congregational nature by constantly using the plural 'churches' rather than the singular 'church' to signify Jerusalem. To understand this diffidence, one must remember

88 *Sions joy*, pp. 24, 44, 60; cf. *A glimpse*, pp. 3, 24–5, 32
89 *Ibid.*, p. 33, see 16–18, 22, 43, 51–2

his earlier warnings about divisions among the godly – after all, this sermon celebrated the signing of peace between England and presbyterian Scotland.

Despite the many continuities underlying the messages preached in *Sions joy* and *A glimpse of Sions glory*, the startling contrast of contexts created a number of glaring discontinuities. Most conspicuously, Burroughs held back from explicitly advocating a congregational polity and from even mentioning any millennial ideas in his parliamentary sermon. The latter seems most strange. Perhaps Burroughs refrained from a public pursuit of the millennium in September 1641 because privately he perceived it already coming into existence. The heady fire of joy and expectation that surged through the beautiful, biblical language of *Sions joy* suggests this sort of solution. Perhaps he just trimmed his sails to fit the new situation. Unwilling to compromise his ultimate aims, however, Burroughs ended his address to the thunderers with a doxology conditionally promising that the preaching brotherhood would support Parliament: 'Bless ye the *Lord*; we will bless the Lord for this, we will bless you in the name of the Lord, and we will stir up all we can to bless God for you.'[90] No matter what strength of opposition might arise, Parliament must complete the reform of church and state.

Stephen Marshall sounded similar themes on the same day, celebrating the deliverance of God's people from danger, warning that troubles lay ahead, and exhorting Parliament to continue tearing down Babylon and building up Zion. Specifically, he cautioned his audience not to hang up their armour. Despite the fact that 'God hath lately done great things for these *two unworthy nations*, great enemies are quelled, great yokes are broken, blessed be his name for it, but all our enemies are not dead,' some sulked in the shadows waiting for revenge.[91] Having secured the civil liberties of the subject, the godly magistrates must remember that the most important task remained incomplete. Echoing the very

90 *Ibid.*, p. 64, cf. 6, 21, 44–7, 60. Burroughs and Thomas Goodwin both refrained from public pursuit of the millennium in 1641–2. In one work, Burroughs hinted at it, concluding that: 'I am confident that Christ shall reign personally, in his flesh I will not say, but spiritually, far more gloriously than he hath done.' Burroughs, *Moses his choice*, p. 487, see 281, 484–7. These passages are capable of millennial construction (as in Capp, *Fifth Monarchy*, p. 47), but seem, more plausibly, to refer to the spread of the congregational churches of Christ across the whole world – the position preached by Holmes in 1641 and Thomas Goodwin in 1642.

91 Marshall, *A peace-offering* (7 Sept. 1641), p. 9, passim. The tormented condition of the saints in the 1630s fulfilled the prophecy about the persecution of the two witnesses of Revelation xi.

words employed by Nathaniel Holmes a little more than three months previously, Marshall reminded the members of Parliament: 'you have *great works* to do, the planting of a new heaven and a new earth amongst us.' Although not as overwhelmingly apocalyptic as his colleague, Marshall also placed the peace with Scotland into the context of the latter days. Like Burroughs, he hinted at his preference for a congregational polity. As both men looked back over the '*mirabilis annus*' in which so many marvellous changes took place, Burroughs and Marshall could only approach the future with optimistic rejoicing.[92] The note of warning sounded by both men took on pressing reality two months later, however, with the outbreak of the Irish rebellion.

The year of expectation signalled a turning point for English puritans. From November 1640, when Parliament started to sit, to November 1641, when news of the Irish revolt spread across England, a heady atmosphere of anticipation and confidence prevailed among those who longed for further religious reform. Parliamentary preachers joined a host of others who expressed their feelings in pulpit and press to perceive in the downfall of the Laudians both a deliverance of God's people from the persecutors and a portent of greater things to come. While the reformers agreed that Babylon was falling and the New Jerusalem springing up in England, they assigned a variety of precise meanings to both of these apocalyptic images. Flushed with optimism, they inclined to minimize the real differences within their own ranks and probable opposition to radical reformation of the Established Church from more conservative people. After all, the reformers repeated, had not the Almighty revealed his hand? Did not rich and poor, powerful and persecuted, join hands to raise the proper foundations of the kingdom of Christ? The face of reform seemed strongly set, but certainly it looked in more than one direction.

One of the most extraordinary manifestations of the year of expectation found congregational divines exercising a virtual monopoly of the parliamentary pulpit between May and September 1641. With differing degrees of openness, these radicals presented their vision of a New Jerusalem. A few short months before they addressed less exalted audiences of exiles or country folk. With such a sudden elevation in fortune,

---

92 *Ibid.*, pp. 22, 40, see 45–6, 50; see Burroughs, *Sions joy*, p. 25. The summer of 1641 also witnessed the first publication of Mede, *Apostasy*, in English and of several shortened versions of Brightman: *Brightmans predictions, The revelation of Mr. Brightmans*, and *Reverend M. Brightmans*. These printed the high points (that is, chronology) of his prophecies without his qualifications.

men like Holmes and Burroughs quite rightly saw the dawning of a new day in contemporary events. The squires who sat in the House of Commons could no longer ignore the possibility of gathered congregations of the godly as an alternative polity to a national church. Peers like Lord Brooke certainly did not disregard it – in fact, the Earl of Warwick and Viscount Say and Sele may well have launched the congregational campaign from behind the scenes.[93] This sustained propagation of the congregational programme opened the first split in the puritan brotherhood, one that grew and became public in the years which followed. The budding rift went beyond polity to include the attitudes of educated reformers toward the sects. Radicals, like Burroughs, Milton, and Lord Brooke, welcomed manifestations of light from the lower orders, while moderate presbyterians and episcopalians perceived them as threats to the hierarchical order of the church, society, state, and universe. However, during the year of expectation almost all reformers agreed to paper over their differences in anticipation of inevitable religious change.[94] They felt genuinely united in joy at the downfall of the Arminians and in hope for further reformation. Doubts and warnings of opposition intruded into their works, but most believed that action and exhortation could overcome any stumbling blocks. New developments in the second year of the Long Parliament jolted this optimism and tempered confidence into militance.

III   FORGING MILITANCE

As members of Parliament arrived in London after the September recess, plots and rumours of plots filled the air and the news-sheets. Reports of the Incident – a conspiracy by reckless royalists to overthrow the ascendancy of the Marquis of Argyll in Scotland – appeared in pamphlets shortly after reaching the recess committee of Parliament through official channels.[95] When the Commons reassembled on 20 October 1641,

93 Of the ten sermons preached to the Commons during this period, only that by F[ord]fell outside this category. Lord Brooke openly propounded a serious consideration of the congregational way. His radical friend, Viscount Say and Sele, gained office in the spring of 1641 and stood near the height of his influence during the summer. The Earl of Warwick's connection included at least Marshall and Burroughs, and probably Holmes as well. See Shipps, 'Lay Patronage,' and Fiennes, *Two speeches of.*

94 For an exception, see Edwards, *Reasons against*, sig. **1, who pointed out that the congregationalists sent their ministers to the Commons and were 'preaching often at *Westminster*'; cf. Liu, *Discord in Zion*, ch. 1.

95 *A great discoverie, The discovery of a late, A true and full relation*, and J.S., *The truth*

John Pym – chairman of the recess committee – included the Incident in his long report to the House. Sir Simonds D'Ewes, speaking next, emphasized the gravity of recent events in a long oration on the danger presented by papists and their allies. Five days later the contagious plaster from a plague sore entered the House of Commons addressed to Pym. Pamphleteers quickly blamed this foul deed upon the machinations of 'Romish dragons.' In November Charles returned from Scotland, determined to restore proper order by standing strong against further reformation in church and state. Having confirmed the abolition of episcopacy and parliamentary approval for important appointments in Scotland, he stubbornly resisted any attempt by the English Parliament to wring similar concessions. In religious affairs the king tipped his hand by translating to new sees four bishops – John Williams, Joseph Hall, Brian Duppa, and Robert Skinner – who all supported *jure divino* episcopacy.[96] During that same November reports of popish plots streamed in from various parts of Great Britain – London, Norwich, Cheshire, Wales, Edinburgh, and, most threatening of all, Ireland. Most contained little substance and merely reflected the panic caused by the Irish rebellion. The latter, detailed in over thirty pamphlets collected by George Thomason before the end of 1641, struck Englishmen with shock and posed some knotty political problems.[97] Ireland, the Incident, and the inflexibility of King Charles confirmed the worst fears of the reformers and dampened those euphoric fevers that prevailed among them during the first year of the Long Parliament.

The road to a New Jerusalem no longer seemed swift, straight, and smoothly paved, but full of obstacles and twistings. Those who preached before the Long Parliament in its second year faced an increasingly polarized audience. Some trod the path of peace and moderation, but they made up a distinct minority who shared St Margaret's pulpit with more fiery spirits.[98] Others concentrated their focus upon the New Jerusalem rather than upon the immediate problems besetting Britain.

96 D'Ewes, *Journal*, pp. 1–15, *A damnable*, sig. A 2, passim, and [Vicars], *All the mercies*, plate 8a. Charles translated the four bishops between 11 November and 19 December 1641.

97 *A new plot, A discovery of a horrible, Bloody newes, A royal message*, [Davis], *A great discovery*, and *Dolefull newes*. Plots of this type were discovered in England right up to the outbreak of fighting; see Clifton, 'Popular fear,' and Hibbard, 'Charles I and Plot.' Pamphlets on the Irish rebellion appear in Thomason numbers E 173–81; see Lindley, 'The impact.'

98 Thomas Cheshire and Edward Reynolds preached sermons of this sort; see notes 12 and 13 above.

Even these came to register a growing confidence in the justice of Parliament's cause and in the likelihood of triumph. Inside and outside of the parliamentary pulpit, most reformers expressed fears that a victory for those around the king would lead either to a revival of the religious uniformity of the 1630s or a clinging to the Elizabethan settlement. Unwilling to return to such bondage, they threw the full weight of their persuasive abilities behind the cause of Parliament. Events forged puritan militance.

While not ignoring the constitutional issues that split the ruling segment of society, the reformers viewed religion as the real issue of contention in 1642. The popish plot interpretation of the 1630s, so often repeated by Pym, took on new meaning as civil war appeared increasingly imminent and parliamentarians identified the evil forces misleading King Charles with the legions of the beast. Preachers transferred to England's hostilities their analysis of the Irish revolt – both became branches of the cosmic conflict between Christ and antichrist. The call for apocalyptic warfare against Spain sounded by James VI ironically recoiled upon the advisers and supporters of his son. Radicals preached a crusade against the company who kept the king from his great council, while more moderate reformers urged Parliament's adherents to take up defensive arms.[99] Learned divines tore the apocalyptic tradition of the oppressed from its normal employment as an ideology of quietism – or, at best, passive resistance – and transformed it into an offensive or defensive weapon against those who failed to support further reformation. Paradoxically, they also appealed to Parliament as God's imperial instrument, when that seemed appropriate. Without abandoning the dream of building a New Jerusalem in England, reformers found that the annihilation of Babylon claimed top priority. After recovering from the shock of the new situation, they supported Parliament – the persecuted and imperial instrument of the Lord of hosts – against a royalist army that dwelt in the tents of antichrist.

Just when news of the uprising in Ireland started to reach London, the Commons heard their first fast sermon after the September recess. Preaching on 5 November Cornelius Burges naturally turned to holy history and presented the Irish rebellion as the most recent manifestation of antichrist's opposition to the church of Christ in Britain, a

99 Hill, *Antichrist*, pp. 78–84, makes this point about the radicals, while Walzer, *Revolution*, pp. 293–9, suggests the interpretation as a whole, but dates the differences to the years after 1642; from their citations, neither appears to have surveyed all of the fast sermons.

continuation of the cosmic warfare of the Armada, Tyrone's rebellion, and the Gunpowder Plot. Pointing to the root of the matter, he implored Parliament to use all of its power 'to destroy popery, and to reduce (if possible) those many thousands of poor seduced souls, that, having not known *the depths of Satan*, are miserable, hoodwinked by antichrist to withstand the light and their own salvation. For, till then, they will never be at an *end* of their *rage* against us.'[100] Although he believed that God sent the Irish revolt to punish England for failing to finish the reformation, the growth of sects in London shocked Burges just as much as the trouble in Ireland.[101] His sermon registered a dampening of the optimistic tone that prevailed hitherto in St Margaret's chapel.

The drums of apocalyptic warfare beat with more resonant tones outside the parliamentary pulpit at first. In London, John Goodwin encouraged Englishmen to help their beleaguered brethren. The persecuted protestants in Ireland made up 'but few in number in respect of the swarms of those antichristian hornets that nestle amongst them.' Goodwin tried to fire the hearts of his compatriots by pointing out that the Irish had 'already consecrated themselves unto the devil and his service upon the lives and blood of many servants of GOD, your brethren in the faith.'[102] The English must suppress this massacre as the Israelites of old had slaughtered the Amaleckites. If not, England faced terrible consequences: 'If *Ireland* ever be brought under the power of the *Romish* faction, the sun of *England*'s prosperities will suddenly be darkened in the midst of the heavens thereof ...'[103] The back door to Britain could not stand open to Babylon without endangering England. Goodwin provided an early example of the heated reaction stirred up in English hearts by the Irish rebellion. His sermon seethed with militant imagery and conditional warnings of dire consequences. Although only calling for monetary contributions at this time, Goodwin prepared his audience to take up arms.

As fierce debate over the Grand Remonstrance split the ranks of the House of Commons and sentiment within the ruling orders started perceptibly to favour the king, pessimism pervaded the parliamentary pulpit. Appropriately taking his text from Jeremiah, Edmund Calamy

---

100 Burges, *Another sermon* (5 Nov. 1641), p. 35, see 13–33
101 *Ibid.*, pp. 60–2
102 [Goodwin], *Irelands advocate*, pp. 27, 29. Goodwin, a controversial congregationalist, preached this sermon on 14 November 1641; in a work finished in May of that year, he supplied his readers with twenty motives for patience. Goodwin, *The returne*, pp. 137–346. See the *DNB*.
103 *Irelands advocate*, p. 32, see 19–20

bemoaned the possibility that England might experience the plagues of Germany, Bohemia, the Palatinate, La Rochelle, and Ireland – all places of victory for catholic arms. He feared that the Almighty had withdrawn his hand of support from England: 'That the sun of our prosperity is ready to set.'[104] Only immediate action could prevent this horrible fate: 'Oh, let us set God on work this day, to destroy the implacable enemies of his church; arise oh Lord, and scatter the Irish rebels! Arise oh Lord, and confound antichrist, and build the walls of Jerusalem!'[105] With the beast roaring so near at hand, only conformity to the Lord's will could cure England's woes.

Calamy's colleague, Stephen Marshall, also feared the withdrawal of divine favour and the extension of Ireland's battle to England. He warned the Commons that 'you can do England no good, if God's wrath, which is kindled against it, be not pacified.' The best pacifier was a full reformation. Until Parliament reformed the church, the showers of blood that antichrist now poured down upon Ireland's soil would continue to hang over England.[106] As Samuel Fawcet explained in a sermon to the Haberdashers Company: 'Now *Ireland* calls for your help, the fire is begun there and who knows whither it may burn, if not timely quenched? Those *Romish Ignatians* and *antichristian brood* have begun that fire there, who doubtless are blowing the coals at this time here amongst us also.'[107] At last, hints of internal strife moved out into the open when John Marston speculated that the judgment of the Lord, withheld when external enemies such as the Scots threatened, might fall on England through civil war: 'But it is not an open enemy that now doth us this dishonour, but the serpents lie in the bosom of the kingdom, and so much are we our own enemies, that there is great cause to fear we may destroy ourselves (we read not of Sion so) and doubtless it is desperate with that state that is ready to stab itself.'[108] The hopes and

104 Calamy, *Englands* (22 Dec. 1641), p. 20, see 16–17. Driven from his lectureship by Bishop Wren, Calamy became one of the leading 'presbyterians' in the Westminster Assembly. See the *DNB*. Since many divines called 'presbyterians' by contemporaries actually supported a moderate or 'primitive' episcopacy, that term will appear within quotation marks.

105 *Ibid.*, pp. 46, 10

106 Marshall, *Reformation* (22 Dec. 1641), p. 24, see 47–8; cf. Calamy, *Englands*, pp. 13–17. These sermons were preached three days after the twelve bishops in the Tower protested to King Charles that all 'laws, orders, votes, resolutions, and determinations' passed by Parliament while crowds restrained the bishops from sitting were null and void; quoted in Zagorin, *Court and Country*, p. 277.

107 Fawcet, *A seasonable*, p. 13, see 15–17, 19, 25; preached in St Mary Stainings on 23 Nov. 1641

108 Marston, *A sermon* (6 Feb. 1642), p. 4

dreams of the reformers, their belief that England stood on the threshold
of a New Jerusalem, lay so dashed that preachers openly wondered
whether or not Zion would arise in the land.

The months which witnessed the low point of expectation in the
parliamentary pulpit, notably November 1641 through January 1642,
also produced a polarization between king and Parliament as seen in
such well-known events as the passage and printing of the Grand Remonstrance by the Commons and the attempt to arrest the 'five members' by King Charles. While clerical politicians sank into depths of
despair, more radical spirits grasped the initiative in the press and in
direct action. Crowds of common people, as at the attainder of Strafford,
swarmed into Westminster and prevented the bishops from sitting in the
Lords. An unprecedented volume of popular pamphlets, scourging the
persons of prelates as well as the office itself, dared point to the serpents
in the bosom of the nation.[109] Petitions demanding the 'root and branch'
abolition of episcopacy arrived from Cheshire, Kent, Somerset, Ulster,
and groups of women in London. Other petitions, ones that linked the
Irish rebellion with England's troubles and called for the removal of
bishops and popish lords from the upper House, streamed in from London, the apprentices of London, Devon, Buckinghamshire, Kent, Essex,
Colchester, Gloucester, Northamptonshire, London, Hertfordshire,
Exeter, Devon, many thousands of poor people in London, Leicester-
shire, Surrey, and Middlesex.[110] This campaign directed by some against
episcopacy and by others against the political power of the bishops,
clearly contained political aims within a plea for reformation. With the
prelates and popish peers dislodged, godly nobles like the Earls of Essex
and Warwick, Viscounts Mandeville and Say and Sele, Lords Brooke and
Wharton, and their allies would dominate the House. It met with some
success. On 14 February 1642 Charles I finally assented to a bill prohibit-
ing all clergy from holding secular office, the last statute of his reign; on
the next day, the Lords passed the militia ordinance.[111]

The pessimistic mood among parliamentary preachers noticeably
shifted shortly afterward, buoyed up as well by the establishment of a
regular series of official monthly fast sermons on 23 February 1642.

109 See Pearl, *London*, pp. 210–36, and notes 30 and 31 above.
110 For the 'root and branch' petitions respectively, see Thomason numbers E 178.4, 669
f4.9, E 131.24, E 148.2, E 134.17, and 669 f4.57. For the others respectively, see 669 f4.33,
E 180.18, E 181.27, E 131.20, E 131.24, E 200.14, E 134.13, E 133.7, E 135.36, E 200.21–3, E
133.15, 669 f4.50, 52, 54, E 131.25, and E 134.24; these appear in chronological order.
111 On the political importance of removing bishops from the Lords, see Christianson,
'The peers.'

Leading off, a recovered Edmund Calamy listed the glories showered by the Almighty on England. Included in this inventory appeared the fact that 'the *first* king that ever wrote in print that the *pope was antichrist was King James* of famous memory.'[112] Implicitly, this praise of the father contained a criticism of the ecclesiastical policy of the son. Calamy proclaimed that the popish plotters of the 1630s remained a danger to England, for they enjoyed 'their former condition under the innovation so well, that they had rather continue in *Babylon* still, than accept of the reformation offered.' Without underplaying the hurdles that lay ahead on the road to reformation, Calamy now stressed the positive help promised by the Lord if Parliament returned his favours and enacted his will: 'The great God hath freed this nation from Egypt, and Babylon, from the gunpowder treason, and from many slaveries. Now if we prove unthankful after all these mercies, we may justly expect to be reinslaved.'[113] Clearly laying out the terrible alternatives in uncompromising tones, Calamy none the less had faith that Parliament would follow the proper path. Confidence began to return.

Stephen Marshall, even more than Calamy, replaced his earlier feelings of desolation with tones of militant hope in the face of enormous odds. Throughout history the rulers of the world often oppressed the saints, he reminded members of the Commons: 'The lamb's followers and servants are often the poor and off-scouring of the world, when kings and captains, merchants and wisemen, being drunk with the wine of the whore's fornications, proceed to make war with the lamb, and to give all their strength unto the beast till the words of God shall be fulfilled.' Such cosmic warfare now raged in Ireland where the catholic confederation, claiming a commission from the crown, persecuted protestants. In England, dangers threatened from the mighty as well, many of whom bent their weight against further reformation. 'How many are there who have, as it were, entered their names into the *dragon's* muster book,' Marshall asked, 'openly bidding defiance against the church of Christ in every good cause?'[114] In the battle of the latter days, those who wished to share Christ's victory, must deliberately enrol in his legions, for 'men are

---

112 Calamy, *Gods free* (23 Feb. 1642), p. 4. The process of establishing a regular programme of monthly fast sermons is traced in Wilson, *Pulpit*, ch. 1–3.

113 *Gods free*, pp. 46, 24–5. Popular pamphlets acknowledged the removal of the bishops from the Lords, but did not undergo the same change of spirit as seen in the parliamentary pulpit; see J.B., *The last will*, and [Overton], *New Lambeth*.

114 Marshall, *Meroz cursed* (23 Feb. 1642), pp. 8, 20. Concentrating upon parliamentary fast sermons, Trevor-Roper viewed this sermon as a prototype for the militant preaching which would henceforth sound from English pulpits; see *Religion*, p. 308.

never numbered among the lamb's followers, their names are not entered into his list, until they be saints.' Only the committed could avoid the fate of Meroz, the neutral of old: 'God's blessing is upon them that come to help him ... Meroz, and with Meroz all others are cursed, who come not out to the help of the Lord against the mighty.'[115] With military language, Marshall sought to implant Parliament in the apocalyptic role of the oppressed and persecuted, royalists and neutrals in the ranks of antichrist. Since England could expect troubles like those besetting Ireland, the godly had a duty to take up arms. They could show no mercy, for 'if this work be to revenge God's church against Babylon,' which Marshall surely believed it was, 'he is a *blessed man that takes and dashes the little ones against the stones.*' Those who took less drastic actions received blessings as well, so long as they fought the battles of the Lord.[116] Reformation became a holy war won by the few and humble, persecuted saints.

Apocalyptic analogies between Ireland and England piled one upon another as the process of polarization moved from Westminster out into the countryside. In the parliamentary pulpit Cornelius Burges painted a picture of Ireland 'swimming in blood, as if that whole kingdom were but one main *lough* of crimson, prepared to satiate the insatiable scarlet drunken whore,' and warned members of the Commons that 'it cannot hurt you to consider, whether this kingdom hath not cause to fear that God will put the cup into her mouth and cause her to drink deep thereof.'[117] Instead of fearing the future now, however, Burges – a moderate puritan – joined his more radical colleagues to demand immediate reformation. His fellow preacher, Simeon Ashe, believed that 'hell and earth are combined against us, because we endeavour reformation.' Anglican bishops itched to persecute the saints again, as they had in the 1630s, and formed the core of the 'malignant party' gathering around King Charles at York. Strongly supporting Parliament's attempts to remove the king's evil advisers, Ashe pointed out that: 'An antichristian party may be better plucked down, if the heads of that faction be removed.' No need to fear if the godly seemed small in number 'in comparison of the malignant party who oppose our hopes and welfare,

---

115 *Meroz cursed*, p. 33 (upon Rev. vii:14), 54
116 *Ibid.*, p. 12. This image became a favourite among the militants.
117 Burges, *Two sermons* (30 March 1642), pp. 29, 41. Not all moderates who feared that the dangers of Ireland threatened England expressed such militant support for Parliament; cf. two other sermons preached on the same day: Love, *Watchmans*, pp. 3–4, 11–12, 15–16, 30, and Piggot, *Hierusalem*, pp. 13–14, 26–8, 30–3.

yet may we pluck up our hearts from this consideration: *That our help standeth in the name of the Lord, who made heaven and earth.*'[118] Follow him and the Almighty would protect England as in the past. Cosmic warfare again threatened the land and the godly must gird themselves in preparation for it. If the destruction of the malignants gathered around the king meant war, Parliament must push through none the less, for such an act paved the way for England's eternal safety.

So much had tempered expectation returned to the parliamentary pulpit that Thomas Goodwin revived the congregational New Jerusalem of the previous year. Outlining the familiar providential and historical interpretation of Revelation, Goodwin seemed uncertain if the true church had experienced its last persecution by the powers of darkness or if civil war in England would fulfil this prophecy. Although some details remained uncertain, the time certainly approached when Christ 'will fully show himself to be *king of the saints* in his *worship*, as well as *king of nations* in his *works*.'[119] Even though 'mountains of opposition' lay in the way, God would build his visible church on earth. Parliament must enact the Lord's will to assure his blessing upon its cause, 'secure the land' from the threats of the royalists, and pave the way for 'a perfect victory over the beast ... his *holiness* the pope.' A properly reformed England could lead the northern nations to an ultimate triumph over antichrist. The culmination of history at the blowing of the seventh trumpet appeared imminent to Goodwin, so he begged Parliament to 'purge and reform the Temple, though you die for it, in the doing of it.'[120] Expectation returned, indeed, entwined with a new militance. As a congregational broadsheet put it in May 1642: 'If any shall this *house*

118 Ashe, *Best refuge* (30 March 1642), pp. 15, 2, 40, see 30–1, 37, 51–2, 58–61. Ejected in the 1630s, Ashe came to London in 1640 as a client of the Earl of Manchester and became a congregationalist by 1644; see the *DNB* and Nuttall, *Visible Saints*, p. 5 n. 2. For similar interpretations, see Harby, *Divi Arminii*, pp. 1–3, 9–12, and Spencer, *The spiritual*, pp. 3, 6–8, 10–14. A lay preacher, Spencer began as a groom to Viscount Say and Sele, became a captain in the parliamentary army, and, eventually, a fifth monarchist; see Capp, *Fifth Monarchy*, pp. 262–3. While highly apocalyptic, Spencer's sermon was not, as Capp contended, a 'millenarian defence of the civil war.'

119 Goodwin, *Zerubbabels* (27 April 1642), p. 36, see 12–16, 32, 46–8, 50, 55–8 (the last to the two witnesses of Rev. xi:1–14). Forced into exile in the 1630s, Goodwin became one of the leading 'dissenting brethren' in the Westminster Assembly; see the *DNB*.

120 *Ibid.*, pp. 19, 42, 48, 58, see 56–8. In addition to applying Mede's interpretation of the 'stone' in Daniel to the triumph of congregationalism like Holmes, Goodwin likened this new church to the rebuilding of the Temple at Jerusalem after the return of the Israelites from their exile in Babylon.

henceforth deride,/and scorning it, in Babel still abide,/Before God's face, as *foes* they must be slain,/whose rule and kingdom proudly they disdain.'[121] Goodwin, however, combined a glorious promise with his conditional warning. Victory over the royalists applied not only to England, or even to Britain, but to the whole world. Civil war still stood on the horizon, yet he already anticipated a complete military rout of Babylon.

Joseph Caryl, his colleague, mustered an explosive appeal for a purge of all the remnants of Babylon in England and only mentioned the New Jerusalem in passing. 'Not to bear evil is mercy,' rang his implacable words, 'not only to the good, but to the evil. You cannot be more cruel to them, than in sparing them.' This redefinition of mercy sounded shocking, but compromise promised equally horrid results to the godly. Analysing the polarization taking place across the land, Caryl emphasized that a royalist triumph held out a return of Britain to Babylon, to Rome. Once again, Arminians had captured the ear of King Charles and revived their popish plot to reverse the reformation.[122] To protect the land from the wrath of the Almighty, Parliament must act as an instrument of the saints and demolish those evil forces who worked against a proper reformation. 'And when the people of God have strength and power, they are as much obliged to cast *Babylon* out from them, *lest they be partakers in her plagues; for God will plague* Babylon *wheresoever he finds her.* There is no safety in being near them who are under the curse of God.'[123] Identifying the royalists with the Laudians and the latter with Babylon, Caryl actually advocated an offensive war against them. In his analysis of these two sermons, John Wilson made the point succinctly: 'As far as the pulpit in St. Margaret's was concerned, civil war had already begun.' Just as significant, however, parliamentary preachers grasped the initiative by framing a militant interpretation of current events in Britain. In the spring of 1642 they ran ahead of most contemporaries to push a clearly apocalyptic justification for fighting a civil war.[124]

121 *A song of Syon*
122 Caryl, *The workes* (27 April 1642), p. 41, see 47, 54; preached upon the text of Rev. ii:2–3. Caryl sat in the Westminster Assembly; see the *DNB*.
123 *The workes*, p. 1, see 32, 40–1, 50
124 Wilson, *Pulpit*, p. 64. Cf. *The envie*, pp. 2–3, 5–6, T.R., *A message*, pp. 1, 4–6, *A short description*, pp. 4–5, 7–9, *A plea*, pp. 3, 4–5, 8 (misnumbered as 7), 9, 11–12, and Robinson, *The petitioners*, pp. 4–7, 9, 15, 19, 23, 32, 40, 49–50. The last two were quite sophisticated works that combined constitutional with apocalyptic arguments.

Before Charles I actually raised his standard, William Sedgwick broke the self-imposed silence of the puritan brotherhood to proclaim the millennium. Aside from an almost hidden millenarianism, he preached a message similar to that of other radicals. The growing commotion in England, he explained, sprang from an attempt by the devil and his disciples to prevent the Long Parliament from reforming the church: '... Let not the present troubles seem strange to you. We could not expect to find the dragon asleep, and to steal away the golden fleece of reformation ... but now Christ comes to do it indeed, and he [the dragon] raves and tears and foams and blasphemes, shakes the very pillars of the kingdom, cracks the foundation of government, and threatens confusion to the whole; but we hope by the help of Christ's hands, the issue will be good. God seldom doth great things without commotion.' Those leagued with Christ need not fear this last fling from the captains of Babylon. Sedwick made war seem like a natural and expected event. He welcomed 'earthquakes, church-quakes, and kingdom-quakes' instead of viewing them as disasters. The Thirty Years War, bemoaned by Calamy some six months before, combined with attacks on episcopacy in England and Scotland to harbinger the glorious demise of antichrist: '... The shaking of the German Empire, that great bulwark of the beast, speaks the wrath of God bordering upon the man of sin. It is nearer than a border; God hath poured out some wrath upon the very throne of the beast. Prelacy is by some late and very sound expositors conceived to be that throne, and we have seen it pulled down in *Scotland*, darkened in England. Yea, may not a strict observer see the beginnings of the dissolution and breakings in the kingdom of the beast itself?'[125] A whirlwind of apocalyptic change swept across Europe, brushing aside the power of Babylon and confirming Sedgwick's hopes that better days lay ahead.

Positive signs, such as the increase of light among Englishmen, converged to show that a congregational Zion, 'the *stone cut off the mountain without hands, that is* the kingdom of Christ,' although 'scorned and trampled on' in the past, now started to become 'firm and strong, as a stone,' in England and Scotland. Could not the godly magistrates see it 'growing bigger and bigger toward a mountain?' Like Holmes and Good-

---

125 Sedgwick, *Zions deliverance*, pp. 10–11, 26. Sympathetic to sectarians from the lower orders, William became known as 'doomsday' Sedgwick to separate him from less radical men with the same surname; see the *DNB*. The May fast sermons contained little apocalyptic thought; see O. Sedgwick, *England's preservation* (25 May 1642), pp. 34–5, and Harris, *A sermon* (25 May 1642), pp. 28–9. Both sat in the Westminster Assembly; see the *DNB*.

win, Sedgwick presented a vision of the congregational New Jerusalem spreading across the world from England: 'This shall be the happy condition of the church, and this I conceive to be a PRAISE IN THE EARTH.'[126] However, he went beyond his colleagues to promise that Christ, through a 'visible, outward and manifest declaration,' would 'take his church by the hand and publicly own his people.' Sedgwick proposed a direct divine intervention, not one through secondary causes. Christ would return to end the power of antichrist and to establish a thousand-year rule of the saints on earth: '*Satan shall be bound and cast into the bottomless pit*, and with him this antichristian malignity, whereby men oppose the ways of God. Wicked men shall be as much below the saints in power as in desert; they are dogs, and as dogs shall they crouch and *bow to the soles of the feet* of God's children, and *shall call them the city of the Lord, the Zion of the holy one of Israel*.'[127] This passage only made sense as a prophecy of the millennium. Both the future binding of Satan – one need hardly state, for a thousand years – and the image of the wicked bowing before the saints – a contemporary symbol for the earthly rule of the elect – almost certainly pointed in this direction.

Parliament shared a responsibility with all of the righteous to prepare a path for the coming millennium by supporting the saints and defeating the enemies of the Almighty. Magistrates had a special duty to 'resolve for God rather than men, though princes.' Sedgwick plunged into the heart of the dispute between Charles I and Parliament with a penetrating radical logic shared by few of the reformers. 'If heaven and earth should make war,' he warned, 'there would be no corner of the world so safe, as on God's and the church's side.'[128] This conditional tone evaporated when Sedgwick came to describe the royalists:

Your adversaries are antichristian, they that will deal with such, must come

---

126 *Zions deliverance*, pp. 26, 17, see 11
127 *Ibid.*, pp. 16–17. For other millennial works, see Duke, *The fulnesse*, pp. 166–7, Fenwick, *Zions rights*, sig. B 1–4, pp. 1, 7, 12–13, 24–5, 30, 54, 58–60. According to Thomason, Duke was the 'cook of Hell at Westminster' – that is, at the tavern with that name. Fenwick, an utter barrister at Gray's Inn, was a Joachimite who believed that he was living in the age of the spirit. *Napiers narration*, a pamphlet with his prophecies, came out in April 1642 and English translations of Mede, *Diatribae* and *A paraphrase*, appeared by June.
128 *Zions deliverance*, pp. 34, 11, see 31–2 for the argument that Parliament should follow the example of David in his quarrel with Saul. The latter became a hotly debated issue as civil war approached; see [Palmer], *Scripture and reason*, pp. 11–13, passim, for both sides.

armed with *the blood of the lamb and the word of their testimony*, *Apocalypse* xii:11. And faith only knows how to use these. You should carry the blood of the lamb always about you, wear it in your hearts, and think you have to do with the enemies of that Christ that shed his blood for you, against those that trample that blood under their feet by their superstition and prophaneness, such are bloody enemies that thirst for the blood of saints.[129]

Sedgwick sought to inculcate a resolute, militant spirit in his listeners by reminding them that England's coming conflict must fit into the ongoing struggle against the forces of Babylon. He set aside all hope of compromise, bolstered stubbornness of spirit, and sounded a trumpet cry of preparation for a crusade against the royalists.

With words ominous in warning, but comforting if followed, Sedgwick assured Parliament that nothing could stand before the success of the saints and besought Parliament to ensure a victory for its cause by seeking first the glory of God: 'Though it lie under mountains of kingdoms, you shall thresh them to dust; though it be buried under nations, and empires, customs, antiquities, he will *drive the nations asunder, scatter the everlasting hills*, nothing shall stand in his way; wherever he finds his glory, he will sieze upon it; and if they yield not speedily, it will cost them dear.' With the Lord of hosts leading against their antichristian enemies, nothing could defy the assaults of the godly. If necessary, all established human institutions would crumble to dust under their blows. Parliament, therefore, must press ahead to build a congregational Zion! 'You must be restless till *Jerusalem rest*, and be established. We are sorry we must require such pains of you, but glad to see your cheerful and indefatigable travail.'[130] England looked like the chosen place, Parliament the chosen instrument, for rooting out antichrist and planting Zion. The abundance of prayer, the multitude of converts, the increase of active public spirits working for reformation, and even the 'nation-quake' of royalist opposition provided signs of England's apocalyptic role: 'There is good hope we are going out of *Babylon*, when the *he-goats go before the flocks*, men of public place and authority are actice for reformation. When the *governors of Israel offer themselves willingly among the people*, there is a blessing at hand.'[131] The days of fulfilment drew near. Parliament had a duty to take

129 *Zions deliverance*, p. 35
130 *Ibid.*, pp. 39–40, 47, see 47–54. Cf. Johnson, *A letter from*, p. 3. Although not published until 1 October 1642, this work – derived from Archer – appears to have circulated in manuscript as early as July.
131 *Ibid.*, pp. 24–5

the offensive and, thereby, win a cosmic victory as well as a civil war.

Such an exceptionally powerful apocalyptic interpretation of the civil war seldom rang from the parliamentary pulpit in 1642 or 1643.[132] Although others pointed in that direction, Sedgwick first identified the royalists with antichrist and he went beyond an apocalyptic appeal for the congregationalist Zion to pursue the millennium in public. The venerable William Gouge, his colleague for the day, made no mention of the prophecies of St John.[133] The Lords listened to Thomas Cheshire urge peace and conciliation on the same day, a theme also followed by Edward Reynolds at the next monthly fast of the Commons. These two echoed the despair of many moderate men in this time of tumult, a cry amplified in many petitions and pamphlets.[134] Such feelings, however, dwelt far from the lips of most parliamentary preachers and those who expressed them shared St Margaret's pulpit with fiery spirits.

Thomas Hill, Reynolds' colleague, stressed the pursuit of truth above all else, a path which led away from compromise. Only abolition of the episcopal government of the Elizabethan settlement promised to establish truth in England. Indirectly identifying episcopacy with Babylon, Hill clearly placed the Laudians in the camp of Babylon by terming them emissaries of the pope. '*Babylon and all her crutches must down; the fight of faith is a good fight* because such soldiers are sure of the victory. The kingdom of Christ shall prevail, though second causes be impotent, yet *the zeal of the Lord of hosts will perform this*.'[135] The spiritual and temporal warfare raging in Ireland would soon shift to England, so Parliament had better assure a victory on both fronts by enacting a proper reformation. '*Truth* is the *armour* by which you are defended against your spiritual enemies,' who included the royalists, 'and enabled for offensive war.' No mere defensive campaign here. Stressing the

---

132 See that by Wilson discussed below and Cheynell, Sions memento (31 May 1643), sig.
A 1, 3, pp. 3–4, 9–12, 16–22, 26–9, 31. Marshall, The song (15 June 1643), and
Wilkinson, Babylons ruine (25 Oct. 1643); one would need to cite nearly every page of
the last two sermons.

133 Gouge, The saints (29 June 1642). Other fast sermons that backed the cause of
Parliament, but had little apocalyptic content, include A. Burges, The difficulty of
(27 Sept. 1643), Carter, Prayers (28 June 1643), Perne, Gospell courage (31 May 1643),
Simpson, Reformations (26 July 1643), Spurstowe, Englands patterne (21 July 1643),
Valentine, A sermon (28 Dec. 1642), Vines, Calebs integrity (30 Nov. 1642).

134 For Cheshire and Reynolds, see notes 12 and 13 above; none of the sermons from 1643
fell into this category.

135 Hill, The trade (27 July 1642), sig. A 4v, see pp. 31, 58–9. A member of the Lord's
committee on ecclesiastical innovations and of the Westminster Assembly, Hill
became master of Trinity College, Cambridge, in 1645; see the DNB.

role of preachers, of the 'sword of the spirit,' in this cosmic conflict, Hill did not, however, underplay the practical importance of physical arms in defeating antichrist and his allies.[136] His zeal for war matched that of the Lord of hosts.

Apocalyptic battle cries reverberated outside of the parliamentary pulpit as well. With skirmishes already starting in the countryside, one pamphleteer asked his countrymen to flock to the support of Parliament against the malignant party around the king – 'unanimously [to] join against the viperous brood of Satan, and locusts of the bottomless pit.'[137] In a more subtle manner, the anonymous 'master of innuendo' took the threads of conspiracy and fear spun by the 'Bishops' Wars,' the Irish rebellion, and the royalist revival and invited his readers to weave them together into a fabric for explaining the troubles that plagued Britain. Of course, he provided a ready-made pattern. Comparing the armies assembled to enforce the prayer book on Scotland with those collecting now around King Charles, he argued that '*papists* and popish persons were then the chief commanders (for the most part) in the *English* armies, and *papists* now and popish persons.' He then went on to imply that Englishmen could not trust their religion and liberties to such deceivers by asking 'whether these aim at the *protestant* religion, whatever they call the *protestant* profession except it be popery in all things – supremacy only excepted, or at the subjects' liberty, let every man of the meanest capacity judge.' To prevent the miseries of Germany and Ireland, parliamentarians must struggle to separate the person of the king from malignant forces 'the badge of whose arch-leader (the devil's first-born) [is] the pope's garments made red with the blood of the saints.'[138] Arguing that the surest road to peace lay in defeating the

---

136 *Ibid.*, p. 14, see 17–19, 28–9, 36–7, 45. A year later he preached an even more fiery apocalyptic sermon, *The militant* (21 July 1643), pp. 4, 7, 9–10, 19–20, 30. Other 'root and branch' fast sermons include Chambers, *A divine* (27 Sept. 1643), pp. 7, 14, 25, and Coleman, *Christians* (30 Aug. 1643), pp. 24, 26, 40–2, 54–5, 64–6, 71.

137 [Jenkinson], *Lamentable*, p. 4, see 3–5; cf. *A conference*, sig. A 2v, 4v, and J. Sedgwick, *Englands condition*, no. 1, pp. 9, 13, 19–20, 24–5, 29–30, 39, 42, no. 2, pp. 11–12. A rector in London, Sedgwick received an invitation from the MPs of Marlborough, Wiltshire, to preach these two sermons there. Not printed until September 1642, internal evidence suggests July as the month in which they were delivered. Sedgwick appears in the *DNB*.

138 *Some more new observations*, pp. 3, 7. A number of anonymous pamphlets share a style similar to that in this one and seem to stem from the same author – someone trained in the Common Law. Henry Parker looked like a candidate, but a note on the title page of Thomason's copy proclaimed: 'not written by the former author of the objections' and he would have known.

power of antichrist in England, he ended by asking 'any seeing man' to decide whether 'now or never must the pope up or down in this kingdom ... that is the quarrel in the land, whether *Michael* or the *dragon, Christ* or the pope shall get safest footing in this island ...?'[139] The popish plot theory of the 1630s took on a refreshed, if somewhat convoluted, reality as the author asked the meanest man to make up his own mind, but weighted the evidence to make any who questioned the thrust of the argument feel unreflective.

In case any had forgotten those days of slavery, John Vicars prepared a manual to help them remember and enjoined all to teach their friends and children about the great and marvellous things done by the Lord for England, Scotland, and Ireland in their adversity. Drawing upon a theme of holy history, Vicars began with the revolt of Satan, but quickly arrived at the present battle fought 'by the *Romish antichrist*, against the *reformed-Christian* in all parts. And the implacable rage of this arch-adversary of the Lord Jesus Christ hath far transcended all the malice and mischief of former ages' cruelties, both of the old *Assyrians* and *Philistines* to the *ancient Israelites*, or the last ten persecuting *heathen Emperors* to the *primitive-Christians*.'[140] Britain, especially England, acted as the key battleground in this cosmic conflict and experienced more deliverances at the hand of the Almighty than any other nation – particularly in the last few years. The text illustrated this theme with numerous historical examples and ended with the revival of the popish plotters in the creation of a royalist party at York. A series of conclusions called upon Englishmen to admire God's special mercies to them, to show their thanks by eradicating episcopacy 'root and branch,' to act in a more faithful and less fearful way, and to remember that the Lord alone provided their strength and salvation. God promised 'that *Babylon* shall fall; yea says the Lord, by the prophet (in respect of the certainty of it): *Babylon is fallen, is fallen ... and all the graven images of her gods, the Lord hath broken to the ground.*'[141] The instruments of

139 *Ibid.*, p. 6
140 Vicars, *Jehovah-Jireh*, p. 2, see pp. 1–4. Thomason's copy was dated to 17 August 1642. The first edition, entitled *Englands remembrancer*, had five pages of text and was collected by Thomason in July 1641. Within little over a year, it grew to 110 pages; eventually it reached four long volumes. A layman, Vicars acted as an important propagandist for the parliamentary cause in the first civil war, one who appealed directly to yeomen, artisans, and apprentices. See the *DNB*.
141 *Jehovah-Jireh*, p. 106, see 99–110; see [Vicars], *All the memorable*, which illustrated sixteen important scenes from the history. For similar views published in August 1642, see Mocket, *The churches*, pp. 40–1, 44–5, 56–7, 60–2, 69, 75, 79, M.B., *A description*, sig. A IV, and *A new remonstrance*, sig. A 2–3, 4v.

Babylon had captured the person of the king and now tried to subvert the laws and religion of England. Although not mentioned explicitly, the whole thrust of Vicar's work clearly enforced on Englishmen the duty of making St John's prophecy come true by actively supporting Parliament.

When King Charles raised his standard and finally made war a reality – not just a probability – open justification of resistance to his forces became a necessity. Taking up the gauntlet in the parliamentary pulpit, William Carter told the Commons that God sometimes commanded brother to fight against brother. In fighting the royalists, Parliament played an apocalyptic role of even greater universal significance than the reformation of the sixteenth century:

God hath put into your hands, *a work of his*, the greatest that hath been on foot for God in these islands for many hundred years; the safety, peace, and welfare of the kingdom, I may say the three kingdoms, nay in a great degree of all the kingdoms of the world, wherein the true religion is professed ... God hath called you to the purging of the land of those locusts and caterpillers ... which by interpreters are applied to the *Saracens* in the east, and to the monks and friars, and whole popish hierarchy in these western kingdoms; it is true, the time of their chiefest power is past ... yet multitudes we have amongst us still, and the design is that they may again prevail ... 'Tis not long since we had experience how they grew upon us ... And how slender was the *meat-offering* left for God, when as so many burning and shining lights were quite put out, such a famine of the word in the most places of the kingdom, and such a bondage laid upon men's souls?[142]

The forces rallying around King Charles represented a 'design' to bring the Laudians and their allies back into power in Britain. If successful, they would attempt to reverse the reformation, as in the 1630s when they deprived England of its best ministers, its 'shining lights.' Parliamentarians, therefore, not only had a justification but an obligation to take up arms – a divine command to fulfil divine prophecy and holy history by extirpating these foes: 'God is resolved upon it; he will have the *locusts* purged, I mean, so as they shall not hurt his people.'[143] Just as he ordered the Israelites to quell the tribe of Benjamin in Old Testament

142 Carter, *Israels peace* (31 Aug. 1642), pp. 23–5, see 1–2, 19, 44; on the appropriate text, Judges xx:26–8. Little is known about Carter; see Wilson, *Pulpit*, p. 119.
143 *Israels peace*, p. 27. Other parliamentary preachers who professed to pray for peace but took militant apocalyptic stances included Bridges, *Joabs counsell* (22 Feb. 1643), pp. 12–13, 16–23, Corbet, *God's providence* (28 Dec. 1642), pp. 13–14, 20, 28, 30, and Hodges, *A glimpse* (28 Sept. 1642), sig. B 1, pp. 17, 19, 20, 33, 42. Those tracing the

times, the Lord of hosts now demanded his godly Englishmen shed the blood of their malignant brothers. Carter openly professed a desire for peace, but in reality proposed a crusade against the royalists.

A month later, Thomas Wilson also drew upon the Old Testament and compared England's situation with that of the children of Israel when they stood on the borders of the promised land. The Anglican hierarchy, for him, represented an antitype of Jericho – a bulwark blocking the way of the Lord's people: 'Prelacy, purple prelates, and their clergy, hinder the passage of God's redeemed ones into Caanan, heaven, and shall down.'[144] Wilson equated episcopacy with Babylon and believed that bishops, led by the Laudians, must be removed from the presence of the king before they began the persecutions of the 1630s again. By now, this theme had become a standard weapon in the apocalyptic arsenal of the parliamentary cause. Wilson admonished Parliament to take decisive action against the aggressors:

Remove the wicked from before ... (as special servants and chaplains in ordinary to) the king ... *Leave no frogs* that creep into kings' chambers, provoking them by their croaking to make war; they are known by the gutter whence they come, out of the mouth of the dragon, out of the mouth of the beast and the false prophet; they are spirits of devils, which go forth unto the kings of the earth, to gather them to battle, prince against his principality, king against Parliament, kingdom against kingdom, nation against nation, England against Scotland ... Here is a work for the power of a Parliament, that the king may have no croakers in his chamber or court, to be offensive to his royal ears, that the kingdom, distracted and bleeding, may have justice and peace; this (God commanding you so) do according to your wisdom, given you of God.[145]

lineage of the royalists through the bishops or Arminians to Babylon included Arrowsmith, *The covenant* (25 Jan. 1643), pp. 15, 25, 28, Ellis, *The sole path* (22 Feb. 1643), pp. 22–3, 42, 48, 64, Greenhill, *The axe* (26 April 1643), pp. 12–14, 35, 46. Lightfoot, *Elias* (29 March 1643), pp. 2, 6, 8–9, 12, 16, 19, 26, Tuckney, *The balme* (30 Aug. 1643), pp. 25–6, 30, 32, 37–9, 40, and Whittaker, *Eirenopoios* (25 Jan. 1643), pp. 1, 17–18, 26, 27, 34, 60–1.

144 Wilson, *Jerichoes down-fall*, p. 5, see 14–16, 32–3, 36, 41. Wilson had come to identify the Established Church with Babylon. For works from September and October 1642 that contained a similar message, see J. Goodwin, *Anti-Cavalierisme*, p. 2, [Woodward], *The churches*, pp. 47–9, 96, 109, *The aphorismes*, pp. 1, 4, 8, and *Englands complaint*, pp. 3–4. Lamont has pointed out that Prynne did not write *The aphorismes*.

145 *Jerichoes down-fall* pp. 33–4 (upon Rev. xvi:13 and xviii); cf. *The aphorismes*, pp. 57–60, and *Englands complaint*, pp. 5–6

Parliament need not fear the seeming strength of those forces surrounding King Charles, for the example of 'Arch-B[ishop] W[illiam] L[aud],' now locked in the Tower, provided a recent demonstration that 'when the wicked spring as the grass, and all the workers of iniquity do flourish, it is that they shall be destroyed forever.'[146] An eternal Nemesis stood with the parliamentarians.

The prophecies of St John pointed to an imminent fall of Babylon and also instructed the godly on their behaviour. Looking directly at Ireland and, by undisguised implication, at the outbreak of fighting in England, Wilson propounded an apocalyptic vision of cruel, offensive revenge against those who persecuted the saints: '... Cruel *men have shed blood*, the blood of saints, the blood of prophets, and in justice *they must have blood to drink*, for they are worthy, *Revelation* xvi:5,6. Reward Babylon as she hath rewarded you, *double to her double*, in the cup she hath filled, *fill to her double*, xviii:6.' Such shedding of blood, a double *lex talionis*, was angelical, holy, happy, and honourable, for those involved in it poured vials of wrath upon the body of the beast. Now that the persecuted rose up against their oppressors, no power on earth could stop them: The 'kingdom of saints are a peerless people. It is the honour of the saints to triumph over all contrary royalty and nobility, *to bind kings in chains, and nobles with fetters of iron* ...'[147] The wilderness lay behind and only the crumbling walls of an episcopal Jericho prevented the godly from entering their New Jerusalem. By following God's will Parliament could gain a victory at home and pave the way for the establishment of Christ's congregational kingdom on earth.[148] Like other radicals, Wilson looked forward to the 'root and branch' extirpation of episcopacy, showed sympathy with the sects and hostility toward such symbols of the Established Church as the godly prince and the bishop martyrs, and transformed the English civil war into an apocalyptic crusade. Not all militant members of the puritan brotherhood agreed with this vision.

In his message to the Commons at the October fast, Thomas Case illustrated the different approach of the 'presbyterians.' To be sure,

146 *Ibid.*, p. 16; see note 21 above
147 *Ibid.*, pp. 40, 20, see 41–2; cf. Goodwin, *Anti-Cavalierism*, pp. 31–9, and [Woodward], *The churches*, sig. a 2r, b 3v, c 2v, pp. 83–4.
148 *Ibid.*, pp. 26, 36, 42, 44–5. From his stress on gathered congregations, Wilson must have held this view. Cf. Goodwin, *Anti-Cavalierisme*, pp. 49–51, and [Woodward], *The churches*, pp. 26, 74, 83, 106–9; see Caryl, *The nature* (joint, 6 Oct. 1643), pp. 20–1, 37, 40–3, and Temple, *Christs government* (26 Oct. 1642), pp. 4, 23–4, 32, 35, 46–8, 50

England's situation struck him as a continuation of the ongoing warfare between God's children and Satan's supporters. In the past this took the form of a struggle between catholic and protestant, however in the present there appeared 'among Christians, no such antipathy between *papists* and *protestants* as there is between *protestants* and *protestants.'* In England, at least, the battleground had shifted: 'At this day no hatred so *mortal*, no enemies so *irreconcilable* as the *malignant protestants*, and those whom they scorn by that new-name, roundhead, that poor despised party that stand up for reformation, the *protestant* indeed.'[149] Even a moderate like Case now appropriated the socially degrading name of roundhead – a symbol of derision for those sects that he found so distasteful. While identifying the parliamentarians with the persecuted and oppressed, Case still called the royalists protestants – malignants, irreconcilable to the truth, but protestants still, a point not granted by the radicals. Around the king, however, stood 'enemies to God, that are up in arms against him and his people in this kingdom.' As those trying to destroy the Zion of further reformation in England, they deserved defeat.[150] An unwillingness to distort did not blunt the militance exhibited by Case.

In the strength of his aggressive attitude, Case argued clearly for a defensive war: 'We must do somewhat, but it is not till our enemies force us to it, when we must either *kill*, or be *killed.'* Those who stood as neutrals in the civil war, who refused to contribute to the cause of Parliament, he uncompromisingly branded as *'antichristian enemies* of Jesus Christ who destroy his poor people.'[151] Not as quick to condemn all royalists to perdition as the radicals, Case also exhibited moderation by attacking the sects and by appealing to the tradition of the martyr bishops of Mary's reign. Like those of a similar temper, Case shared an apocalyptic interpretation of the civil war with more radical colleagues, but broke with them in showing more discrimination toward the royalists, in viewing the war as defensive, not offensive, and in exhorting Parliament to establish a national church instead of congregational churches.[152]

149 Case, *Gods rising* (26 Oct. 1642), p. 4. A prominent 'presbyterian' in the Westminster Assembly, Case experienced trouble with the authorities in the 1630s; see the *DNB* and Wilson, *Pulpit*, pp. 113–14.
150 *Gods rising*, p. 14, see 14–16; cf. *The aphorismes*, p. 58
151 *Ibid.*, pp. 5, 41–2; cf. Ward, *An encouragement*, pp. 1–3, 9–10, 13–14
152 *Ibid.*, p. 44. For other reformers troubled about the growth of the sects, see C. Burges, *Another sermon*, p. 60, and *Two sermons*, p. 46, and Brinsley, *The healing*, pp. 22–4,

In the midst of this sermon Case received a note from Lord Wharton which 'permitted the preacher to make a dramatic announcement of the divine intervention at Edgehill.' With this great battle the civil war began in earnest. Case explicitly laid the cause of the hostility at the door of religion:

And what is the quarrel all this while, is it not *religion* and the *truth* of God? The truth of *doctrine*, the truth of *discipline*, the truth of *worship*? May not the *Parliament*, and the *Parliament's* friends cry to God: *For thy name's sake, oh Lord, are we killed all the day long*? Surely had not the *gospel* and the *government* of Jesus Christ been precious in their eyes, they might have compounded for their civil liberties upon infinitely cheaper terms then it hath cost them already, and yet the Lord knows what it may cost them more![153]

This analysis of the cause of the civil war stated in a succinct and cogent way one of the basic ideas that lay behind all of the pronouncements of the reformers. They fought for religion. However, religious disputes display bewildering variations. Significantly, these divines and laymen chose to interpret their quarrel with the royalists in apocalyptic terms. Because they conceived of those who opposed the aims of Parliament not merely as people with religious ideas which diverged from the truth (the reformers differed among themselves in their visions of the true church), but as associates of antichrist in a cosmic conflict, the reformers pressed for an uncompromising position. They pushed ahead, rather than held back, the polarization of the political nation. The horrors of holy war paled to insignificance when compared to the threat of a successful revival of the popish plot of the 1630s, a return of Britain to Babylon.

Between 1640 and the outbreak of war in 1642 the apocalyptic visions of English reformers helped them to explain and understand exciting contemporary events. When the Laudians lost their power with the opening

36–8, 90, 101–2, 116, 138; most royalists fit into this category. Those parliamentary preachers employing an interpretation similar to that of Case included Bowles, *Zeale* (joint and Assembly, 7 July 1643), pp. 4, 17, 23, 32, 34, A. Burges, *The difficulty*, pp. 7, 13–14, Calamy, *The noble-mans* (Lords, 15 June 1643), pp. 24, 30, 46–7, 56–8, Herle, *A payre* (30 Nov. 1642), pp. 12, 25, 44, and *Davids song* (Lords, 15 July 1643), pp. 4, 22–7, Ley, *The fury* (26 April 1643), pp. 2, 20, 32, 41–2, 74, Newcomen, *The craft* (5 Nov. 1642), sig. A 3v, pp. 12, 16, 21, 28–33, 36, 45, 49–51, 53–5, and Palmer, *The necessity* (21 June 1643), sig. A 2, pp. 3, 11–12, 42–4, 61.

153 Wilson, *Pulpit*, p. 66, and Case, *Gods rising*, p. 34

of the Long Parliament, the prophecies made by the protesters of the 1630s seemed, indeed, to come true. A bright new vista suddenly sprang up before those previously persecuted and now restored to respectability. A full reformation, for which they had suffered, prayed, and preached, at last would be enacted in England. The promise of a long-awaited New Jerusalem loomed on the horizon during the year of expectation, that first miraculous year of the Long Parliament. However various their visions, the reformers joined to rejoice at this pleasing prospect.

When rebellion in Ireland and subsequent polarization of the English political nation raised the spectre of strong opposition to further reform of the Established Church, despair overtook some of the brethren. But their vision did not long remain dimmed, and even when pessimistic they pressed the cause of reformation. Hope sprang up again, despite the gathering omens of civil war in England. The revival of a malignant faction around the king merely meant that peaceful means no longer sufficed to rid Britain of the threat of Babylon. Since the Almighty fulfilled their prophecies in the past, the reformers confidently expected a military victory, especially since the Long Parliament seemed to support the cause of the Lord of hosts. Before fighting broke out on a large scale, preachers and laymen girded parliamentarians with the apocalyptic armour of faith and prepared them to excel in temporal, as well as spiritual, warfare.

Although united in opposition to the royalists, whom they identified with the bishops or the Laudians, the reformers remained a divided group. As the deliberations of the Westminster Assembly later demonstrated, few English divines and fewer laymen desired a congregational Zion. More conservative spokesmen attacked the explosion of sects in England and argued for a defensive war against the evil ministers of the crown.[154] Radicals, from 'root and branch presbyterians' to congregationalists to separatists, welcomed tub preachers as manifestations of light from the common people and stressed an offensive war. In a real

---

154 Pennington, 'The rebels of 1642' in Parry, *English Civil War*, ch. 2; see ch. 1 by Manning for the types of social fears which fed hatred of the sects. The arguments of various divines for a defensive war appeared in [Palmer], *Scripture and reason*. When dealing with the constitutional argument, even a radical like Jeremiah Burroughs put forth a plea for defensive arms; see *The glorious*, pp. 7, 11–12, 15, 17–18, 27–8, 36, 42, 45, 54, 55b, 56b–7b, 72–3, 105. When discussing religious motivation, however, Burroughs stressed an offensive war; *ibid.*, pp. 5–6, 56b–7b, 72–3, 145–6. In this pamphlet, there are two sets of pages 49 through 70.

sense, the argument between Oliver Cromwell and the Earl of Manchester over the prosecution of military operations in 1644–5 implicitly took place in pulpit and pamphlet before substantial combat started.

Most reformers agreed, however, that England's troubles formed an important part of that annihilation of antichrist predicted by St John for the latter days of the earth. They viewed their opponents through apocalyptic lenses. Henry Burton argued that civil war in Britain began the Battle of Armageddon:

And now is this war begun professedly in *Ireland* by the rebels there ... for the rooting out of all protestants, and of the protestant religion, which war they intended to perfect in *England* and *Scotland*. So as this outrageous war in the rebellion of *Ireland*, and in the raising of popish forces in *England* against the true protestants, under the infamous name of roundheads, which war is fomented by all papists and popishly affected within the land and without; among whom our prelates with their priests are not the least incendiaries and bellows-blowers ... This war (I say) so furiously and universally by them prosecuted, is a most certain immediate forerunning sign of the imminent ruin of the whole kingdom of the beast ... For the enemy hath said: *I will pursue, I will overtake them, I will divide the spoil, my lust shall be satisfied upon them, I will draw my sword, my hand shall destroy them* [Exodus xv:9]. The very language of our antichristian enemies at this time, the Cavaliers at *York* ... therefore, certainly the ruin of this cursed faction is near at hand, which shall be with a fearful destruction, forasmuch as they make open war against the Lord and his anointed people ...[155]

Egypt and Babylon, the children of Israel and God's elect nation of England, the Old Testament and the Book of Revelation, all entwined together into a militant message that stressed the active intervention of the Almighty on the side of the saints. Few reckoned on the judgment day arriving quite so soon and some looked forward to a thousand-year reign of the saints on earth first. However, most reformers agreed with the thrust of Burton's theme – that the royalists must be slain all the day long, for they upheld the power of antichrist.

155 Burton, *A narration*, p. 27; cf. Hughes, *Signes*, pp. 13–17, 19–22. The passage quoted from Exodus by Burton was the cry of those Egyptians who pursued the children of Israel into the Red Sea; he did not compare Charles I to the Pharoah.

Conclusion

The common opinion that the pope is antichrist doth prevail more with the vulgar that can't dispute against particular doctrines of Rome, than all the direct arguments that are used.

Richard Baxter, Baxter Treatises, iii, fo. 306v, as quoted in Lamont, 'Richard Baxter,' p. 80

Writing not long after the nominated Parliament of saints returned its power into the hands of Oliver Cromwell, thereby sealing the era of expectations, Richard Baxter still perceived a weak necessity for maintaining the apocalyptic tradition. Identification of the papacy with antichrist no longer functioned as a powerful offensive weapon of hope for him. Instead, it crumbled into an indirect argument to keep the common people steadfast in the protestant cause. In Baxter's private remark, caution and half-doubt replaced the buoyant spirit of prophecy and triumph sounded by generations of English protestants. Even before he wrote it, respectable congregational divines renounced their pursuit of the millennium.[1] No food for the learned here. The insight first enunciated by John Bale still continues to inspire people today, but Newton was the last great thinker who attempted systematically to come up with an enduring solution to the number of the beast.[2] The vision fit for thousand-page treatises by intellectuals moved to the fringes of learned society.

From its first appearance in Bale's *The image of bothe churches* until

1 Liu, *Discord in Zion*, ch. 2 and 3
2 See Manuel, *Religion of Newton*.

the late seventeenth century, the historical paradigm that explained England's break from Rome by identifying the papacy with antichrist operated on a multiplicity of levels. Throughout this period, reformers used it as a popular argument to convert people to protestantism. The common people took it up as well, made it their own, and have continued to repeat it to the present day. During the Tudor and early Stuart periods, however, Bale's paradigm presented a viable framework for explaining holy history and current events. Its problems and puzzles taxed the ingenuity and skills of scholars, giving rise to fruitful research. Savants from diverse social backgrounds displayed an immense range of learning in unlocking the historical secrets of biblical prophecy – witness the works of a king, a gentleman mathematician, a parish minister, a university don, and a bishop (James VI and I, Napier, Brightman, Mede, and Bale). At these heights, reformers developed Bale's insight into an intellectual system of magnitude and power. Often their works appeared in Latin as well as English and their pursuit reciprocated with that carried on by continental scholars, whether catholic or protestant, in a lively debating and sharing of insights. Foxe's *Actes and monuments* demonstrated Bale's historical application of Revelation at length, Napier and Brightman projected it into the future, James VI and I (following Knox) applied it to secular warfare, and Mede transformed it into the millennium. One needed considerable chronological, historical, and exegetical skills to operate in competition or co-operation with the likes of Foxe, Napier, Brightman, and Mede. As the tradition developed and scholars solved particular problems, it took a higher and higher degree of energy and intellectual capacity to grasp the whole and make an original contribution. With the enormous weight of his learning, Joseph Mede both reached the peak of chronological interpretation and sounded its scholarly death-knell. After Mede no one could provide a more systematic account based upon Bale's assumptions. Few tasks remained – tinkering with Mede's synchronisms or applying them to the most recent period of history, to the present, and to the future.[3] The creative force of the apocalyptic tradition slowly evaporated.

In addition to operating as an explanatory system at the top of the intellectual hierarchy, the apocalyptic tradition played an important role in differentiating the ecclesiastical positions of English protestants

3 Both Firth, 'Apocalyptic Tradition,' and Bauckham, 'Prophecy,' unfold the intellectual tradition at length and refer to continental protestant developments. Firth, pp. 274–6, stresses the poverty of intellectual development in the tradition after Mede.

from all degrees of society. From the very beginning it justified the break from Rome with vivid, easily understood, powerful imagery. Before many years passed, however, English protestants began to apply some of these symbols against each other. If the medieval church represented Babylon and the papacy stood for antichrist or the beast, then where did one locate the reformed Church of England? The mainstream firmly placed the Established Church into the compass of those making up the true church of Christ; separatists saw it as an integral part of the false church – of Babylon; radical puritans as a mixture of true and false – as Laodicea; and 'root and branch' radicals argued that its government remained a part of the false church – that bishops were antichrists. Articulated before the end of the sixteenth century, each stream played a significant role in the religious disputes of the following century and overlapped into social and political events. Once announced or codified, they entered into church controversy at all intellectual levels, from lengthy scholarly treatises down to four-page pamphlets, broadsheets, and doggerel verse. With such a plethora of publications, Occam's razor cut away any necessity for Michael Barkun's hypothesis of a rural oral tradition in early modern England.[4] One must clearly differentiate between oral communication and a true oral tradition. The word in the mouth and the word in the ear influenced many people, indeed; but whether they listened to sermons or passed on Henry Barrow's four points by word of mouth, people derived their apocalyptic insights and arguments from written sources. After the early sixteenth century Bale's assumptions ruled without dispute from Joseph Mede down to a tub preacher like John Hunt.

Although disputing – sometimes ferociously – among themselves about the nature of their national church, English protestants came to see a special role for their own nation and church in the apocalyptic plan of the Lord. Through hindsight, one could find material for such an interpretation in Bale and Foxe, but the idea of England as an 'elect nation' fully entered systematic apocalyptic thought only with Brightman. It grew into an increasingly powerful component in the early seventeenth century and flourished in the 1640s. As in the middle ages, so in their present, England stood as a central fortress for God's elect. Even reformers who rejected the notion of a national church found it difficult to escape from the fixed belief that the Almighty would reveal his reformation first to his Englishmen, then to the rest of the

4 Barkun, *Diasaster*, pp. 68–74, 91–7

world. One of the most mighty thrusts in nascent English nationalism (or Scottish, for that matter), apocalyptic thought charged such important symbols of national pride as the victory over the Armada with eternal significance. It created a means of categorizing all foreign powers into either the camp of good or that of evil and reinforced the already strong tendency to explain domestic troubles in moral terms. Such troubles resulted from the machinations of evil people, of the agents of antichrist. In an age of religious and political dispute, the ideological component of foreign and domestic policy gained a strongly polarized momentum from the apocalyptic tradition. People who view their opponents as the consorts of Satan, rather than as ordinary men and women, make poor compromisers and relentless enemies.

Although continually asserted during the sixteenth and early seventeenth centuries, apocalyptic visions acquired a special reality and urgency at times of political and religious crisis. Hence, the period of conservatism in the latter part of the reign of Henry VIII, the reign of Queen Mary, the northern rising and Armada crises of Elizabeth's reign, the Gunpowder Plot, the Thirty Years War, the ascendency of Arminians during the eleven years of personal rule by Charles I, and the Irish Rebellion of 1641 all heightened the feeling that protestantism itself stood threatened in Britain and Europe. Because it helped to maintain a militant or hopeful posture in the face of danger, English reformers turned even more forcefully to the apocalyptic armoury at such times. Until the civil war, however, even separatists advocated nothing more than passive disobedience to the magistrate. Active opposition to reformation fulfilled the prophecies of spiritual warfare and, thereby, reinforced the whole framework. Persecution confirmed apocalyptic feelings and, eventually, transformed spiritual into physical warfare.

Times of crisis, then, provided both a test of specific prophecies and a trial of the worthiness of the Lord's instruments. The imperial tradition of apocalyptic thought normally reinforced the already strong hierarchical assumptions of society, but even it could become a means of justifying unusual action. If the godly prince refused to fulfil his proper role as commander of the saints, then lesser magistrates might force him to it. Hence, the shift of the imperial mantle from King Charles to Parliament which took place in 1641 and after. The desire for parliamentary control of the king's advisers got militant support from reformers who believed that the powers of cosmic evil had captured the ear of the king. The tradition of the persecuted and oppressed, on the other hand, could apply to the magistrate as well. Radicals, however, also spun a justification for social and political initiative coming from the lower orders – those below the political nation – that came into conflict with traditional social assumptions. Ministers, apprentices, and artisans were supposed to obey their superiors, not lead them. The separatist practice of participatory congregationalism combined with a strong emphasis upon the tradition of the persecuted and oppressed to produce the Levellers and Diggers – granted, under the hot-house conditions of civil war and social dislocation, of disaster. The combination of the imperial tradition and that of the persecuted and oppressed by parliamentary preachers on the eve of the English civil war helped them to appeal to all levels of society to take up arms for Parliament.

The fear of popery that gripped the English people in the sixteenth and seventeenth centuries should no longer seem merely an irrational anxiety. It sprang from a highly rationalized, articulate, explanatory framework of thought – one based upon the assumption that human action reflected a universe polarized between good and evil, and built upon the belief that the papacy, throughout the ages, represented antichrist, the human leader of evil. For Baxter in the Interregnum the apocalyptic tradition had become mainly a mode of keeping the common people true to the protestant cause, but for his predecessors it meant much more. Through its fruitful imagery they communicated a glimpse of ultimate reality with a rich language of hope, fear, steadfastness, expectation, and eventual triumph which explained the relevance of contemporary events to the timelessness of eternity.

The early works of John Lilburne

Three scholars have attempted to work out the chronology of the composition of Lilburne's early works; see Gregg, *Free-born John*, p. 400, Haller, *Rise of Puritanism*, pp. 432–40, and Wolfe, *Milton in the Puritan Revolution*, pp. 469–71. All employ a different sequence from that given here which follows the dates given in the pamphlets unless other evidence forces another conclusion.

1 *The Christian mans trial*, written 12 March 1638, see p. 16

2 *A worke of the beast*, no date given, but published in 1638

3 *Come out of her my people*, written in September? 1638 according to Haller

4 *An answer to nine arguments*, written as a letter in 1638 (viz. age 21), see p. 43. The last two were written as letters to sympathizers around the same time. The order could be reversed, but both probably came prior to the next work.

5 *The poore mans cry*, finished on 20 December 1638 (age 22), see p. 14. It was probably written in October 1638, the petition on p. 15 being clearly *ante* the next work.

6 *Coppy of a letter*, attached to *Innocency and truth justified*, written in November 1638 (age 21, p. 21), obviously after the petition mentioned in it on pp. 17–20. Although Lilburne claimed to have written many petitions while in prison, the one in *The poore mans cry* was clearly the petition that won him the hearing which he described to a sympathizer in *Coppy of a letter* and, therefore, it was composed before the latter work. Internal evidence bears out this conclusion.

7 *A cry for justice*, in *A picture of the council of state*, written in May? 1639, see p. 26

8 *To all the brave apprentizes*, in *Innocency and truth justified*, finished on 10 May 1639, but it mentioned that *A cry for justice* was already in print.

9 *A ... letter written by*, written on 4 October 1640, see p. 8

10 *To the honourable House of Commons*, in *Innocency and truth justified*, composed in November 1640 for the Long Parliament, for Lilburne mentioned that he had suffered close imprisonment for two and a half years, see p. 66; his close imprisonment began after his punishment on 18 April 1638.

Although no known copies survive, both *To all the brave apprentizes* and *A cry for justice* were printed in 1639. Laud noted in his diary that he had received copies of these two works on 4 June 1639. Laud, *Works*, III, p. 232

Attribution of *A glimpse of Sions glory*

The most recent thorough attempt to attribute this anonymous pamphlet appeared in John F. Wilson, '"A glimpse of Syons glory,"' *Church History*, xxxi, 1962, pp. 66–73, and it received some further support in A.R. Dallison, 'The authorship of "A glimpse of Syons glory,"' in Toon, ed., *Puritan Eschatology*, appendix II, pp. 131–6. Wilson demonstrated that this tract most probably derived from notes made by one of the listeners to a sermon preached at the gathering of a congregational church in the Netherlands. After carefully narrowing the field of candidates down to Jeremiah Burroughs and Thomas Goodwin, he opted for the latter, mainly on the basis of a variant title page that listed the author as 'T.G.' Wilson's argument appears sound and convincing, but some additional positive and negative evidence points to Burroughs. As already indicated, works that Burroughts published in 1641 contain remarkable parallels to the interpretation, imagery, and language of *A glimpse*. A case for accepting Burroughs, then, presumably exists and one for rejecting Goodwin remains to be constructed.

The most important reason for questioning the attribution of *A glimpse* to Goodwin springs from the fact that the anonymous pamphlet omits the key image of Goodwin's apocalyptic thought from this period. Both in his sermons from the late 1630s and in his parliamentary sermon of 1642, Goodwin described the reformation as an historical event that unfolded in three stages and used the rebuilding of the Temple in Jerusalem after the return of Israel from Babylon as an Old Testament type of the reformation. Hence, the ruins of the Temple typified the earliest stirrings of reform in the medieval church, the outer court of the Temple the sixteenth-century reformation, and the holy of holies the visible kingdom of Christ in congregational churches. See Goodwin,

Works, III, pp. 79–81, and *Zerubbabels encouragement*, pp. 12–16, 30, 32. Since this symbol loomed so important in Goodwin's apocalyptic vision immediately prior to and after 1641, one can strongly presume that he would have employed it in that year. The fact that nothing approaching this image appears in *A glimpse* tells heavily against Goodwin's authorship. Stanley Fienberg, while working on his doctoral thesis on Goodwin, informed me that *A glimpse* was not at all in Goodwin's style and accepted my attribution of the pamphlet to Burroughs. I would like to thank him for his support.

Bibliography

The bibliography is divided into two sections: Primary Sources (government document series come at the end) and Secondary Works (unpublished theses come at the end). Unless otherwise noted, the place of publication was London. STC = *A Short-Title Catalogue of Books ... 1475–1640*, ed. A.W. Pollard and G.R. Redgrave; W = *Short-Title Catalogue of Books, 1641–1700*, ed. Donald Wing.

PRIMARY SOURCES

Abbot, George. *The reasons ... for upholding papistry unmasked*, 1604, STC 37
   [ ]. *A treatise of ... the true church*, 1624, STC 39
Abbot, Robert. *Antichristi demonstratio*, 1603, STC 43
An answer to the petition sent from the Universitie of Oxford, 1641, WA3430
Andrewes, Lancelot. *Works*, ed. J.P. Wilson and J. Bliss, 9 vol., Oxford 1851–4
The aphorismes of the kingdome, [1642], WP3893
Archer, [John]. *The personall raigne of Christ upon earth*, 1642, WA3615
Arrowsmith, John. *The covenant-avenging sword brandished*, 1642[3], WA3773
Ashe, Simeon. *The best refuge for the most oppressed*, 1642, WA3949
Aston, Sir Thomas. *A remonstrance against presbitery*, 1641, WA4078
[Aylmer, John]. *An harborowe for faithfull and true subjects*, 1559, STC 1005

B., J. *The last will and testament of superstition*, 1642, WB108

B., M. *A description of a prerogative royal*, 1642, wB134

B., T. *Newes from Rome*, 1641, wB193

Bale, John. *The image of bothe churches*, 1550, STC 1299

. *Select Works*, ed. Henry Christmas, Parker Society, Cambridge 1849

. *The vocacyon of Johan Bale to the bishoprick of Ossorie in Irelande*, 1553, STC 1307

[Bancroft, Richard]. *Daungerous positions and proceedings*, 1593, STC 1344

Barrow, Henry. *The Writings 1587–1590*, ed. Leland Carlson, English Nonconformist Texts, III, 1962

. *The Writings 1590–1591*, ed. Leland Carlson, ENT, V, 1966

. *The Writings of John Greenwood and Henry Barrow 1591–1593*, ed. Leland Carlson, ENT, VI, 1970

Bastwick, John. *The answer of J. Bastwick ... to the information of Sir J. Bancks*, 1637, STC 1568

. *The confession of the faithfull witnesse of Christ*, 1641, wB1059

. *Elenchus papisticae religionis*, 1627, STC 1571

. *Flagellum pontificis*, 1634, 1641, wB1062

. *The letany of J. Bastwick* [part 1], 1637, STC 1572

. *The answer of J. Bastwick to the exceptions against his letany* [part 2], 1637, STC 1573

. *The vanity and mischiefe of the old letany* [part 3], 1637, STC 1574

. *A more full answer of J. Bastwick* [part 4], 1637, STC 1575

. Πραξεις τῶy επισκπωy, *sive apoligeticus ad praesules Anglicanos*, 1636, STC 1576

Baxter, Richard. *Reliquiae Baxterianae*, ed. M. Sylvester, 1696, wB1370

Beard, Thomas. *Antichrist the pope of Rome*, 1625, STC 1657

The beast is wounded or information from Scotland, Amsterdam 1638? STC 22032

[Bernard, John]. *The anatomy of the service-book*, [1641], wB1998

[Bernard, Richard]. *A short view of the prelatical Church of England*, 1641, wB2033

Bible, Geneva 1560, STC 2093

Bilson, Thomas. *The true difference between Christian subjection and unchristian rebellion*, Oxford 1585, STC 3071

The bishops manifest, 1641, wB3029

Bloody newes from Norwich, 1641, wB3274

Bond, John. *King Charles his welcome home*, [1641], wB3579

Bowles, Oliver. *Zeale for Gods house quickened*, 1643, wB3884

Bridge, William. *Babylons downfall*, 1641, wB4448

Bridges, Walter. *Joabs counsell and King Davids seasonable hearing it*, 1643, wB4483A

A briefe relation, Amsterdam 1638, STC 1570

Brightman, Thomas. *Antichristi pontificorum*, Hamburg 1610

. *A most comfortable exposition of Daniel*, Amsterdam 1635, STC 3753

. *A revelation of the Revelation*, Amsterdam 1615, STC 3755

. *The workes of*, 1644, wB4679

Brightmans predicitions and prophecies, 1641, wB4690

Brinklow, Henry. *The true coppy of the complaint of Roderyck Mors*, [1642], wB4696

Brinsley, John. *The healing of Israels breaches*, 1642, wB4716

B[rome], A[lexander]. *A Canterbury tale*, 1641, wB4847

The brothers of the separation, 1641, wB4986

Broughton, Hugh. *Certayne questions ... handled between Mr. H. Broughton and Mr. Henry Ainsworth*, Amsterdam 1605, STC 3848

. *A most humble supplication to the king*, Amsterdam 1609, STC 3872

. *A petition to the king for authority to expound the Apocalyps*, Amsterdam 1611, STC 3876

. *A revelation of the holy Apocalyps*, Amsterdam 1610, STC 3883

Browne, Robert. See under Robert Harrison

Bullinger, Heinrich. *A hundred sermons upon the Apocalypse*, 1561, STC 4016

Burges, Anthony. *The difficulty of and encouragements to a reformation*, 1643, wB5643

Burges, Cornelius. *Another sermon*, 1641, wB5668

. *The first sermon*, 1641, wB5671

. *Two sermons*, 2nd ed., 1645, wB5688

[Burroughs, Jeremiah]. *A glimpse of Sions glory*, 1641, wK711

[ ]. *The glorious name of God*, 1643, wB6074

. *Moses his choice*, 1641, wB6094

[ ]. *The petition for the prelates briefly examined*, 1641, wP1749

. *Sions joy*, 1641, wB6119

Burton, Henry. *An apology to an appeale*, 1636, STC 4134

H.B. *Babel no Bethel*, 1629, STC 4136

H.B. *The baiting of the popes bull*, 1627, STC 4137

. *A censure of simony*, 1624, STC 4139

H.B. *The Christians bulwarke*, Oxford 1632, STC 4140

[ ]. *A divine tragedie*, Amsterdam 1636, STC 20459

. *A divine tragedie*, 1641, wB6161

. *Englands bondage and hope of deliverance*, 1641, wB6162

. *For God and the king*, Amsterdam 1636, STC 4141

H.B. *Grounds of Christian religion*, 1631, STC 4143

H.B. *Israels fast*, 1628, STC 4146

. *The law and the gospel reconciled*, 1631, STC 4152

[ ]. *Lord bishops none of the Lords bishops*, 1640, STC 20467

. *A narration of the life of Mr. Henry Burton*, 1643, wB6169

H.B. *A plea of an appeal*, 1626, STC 4153

[ ]. *The protestation protested*, 1641, wB6171

[ ]. *A replie to a relation of the conference between William Laude and Mr. Fisher the Jesuit*, 1640, STC 4154

H.B. *The seven vials*, 1628, STC 4155

. *The sounding of the two last trumpets*, 1641, wB6172

H.B. *Truths triumph over Trent*, 1629, STC 4156

H.B. *A tryall of private devotions*, 1628, STC 4157

Byfield, Richard. *The power of the Christ in God*, 1641, wB6392

Calamy, Edmund. *Englands looking-glasse*, 1642, wC237

. *Gods free mercy to England*, 1642, wC253

. *The noble-mans patterne of true and real thankfulnesse*, 1643, wC261

C[anne], J[ohn]. *The informer*, Amsterdam 1641, wC58A

. *The necessitie of separation*, Amsterdam 1634, STC 4574

. *A stay against straying*, Amsterdam 1639, STC 4575

[ ]. *Syons prerogative royal*, Amsterdam 1641, wS3871

Canterburies pilgrimage, 1641, wC459

Carter, Thomas. *Prayers prevalencie for Israels safety*, 1643, wC668

Carter, William. *Israels peace with God*, 1642, wC679A

C[artwright], T[homas]. *A replye to an answere*, [1574], STC 4711

. *The second replie*, Zurich 1575, STC 4714

. *The rest of the second replie*, 1577, STC 4715

Caryl, Joseph. *The nature, solemnity, grounds, property, and benefits of a sacred covenant*, 1643, wC782

. *The workes of Ephesus explained*, 1642, wC790

Case, Thomas. *Gods rising, his enemies scattering*, 1644, wC830

. *Gods waiting to be gracious unto his people*, 1642, wC831

. *Two sermons*, 1641, wC845

Chambers, Humfry. *A divine ballance to weigh religious fasts in*, 1643, wC1915

Cheshire, Thomas. *A sermon*, 1642, wC3781
    . *A sermon preached in Saint Paules Church on the tenth of October 1641*, 1641, wC3780

Cheynell, Francis. *Sions memento, and Gods alarum*, 1643, wC3816

Chidley, Katherine. *The justification of the independent churches of Christ*, 1641, wC3832

Clarendon, Edward Hyde, Earl of. *The History of the Rebellion and Civil Wars in England begun in the Year 1641*, ed. W. Dunn Macray, 6 vol., Oxford 1888

Coachman, Robert. *The cry of a stone*, 1642, wC4746

Coleman, Thomas. *The Christians course and complaint*, 1643, wC5050

A conference betweene the pope, the emperour and the king of Spaine, 1642, wC5727

A copie of a letter written from his holinesse court at Rome, 1642, wC6171

Corbet, Edward. *God's providence*, 1642[3], wC6241

Cosin, John. *A collection of private devotions*, ed. P.G. Stanwood, Oxford 1965
    . *Works*, ed. J. Sampson, 5 vol., Oxford 1843–55

Cranmer, Thomas. *Works*, ed. G.E. Duffield, Philadelphia 1965

A damnable treason, 1641, wD157

[Davis, John]. *A great discovery of a damnable plot at Raglan castle*, 1641, wD420

De la March, John. *A complaint of the false prophet's mariners*, 1641, wD868

D'Ewes, Simonds. *The Autobiography of Sir Simonds D'Ewes*, ed. J.O. Halliwell, 2 vol., 1845
    . *The Journal of Sir Simonds D'Ewes*, ed. W.H. Coates, New Haven 1942

A discovery of a horrible and bloody treason, 1641, wD1636

The discovery of a late and bloody conspiracie at Edenburgh, 1641, wD1637

A discovery of the arch-whore, [1642], wD1649

A discovery of the great fantasie, or, phantasticall conceitednesse, 1642, wD1651

A divine pater-noster, [1642], wD1725

Dolefull newes from Edinborough, 1641, wD1839

Dow, Christopher. *Innovations unjustly charged upon the present church and state*, 1637, STC 7090

Downame, George. *A treatise concerning antichrist proving the pope is antichrist*, 1603, STC 7120

Duke, Francis. *The fulnesse and freenesse of Gods grace*, 1642, wD2501

Du Perron, Jacques. *The copy of a letter sent from*, 1641, wD2637

E., E. *The bishops downefall or the prelats snare*, 1642 wE664

E., I. *The land of promise*, 1641, wE11

Edwards, Thomas. *Reasons against the independent government*, 1641, wE233

Ellis, John. *The sole path to a sound peace*, 1643, wE592

Englands complaint or the church her lamentation, [1642], wE2952

Englands glory in her royall king, 1641, wE2969

Englands petition, to her gratious king, Amsterdam [1641], wE3011

The envie of the popish prelates, 1642, wE3140

Fairclough, Samuel. *The troublers troubled*, 1642, wF109

False prophets discovered, 1642, wF346

Fawcet, Samuel. *A seasonable sermon*, 1641, wF562

[Fenwick, John], V., V.N. *The downfall of the pretended divine authoritie*, [1641], wV14

Fenwick, William. *Zions rights and Babels ruine*, 1642, wF725

Fiennes, William, Viscount Say and Sele. *Two speeches of*, 1641, wS796

Forbes, Patrick. *An exquisite commentarie upon the Revelation of St. John*, 1613, STC 11149

F[ord?], T[homas]. *Reformation sure and steadfast*, 1641, wF1515

Foxe, John. *Actes and monuments*, 1563, 1570, 1576, 1583, STC 11222–5
    . *Eicasmi sev meditationes in sacram Apocalypsin*, 1587, STC 11237

Franklin, Thomas. *An epistle written from Lucifer*, 1642, wF2089

Frere, Walter, and Charles Douglas, eds. *Puritan Manifestoes*, 2nd ed., 1954

Fuller, Nicholas. *The argument of N. Fuller in the case of T. Lad and R. Maunsell his clients*, 1607, STC 11460

Fuller, Thomas. *The Church History of Britain*, 3 vol. 1837

Gardiner, Samuel Rawson, ed. *Constitutional Documents of the Puritan Revolution 1625–1660*, Oxford 1906
    . *Documents Relating to the Proceedings against William*

Prynne, Camden Society, new series, XVIII, 1877

Gauden, John. *The love of truth and peace*, 1641, wG362

Geree, John. *The down-fall of antichrist*, 1641, wG595
. *Vindiciae voti*, 1641, wG605

Goodwin, John. *Anti-Cavalierisme*, [1642], wG1146
[ ]. *Irelands advocate*, 1641, wG1178
. *The returne of mercies*, 1641, wG1199

Goodwin, Thomas. *Works*, ed. T. Smith, 11 vol., Edinburgh 1861–4
. *Zerubbabels encouragement to finish the temple*, 1642, wG1268

Gouge, William. *The saints support*, 1642, wG1397

Great Brittans ruine plotted, 1641, wG1669

A great discoverie of a plot in Scotland, 1641, wG1685

Greenhill, William. *The axe at the root*, 1643, wG1848

Greenwood, John. *The Writings of John Greenwood 1587–1590, together with the Joint Writings of Henry Barrow and John Greenwood 1587–1590*, ed. Leland Carlson, ENT, IV, 1962
. *The Writings of John Greenwood and Henry Barrow 1591–1593*, ed. Leland Carlson, ENT, VI, 1970

Greville, Robert, Lord Brooke. *A discourse opening the nature of that episcopacie which is exercised in England*, 1642, wB4912

Grindal, Edmund. *Remains*, ed. William Nicholson, Parker Society, Cambridge 1863

A guide unto Sion, Amsterdam 1638, 1639, 1640, STC 26125–7

H., J. *King Charles his entertainment*, 1641, wH73A

[Hall, Joseph]. *A survay of that ... libell*, 1641, wH418

Harby, Thomas. *Divi Arminii mactatorum renata*, 1642, wH682

Harris, Robert. *A sermon*, 1642, wH875

Harrison, Robert. *The Writings of Robert Harrison and Robert Browne*, ed. Albert Peel and Leland Carlson, ENT, II, 1953

Here begynneth the byrthe and lyfe of antechryst, 1520? STC 670

Herle, Charles. *Davids song of three parts*, 1643, wH1556
. *A payre of compasses for church and state*, 1642, wH1561

Heylyn, Peter. *A briefe and moderate answer*, 1637, STC 13269

H[eywood], T[homas]. *A true discourse of the two infamous upstart prophets*, 1636, STC 13369

Hill, Thomas. *The militant church triumphant over the dragon and his angels*, 1643, wH2024
. *The trade of truth advanced*, 1642, wH2031

Hodges, Thomas. *A glimpse of Gods glory*, 1642, wH2314

Ho[l]mes, Nathaniel. *The new world*, 1641, wH2570
. *The peasants price*, 1642, wH2571
Hooker, Richard. *Of the laws of ecclesiastical polity*, ed. Christopher Morris, 2 vol., 1963
Hughes, Lewis. *Certaine grievances or errours of the service-book*, 1641, wH3314
. *Signes from heaven*, 1642, wH3318
Hunt, James. *A plaine and briefe discovery of those two beasts that are written, Revelation 13*, 1643, wH3731
. *The sermon and prophecie of*, 1641, wH3733
. *The spirituall verses and prose of*, 1642[3], wH3737
. *These spirituall verses of*, 1642, wH3739

James VI and I. *The workes of ... James by the grace of God king of Great Britain*, ed. James [Montague], bishop of Winton, 1616, STC 14344
. *A meditation upon the Lords prayer*, 1619, STC 14384
[Jenkinson, William], *Lamentable and sad newes from the north*, 1642, wJ617
Jewel, John. *An apology of the Church of England*, ed. J.E. Booty, Ithaca 1963
. *Certaine sermons*, 1583, STC 14596
. *Works*, ed. John Ayre, 4 vol., Parker Society, Cambridge 1840–50
Johnson, Robert. *A letter from Mr. Robert Johnson*, 1642, wJ815
Junius, Franciscus [François du Jon]. *A brief commentary upon the Revelation of St. John*, 1592, STC 7297, reprinted in 1594, 1596, and 1600 under slightly different titles, STC 2988–91, STC 7296

Kenyon, J.P., ed. *The Stuart Constitution 1603–1688: Documents and Commentary*, Cambridge 1966

L., J. *Englands doxologie*, 1641, wL28
Laud, William. *A relation of the conference between W. Lawd ... and Mr. Fisher the Jesuite*, 1639, STC 15298
. *A speech delivered in the starr-chamber at the censure of J. Bastwick, H. Burton, and W. Prynne*, 1637, STC 15306
. *Works*, ed. W. Scott and J. Bliss, 7 vol. in 9, Oxford 1847–60
Leighton, Alexander. *An appeal to the Parliament, or Sions plea against the prelacy*, Amsterdam 1628, STC 15430
[ ]. *A decade of grievances*, 1641, wL1023
. *Speculum bellisaeri: or the looking-glasse of the holy war*,

Amsterdam 1628, STC 15432

Ley, John. *The fury of warre, and the folly of sinne*, 1643, wL1879

A licht for the ignorant, Amsterdam 1638, STC 15591

A light for the ignorant, 1641, wL2138

Lightfoot, John. *Elias redevivus*, 1643, wL2053

Lilburne, John. *An answer to nine arguments*, 1645, wL2081

. *The Christian mans trial*, 2nd ed., [1641], wL2089

. *Come out of her my people*, Amsterdam 1638, STC 15596

. *Copie of a letter ... to Mr. William Prinne esq.*, 1645, wL2092

. *Innocency and truth justified*, 1646, wL2118

. *A letter sent from Captaine Lilburne*, 1643, wL2134

. *A ... letter written by*, [1640?], STC 15597

. *A picture of the councel of state*, 1649, wL2154

. *The poore mans cry*, Amsterdam 1639, STC 15598

. *A worke of the beast*, Amsterdam 1638, STC 15599

Love, Richard. *The watchmans watchword*, Cambridge 1642, wL3193

Loveday, Samuel. *An answer to the lamentation of cheap-side crosse*, [1642], wL3232

The Marprelate Tracts, Leeds 1967

Marshall, Stephen. *Meroz cursed*, 1641[2], wM762

. *A peace-offering to God*, 1641, wM766

. *Reformation and desolation*, 1642, wM770

. *A sermon*, 1641, wM776

. *The song of Moses*, 1643, wM789

Marston, John. *A sermon*, 1642, wM817

Mayer, John. *An antidote against popery*, 1625, STC 17729

. *Ecclesiastica interpretatio*, 1627, STC 17731

Mede, Joseph. *The apostasy of the latter times*, 1641, wM1590

[ ]. *Clavis apocalyptica*, Cambridge 1627, STC 17766

. *Diatribae*, 1642, wM1596

. *The key of the Revelation*, trans. Richard More, 2 parts, 1643, wM1600

. *A paraphrase and exposition of the prophesie of St. Peter*, 1642, wM1605

. *Works*, 1648, wM1585

Milton, John. *Complete Prose Works*, ed. Don Wolfe *et al.*, 8 vol., New Haven 1953+

Mocket, Thomas. *The churches troubles and deliverance*, 1642, wM2305

A most sad and serious lamentation, 1642, wM2919

Napier, John. *A plaine discovery of the whole Revelation of Saint John,* Edinburgh 1593, London 1611, STC 18354, 18356A

Napiers narration, or an epitome of his booke on the Revelation, 1641[2], wN153

A new plot against the Parliament, 1641, wN706

A new remonstrance wherein is declared who are the malignant party, 1642, wN745

Newcomen, Matthew. *The craft and cruelty of the churches adversaries,* 1643, wN907

——. *Jerusalems watch-men,* 1643, wN911

Newes from Ipswich, see under White pseudonym

Notestein, Wallace, and Frances Relf, eds. *Commons Debates for 1629,* Minneapolis 1921

The organs funerall, [1642], wO423

[Overton, Richard]. *Canterburys will,* 1641, wC461

[ ]. *Mercuries message,* 1641, wM1748

[ ]. *Mercuries message defended,* 1641, wM1747

——. *New Lambeth fayre,* 1642, wO631

[ ]. *Vox borealis,* 1641, wV712

P., R. *The bishop's looking-glasse,* 1641[2], wP96

Palmer, Herbert. *The necessity and encouragement of utmost venturing for the churches help,* 1643, wP242

[ ]. *Scripture and reason pleaded for defensive armes,* 1643, wP244

The papists petition in England to their diabolicall center of impiety the pope, 642, wP317

Pareus, David. *A commentary upon the divine Revelation,* Amsterdam 1644, wP353

A parte of a register, Middelburg 1593, STC 10400

Peel, Albert, ed. *The Seconde Parte of a Register,* 2 vol., Cambridge 1915

Perne, Andrew. *Gospell courage,* 1643, wP1577

Piggot, John. *Hierusalem bedewed with teares,* 1642, wP2221

A plea for the Parliament, 1642, wP2522

Ponet, John. *An apologie fullie aunswering ... Stephen Gardiner,* Zurich 1555, STC 20175

——. *A notable sermon,* 1550, STC 20177

J.P. *A shorte treatise of politike power,* Strasburg? 1556, STC 20178

Porter, H.C., ed. *Puritanism in Tudor England,* 1970

The prentices prophecie, 1642, wA3587

Price, William. *A sermon*, 1642, wP3402

Prynne, William. *Anti-Arminianism*, 2nd ed., 1630, STC 20458

    . *The antipathie of the English lordly prelacie both to regal monarchy and civil unity*, 1641, wP3891

    [ ]. *A breviate of the prelates intollerable usurpations*, [W. Huntley, pseudonym], 3rd ed., Amsterdam 1637, STC 20454

    . *A briefe survay and censure of Mr. Cozens his couzening devotions*, 1628, STC 20455

    [ ]. *Certain quaeries propounded to the bowers at the name of Jesus*, 4th ed., Amsterdam 1636, STC 20456

    . *The Church of Englands old antithesis to new Arminianism*, 1629, STC 20457

    . *God no imposter nor deluder*, 1629, STC 20460

    . *Healthes sickness*, 1628, STC 20462

    . *Histrio-mastix*, 1633, STC 20464

    . *Lame Giles his haltings*, 1630, STC 20465

    [ ]. *A looking-glasse for all lordly prelates*, 1636, STC 20466

    [ ]. *The Lords day the sabbath day*, 2nd ed., 1636, STC 20468

    [ ]. *A new discovery of the prelates tyranny*, 1641, wP4018

    . *The perpetuitie of a regenerate mans estate*, 1626, STC 20471

    [ ]. *A quench-coale*, Amsterdam 1637, STC 20474

    [ ]. *XVI new quaeres ... to our lord prelates*, 1637, STC 20475

    [ ]. *A soveraigne antidote*, 1642, wP4087

A.B.C. *The unbishoping of Timothy and Titus*, Amsterdam 1636, STC 20476

    . *The unlovelinesse of love-lockes*, 1628, STC 20477

    [ ]. *A vindication of Psalme 105:15*, 1642, wP4125

Questions to be disputed on the counsell of the lords spirituall, 1641, wQ187

Quintine, Michael. *A brief treatise containing a full discovery*, 1641, wQ227

R., T. *A message of peace*, 1642, wR88

Reasons why the hierarchy or governement of the church, 1641, wR588

The recantation of the prelate of Canterbury, 1641, wR613

The revelation of Mr. Brightmans revelation, 1641, wR1190

The reverend M. Brightmans judgement or prophecies, [1641], wB4682

Reynolds, Edward. *Eugenia's teares*, 1642, wR1247

    . *Israels petition in time of trouble*, 1642, wR1256

Ridley, Nicholas. *Works*, ed. H. Christmas, Parker Society, Cambridge 1841

R[itor], A[ndrew]. *A treatise of the vanity of childish-baptisme*, 1642, wR1542

Robinson, T. *The petitioners vindication*, 1642, wR1715

A royal message, 1641, wC2765

S., G. *Sacrae heptades, or seaven problems concerning antichrist*, Amsterdam 1625, STC 21492

S., J. *The truth of the proceedings in Scotland*, 1641, wS101

Sandys, Edwin. *Sermons*, ed. John Ayre, Parker Society, Cambridge 1841

Sclater, William. *Papisto-mastix*, 1642, wS919

Sedgwick, John. *Englands condition parallel'd with Jacobs*, 1642, wS2360

Sedgwick, Obadiah. *England's preservation*, 1642, wS2372
    . *Haman's vanity*, 1643, wS2374

Sedgwick, William. *Scripture a perfect rule for church government*, [1643], wS2388
    . *Zions deliverance and her friends duty*, 1642, wS2392

A short, compendious, and true description of the round-heads and the long-heads, 1642, wS3581

Simpson, Sidrach. *Reformations preservation*, 1643, wS3825
    . *A sermon*, 1643, wS3826

Sleidanus, Joannes. *A briefe chronicle of the foure principall empyres*, 1563, STC 19849
    . *A famouse cronicle of oure time*, 1560, STC 19848

Smectymnuus. *An answer to a booke entitled, An humble remonstrance*, 1641, wM748
    . *A vindication*, 1641, wM798

Some more new observations concerning the king and Parliament, 1642, wS4527

A song of Syon or the beauty of Bethell, 1642, wS4678

Spencer, John. *The spiritual warfare*, 1642, wS4955

Spurstowe, William. *Englands patterne and duty in it's monthly fasts*, 1643, wS5094

A strange prophecie against bishops, 1641[2], wS5917

S[winnock], G[eorge]. *The life and death of Mr. Thomas Wilson*, 1672, wS6277

Symonds, Joseph. *A sermon*, 1641, wS6358

[Taylor, John]. *The Brownists conventicle*, 1642, wT436
    . *A delicate, dainty, damnable dialogue*, 1642, wT447
    [ ]. *The discovery of a swarme of separatists*, 1641, wT452
    [ ]. *The divisions of the Church of England*, 1642, wT454
    [ ]. *The hellish parliament*, 1641, wT465
    . *A plea for prerogative*, 1642, wT496
    [ ]. *The popes benediction*, 1641, wT497
    [ ]. *Religions lotterie*, 1642, wT505
    . *A swarme of sectaries*, 1641, wT514
Taylor, Thomas. *A mappe of Rome in five sermons on the gunpowder treason*, 1619, STC 23837
Temple, Thomas. *Christs government in and over his people*, 1642, wT634
The times dissected, 1641, wT1288
Thomason, George. See under G.K. Fortescue among the secondary works.
Trinterud, Leonard J., ed. *Elizabethan Puritanism*, New York 1971
Triple episcopacie, 1641, wT2287
A true and full relation of the horrible and hellish plot, 1641, wT2481
Tuckney, Anthony. *The balme of Gilead*, 1643, wT3210

The untrussing of above one hundred popis-h points, 1642, wU103
Ussher, James. *Vox Hibernae*, 1642, wU228

Valentine, Thomas. *A sermon*, 1643, wV26
[Vicars, John]. *All the memorable & wonder-strikinge parlamentary mercies*, [1642], wA944
    . *Englands remembrancer*, 1641, wV303
    . *Jehovah-Jireh, God in the mount, or Englands remembrancer*, 1641[2], wV312
Vines, Richard. *Calebs integrity in following the Lord fully*, 1642, wV546

W., I. *A discoverie of the beasts*, Amsterdam 1641, wW41
[Walker, George]. *A true copie of the disputation*, 1641, wW366
Ward, John. *An encouragement to war*, [1642], wW776
Ward, Richard. *The principall duty of parliament-men*, 1641, wW805
Wentworth, Thomas, Earl of Strafford. *The Earl of Strafforde's Letters and Dispatches*, ed. William Knowler, 2 vol., 1739

White, M. [pseudonym]. *Newes from Ipswich*, [1636], STC 20469
Whitgift, John, *An answere to a certen libel*, 1572, STC 25427
   . *The defense of the aunswere*, 1574, STC 25430
Whittaker, Jeremiah. *Eirenopoios, Christ the settlement of unsettled times*, 1642[3], wW1712
Wickins, Nathaniel. *Wood-street-compters plea*, Amsterdam 1638, STC 25587
Wilkinson, Henry. *Babylons ruine, Jerusalems rising*, 1644, wW2221
Wilkinson, John. *An exposition of the 13. chapter of the Revelation of Jesus Christ*, Amsterdam 1619, STC 25647
Williams, Charles H., ed. *English Historical Documents*, v, *1485–1558*, 1967
Wilson, Thomas. *Davids zeal for Zion*, 1641, wW2947
   . *Jerichoes down-fall*, 1643, wW2948
[Woodward, Hezekiah]. *The churches thank-offering to God her king, and the Parliament*, 1642, wW3484
Wrens anatomy, 1641, wW3680

Calendar of State Papers, Domestic Series, Charles I, ed. J. Bruce, W.D. Hamilton, and S.C. Lomas, 23 vol., 1858–97 (*CSPD*)
Historical Manuscripts Commission (*HMC*). Fourth Report, 1874
   . Ninth Report, 3 parts, 1883–4
   . De L'Isle and Dudley manuscripts, VI, Sidney Papers, 1626–98, ed. G.D. Owen, 1966
Journals of the House of Commons 1547–1714, 17 vol., 1742+ (CJ)
Letters and Papers, Foreign and Domestic, of the Reign of Henry VIII, ed. J.S. Brewer, James Gairdner, and R.H. Brodie, 21 vol. in 33 parts, 1862–1910

SECONDARY WORKS

A Books and articles

Anglo, Sydney. 'An early Tudor programme for plays and other demonstrations against the pope,' *Journal of the Warburg and Courtauld Institutes*, xx, 1957, pp. 176–9
Ball, Bryan W. *A Great Expectation: Eschatological Thought in English Protestantism to 1660*, Leiden 1975
Barkun, Michael. *Disaster and the Millennium*, New Haven 1974
Bennett, H.S. *English Books and Readers 1603–1640*, Cambridge 1970

Bindoff, S.T., Joel Hurstfield, and C.H. Williams, eds. *Elizabethan Government and Society: Essays Presented to Sir John Neale*, 1961

Booty, John E. *John Jewel as an Apologist of the Church of England*, 1963

Bousset, Wilhelm. *The Antichrist Legend: A Chapter in Christian and Jewish Folklore*, trans. A.H. Keane, 1896

Breslow, Martin A. *A Mirror of England: English Puritan Views of Foreign Nations 1618–1640*, Cambridge, Mass. 1970

Bruce, F.F. *The English Bible*, 1961

Burrage, Champlain. *The Early English Dissenters*, 2 vol. Cambridge 1912

Burrell, Sidney. 'The apocalyptic vision of the early covenanters,' *Scottish Historical Review*, xliii, 1964, pp. 1–24
. 'The covenant idea as a revolutionary symbol,' *Church History*, xxvii, 1958, pp. 338–50

Burridge, Kennelm. *New Heaven, New Earth: A Study of Millenarian Activities*, New York 1969

Capp, Bernard S. *The Fifth Monarchy Men: A Study in Seventeenth-century English Millenarianism*, 1972
. '*Godly Rule* and English millenarianism,' *Past and Present*, 52, 1971, pp. 106–17
. 'The millennium and eschatology in England,' *Past and Present*, 57, 1972, pp. 156–62

Christianson, Paul. 'From expectation to militance: reformers and Babylon in the first two years of the Long Parliament,' *Journal of Ecclesiastical History*, xxiv, 1973, pp. 225–44
. 'The peers, the people, and parliamentary management in the first six months of the Long Parliament,' *Journal of Modern History*, xlix, 1977

Clebsch, William A. *England's Earliest Protestants 1520–1535*, New Haven 1964

Clifton, Robin, 'The popular fear of catholics during the English revolution,' *Past and Present*, 52, 1971, pp. 23–55

Clouse, Robert. 'John Napier and apocalyptic thought,' *Sixteenth Century Journal*, v, 1974, pp. 101–14

Cohn, Norman. *The Pursuit of the Millennium: Revolutionary Messianism in Medieval and Reformation Europe and its bearing on Modern Totalitarian Movements*, 2nd ed., New York 1961

Collinson, Patrick. *The Elizabethan Puritan Movement*, 1967

Coolidge, John S. *The Pauline Renaissance*, Oxford 1970

Dickens, A.G. *The English Reformation*, 1964

Dixon, Richard W. *History of the Church of England from the Abolition of the Roman Jurisdiction*, 6 vol., Oxford 1872–1902

Fairfield, Leslie P. 'John Bale and protestant hagiography in England,' *Journal of Ecclesiastical History*, xxiv, 1973, pp. 145–60
. '*The vocacyon of Johan Bale* and early English autobiography,' *Renaissance Quarterly*, xxiv, 1971, pp. 327–40

Fixler, Michael. *Milton and the Kingdoms of God*, 1964

Fortescue, G.K., ed. *Catalogue of the Pamphlets, Books, Newspapers, and Manuscripts relating to the Civil War, the Commonwealth, and Restoration, Collected by George Thomason 1640–1661*, 2 vol., 1908

Froom, Le Roy. *The Prophetic Faith of Our Fathers*, 4 vol., Washington 1946–54

Gardiner, Samuel R. *History of England from the Accession of James I to the Outbreak of the Civil War 1603–1642*, new ed., 10 vol., 1894

George, Charles H. 'Puritanism as history and historiography,' *Past and Present*, 41, 1968, pp. 77–104

Greenslade, Stanley L., ed., *The Cambridge History of the Bible*, Cambridge 1963

Greg, W.W. *Some Aspects and Problems of London Publishing between 1550 and 1650*, Oxford 1956

Gregg, Pauline. *Free-born John: A Biography of John Lilburne*, 1961

Haller, William. *Foxe's 'Book of Martyrs' and the Elect Nation*, 1963
. *Liberty and Reformation in the Puritan Revolution*, New York 1955
. *The Rise of Puritanism; Or, the Way to the New Jerusalem as Set Forth in Pulpit and Press from Thomas Cartwright to John Lilburne and John Milton*, New York 1938

Hill, Christopher. *Antichrist in Seventeenth Century England*, Oxford 1971
. *Puritanism and Revolution: Studies in Interpretation of the English Revolution of the 17th Century*, 1958
. *Society and Puritanism in Pre-Revolutionary England*, 1963

Hobsbawm, Eric. *Primitive Rebels: Studies in Archaic Forms of Social Movement in the 19th and 20th Centuries*, 1958

Holden, William. *Anti-Puritan Satire 1572–1642*, New Haven 1954

Holsti, Ole. *Content Analysis for the Social Sciences and Humanities*, Don Mills, Ont. 1969

Huehns, Gertrude. *Antinomianism in English History: With Special Reference to the Period 1640–1660*, 1951

Hughes, Philip. *The Reformation in England*, 3 vol., 1951–4

Johnson, A.F. 'The exiled English church in Amsterdam and its press,' *Library*, 5th ser., v, 1951, pp. 219–42

⸻ . 'J.F. Stam, Amsterdam, and English Bibles,' *Library*, 5th ser., ix, 1959, pp. 185–93

Jordan, Wilbur K. *The Development of Religious Toleration in England*, 4 vol., Cambridge, Mass. 1932–40

King, Peter. 'Bishop Wren and the suppression of the Norwich lecturers,' *Journal of Ecclesiastical History*, ix, 1968, pp. 237–54

Kirby, Ethyn Williams. 'Sermons before the Commons, 1640–42,' *American Historical Review*, xliv, 1939, pp. 538–48

Knappen, Marshall M. *Tudor Puritanism: A Chapter in the History of Idealism*, Chicago 1939

Koebner, Richard. '"The imperial crown of the realm": Henry VIII, Constantine the Great, and Polydore Vergil,' *Bulletin of the Institute of Historical Research*, xxvi, 1953, pp. 29–52

Kuhn, Thomas. *The Structure of Scientific Revolutions*, Chicago 1962

Lamont, William M. 'Episcopacy and a "godly discipline," 1641–6,' *Journal of Ecclesiastical History*, x, 1959, pp. 74–89

⸻ . *Godly Rule: Politics and Religion 1603–60*, 1969

⸻ . *Marginal Prynne 1600–1669*, 1963

⸻ . 'Prynne, Burton, and the puritan triumph,' *Huntington Library Quarterly*, xxvii, 1963–4, pp. 103–13

⸻ . 'Puritanism as history and historiography: some further thoughts,' *Past and Present*, 44, 1969, pp. 133–46

⸻ . 'Richard Baxter, the Apocalypse and the mad major,' *Past and Present*, 55, 1972, pp. 68–90

⸻ . 'The rise and fall of Bishop Bilson,' *Journal of British Studies*, vii, 1966, pp. 22–32

Lanternari, Vittorio. *The Religions of the Oppressed: A Study of Modern Messianic Cults*, trans. Lisa Sergio, New York 1965

Lindley, Keith J. 'The impact of the 1641 rebellion upon England and Wales, 1641–5,' *Irish Historical Studies*, xviii, no. 70, 1972, pp. 143–76

Liu, Tai. *Discord in Zion: The Puritan Divines and the Puritan Revolution 1640–1660*, The Hague 1973

Lorimer, Peter. *John Knox and the Church of England*, 1895

Maclear, James F. 'New England and the fifth monarchy: the quest for the millennium in early American puritanism,' *William and Mary Quarterly*, 3rd ser., xxxii, 1975, pp. 223–60

⸻ . 'Puritan relations with Buckingham,' *Huntington Library*

Quarterly, xxi, 1957–8, pp. 111–32

Maclure, Millar. *The Paul's Cross Sermons 1534–1642*, Toronto 1958

Manuel, Frank E. *The Religion of Isaac Newton*, Oxford 1975

Marchant, Ronald. *The Puritans and the Church Courts in the Diocese of York, 1560–1642*, 1960

Miller, John. *Popery and Politics in England 1660–1688*, Cambridge 1973

Miller, Perry. *Orthodoxy in Massachusetts 1630–1650*, Boston 1933

Morgan, Edmund. *Visible Saints: The History of a Puritan Idea*, New York 1963

Morris, Christopher. *Political Thought in England from Tyndale to Hooker*, Oxford 1953

Morton, A.L. *The World of the Ranters: Religious Radicalism in the English Revolution*, 1970

Neale, John E. *Elizabeth I and Her Parliaments 1559–1581*, 1953
    . *Essays in Elizabethan History*, 1958

Notestein, Wallace. *Four Worthies: John Chamberlain, Anne Clifford, John Taylor, Oliver Heywood*, New Haven 1957

Nuttall, Geoffrey F. *Visible Saints: The Congregational Way 1640–1660*, Oxford 1957

Olsen, Viggo Norskov. *John Foxe and the Elizabethan Church*, Berkeley 1973

Owen, H. Gareth. 'A nursery of Elizabethan nonconformity 1567–72,' *Journal of Ecclesiastical History*, xvii, 1966, pp. 65–76

Parry, R.H., ed. *The English Civil War and After 1642–1658*, 1970

Pearl, Valerie. *London and the Outbreak of the Puritan Revolution*, Oxford 1961

Pearson, A.F. Scott. *Church and State: Political Aspects of Sixteenth-Century Puritanism*, Cambridge 1928
    . *Thomas Cartwright and Elizabethan Puritanism*, Cambridge 1928

Peel, Albert. *The Brownists in Norwich and Norfolk about 1580*, Cambridge 1920
    . *The First Congregational Churches*, Cambridge 1920

Pierce, William. *An Historical Introduction to the Marprelate Tracts*, 1908

Pineas, Ranier. *Tudor and Early Stuart Anti-Catholic Drama*, Nieuwkoop 1972

Pocock, J.G.A. *The Ancient Constitution and the Feudal Law*, Cambridge 1957

Pollard, A.W., and G.R. Redgrave, eds. *A Short-Title Catalogue of Books*

Printed in England, Scotland, and Ireland and of English Books Printed Abroad 1475–1640, 1926

Porter, H.C. *Reformation and Reaction in Tudor Cambridge*, Cambridge 1958

Prescott, Hilda M.F. *Mary Tudor*, New York 1963, originally 1940

Reeves, Marjorie. *The Influence of Prophecy in the Later Middle Ages: A Study of Joachimism*, Oxford 1969

Richardson, R.C. *Puritanism in North-west England: A Regional Study of the Diocese of Chester to 1642*, Manchester 1972

Ridley, Jasper. *Nicholas Ridley*, 1957

Robertson, D.B. *The Religious Foundations of Leveller Democracy*, New York 1951

Rostenberg, Leona. *Literary, Political, Scientific, Religious & Legal Publishing, Printing & Bookselling in England 1551–1700: Twelve Studies*, 2 vol., New York 1965

Rupp, E. Gordon. *Six Makers of English Religion*, 1957

Russell, Conrad, ed. *The Origins of the English Civil War*, 1973

Rutman, Darrett. *American Puritanism: Faith and Practice*, New York 1970

Sachse, William. 'The migration of New Englanders to England, 1640–1660,' *American Historical Review*, liii, 1948, pp. 251–78

Schwarz, Marc L. 'Viscount Saye and Sele, Lord Brooke and aristocratic protest to the first Bishops' War,' *Canadian Journal of History*, vii, 1972, pp. 17–36

Seaver, Paul S. *The Puritan Lectureships: The Politics of Religious Dissent 1560–1662*, Stanford 1970

Shaw, William A. *A History of the English Church during the Civil Wars and under the Commonwealth*, 2 vol., 1900

Siebert, Frederick S. *Freedom of the Press in England 1476–1776*, Urbana, Ill. 1952

Smith, Edward O. 'The Elizabethan doctrine of the prince as reflected in the sermons of the episcopacy, 1559–1603,' *Huntington Library Quarterly*, xxviii, 1964–5, pp. 1–17

Spencer, Lois. 'The politics of George Thomason,' *Library*, 5th ser., xiv, 1959, pp. 11–27

——. 'The professional and literary connexions of George Thomason,' *Library*, 5th ser., xiii, 1958, pp. 102–18

Sprunger, Keith. *The Learned Doctor William Ames: Dutch Backgrounds of English and American Puritanism*, Urbana 1972

Strong, Roy C. *Van Dyck: Charles I on Horseback*, 1972

Sykes, Norman. *Old Priest and New Presbyter*, Cambridge 1956

Thomas, Keith V. *Religion and the Decline of Magic: Studies in Popular Beliefs in Sixteenth and Seventeenth Century England*, 1971

Thrupp, Sylvia L., ed. *Millennial Dreams in Action*, Comparative Studies in Society and History, supplement II, The Hague 1962

Toon, Peter, ed. *Puritans, the Millennium and the Future of Israel: Puritan Eschatology*, Cambridge 1970

Trevor-Roper, Hugh R. *Religion, the Reformation and Social Change*, 1968

Tuveson, Ernest Lee. *Millennium and Utopia: A Study in the Background of the Idea of Progress*, New York 1964, originally 1949
    . *Redeemer Nation: The Idea of America's Millennial Role*, Chicago 1968

Vann, Richard T. *The Social Development of English Quakerism, 1650–1750*, Cambridge, Mass. 1969

Walzer, Michael. *The Revolution of the Saints: A Study in the Origins of Radical Politics*, Cambridge, Mass. 1966

White, B.R. *The English Separatist Tradition from the Marian Martyrs to the Pilgrim Fathers*, Oxford 1971

Wiener, Carol Z. 'The beleaguered isle: a study of Elizabethan and early Jacobean anti-catholicism,' *Past and Present*, 51, 1971, pp. 27–62

Williams, jr., Franklin B. *Index of Dedications and Commendatory Verses in English Books before 1641*, 1962
    . 'The Laudian imprimatur,' *Library*, 5th ser., xv, 1960, pp. 96–104

Willson, David Harris. *King James VI and I*, 1956

Wilson, John F. 'Another look at John Canne,' *Church History*, xxxiii, 1964, pp. 34–48
    . 'A glimpse of Syons glory,' *Church History*, xxxi, 1962, pp. 66–73
    . *Pulpit in Parliament: Puritanism during the English Civil Wars 1640–1648*, Princeton 1969

Wing, Donald, ed. *Short-Title Catalogue of Books Printed in England, Scotland, Ireland, Wales, and British America and of English Books Printed in Other Countries 1641–1700*, 3 vol., New York 1945

Wolfe, Don. *Milton in the Puritan Revolution*, New York 1941.
    . 'Unsigned pamphlets of Richard Overton: 1641–1649,' *Huntington Library Quarterly*, xxi, 1958, pp. 167–201

Zagorin, Perez. *The Court and the Country: The Beginning of the English Revolution*, 1969

B *Unpublished theses and essays*

Bauckham, Richard. 'Interpretations of Prophecy in Tudor Protestantism,' Archbishop Cranmer Prize Essay, Cambridge 1972
Clouse, Robert G. 'The Influence of John Henry Alsted on English Millenarian Thought in the Seventeenth Century,' PH D thesis, State University of Iowa 1963
Firth, Katherine. 'The Apocalyptic Tradition in Early Protestant Historiography in England and Scotland,' D PHIL thesis, Oxford 1971
Gilsdorf, Althea Joy Bourne. 'The Puritan Apocalypse: New England Eschatology in the Seventeenth Century,' PH D thesis, Yale 1964
Hazelip, Herbert H. 'Stephen Marshall: Preacher to the Long Parliament,' PH D thesis, University of Iowa 1967
Hibbard, Caroline M. 'Charles I and the Popish Plot,' PH D thesis, Yale 1975
Hughes, Richard T. 'Henry Burton: A Study in Religion and Politics in Seventeenth Century England,' PH D thesis, University of Iowa 1972
Shipps, Kenneth W. 'Lay Patronage of East Anglian Puritan Clerics in Pre-Revolutionary England,' PH D thesis, Yale 1971
Tyacke, N.R.N. 'Arminianism in England in Religion and Politics, 1604–1640,' D PHIL thesis, Oxford 1968
Williamson, Arthur H. 'Antichrist's Career in Scotland: The Imagery of Evil and the Search for a Scottish Past,' PH D thesis, Washington University 1973
Wilson, John F. 'Studies in Puritan Millenarianism under the Early Stuarts,' TH D thesis, Union Theological Seminary, New York 1962

Index

The major discussion of major figures is indicated in bold type.